OXFORD MEDICAL PUBLICATIONS

A Guide to Effective Care in Pregnancy and Childbirth

A GUIDE TO EFFECTIVE CARE IN PREGNANCY AND CHILDBIRTH

Murray Enkin, Marc J. N. C. Keirse,
Iain Chalmers

with the editorial assistance of
Eleanor Enkin

Oxford New York Tokyo Toronto
OXFORD UNIVERSITY PRESS

Oxford University Press, Walton Street, Oxford OX2 6DP

Oxford New York Toronto
Delhi Bombay Calcutta Madras Karachi
Petaling Jaya Singapore Hong Kong Tokyo
Nairobi Dar es Salaam Cape Town
Melbourne Auckland

and associated companies in
Berlin Ibadan

Oxford is a trade mark of Oxford University Press

Published in the United States
by Oxford University Press, New York

First published 1989
Reprinted with corrections, 1990 (four times), 1991 (twice)

British Library Cataloguing in Publication Data
Enkin, Murray
A guide to effective care in pregnancy and
childbirth.
1. Woman. Pregnancy & Childbirth
I. Title   II. Keirse, Marc J. N. C.   III. Chalmers, Iain
618.2
ISBN 0-19-261916-0 (Pbk.)

Library of Congress Cataloging in Publication Data
(Data available)

Printed and bound in Great Britain by
Biddles Ltd, Guildford and King's Lynn

To Eleanor, Nelly, and Jan,
who make everything worthwhile.

Preface

Over ten years ago we embarked upon a systematic review of the effects of care during pregnancy and childbirth. We began by agreeing which type of studies were likely to provide the best evidence for evaluating care. As well as using the MEDLINE database to identify studies that met our criteria, we organized a systematic hand search of over 60 key journals, from the 1950 issues onwards. In addition, we wrote to over 40 000 obstetricians and paediatricians in 18 countries in an attempt to identify unpublished studies and wrote to the authors of many published studies to try to obtain relevant unpublished data. Having assembled the raw material for our review in these ways, we and our collaborators set about conducting a systematic synthesis of this wealth of data, using methods to reduce bias and random error.

This process has already resulted in two publications: a 1500-page, two-volume book, entitled *Effective care in pregnancy and childbirth*; and an electronic publication called *The Oxford database of perinatal trials*. The latter is updated on a continuing basis as new evidence becomes available.

We believe that the information contained in these publications is important to anyone involved in the care of childbearing women, as well as to women themselves. Unfortunately, their size and high cost will inevitably limit their availability and accessibility. It is with this in mind that we have prepared *A guide to effective care in pregnancy and childbirth*, to make the main conclusions of the other two publications more readily available, in a more portable format, and at a more affordable price.

In order to achieve this, we have been forced to omit the data and references on which the conclusions presented in this book have been based. This information can, however, be obtained by consulting the other two publications, which should be available in most medical libraries. We hope that, between them, these three publications will serve the needs of those providing and receiving care during pregnancy and childbirth.

Murray Enkin, Marc Keirse, Iain Chalmers

Acknowledgements

We are grateful to Alison Macfarlane, who first suggested that we prepare this book. We owe special thanks to the authors of each chapter of *Effective Care in Pregnancy and Childbirth*, from which all of the text of this book has been derived. They spent many hours reviewing and analysing the data on which their contributions to the larger book were based. The credit for these analyses is theirs; the blame for any errors that may have crept in during our condensation of their work rests with us.

We acknowledge with particular gratitude the help we received from the Rockefeller Foundation, through the good offices of Dr. Kenneth Warren. Not only did the Foundation grant us time to work together as scholars in residence at its Study Center in the Villa Serbelloni, Bellagio, Italy; it also helped to fund the additional travel and communication that was necessary to complete our work. We are grateful to McMaster University, Leiden University, and the Department of Health (UK) for granting us the time necessary to work on this project.

We received helpful comments on draft manuscripts, not only from chapter authors of *Effective Care in Pregnancy and Childbirth*, but also from Beverley Beech, Susan Boron, Brian Hutchison, Karyn Kaufman, Andy Oxman, and Leonie Somorjay. We acknowledge this help with gratitude, as well as that provided by Oxford University Press at all stages of the preparation of this book.

Finally, we thank Eleanor Enkin, Nelly Keirse, and Jan Chalmers, who helped in every conceivable way, from direct assistance with the work, to the emotional support which kept us going. Our task could not have been accomplished without them.

Murray Enkin, Marc Keirse, Iain Chalmers.

Contents

Contents

The data on which the conclusions of this book are based (and references to published sources of these data) can be found in Chalmers, Enkin, and Keirse (ed.): *Effective care in pregnancy and childbirth*. Oxford University Press (1989).

1

Effective care in pregnancy and childbirth

Care during pregnancy and childbirth should be effective. While no one is likely to disagree with this principle, marked disagreement exists as to what constitutes effective care. The disagreement arises from differences of opinion both about the objectives of care, and about the best means of achieving them.

The objectives of care, or the relative emphases placed on particular objectives, depend on what individuals or communities think is most important. This may range from enjoyment of the experience of childbirth, to shaving another fraction of a percentage point off the perinatal mortality rate, regardless of the costs. This diversity has resulted in widely differing recommendations for care during pregnancy and childbirth.

Differing views about the objectives of care also help to explain the disparate indicators used to assess the effects of care. Some people rate women's satisfaction with the care that they have received as the most important measure of its effectiveness; others seem to regard indirect measures of the baby's wellbeing, such as fetal heart-rate tracings or estimates of the acid-base status of umbilical cord blood, as more important.

In preparing this book, we have not attempted to assess the desirability of different objectives of care during pregnancy and childbirth. These will always remain a matter for individual judgement, and they are unlikely to be influenced by the kind of evidence reviewed in the chapters that follow. What we have tried to do, however, is to give systematic attention to the second reason for disagreements about what constitutes effective care: the differences of opinion about how to attain the various objectives considered to be important.

These differences of opinion are manifested in dramatic variations in the patterns of care from country to country, from community to community, from institution to institution, and from one caregiver to another. The variations exist throughout the various phases of care during pregnancy and childbirth. A variety of methods are used to assess the risk status of the mother and the wellbeing of the fetus. Strongly held opinions differ as to whether pregnant women should take iron or vitamin supplements routinely during pregnancy; whether the cervix should be examined each time a woman attends for antenatal care; and whether or not all women should have an ultrasound examination. There is disagreement about whether women who have an uncomplicated twin pregnancy, or who develop non-albuminuric hypertension, should be hospitalized for bed rest. There is no agreement about the place of external version for breech presentation, cervical cerclage for 'incompetent cervix', corticosteroids for fetal lung maturation, or betamimetics for inhibition of preterm labour. Some people believe that women should not be permitted to eat or drink once labour has started, and that intravenous fluids should be administered routinely; others believe that such restriction is not warranted. There is no consensus about many of the suggested indications for caesarean section and operative vaginal delivery, or about the relative merits of forceps delivery and vacuum extraction. People disagree as to when and how an episiotomy should be performed, and about the best method and suture material to use for its repair. Professionals often present women experiencing difficulties with breastfeeding with conflicting advice about how to overcome these problems. The list of examples that could be cited is endless.

A number of factors may explain these variations in the patterns of care. Some relate to differences in the needs of childbearing women and their babies. Others reflect differences in culture, tradition, status, and fashion; differences in the availability of buildings, personnel, hospital beds, and equipment; differences in the need to provide opportunities for clinicians in training to gain experience; differences in the extent to which malpractice litigation is feared; differences in the extent to which doctors are paid on a 'piecework' basis; and differences in commercial pressures from drug and equipment manufacturers and others.

The focus of *Effective care in pregnancy and childbirth*, however, relates to another important, but rather different determinant of variations in practice. This is the collective uncertainty that exists among those who provide care about the effectiveness and safety of many of the elements of care given during pregnancy and childbirth.

Sometimes the basis for selecting one of a number of alternative forms of care is based on no more than an informal impression that it is superior. Such impressions about the effects of care are sometimes right, and sometimes wrong. The impression that women were less likely to sustain injury during delivery with the vacuum extractor than during delivery with forceps has been borne out by the results of formal studies mounted to investigate this possibility. Other impressions, such as those that led obstetricians to believe that diethylstilboestrol could prevent miscarriages and fetal death have been refuted by the results of properly controlled studies, all too often only after irreparable damage has already been done. Assessing the validity of informal impressions about the effects of care by formal evaluation is therefore essential. Unless this is done, effective forms of care will not be recognized as such, and brought into use as promptly as possible; ineffective or harmful forms of care will not be detected efficiently, and may therefore do harm on a wider scale than necessary.

In the next chapter we outline the rationale, materials, and methods that have been used to arrive at the conclusions presented in subsequent chapters in this book.

2

Evaluating care in pregnancy and childbirth

This chapter is derived from the chapters by Iain Chalmers (1); Iain Chalmers, Jini Hetherington, Diana Elbourne, Marc J. N. C. Keirse, and Murray Enkin (2); Patrick Molinde and Adrian Grant (3); Jane Robinson (4); and Miranda Mugford and Michael F. Drummond (5) in EFFECTIVE CARE IN PREGNANCY AND CHILDBIRTH.

---

1. Introduction

The number of formal studies that attempt to address uncertainties about the effects of many aspects of care during pregnancy and childbirth is overwhelming. Not all of these studies, however, provide reliable information. If judgements about the effects of care based on formal studies are to be valid, careful consideration must be given to the strengths and weaknesses of the methods used by the investigators. In this way a rational basis can be established for selecting those studies that are most likely to provide useful evidence.

Formal studies can be arranged in a hierarchy that reflects the likelihood that biases (systematic errors) will result in misleading conclusions. In addition, it is possible to estimate the extent to which the play of chance (random errors) may be misleading.

2 Minimizing systematic errors (biases)

Sometimes past experience provides a sufficient basis for making a valid assessment of the effects of care. This will only be the case when these effects are dramatically different from what would have been expected on the basis of past experience. For example, case reports have shown that prostaglandin administration may be life-saving when used to treat otherwise uncontrollable haemorrhage when the uterus fails to contract after delivery. Dramatic effects such as this are rare. Usually, one is trying to detect more modest differences (which are nevertheless important) in the effects of alternative forms of care. Single case reports, and case series without formal comparison groups (controls), cannot provide a secure basis for evaluating the effects of care unless the effects are unambiguous. Such studies are subject to a variety of biases that may be sufficiently large either to mask real differences between alternative forms of care, or to suggest that differences exist when, in fact, they do not.

Bias may also affect studies that do have formal comparison groups. In the sections that follow we discuss two of the most important sources of bias. The first of these occurs during the selection process that leads people to receive a particular form of care when alternative forms of care exist; the second results when those providing, receiving, or evaluating care know which one of two or more alternative forms of care has been received.

2.1 *Minimizing bias in the selection of controls*

Uncontrolled observations of events following a particular form of care usually leave questions unanswered about what might have happened if a different form of care (or no care at all) had been provided. Judgements about the effects of care should thus be supported by comparisons between what happens to people who have received a particular form of care with the experience of 'controls' who have received an alternative form of care.

Differences between the experiences of people who have received alternative forms of care can either be due to the differential effects of the different forms of care, or to differences in the pre-treatment characteristics (prognoses) of the people who received these forms of care. The extent to which it is possible to attribute the differences in outcome to the effects of the treatment thus depends on the extent to which the people who received the different forms of care are comparable in every other respect that matters. The challenge is thus to select comparison groups that are comparable in every important respect.

2.1.1 *Studies using historical controls*   One approach to the selection of controls involves making comparisons between people who have received a recently introduced form of care with similar people who received a different form of care in the past. The use of such 'historical controls' sometimes leads to valid inferences, but at other times it can be seriously misleading. For example, it was the results of studies using historical controls which suggested that administration of diethylstilboestrol during pregnancy led to a dramatic decrease in the risk of miscarriage and stillbirth.

Even when outcome following current treatment appears to differ substantially from outcome following earlier forms of care, this may simply be a reflection of changes in other, undocumented, factors that have modified the outcome over time. Without concurrent comparisons between alternative forms of care there is no way of knowing which of the studies using historical controls provide reliable data about the effects of care, and which do not. The most useful role for comparisons using historical controls may therefore be as 'screening tests' for promising new forms of care, which can then be assessed in controlled, prospective experiments.

2.1.2 *Case-control studies*   The underlying principle of a case–control study is straightforward: groups of people who have, and who have not, experienced a particular outcome are assembled; then the frequencies with which each has received the form of care in question are compared. This approach is particularly valuable when the postulated outcome of care is either very infrequent, or when it cannot be ascertained for some months or years after the form of care in question has been received. For example, when cases of cerebral palsy were compared with controls, no difference in the frequency of substandard care during labour and delivery was detected, thus casting further doubt on the widespread belief that the quality of intrapartum care is an important factor in the aetiology of cerebral palsy.

Although case–control studies may sometimes offer the only practicable research strategy for evaluating some of the postulated effects of care during pregnancy and childbirth, they are subject to a variety of biases that restrict their value. Some of these biases may be eliminated by careful matching of cases and controls, but it is never possible to know with any certainty how successful measures to reduce selection and other biases have been. Thus, conclusions about causes and effects based upon case–control studies are often insecure. No amount of matching using information about known confounding factors can ever eliminate the effect of unrecognized confounding factors.

Like the results of studies using historical controls, the results of case–control studies are sometimes supported and sometimes not supported by the results of studies that are less subject to bias. In many instances, however, there are simply no unbiased comparisons available against which to assess the validity of inferences based on the results of case–control studies. In these circumstances, consistent findings from a number of well-designed case–control studies may provide the best evidence that is ever likely to be available.

2.1.3 *Studies using non-randomized, concurrent controls*   A common approach to controlled evaluation of care involves comparison of two or more groups of individuals who happen to have received different forms of care concurrently. Before making causal inferences about the effects of care on the basis of the results of such studies, however, one must be convinced that 'like has been compared with like'.

There are a number of ways in which bias can affect comparisons between non-randomized, concurrent groups receiving different forms of care. For example, many such comparisons have been made between very-low-birthweight infants delivered by caesarean section and other such babies delivered vaginally. In most reports of such comparisons, infants delivered by caesarean section have been more likely than those delivered vaginally to survive. Some people have concluded from these observations that caesarean section is the preferred method of delivery for very-low-birthweight babies. This conclusion cannot be justified, however, unless the two groups of babies compared can be shown to be at comparable prior risk of death and morbidity. As it is, caesarean section is less likely to be used to deliver babies whose chances of survival are judged to be minimal anyway; vaginal delivery, on the other hand, is more likely to have occurred when labour has been precipitate, in itself a risk factor for poor outcome. These and other factors of prognostic importance thus introduce bias into comparisons of the two methods of delivery in these non-randomized comparisons.

The potential of such analyses will improve if risk markers can be identified that make it possible to estimate prognosis in individual patients with a high degree of accuracy. Nevertheless, as in studies using historical controls and in case–control studies, the conclusions drawn from such studies may be invalid because important selection biases have not been controlled adequately.

2.1.4 *Studies using randomized controls* There is only one certain way to overcome the bias that results from people at different prior risk selectively receiving one of the alternative forms of care being compared. This is to conduct a prospective experiment in which the play of chance (randomization) is used to decide which of the alternative forms of care a particular woman or baby should receive. Randomization not only controls selection biases from factors known to be important, it is the *only* known way to control for *unknown* selection biases.

Randomization does not guarantee, nor does it need to guarantee, that the comparison groups that result will be exactly matched in respect of all characteristics of prognostic importance. What randomization does guarantee is that the members of the comparison groups will be selected by chance, rather than by any biased form of selection. The statistical test procedures used to compare the subsequent experiences of the two groups take into account the probabilities that chance imbalances may affect the study results.

The logic underlying the use of randomized controls in prospective experiments to create comparable groups of people for the comparison of alternative forms of care has great force once it has been clearly perceived. Indeed, the randomized controlled trial has become widely accepted as the methodological 'gold standard' for comparing alternative forms of care.

The fact that a formal comparison of two or more alternative forms of care is reported to be a randomized controlled trial is not a guarantee that selection bias has been eliminated. Unless adequate precautions are taken, potential participants in a 'randomized' comparison may be selectively recruited into the study, depending on their or their caregivers' prior knowledge of the group to which they have been allocated. Futhermore, they may be selectively 'withdrawn' from the study, either before or after formal entry.

The selection bias that results from tampering with the make-up of the randomized groups in these ways can sometimes be a more important determinant of the differences in outcome than the effects of the forms of care being compared; comparisons of the experimental groups can then be misleading. For these reasons it is important to take into account the quality of studies purporting to be randomized comparisons of alternative forms of care when assessing whether the results should be used to guide practice.

2.2 *Minimizing other biases*
The second major source of bias results from knowledge among those receiving, providing, or evaluating care concerning which of the alternative forms of care has been received. These biases can be reduced and sometimes eliminated by keeping those administering

or receiving care unaware of the particular form of care that is being used. This process is known as 'masking' or 'blinding'.

Masking is worth while when one or more of the forms of care being compared is likely to have psychologically-mediated effects on the outcomes of interest, because the expectation that a form of care will have certain effects may result in a self-fulfilling prophecy. This phenomenon is known as the 'placebo effect' (literally, 'I will please') when the effects are pleasant or beneficial in some other way; when the effects are unpleasant or unwanted, it is referred to as 'symptom suggestion'.

Another reason for trying to keep caregivers unaware of the forms of care being compared is to reduce the extent to which they may adjust their care in other ways in the light of this knowledge. This 'co-intervention' may make the results of the comparison more difficult to interpret.

Lastly, knowledge of which form of care has been received can affect people's perception of the outcomes. This can occur, for example, if the people assessing the outcome of treatment consciously or unconsciously believe that one of the forms of care being compared is superior to the other; they may tend to record the outcomes in ways that confirm their expectations.

Protection against these observer biases is most secure when the outcome in question is unambiguous (death is the obvious example). Observer biases among those assessing less unambiguous outcomes of care, for example neonatal jaundice, can be reduced, and sometimes abolished, by masking which care has been received. When it is either not practicable or not possible to mask the identity of the alternative forms or care, observer bias may be eliminated by having the outcomes assessed by 'independent' observers who are not aware of the treatment allocation.

3 Minimizing random errors (the play of chance)

Even after successful control of selection biases and other biases that may distort comparisons of alternative forms of care, the results of such comparisons may still be misleading because of *random errors* resulting from the play of chance. Unlike systematic errors, random errors are reduced by increasing the size of the sample studied.

Tests of statistical significance are used to assess the likelihood that the observed differences between alternative forms of care may simply be a reflection of random errors (chance). These tests are used to prevent people inferring that a real difference exists when it does not. Unfortunately, differences between alternative forms of care that are not statistically significant tend to be dismissed as simply reflecting the play of chance. Often, this conclusion is not warranted. Failure to detect a difference does not mean that a difference does not exist.

Random errors will be reduced as samples yielding larger numbers of the outcomes of interest are studied. This can be achieved both by conducting larger trials than has been usual in the past, and by incorporating all the available data from broadly similar trials within a particular field of enquiry in systematic overviews (meta-analyses).

Estimating the range within which the true differential effects of alternative forms of care is likely to lie, by calculating a confidence interval for the statistical estimate of the differences in the outcome of care, provides further protection against being misled by random error.

4 Applying the results of research

Even if one is reasonably certain that systematic and random errors have been adequately controlled in a particular study or in an over-view of similar studies, that is, that the study is 'internally valid', questions may remain about the extent to which this research evidence constitutes a valid basis for guiding care of individual women or babies. This 'external validity' of research may be com-promised either because there are crucial differences between par-ticipants in formal comparisons of care and people receiving care in other contexts, or because there are differences in the nature of the care given within formal comparisons and that provided in usual clinical practice.

Sometimes the limited applicability of the study or overview results may be relatively clear. The results of trials assessing the value of prophylactic folic acid for pregnant women in developing countries, for example, may well not be relevant in relatively well-nourished populations. More usually, however, it will not be possible to conclude with any confidence that the results of controlled trials are not applicable in practice. For a particular form of care to have opposite effects in particular subcategories of individuals would be very rare indeed. Any real differences in the effects of care that do exist between participants in controlled trials and apparently similar people seen in the context of everyday clinical practice are more likely to be differences in the magnitude of effects than differences in the direction of the effects. Judgements to guide practice must then be made more in terms of whether the magnitude of the differential effect is sufficient to warrant modification of usual clinical practice. These judgements will often involve social and economic dimensions.

5 Conclusions

The consequences of being misled by systematic errors (biases) and random errors (the play of chance) are that some women and babies will be denied effective care during pregnancy and childbirth, while others will receive care that is ineffective or actually harmful. In the

modified to only a limited extent by policies of social and financial support for childbearing families. In complex societies, fiscal, economic, social and other policies interact.

2 Social and financial support

Most industrialized countries provide direct financial aid to childbearing families, although the amount women receive varies dramatically among countries. In addition to maternity benefits, there are other aspects of the welfare and taxation system to be considered, such as family or tax allowances. In the Netherlands, for example, provision for 'maternity aides' is an integral part of the maternity system. These specially trained women provide support for up to seven days postpartum for the substantial proportion of women who are at home for some or all of this period.

Most industrialized countries also have legislation intended to protect the fetus, newborn, and mother from the general and specific harmful effects of work, to protect employment by enabling parents to keep jobs while caring for children, and to provide income maintenance for parents during breaks in employment. Many countries have laws that restrict the type of work that pregnant women can do. Contact with low temperatures, lead, ionizing radiation, and other hazards, for example, may be controlled by law. Women may be barred from night work, or long working hours. In some countries employers may not allow a woman to work in the period just before or just after delivery.

There has been considerable debate about this type of legislation, because, while it has laudable aims, it can restrict women's employment opportunities and result in their losing earnings during the childbearing period. Legislation of this nature, in the absence of adequate unemployment benefits or alternative work, may lead some women to conceal their pregnancies and to avoid seeking care. One way to avoid this effect is to have laws that protect women from dismissal on the grounds of pregnancy, and that offer alternative work or compensation to women if their usual jobs are thought to be dangerous.

The other main area of legislation concerns leave, reinstatement, and income maintenance during maternity or parental leave. Most industrialized countries allow all employed women to have paid leave around the time of birth. For legislation to be effective in protecting parents and infants from stress and hardship, the level of income replacement during leave must be adequate. In some countries the maternity allowance is the same as, or close to the woman's usual earnings, while in others it is fixed at a lower rate. If benefits are too low, women will be more likely to work during their period of maternity leave.

There is no evidence at present on which to determine the optimal length of leave. Some types and aspects of work seem more likely than others to compromise health during pregnancy. Different women may have different requirements, and more flexible leave arrangements are needed to allow some pregnant women to take time off earlier in pregnancy.

3 Access to care

The best care will not be effective if it is not available to those who need it. The cost of getting care can be a major impediment to access. There is a close association between the lack of insurance for medical cost coverage for low-income people and low uptake of medical services. In many countries teenagers and socially marginal women may delay seeking care because of feeling ill at ease in conventional care settings. They are made uncomfortable by their difficulty in communication with staff and the frequent impossibility of following the advice they are given, and often because of the reactions of caregivers. In general, women from lower social classes tend to be less well informed about the progress of pregnancy and birth, about problems, and about preventive and curative care. In giving greater priority to the preventive aspects of care rather than to the alleviation of symptoms, the current system of antenatal care is more adapted to the usual behaviour of middle- and upper-class women.

4 Psychological support

The interests of mothers are sometimes forgotten by those who profess an interest in promoting maternal and child health. The social, psychological, and physical problems experienced by pregnant women are often substantial, and those providing care must be sufficiently aware of them. Social and psychological support should be an integral element of all of the care provided for pregnant women.

Evidence from controlled trials suggests that enhanced social and psychological support during pregnancy has a number of beneficial psychological and behavioural effects. Women who received such enhanced support are less likely than women in the control groups to feel unhappy, nervous, and worried during pregnancy, and less likely to have negative feelings about the forthcoming birth. Supported mothers are more likely to communicate effectively with staff, to feel 'in control' during their pregnancies, to attend antenatal classes, and to be satisfied with the care they receive. These women are also more likely to enjoy a worry-free labour and to breastfeed their babies.

5 Unhappiness after childbirth

Lack of social and psychological support during the days and weeks following delivery is one of the main reasons that unhappiness after childbirth is such a common problem. This has traditionally, and wrongly, been seen as a medical subject, labelled postpartum depression. There is no persuasive evidence to support traditional explanations of so-called postpartum depression: no intrinsic, biochemical explanation of women's unhappiness after childbirth has been uncovered and psychoanalytic explanations of postpartum depression cannot be validated empirically. Mothers of young children are often depressed, and are no less likely to be so six months or a year after delivery than in the first few weeks or months following childbirth. Sociological and psychological studies have provided strong evidence of a relationship between some social conditions and postpartum depression: the social conditions linked with depression are only rarely 'out of the ordinary'; more often, they correspond to social expectations about what normal womanhood and normal motherhood must be.

Because many of the social factors leading to postpartum unhappiness are rooted in society's expectations of new mothers, the solutions lie mainly in social change. There is considerable scope, however, for professionals working in the maternity services to reduce the difficulties and unhappiness experienced by women after childbirth. In particular they should be more ready to listen to women, to learn about their social circumstances, and to provide them with information which will lead to more realistic predictions about the experience of pregnancy, childbirth, and early parenthood.

If, in spite of the best efforts being made to prevent the problem, women do become seriously depressed, then encouraging them to talk about their feelings to a non-judgmental person has been shown in a controlled trial to increase their chances of early recovery.

6 Caregivers

Both access to care, and the extent to which care meets the social and psychological needs of women, depend to a large extent on the nature and training of those who provide care during pregnancy and childbirth.

As technical advances became more complex, care has come to be increasingly controlled by, if not carried out by, specialist obstetricians. The benefits of this trend can be seriously challenged. It is inherently unwise, and perhaps unsafe, for women with normal pregnancies to be cared for by obstetric specialists, even if the required personnel were available. Specialists caring for women with both normal and abnormal pregnancies, because of time constraints, have to make an impossible choice: to neglect the normal pregnancies in order to concentrate their care on those with pathology, or to spend most of their time supervising biologically normal processes, in which case they would rapidly lose their specialist expertise.

Midwives and general practitioners, on the other hand, are primarily oriented to the care of women with normal pregnancies, and are likely to have more detailed knowledge of the particular circumstances of individual women. The care that they can give to the majority of women whose pregnancies are not affected by any major illness or serious complication will often be more responsive to their needs than that given by specialist obstetricians.

Optimal care can only occur when both primary and secondary caregivers recognize their complementary roles. There is no place for rivalry or competition between those whose expertise is in the supervision of health and the detection of disease, and those whose specialty is the management of disease and the restoration of health. The responsibility for achieving the co-operative interaction that is so necessary depends on an understanding and acceptance of this by all concerned.

7 Conclusions

When resources of money, time, and energy are limited, the possibilities of making choices that promote health are also limited. People may behave in a way that seems irrational to an outsider, but which is the best choice for them. Pregnant women may have other priorities besides care, such as finding the time and money to provide for children already in the household. A pregnant woman does not leave her work, community, and family responsibilities behind when she steps into the clinic or doctor's office.

Persons providing maternity care share the collective responsibility for ensuring that effective care is not only known, but is also available, accessible, and affordable to all women who require it. Social and psychological support of pregnant women should be an integral part of all forms of care given during pregnancy and childbirth, so that more women and their babies can begin to enjoy their beneficial effects.

4

Advice for pregnancy

This chapter is derived from the chapter by Judith Lumley and Jill Astbury (16) in EFFECTIVE CARE IN PREGNANCY AND CHILDBIRTH.

1 Introduction

The most common form of remedy offered to pregnant women comes in the guise of 'advice'. Unlike ordinary advice, however, there is frequently no option of refusal. Those believed to be authorities on reproduction, such as obstetricians and childbirth educators, can give advice that appeals powerfully to the pregnant woman's desire for a perfect pregnancy and a perfect child. The effectiveness of this advice must be questioned and evaluated as rigorously as must every other intervention carried out during pregnancy.

2 Prepregnancy advice

The appeal of prepregnancy advice is easy to understand. Care that commences after pregnancy is diagnosed does not as yet have a significant impact on rates of preterm delivery, one of the major causes of perinatal death and disability. It has even less to offer for the other major form of adverse outcome of pregnancy, congenital mal-formations, since almost all birth defects are already determined by the time of the earliest antenatal visit.

The fundamental problem with advice before pregnancy is the threadbare state of our knowledge about how to avoid preterm delivery, birth defects, stillbirths, or fetal growth retardation. Apart from ensuring that the woman has been immunized against rubella and will not be taking any unnecessary drugs, what sensible advice can be given? Smokers need practical assistance for quitting rather than advice. Suggestions to adopt a prudent diet, although probably beneficial as general dietary guidelines, are not warranted in terms of preventing malformations or low birthweight. Supplementation with trace minerals and vitamins cannot be justified in the present state of knowledge. Evidence on the effects of physical activity, work, exercise, and travel is still inconsistent.

The possible unwanted side-effects of prepregnancy advice include reduced self-confidence, reduced self-reliance and increased anxiety for the woman. For advice-givers the side-effects may be a reduced awareness of the social factors beyond individual health behaviours that are associated with adverse pregnancy outcomes, and a misguided though sincere belief that they have the answers.

It would be premature to make any judgements about prepregnancy advice except to say that on the basis of present knowledge its beneficial effects are likely to be extremely modest, and it cannot automatically be regarded as harmless.

3 Sexual activity

Advice on the subject of sexual activity in pregnancy is often poorly given: inexact, inexplicit, euphemistic, and misleading, allowing no opportunity for clarification and discussion of alternatives, not to mention being downright dangerous in terms of unintended side-effects. Moreover, there are little or no data to support the various forms of advice given. The many studies reported on the effects of sexual activity in pregnancy are methodologically unsound and contradictory. It is clear that, on the basis of available evidence, any prohibition of sexual activity is wholly inappropriate.

Those who give advice, counselling or reassurance should bear in mind what Marie Stopes wrote in 1918, which is still valid today:

'Much has been written, and may be found in the innumerable books on the sex problem, as to whether a man and a women should or should not have relations while the wife is bearing an unborn child. In this matter experience is very various, so that it is difficult or impossible to give definite advice without knowing the full circumstances of each case. I have heard from a number of women that they desire union urgently at this time; while to others the thought is incredible . . .
The accumulating evidence that I have acquired through direct personal confidences about this subject points in absolutely conflicting directions, and there is little doubt that in this particular, even more so than in many others, the health, needs and mental conditions of women who are bearing children vary profoundly'.

4 Smoking

The evidence that cigarette smoking may have harmful effects on the fetus is strong. It is quite clear that maternal smoking reduces average birthweight. The effect of smoking on other perinatal outcomes is more controversial.

Smoking cessation programmes have a definite place in antenatal care. They can be effective for a small minority of smokers in terms of reducing the amount smoked, in decreasing the proportion of women who continue to smoke, and in increasing mean birthweight. Such programmes must, however, be used with understanding, sensitivity, and compassion. Much anti-smoking 'advice' and propaganda ignores the problem of physical and psychological addiction, the meaning of the behaviour for the women involved, and the guilt and anxiety felt by those who continue to smoke in the face of exhortations to give it up. Much health promotional material for use in pregnancy is characterized by its particularly strident tone.

The campaign against smoking in pregnancy has not been free of unwanted side-effects: many smokers spend the whole of their pregnancy in a state of guilt and inadequacy. We do not know what the effects of such chronic stress and anxiety might be on the course of pregnancy and labour, or on the ultimate relationship with the child. We do know that more than half of the smoking women worry about smoking during pregnancy and that 10 per cent of smokers actually smoke more heavily in pregnancy. The global nature of much anti-smoking exhortation means that any bad outcome of pregnancy (including malformations and mental retardation) may be retrospectively blamed on smoking, even when this could not have been the cause. Sometimes health professionals unwittingly reinforce the self-blame.

Recognition of the social and environmental context in which individuals take up or continue certain behaviours has led some people to condemn health-education activities addressed to individuals as 'victim blaming'. Interventions that focus on self-help and behavioural strategies are less likely to be perceived in this way, and, in relation to quitting smoking, are soundly based. The current evidence shows that they are more effective than advice.

At the same time, obstetricians, family practitioners, and midwives should support the population strategies towards a progressive reduction in cigarette smoking in the whole of society: to increase cigarette excise taxes; to ban all forms of tobacco advertising; to enforce the laws that prohibit sales to children and adolescents; to make public areas non-smoking; and to develop smoking policies for institutions and workplaces. The aim should be to make healthy choices easy choices.

5 Alcohol

The damaging effects of excessive alcohol consumption in pregnancy are well known. They include fetal growth retardation; mental retardation and a dysmorphic syndrome with variable features (at much higher levels of consumption); and altered neonatal behaviour.

Developmental abnormalities are associated only with regular consumption of at least 28.5 ml alcohol (two standard drinks) per day, though one case has been reported following a single massive exposure to alcohol in the early weeks of pregnancy.

Campaigns to increase public awareness of the dangers of alcohol during pregnancy run the risk of arousing anxiety in some women already pregnant, partly because of the uncertainty about the safe lower limit for alcohol intake and also because of the possibility that the most dangerous time for dysmorphic effects may be the first trimester. The very first weeks of pregnancy are often reported to be a period of high anxiety and depression that may increase drinking to relieve tension.

Policy development on alcohol and pregnancy requires, first of all, clarification as to the degree of risk around conception for low levels of regular alcohol consumption (fewer than two standard drinks a day), and for weekly or monthly 'binge' drinking. No formal trials of interventions to reduce high levels of consumption in pregnancy have been reported, and it may be that the priority is better detection of heavy drinkers.

6 Work

When the American College of Obstetricians and Gynecologists issued its guidelines on work in pregnancy in 1977, the most striking exclusion was any mention of housework and child care as work, whether in regard to exposure to toxic chemicals (pesticides, household spray cleaners?) or lifting heavy weights (a toddler plus a folding push chair? a handicapped seven-year-old?). For example, although women who have previously given birth to infants weighing less than 2 kg are strongly advised not to work, no one has suggested that such women be provided with free child care and daily household help throughout pregnancy. Equally, discussions of whether pregnant women should work usually pay scant attention to the implications for family health and welfare of the concomitant reduction in family income. In fact, the benefits of paid employment are rarely mentioned.

The main cause of confusion results from regarding paid employment as a single category, lumping together women working with much less physical effort or stress than they would have at home with women whose work involves standing all day, or carrying heavy loads, or exposure to extremes of temperature or humidity.

General advice on employment in pregnancy is clearly inappropriate. Where working conditions meet the criteria for occupational fatigue, women's requests for a change of work during pregnancy should be supported by those providing antenatal care. Apart from this situation it is extremely difficult to weigh up the net benefits and risks.

7 Conclusions

The images that underlie advice in pregnancy are threefold: the perfect child, the perfect mother, and the perfect birth. The perfect child, attainable by following the right instructions, is of course a mirage. With the implied promise to be a perfect mother and have the perfect birth, a pregnant woman is exhorted to lead a selfless, healthy life, uncontaminated by sex, cigarettes, alcohol, employment, or anxiety. The evidence for most of these exhortations is slight. Where the evidence is stronger, the flaw has been in the way that research and prescription fail to take into account the real lives and responsibilities of women.

5

Dietary modification in pregnancy

This chapter is derived from chapters by: David Rush (17); Jane Green (18); and Kassam Mahomed and Frank Hytten (19) in EFFECTIVE CARE IN PREGNANCY AND CHILDBIRTH.

1 Introduction
2 Diet and birthweight
3 Diet and pre-eclampsia
4 Iron and folate
5 Conclusions

---

1 Introduction

The relation between the diet of the mother and the wellbeing of the fetus and infant continues to be a matter of uncertainty and controversy. Observational studies have generated conflicting and uncertain results, because their results tend to reflect too many other aspects of the pregnant woman's life that vary with diet and nutrition. Whenever limits to nutritional intake are imposed by economic, educational, social, or other constraints, there are likely to be accompanying stresses, such as exposure to infection, the need for physical labour, inadequate housing, or frequent family disruption.

Adequately controlled studies have not been large enough to allow firm conclusions to be drawn. Nevertheless, much important information has been obtained.

2 Diet and birthweight

Two main conclusions can be drawn from studies on dietary modification. First, dietary restriction can cause marked decreases in birthweight. During famine, mean birthweight can be depressed by as much as 550 grams, and iatrogenic dietary manipulation and restriction can have almost as marked an effect. Although the extent to which such decreases in birthweight are associated with perinatal mortality and morbidity is unknown, there can be no justification for allowing pregnant women to go hungry, or for imposing dietary restriction or major manipulation of the dietary constituents upon them.

Second, attempts at nutritional supplementation, while well intentioned, have not always had the desired effect. It is now clear that high-density protein supplements are associated with a decrease rather than increase in mean birthweight. Although increments (on average, about 30 to 50 g) in mean birthweight have been found in association with programmes of aggressive nutritional counselling and/or supplementation with preparations of relatively low protein density in poorly nourished populations, the magnitude of the increments in birthweight is lower than had been hoped.

3 Diet and pre-eclampsia

Attempts to use dietary manipulation to prevent pre-eclampsia continue to influence antenatal care, despite the fact that the evidence and arguments on which they are based are unconvincing. Presently available evidence provides no justification for any form of dietary intervention with the aim of preventing pre-eclampsia. In particular, women should not be told to restrict their diet to reduce 'high' weight gain. The still widespread idea that this helps to prevent pre-eclampsia was based on false arguments. Equally, there is no evidence to support the alternative view that eating sufficient amounts of a good diet will reliably protect against pre-eclampsia.

We know too little about the effects of high or low salt consumption on the development of pre-eclampsia to be able to offer well-informed advice. The intriguing but unconfirmed results of one study, in which the incidence of pre-eclampsia was lower in women advised to eat more salt than those advised to eat less, suggest that women should be very cautious about restricting salt intake during pregnancy.

4 Iron and folate

The normal haematological adaptations to pregnancy are frequently misinterpreted as evidence of iron deficiency, and iron is inappropriately prescribed. Iron supplements have been given with two objectives in view: to try to return the blood picture towards the normal non-pregnant state, a strange objective when millions of years of evolution have determined otherwise; and to improve the clinical outcome of the pregnancy and the future health of the mother. The first objective can certainly be accomplished; the key question is whether or not in achieving the 'normalized' blood picture we benefit the woman and her baby.

An individual's haemoglobin concentration depends much more on the complex relation between red-cell mass and plasma volume than on deficiencies of iron or folate. The advent of electronic blood counters has given an opportunity for more appropriate criteria to be applied to the diagnosis of anaemia. Mean cell volume may be the most useful; it is not closely related to haemoglobin concentration, and declines quite rapidly in the presence of iron deficiency.

Treatment of a low haemoglobin with iron in pregnancy is seldom necessary. A low haemoglobin without other evidence of iron deficiency requires no treatment; indeed treatment may be harmful. If there is genuine evidence of iron deficiency, iron treatment is needed, and the usual approach is to give iron salts by mouth. There is no convincing evidence that the addition of copper, manganese, molybdenum, or ascorbic acid improves the efficiency with which the iron is used.

The cause of megaloblastic anaemia in pregnancy is almost always folate deficiency. A megaloblastic picture in the peripheral blood occurs at a late stage of folate deficiency and is rare; the condition is more often diagnosed from the finding of megaloblastic changes in the bone marrow during the investigation of an anaemia not responding to iron. Under these circumstances treatment with folic acid supplementation is rapidly effective.

The evidence suggests that, excepting genuine anaemia resulting from iron or folate deficiency, the best reproductive performance is associated with levels of haemoglobin that are traditionally regarded as pathologically low. There is little doubt that supplementation with iron can change the blood picture towards its non-pregnant state, but this 'normalization' of the blood picture has not been shown to confer any benefit on either mother or baby.

Women do not feel any subjective benefit from having their haemoglobin concentration raised. A possible advantage claimed for a high level of haemoglobin in pregnancy is that the woman is in a stronger position to withstand haemorrhage. There is no evidence to support this claim. Indeed, as a low haemoglobin in healthy pregnant women generally implies a large circulating blood volume, it is at least possible that women with a *low* haemoglobin might better withstand a given loss of blood.

In the very few randomized trials where clinical outcome was examined, iron supplementation had no influence on the frequency of proteinuric hypertension, antepartum haemorrhage, or maternal infection. There is cause for concern in the findings of two well-conducted trials that iron supplementation resulted in an increase in the prevalence of preterm delivery and low birthweight. Perhaps there is a primary adverse effect on fetal growth due to the increased viscosity of maternal blood that follows the iron-induced macro-cytosis and increased haemoglobin concentration, impeding uteroplacental blood flow.

In well-nourished women the addition of folate to iron supplements has no evident beneficial effects. In less well-nourished women the addition of folate may be more important, although the evidence is sketchy. Folate itself seems to have little influence on clinical outcome, although there are indications of possible benefit to fetal growth in ill-nourished communities, and in young pregnant teenagers when both fetal and maternal growth are competing.

5 Conclusions

There is no evidence that dietary restriction of any sort confers any benefit to pregnant women or their offspring. Nutritional supplementation with supplements of relatively low protein density may result in a modest increment in birthweight, but no other substantive benefits have yet been documented.

Since the increase in mean birthweight associated with nutritional counselling and supplementation has been relatively small, further trials of these interventions must concentrate on subsets of women in which a beneficial effect is most likely to be demonstrated. Further research is also needed to determine whether the observed small increments in birthweight are associated with decreased perinatal morbidity and mortality, and with improved long-term growth and development of the infant. Since there is some evidence that antenatal feeding may influence subsequent development independent of changes in birthweight, the possibility of such effects must be considered.

While there is an obvious need for further research into the best means of promoting optimal nutrition in pregnancy, hungry women cannot wait for the results of such studies. They must have access both to adequate amounts of food and to informed care.

In spite of persistent recommendations that iron and folate supplementation is an important aspect of antenatal care, the evidence that it benefits the mother and her fetus is, to say the least, unconvincing. There is no clinical benefit to be seen either in the pregnancy itself or in the infant, and the only beneficial results may be to build up the woman's iron stores. On the other hand there are hints that the reversal of the normal fall in haemoglobin concentration and the iron-induced macrocytosis may increase blood viscosity to a degree that could impair uteroplacental blood flow.

True anaemia should be sought in all pregnant women and treated if found, but to treat all pregnant women as if they were iron-deficient is both therapeutically misguided and possibly harmful.

6

Antenatal classes

This chapter is derived from the chapter by Penny Simkin and Murray Enkin (20) in EFFECTIVE CARE IN PREGNANCY AND CHILDBIRTH.

1 Introduction
2 Content of antenatal classes
3 Effects of antenatal classes
4 Conclusions

---

1 Introduction

'Natural childbirth' and 'psychoprophylaxis' began as alternatives to what was perceived as overmedicalized obstetrics, with its liberal use of pain-relieving drugs and operative delivery. A variety of different programmes appeared at about the same time, all with a single common aim: the use of psychological or physical, non-pharmaceutical modalities for the prevention of pain in childbirth.

Modern antenatal classes have expanded their horizons beyond that simple primary goal. Most classes today attempt to accomplish other goals as well, including good health habits, stress management, anxiety reduction, enhancement of family relationships, feelings of 'mastery', enhanced self-esteem and satisfaction, successful infant feeding, smooth postpartum adjustment, and family planning. All aim to enhance the woman's sense of confidence as she approaches childbirth.

Because of their complex, often disparate goals and ideologies, one cannot make general statements about the effects of antenatal classes as if they were a single entity. Research on the effectiveness of antenatal classes over the years reflects their changing emphasis. The early studies focused on the effects of class attendance on labour pain, medication use, and other qualities of labour. Today the emphasis has shifted to study of the psychological effects, parenting behaviours, and the effectiveness of specific teaching, counselling, or labour coping techniques.

2 Content of antenatal classes

Most antenatal classes involve the use of group sessions to establish a community of experience, and include voluntary muscular relaxation, specific breathing patterns to serve as a focus of attention or distraction, and verbal suggestion for both pain reduction and for appropriate behaviour. They aim to provide accurate and reliable information about pregnancy, birth, and the experiences which women will undergo or encounter.

The information content of modern antenatal classes may include the relation of pregnancy symptoms to underlying mechanisms, and suggest ways of alleviating these symptoms. The emotional shifts of pregnancy may be explored, and issues of sexuality, and relationship to spouse and other children may be discussed as well.

Antenatal classes allow an opportunity to review the mechanisms of labour and birth in adequate detail, and to explain medical and obstetrical terminology. Information need not come from the instructor alone. Discussion with other participants allows for the reassurance and sense of community that comes from sharing experience and information.

In addition to knowledge and information, most antenatal classes attempt to impart skills for coping with the stress of labour. These often include a variety of relaxation techniques, various forms of attention-focusing and distraction techniques, numerous comfort measures, various types of controlled breathing patterns, and the teaching of labour support skills to the partners (husbands or others) of the pregnant woman.

Finally, the antenatal class is a vehicle for attitude modification, towards, on the one hand, increased self-reliance and questioning on the part of the woman or couple, or, on the other, to increased compliance with and adherence to prescribed medical regimens.

3 Effects of antenatal classes

Randomized controlled studies have shown antenatal classes to result in the use of significantly less analgesic medication during labour. No other important effects of antenatal classes have been demonstrated.

A number of non-randomized cohort studies have reported a variety of other beneficial effects of antenatal classes, but the self-selection of the study and control groups introduces such major biases that the results of these studies must be largely discounted.

There are few studies comparing the pain-relieving effects of different methods of childbirth preparation. The two major methods, Read's natural childbirth and Lamaze's psychoprophylaxis, have never been compared systematically.

While a reduction in the use of pain medications was found, it cannot be assumed that this reduction is necessarily associated with less pain. The use of pain medications is related only in part to the pain experienced by the woman. Other factors such as availability (many hospitals do not have 24-hour anaesthesia services), quality of labour support, wish of the mother, or hospital customs, may be major determinants of whether she will receive medication, what kind, and how much.

For these reasons many investigators have attempted to evaluate the pain of labour using outcome variables other than medication use. Two findings have been consistently reported: first, that there is a wide variation in the pain experienced by women; second, that the average level of pain experienced by women in labour is high.

If the benefits of antenatal education are difficult to document in a systematic manner, the adverse effects and potential hazards are even more elusive. The extent to which fear is created rather than alleviated by classes, and whether women succumb to peer or educator pressures to conform, or refuse needed medication or intervention is completely unknown. There has been little systematic evaluation of the extent to which negative feelings of anger, guilt, or inadequacy are engendered when a woman's or her partner's expectations, possibly raised by the antenatal classes, are not met.

As antenatal classes have become more popular, they have begun reaching more women from less privileged classes. While antenatal classes appealed primarily to the middle classes in years past, they are now routinely offered in many clinics, health departments, and schools for pregnant adolescent women.

The effects of an antenatal class depend not only on the characteristics of those who attend and the competence and skills of the teacher, but also, to a large extent, on the underlying objectives of the programme. Some classes are taught by independent childbirth educators or co-ordinated by large consumer groups. Others are offered by official health agencies; still others by doctors for their own patients or by hospitals for the women who plan to deliver there. The curricula outlined for these classes may be similar, and there may be little difference in the information taught, or the skills imparted. Nevertheless, there may be great differences in the attitudes that are encouraged. As a general rule community-sponsored childbirth education classes are structured to incorporate the interests of parents into the curriculum; hospital-based classes may be required and expected to explain existing policies to parents, not to question, nor to offer alternatives, nor to help parents decide their own birth plans.

It is possible that the actual existence of antenatal classes is more important than the details of what is taught; that 'the medium is the message'.

The number of women attending antenatal classes is now substantial. The full impact of childbirth education cannot be assessed solely by its effect on the individual woman giving birth, for there may be indirect effects that engender significant changes in the ambience in which all women give birth. Once a critical mass of mothers becomes aware of the fact that options are available to them, major changes in obstetrical practice may ensue.

If information on risks, benefits, and alternatives to conventional care remains a major focus among a significant proportion of antenatal classes, we may expect increasingly influential and well-informed consumer involvement in the future patterns of childbirth practices. If, on the other hand, the ideology of classes continues shifting to reflect an acceptance of conventional obstetric practices, the group consciousness among expectant parents may fade, reducing their impact and their influence on the direction of maternity care.

4 Conclusions

The widespread popularity of antenatal classes testifies to the desire of expectant parents for childbirth education. As there are benefits in terms of amount of analgesic medication used and in some aspects of satisfaction with childbirth, and as significant adverse effects have not been demonstrated, such classes should continue to be available. The objectives of the classes must be made clear to the participants and unrealistic expectations of what the classes can achieve must be avoided. A variety of different types of classes, whose goals are explicitly stated, may help women or couples choose the programme most likely to meet their needs.

7

Formal risk scoring

This chapter is derived from the chapter by Sophie Alexander and Marc J. N. C. Keirse (22) in EFFECTIVE CARE IN PREGNANCY AND CHILDBIRTH.

1 Introduction
2 Utility of scoring
3 Conclusions

1 Introduction

Identification of pregnancies that are at greater than average risk is a fundamental component of antenatal care. In theory, an approach that substitutes rationally based risk scoring for the rather nebulous process of clinical impression should be more accurate than the less formal risk assessment that is part of daily clinical practice. As for many other tests the validity and utility of risk scoring systems remain to be determined.

The primary purpose of a risk scoring system is to permit classification of individual women into different categories, for which different actions can then be planned. The great variety of scores that are used in pregnancy and childbirth aim to identify individuals at high risk and to discriminate between levels of risk.

There are many practical difficulties involved in the use of scoring systems. Often the risk markers are poorly defined. Does 'bleeding' for example, include spotting, or bleeding from a local lesion in the vagina or cervix? The need to dichotomize continuous variables that are as different from each other as blood-pressure (how high ?), or smoking (how much ?), imposes a rigidity that can often be counter-productive. With formalized risk scoring, a woman may be assigned to a high-risk group because of fixed definitions of the risk markers, whereas a capable clinician could have assessed the situation more sensitively by the use of clinical judgement.

The reproducibility of scoring systems tends to be low. Apart from the still small number of antenatal clinics where details of each pregnant woman are transferred interactively to a computer (an approach that remains unevaluated), scoring is done by a busy clinician, with pen and paper. To be feasible, there should be not too many questions, values should be restricted to integers, and addition is preferable to multiplication in deriving the score.

Some scoring systems require women to be scored only once; at the opposite extreme, some require reassessment at each antenatal visit. Reassessment allows the inclusion of complications appearing in the current pregnancy, and revision of the score upwards or downwards depending on the course of the pregnancy. Little is known about the benefits of re-evaluation.

Scoring is more effective in second or later pregnancies than in women pregnant for the first time. The poor predictive value of the scoring systems for nulliparae is, at least in part, inherent in the choice of risk markers, many of which relate to characteristics of the past obstetric history.

An ideal scoring system should allow assignment to a risk group in time for appropriate action to be taken. Scoring systems will perform better at least in assessing the risk, though not in offering possibilities or opportunities to influence the level of risk, if they are implemented late in pregnancy or if they allow for readjustment during pregnancy. This leads to the paradox that the most precise risk prediction is made at a time when there is little or no further need for it, whereas the potentially more useful early identification of risk is relatively imprecise.

Both the positive and the negative predictive values of all scoring systems are poor. Depending on the cut-off point and the test chosen, only between 10 and 30 per cent of the women who are allocated to the high-risk groups actually experience the adverse outcome for which the scoring system declares them to be at risk. Among mothers who deliver preterm or low-birthweight infants, between 20 and 50 per cent have low risk scores.

2 Utility of scoring

It may be useful to the clinician to know which pregnancies under his or her care are most likely to result in an adverse outcome. To the individual woman, being labelled as 'high-risk' will be beneficial only if something can be done either to decrease the risk or to reduce its consequences.

Although often referred to as risk factors, most of the elements that are incorporated in the scores are merely risk markers, indicating that a statistical association with the outcome that is being scored for exists. These risk markers do not cause the outcome. The most important of them, such as parity, prepregnancy weight, height, and past reproductive performance, cannot be altered by any intervention. For the individual woman labelled as being at increased risk, both the threat of adverse outcome and the inability to change its markers may create anxiety, with no possibility of improving the pregnancy outcome.

The most powerful way to test the effectiveness of formal risk scoring systems is to mount randomized controlled trials in which formal risk scoring is a component of the antenatal care of some women, while a control group receive the usual antenatal care without formal risk scoring. No such trials have been published, although two are ongoing at present.

A number of observational studies have claimed a reduction in preterm births following introduction of systematic scoring. They attributed this improvement to better selection of those women who required treatment, and to better 'systematization of interventions'. In many settings there was an increase in the frequency with which interventions of dubious value were performed. Although some authors expressed the belief that their prevention policy had played a part in the overall reduction of preterm birth rates, most of the improved results occurred in the women scored to be at low risk.

3 Conclusions

Formal risk scoring systems are a mixed blessing for the individual woman and her baby. They may help to provide a minimum level of care and attention in settings where these are inadequate. In other settings, however, formal risk scoring results in a variety of unwarranted interventions. The introduction of risk scoring into clinical practice carries the danger of replacing a potential risk of adverse outcome with the certain risk of dubious treatments and interventions.

The potential benefits of risk scoring have been widely publicized, but the potential harm is rarely mentioned in the current literature. Such harm can result from unwarranted intrusion in women's private lives, from superfluous interventions and treatments, from creating unnecessary stress and anxiety, and from allocating scarce resources to areas where they are not needed.

Screening for genetic disease

This chapter is derived from the chapter by Michael Daker and Martin Bobrow (23) in EFFECTIVE CARE IN PREGNANCY AND CHILDBIRTH.

1 Introduction

Prenatal screening for congenital abnormalities and genetic disorders has become increasingly important since the development of amniocentesis in 1969. The planning of a genetic screening programme involves defining the high-risk populations in which screening procedures are justifiable. This requires careful consideration of a number of factors, including the prevalence of the condition in the population to be tested, the severity of the disorder, the sensitivity and specificity of the available tests, and the cost.

Costs are not wholly financial, and it is equally important to weigh the human costs. Although screening programmes may bring reassurance to some women who are tested, for others they may generate anxiety by merely raising the question of abnormality. The consequences of erroneous diagnoses must be a matter for particularly careful consideration.

2 Methods of screening

2.1 *Ultrasound*

Many structural abnormalities of the fetus are now diagnosable directly by ultrasound, and the introduction of real-time scanning has opened the way for the screening of antenatal populations. Scanning for fetal abnormality is carried out between 16 and 22 weeks gestation, and may include a general assessment of the fetal anatomy (head, heart, stomach, bladder, kidney, and spine). Where the initial scan shows possible evidence of fetal abnormality a more detailed examination will be required.

Neural tube defects are among the more common birth defects. The frequency varies according to ethnic group, being relatively common among Caucasians, less so in Mongolians, and rare in Negroes. There are also geographical, temporal, and socioeconomic variations in occurrence. Affected pregnancies have elevated amniotic fluid alpha-fetoprotein levels, and over 98 per cent of open lesions can be detected by this test.

Since amniocentesis is an invasive procedure, amniotic fluid alpha-fetoprotein screening is only offered to women at known increased risk of having an affected fetus. Serum alpha-fetoprotein determination has made screening of the general population feasible where there is a high incidence of neural tube defects. When the initial result from a serum test shows an elevated level of alpha-fetoprotein, a repeat sample should be requested. If the second test also shows elevated levels of alpha-fetoprotein, the woman should undergo amniocentesis to allow the more sensitive amniotic fluid alpha-fetoprotein assay to be carried out.

With increasing expertise in the use of ultrasound, most neural tube defects are directly detectable by this technique. Some of these abnormalities, such as anencephaly and severe spina bifida, will be picked up as a result of routine scanning during early pregnancy. The smaller lesions, however, will require a more detailed examination by an experienced ultrasonographer. As a method of mass screening for neural tube defects, therefore, ultrasound has not yet been shown to be as effective as alpha-fetoprotein.

2.2 Cytogenetic techniques

Studies on newborn infants show a worldwide frequency of chromosome disorders of about 6 per 1000 births. The total population load of chromosome abnormalities is far greater still, as the majority of affected embryos are spontaneously miscarried early in pregnancy. About 50 per cent of all clinically recognizable spontaneous abortuses are chromosomally abnormal.

Over the past fifteen years there has been a steady rise in demand for prenatal diagnosis for chromosome disorders. The majority of referrals for prenatal chromosome diagnosis are for older women (aged 35 and over) who have an increased risk of carrying a fetus with Down's syndrome (trisomy 21) and most other chromosomal trisomies. Up to the age of about 29 there is little effect of maternal age on the birth frequency of Down's syndrome (the incidence ranging from approximately 0.5 to 1.0 per 1000 live births). Between the ages of 30 and 34 the frequency begins to rise slightly: by age 35 it is

2 to 3 per 1000 live births, and 8 or 9 per 1000 at the age of 40. Currently, many laboratories use an age of 35 as the cut-off point for offering prenatal diagnosis, a decision governed partly by available resources. However, combinations of serum alpha-fetoprotein results and maternal age can improve the selection of women for cytogenetic study in pregnancy. The techniques in current use for the prenatal diagnosis of chromosome disorders are amniocentesis and chorionic villus sampling.

2.2.1 *Amniocentesis* The overall safety of early second trimester amniocentesis has been well established from several large studies. The chief risk is that of the additional risk of miscarriage associated with the procedure, which approximates to 0.5 per cent. Amniotic fluid cell chromosome studies have two major drawbacks. First, it usually takes from two to three weeks from the time the sample is taken until the result is given out. Many women find this long wait in itself to be distressing. Second, amniocentesis cannot be carried out until the sixteenth week of pregnancy, so that, should termination be indicated, it will have to be carried out at a relatively late stage in pregnancy. Culture failure occurs in about 2 per cent of samples. In these cases a repeat sample becomes necessary, and the pregnancy is likely to be rather advanced for termination before the result is finally available.

2.2.2 *Chorionic villus sampling* Chorionic villus sampling could become an attractive alternative to amniocentesis or fetal blood sampling, since it can be performed in the first trimester. It involves the use of a cannula (or biopsy forceps) under ultrasound guidance, to take a small biopsy of villi from the chorion frondosum. A majority of obstetricians take samples by the transcervical route; some advocate a transabdominal approach on the grounds that this is less likely to cause intrauterine infection.

The advantages of first trimester diagnosis are obvious, but there are still problems, both obstetrical and cytogenetic, that need to be resolved. The relatively low (1 to 4 per cent) early fetal loss rate is encouraging, although to some extent it probably reflects careful selecting out of women in whom the obstetrician is not prepared to perform the biopsy. The precise safety of the technique and all questions relating to possible long-term effects on the developing fetus, require further investigation. Several randomized trials are currently being undertaken in various countries, and these should provide objective information on the subject over the next few years.

Apart from technical difficulties, there are other important aspects of prenatal diagnosis by chorionic villus sampling that require consideration. A number of chromosomally unbalanced conceptuses are miscarried spontaneously in early pregnancy, so that a significant

nancy. It may be detected for the first time in pregnancy, but does not regress after delivery. The two conditions may occur together in the same woman. They constitute an important cause of maternal, fetal, and neonatal morbidity and mortality.

Since the cause of the pregnancy-induced hypertensive disorders is not understood, definition and diagnosis are based on the signs that are considered to be most characteristic: hypertension, proteinuria, and oedema. These signs, of which the presence of an elevated blood-pressure is a prerequisite, are not the disease, but constitute secondary features of an underlying circulatory disorder. As signs they are non-specific; they can be induced by pregnancy itself, as well as by a variety of conditions unrelated to, but coinciding with pregnancy. Hypertension and proteinuria are usually asymptomatic and must be detected by screening.

2 Hypertension

The diagnosis of hypertension is made only when blood-pressure passes a predefined threshold. Many pregnancies develop normally in spite of the raised blood-pressure, indicating that adequate uteroplacental and maternal organ flows are maintained. A certain degree of hypertension may well be beneficial to maintain perfusion pressures in the face of an elevated vascular resistance.

Many factors such as age, parity, and race cause marked variability in blood-pressure between individuals, while others, such as time of day, level of activity, emotions, and posture may result in variations within the same pregnant woman. Measurements by doctors or mid-wives in antenatal clinics are usually higher than those obtained at home ('white coat hypertension').

Although measurement of blood-pressure is the mainstay of screening, diagnosis, and decision-making in pregnant women, the inherent technical and sampling errors, whether by auscultation or by automatic devices, constitute an important limitation of the ac-curacy and precision of this measurement.

Hypertension in pregnancy can be defined either as a diastolic pressure above a predetermined cut-off point, or as a rise from a woman's pre-existing blood-pressure level. Pregnant women with a diastolic blood-pressure between 90 and 100 mm Hg in the second half of pregnancy experience an increased incidence of proteinuria and perinatal death. For that reason, a diastolic blood-pressure level somewhere between 90 and 100 mm Hg may be considered to be a threshold between women at low risk and women with an increased risk of pregnancy complications.

A diagnosis of hypertension so defined is not a diagnosis of a disease, but a marker of an increase in risk, and an indication for careful monitoring of mother and fetus. It is clinically important to realize that, in view of the physiological blood-pressure changes in pregnancy, a diastolic blood-pressure of 90 mm Hg in mid-pregnancy is more abnormal than such a pressure would be if it occurred for the first time at term.

The absolute level of blood-pressure is far more important than the rise, both in relation to the occurrence of proteinuria and in terms of prognosis. Pregnancy-induced hypertensive disorders rarely occur before 20 weeks' gestation. Hypertension and/or proteinuria diagnosed before 20 weeks will usually be due to pre-existing chronic hypertension or renal disease. Hypertension may also be diagnosed for the first time during labour; such hypertension will often be transitory, due to effort and/or anxiety.

The differential diagnosis between pregnancy-induced hypertension and pregnancy associated with chronic hypertension can be difficult. In comparison with pregnancy-induced hypertension or pre-eclampsia, which usually occurs in young nulliparous women, women with chronic hypertension tend to be older and parous. Many women with chronic or renal hypertension show an even greater physiological fall in blood-pressure during the first half of pregnancy than do normotensive women, with an exaggerated rise in the third trimester. The earlier in pregnancy that hypertension is noted, the more likely it is to be chronic hypertension.

Chronic hypertension is a major predisposing factor for pre-eclampsia ('superimposed pre-eclampsia'). The maternal and fetal risks of chronic hypertension in pregnancy seem to be mainly attributable to the development of superimposed pre-eclampsia; the majority of chronically hypertensive women who do not develop pre-eclampsia have a normal perinatal outcome.

3 Proteinuria

Renal protein excretion increases in normal pregnancy, and proteinuria is not considered abnormal until it exceeds 300 mg per 24 hours. An increase in protein output will usually, but not always, lead to higher concentrations in random urine samples. The volume and concentration of urine will affect protein concentration and may give rise to erroneously high or low results of tests on random urine specimens.

Proteinuria may be a temporary phenomenon due to pregnancy-induced renal lesions, or it may be an expression of pre-existing renal disease coinciding with pregnancy. In the first case it should disappear at some time after delivery; in the latter it will remain present.

Proteinuria is a late sign of pre-eclampsia, but it is associated with an increased risk of poor fetal outcome. The overall correlation between the degree of elevation of blood-pressure and the occurrence of proteinuria is weak. On the other hand, the magnitude of protein loss correlates positively with the severity of renal lesions. Thus urine testing is a vital part of the screening process for hypertensive disorders in pregnancy.

In practice, screening for proteinuria is usually done with reagent strips or 'dipstick' tests, which will start detecting protein (albumin) concentrations of approximately 50 mg per litre. Protein concentrations depend on urine volume and specific gravity. Dipsticks may give up to 25 per cent false positive results with a trace reaction, and 6 per cent false positive results with a one + reaction on testing of random specimens from women with normal 24-hour total protein excretion.

The definitive test for proteinuria in pregnancy is determination of total protein excretion in a 24-hour urine collection, using a reliable quantitative method (for example, Esbach's). This is too complicated to be used for screening, but should be performed whenever significant proteinuria is detected on screening of a random urine specimen. Alternative approaches to the measurement of 24-hour protein excretion, such as determination of the protein/creatinine index in random urine specimens, await validation.

4 Oedema

Moderate oedema occurs in 50 to 80 per cent of healthy normotensive pregnant women. This physiological oedema of pregnancy is often confined to the lower limbs, but it may also occur in other sites, such as the fingers or face, or as generalized oedema. Most pregnant women note that the rings on their fingers become tight in the course of the third trimester. Physiological oedema usually develops gradually, and is associated with a smooth rate of weight gain. The finding that pregnant women with generalized oedema without hypertension or proteinuria have larger babies than women without obvious oedema strongly suggests that oedema is a part of the normal maternal adaptation to pregnancy.

Oedema affects approximately 85 per cent of women with preeclampsia. It may appear rather suddenly, and may be associated with a rapid rate of weight gain. It cannot be differentiated clinically from oedema in normal pregnancy. Pregnant women without oedema, and with early- or late-onset oedema, all have a similar incidence of hypertension.

The combination of hypertension and oedema, or hypertension and increased maternal weight gain, is associated with a lower fetal death rate than is hypertension alone. Pre-eclampsia without oedema ('dry pre-eclampsia') has long been recognized as a dangerous variant of the condition, with a higher maternal and fetal mortality than pre-eclampsia with oedema.

As oedema in pregnancy is common and does not define a group at risk, it should not be used as a defining sign of hypertensive disorders in pregnancy.

5 Biochemical and biophysical tests

A number of tests have been devised to demonstrate the presence or absence of an abnormal vascular responsiveness before the clinical onset of pregnancy-induced hypertension. These include the cold-pressor test, the flicker fusion test, the isometric exercise test, the roll-over test, and infusions of catecholamines or vasopressin. Evaluation of these tests has shown them to be worthless, and they are of historical interest only. The angiotensin sensitivity test is useful in a research setting, but is too complicated and time-consuming to be of clinical use.

There is insufficient evidence to warrant the use of uric acid levels as a screening test to predict the later development of pregnancy-induced hypertension. In women with established pre-eclampsia, however, serum uric acid levels appear to reflect fetal prognosis. For that reason uric acid levels can be used in the care for women with pregnancy-induced hypertension to monitor the course of the disease.

6 Conclusions

Hypertension and pre-eclampsia are usually asymptomatic; screening and diagnosis depend mainly on careful determination of blood-pressure and proteinuria. The occurrence of pregnancy-induced hypertension is relatively rare before 28 weeks of pregnancy, but when it occurs it frequently leads to pre-eclampsia with its associated high rate of perinatal morbidity and mortality. On the other hand, pregnancy-induced hypertension occurs much more frequently late in the third trimester, when antenatal visits are usually increased in frequency, but the maternal and fetal risks of late-onset disease are much smaller. Therefore, although routine antenatal screening for hypertensive disorders before 28 weeks' gestation may have a low productivity in terms of the number of positive diagnoses per visit, it has a high potential in terms of prevention of maternal and fetal morbidity and mortality. For that reason the number of antenatal visits of nulliparae in the second trimester should certainly not be reduced, but might even be increased to once per 3 weeks; such visits may be confined to a brief discussion and measurement of blood-pressure and urinalysis for protein.

Simple blood-pressure measurement remains an integral part of antenatal care; it should be performed in a standardized fashion by a skilled midwife or nurse, or by the attending physician. Errors in blood-pressure measurement cannot be abolished by spending money on automated equipment. The mercury sphygmomanometer

tal mortality. The effects of treatment with insulin on perinatal mortality have been examined in only one randomized controlled trial. Thirteen of 307 women (4.2 per cent) with a positive glucose tolerance test treated with insulin experienced a perinatal loss, compared to 15 of 308 such women (4.9 per cent) who were treated with diet alone. This small difference is neither statistically nor clinically significant.

The 'adverse outcome' most frequently associated with gestational diabetes is 'fetal macrosomia' (a larger than average baby). Up to 30 per cent of infants of mothers with an abnormal glucose tolerance test have a birthweight of more than 4000 g. A heavy mother and post-term pregnancy, however, are much more strongly associated with fetal macrosomia than is gestational diabetes. Clinical judgement based on assessment of prepregnant weight, weight gain, and a pregnancy past 42 weeks without any reference to glucose tolerance is more predictive of fetal macrosomia than is the glucose tolerance test. Wide application of glucose tolerance testing to pregnant women would thus be of limited value in identifying women at increased risk of fetal macrosomia.

Treating women who have gestational diabetes with insulin can reduce the incidence of macrosomia. A number of studies have confirmed this effect. Despite the observed reductions in birthweight that can be achieved by insulin therapy, there is no convincing evidence of a decrease in the incidence of either operative delivery or birth trauma. There is also no evidence that such treatment reduces the incidence of neonatal jaundice or hypoglycaemia.

3 Effects of glucose tolerance testing

The diagnosis of gestational diabetes, as currently defined, is based on an abnormal glucose tolerance test. This test is not reproducible at least 50 to 70 per cent of the time, and the increased risk of perinatal mortality and morbidity said to be associated with this 'condition' has been considerably overemphasized. No clear improvement in perinatal mortality has been demonstrated with insulin treatment for gestational diabetes, and screening of the pregnant population with glucose tolerance testing is unlikely to make a significant impact on perinatal mortality.

An abnormal glucose tolerance test is associated with a two- or threefold increase in the incidence of macrosomia, but the majority of macrosomic infants will be born to mothers with a normal glucose tolerance test. Thus far, no improvement in neonatal outcome has been demonstrated from insulin treatment for gestational diabetes, nor has there been any demonstrated benefit to the mother or infant from reducing the incidence of macrosomia by insulin therapy.

There is, in addition, a great potential for doing more harm than good by performing a glucose tolerance test. A positive test labels the woman as having a form of diabetes. Her pregnancy is likely to be considered as 'high-risk', invoking an extensive and expensive programme of tests and interventions of unproven benefit. A negative glucose tolerance test, on the other hand, also has a potential for harm by falsely reassuring the physician and the woman that the risk, engendered by the indication for the test, has been removed.

4 Conclusions

Except for research purposes, all forms of glucose tolerance testing should be stopped. Women in whom overt diabetes is suspected should be followed with repeated fasting or blood glucose estimations two hours after meals throughout pregnancy, or simply with repeated urinalyses.

There is a need for population-based research to establish the true risk, if any, associated with sub-diabetic degrees of hyperglycaemia during pregnancy. Once the degree of risk is appropriately identified, therapies designed to reduce that risk must be investigated by randomized trials before being introduced into clinical practice.

11

Assessment of fetal size and growth

This chapter is derived from the chapter by Douglas Altman and Frank Hytten (26) in EFFECTIVE CARE IN PREGNANCY AND CHILDBIRTH.

1 Introduction
2 Size and growth
3 Diagnosis of fetal growth retardation
4 Estimation of fetal size and growth
5 Conclusions

---

1 Introduction

Two questions should be considered in any approach to the assessment of fetal size or fetal growth: first, with what success does the technique used detect the small or slowly growing fetus; and second, does the successful detection of the small fetus lead to more effective care during pregnancy?

An attempt to answer the first question is usually made by comparing the intrauterine measurement with either birthweight or birthweight for gestational age. That the detection of a relatively small fetus should predict a relatively small newborn infant is neither surprising nor particularly useful.

The second question is more difficult to answer. If the technique could detect the poorly growing and compromised fetus who would be safer outside the uterus than remaining within it, then the clinical value would be obvious. Despite the fact that perceived impairments of fetal growth result in a great deal of obstetrical intervention, there is little information to help determine whether or not this is of value.

2 Size and growth

Fetal size and fetal growth are often confused in clinical practice. It is common to see 'birthweight-for-gestation age' standards described as 'fetal growth charts', and a weight-for-gestation below some arbitrary centile referred to as 'intrauterine growth retardation'. There are two main reasons why this may lead to false conclusions. First, birthweights at a given length of gestation may not be a good reflection of fetal weights at the same gestation. There is increasing evidence that the birthweights of babies born at a particular gestational age are not representative of fetal weights at that gestational age. Second, some authors have made inferences about fetal growth by taking differences between cross-sectionally derived mean or median birthweights at consecutive weeks of gestation. This approach is grossly misleading. Infants below a particular centile may be 'light-for-gestational age' without necessarily being 'growth retarded'.

It is essential to maintain the distinction between 'light-for-gestational age' and 'intrauterine growth retardation'. The distinction between size and growth is critical. Growth cannot be estimated from less than two measurements of size, and the argument that size at some time in late pregnancy and a presumed zero size at conception can represent those two measurements is philosophically dubious and clinically useless. What the clinician would like to know is whether fetal growth has deviated from its normal progression.

An assessment of fetal size in early pregnancy can be valuable in estimating or confirming the duration of the pregnancy, but a single estimate of fetal size in late pregnancy is of little or no clinical help. In any population of fetuses 10 per cent will, by definition, have a weight below the 10th centile and it is absurd to define in advance the proportion of babies that will suffer from 'intrauterine growth retardation'.

The term 'intrauterine growth retardation' should be restricted to those fetuses where there is definite evidence that growth has faltered. Such infants may not necessarily be particularly 'light-for-gestational age'; a fetus whose weight falls from the 90th centile to the 30th in a short period of time is almost certainly in greater peril than a fetus who has maintained a position on the 5th centile.

The estimation of growth rather than size is important, because the object of antenatal surveillance is to anticipate or demonstrate clinical problems that can be helped by appropriate action. Establishing that a fetus is small does not expose a clinical problem; only the demonstration of impaired growth can do that. This basic point is recognized by those studying child growth but, in general, not by those studying fetal growth. Even when longitudinal data are available, the definition of intrauterine growth retardation remains problematic; but at least any cut-off chosen will be related to the directly relevant assessment of growth, rather than to size alone.

3 Diagnosis of fetal growth retardation

The use of fetal measurements to assess whether or not the fetus is progressing satisfactorily may be considered in the general framework of diagnostic tests, and appraised from the standpoints of their test properties: sensitivity, specificity, and predictive values. It is not clear, however, precisely what one is trying to predict. There is no absolute postnatal criterion of growth retardation that can be used to assess the validity of the 'test'. In the absence of an appropriate outcome measure, authors frequently use some measure of 'relatively low' birthweight, such as being below the 10th centile for gestational age.

Standards for growth are constructed in the same basic way as those for size, and are subject to the same worries about the selection of the sample and the variation in the number of measurements per individual. One needs at least two measurements of size to estimate growth, and the average weekly growth can be calculated by dividing the change in size by the number of weeks between the measurements. Standards can be constructed from the distribution of such changes, relating these either to the mid-point of the time-period concerned or to the average of the two observed sizes.

In estimating fetal growth the benefits of independence from dating inaccuracies are somewhat offset by the problem that measurement error will be greater for an estimate of growth than for one of size, because growth is calculated from two estimates of size. Thus growth arrest should be observed over at least a two- to three-week period to be clinically significant.

4 Estimation of fetal size and growth

The oldest clinical method of estimating fetal size—abdominal palpation—is so inaccurate as to be little better than a blind guess. Twenty per cent of such assessments made just prior to delivery are not within

450 g of the actual birthweight, and the errors are worse at the extremes of the range, where the information is most needed.

A more quantitative approach is to measure the increase in size of the maternal abdomen, which must, at least to some extent, reflect uterine growth. The two most widely practised techniques are the measurement of fundal height (the distance between the upper border of the symphysis pubis and the uterine fundus) and the measurement of abdominal girth at the level of the umbilicus.

There have been several studies of fundal height as an indicator of fetal size, but little investigation of the potential of this measurement for assessing growth. This is understandable, given the considerable inter- and intra-observer variation in measuring fundal height. Nevertheless, several studies have shown quite good sensitivity and specificity of fundal height for predicting low birthweight for gestation. The ability to predict low birthweight is not the same as the ability to detect growth retardation, but fundal height may be useful as a screening test for further investigation.

The most direct approach to the assessment of fetal growth yet available is ultrasonography. Ultrasonography rather than 'birthweight-for-gestational age' should be considered as the 'gold standard' for measuring fetal size and growth.

There is an extensive literature on ultrasound measurement of fetal size. Numerous authors have produced cross-sectional standards (often wrongly called 'growth curves') for ultrasound measurements of different parts of the fetus, notably biparietal diameter, abdominal circumference, crown–rump length, and femur length. Several authors have looked at serial measurements, but most have analysed the data as a sequence of points on cross-sectional 'growth' charts rather than looking at changes in fetal measurements over time. These cross-sectional standards are valuable for estimating fetal size at a given point in pregnancy, provided that one knows the gestational age accurately, but they are not suitable for assessing fetal growth between two points in the pregnancy.

There has been very little research aimed at producing true growth curves based on repeated measurements over time of the same fetus. Such information would provide a far sounder basis for assessing fetal growth, and is arguably the only valid approach for detecting growth retardation. This approach is particularly useful when gestational age is unknown or uncertain.

5 Conclusions

Fundal height could be used as a screening device for referral of women to an obstetrician for further assessment, but many small fetuses will be missed, and many perfectly well-grown fetuses will be considered worryingly small.

Ultrasound techniques have the capacity to detect abnormalities of fetal growth, but have not been effectively exploited. There is a need for prospective studies to examine the differential growth of fetal parts, in large populations, to see whether patterns of growth that are associated with fetal compromise and later infant morbidity can be defined. Such studies should be carried out with scheduled repeated measurements. It is particularly crucial that some sound measures of outcome should be defined. Intervention based on assessments of size or growth should be evaluated in randomized trials before they are accepted into general obstetrical practice.

Ultrasound in pregnancy

*This chapter is derived from the chapter by Jim Neilson and Adrian Grant
(27) in EFFECTIVE CARE IN PREGNANCY AND CHILDBIRTH.*

1 Introduction

Ultrasound imaging has been increasingly used in obstetrical care
since its introduction to medicine. Improvement in resolution and
quality of ultrasound imaging equipment has been rapid. Progress
from the first detection of the gross abnormality of anencephaly in
1972 to the current sophisticated diagnoses of many subtle fetal
anomalies has taken only a few years.

Whether ultrasound imaging should be routinely used for prenatal
screening or only used selectively for specific indications has not, as
yet, been established.

2 Selective use of ultrasound

There is a clear difference between selective and routine use of
ultrasound. The time taken, the detail inspected, and perhaps the
seniority of the ultrasonographer will vary with the reason for the
examination. To identify fetal presentation, for example, takes
seconds and can be carried out by a minimally trained technician. To

investigate thoroughly the cause of raised alpha-fetoprotein levels
may require considerable time and expertise. Routine examinations
must be accomplished quickly for practical reasons, and some fetal
malformations are therefore less likely to be detected than when there
are specific reasons to anticipate their presence. The selective examination should be tailored to answer a specific question posed by
the person who requests the examination.

2.1 Confirmation of fetal life

Ultrasound has the ability to establish rapidly and accurately whether
a fetus is alive or dead, and to predict whether a pregnancy is likely
to continue after threatened miscarriage. This ability has rationalized
the management of threatened abortion in early pregnancy. The
gestational sac can be visualized by 6 weeks menstrual age, and the
fetus by 7 weeks. As soon as the fetus can be demonstrated with
ultrasound, it can be measured and its viability confirmed by detection of heart movement. Fetal life is confirmed by observation of heart
pulsation, and fetal death by its absence. Except in very early pregnancy, there should not be any doubt about the diagnosis. Blighted
ova, which constitute the largest group of early pregnancy failures,
are diagnosed by the failure to detect a fetus on careful examination,
although, when small, the anembryonic pregnancy has to be differentiated by a repeat ultrasound examination from the normal, very early
pregnancy. Missed abortion can be diagnosed by absence of heart
movement. The small group of 'live' miscarriages cannot be predicted
with certainty by ultrasound. These constitute less than 15 per cent of
the total number of miscarriages, and there are no specific ultrasound
features, although a reduction in amniotic fluid volume, diminished
fetal activity, or the presence of large intrauterine haematomas may
suggest a poor prognosis.

2.2 Assessment of gestational age

The use of ultrasound to assess duration of gestation is based on the
facts that, in early pregnancy, fetal growth is rapid, there is little
biological variation in size, and pathological growth retardation is
uncommon. Gestational age can thus be estimated from early measurements of the fetal size. In the first trimester, measurement of the
fetal crown–rump length is usually accurate to within 5 days. After
13 weeks, varying flexion of the fetal trunk makes this measurement
less reliable, but measurement of the biparietal diameter before 18
weeks usually predicts the date of delivery to within 2 weeks. Measurement of femoral length appears to be of similar accuracy to measurement of the biparietal diameter. Measurement of the fetus is of no
value in assessing gestational age after 30 weeks.

The date of delivery can be reliably predicted from the menstrual history in between 75 per cent and 85 per cent of pregnancies. There is at least circumstantial evidence that early ultrasound estimation of gestational age is more accurate than alternative means of assessment, including clinical examinations or the date of quickening. Since it is not possible to identify all the women in whom an accurate knowledge of gestational age may become essential later in pregnancy, there is a case for routine early ultrasonography, and this will be discussed later. When selective ultrasonography is preferred, it would seem sensible to scan women with uncertain dates, and those for whom elective delivery is likely to be indicated.

2.3 Fetal malformation

Ultrasound may be employed in three ways to assist the identification of fetal malformations: to visualize the malformation; to facilitate other diagnostic techniques, such as amniocentesis and chorion villus sampling; and to allow fetal measurement.

A large number of abnormalities can now be detected by modern ultrasound imaging. Some defects, such as anencephaly, are easily identified; some, such as spina bifida, are moderately difficult to detect; and some, such as certain cardiac anomalies, may be very difficult to identify. The presence of one defect may suggest the presence of others and/or of a chromosomal abnormality. Detection rates may vary with the quality of the equipment and expertise of the ultrasonographer, and with whether the examination has been performed because of high-risk features (such as a previously malformed baby or raised alpha-fetoprotein levels) or is part of a screening examination, when less time (and possibly less expertise) would be available.

The use of ultrasound during amniocentesis certainly seems logical to minimize the chances of placental and/or fetal contact during the insertion of the needle into the amniotic cavity. In addition, the presence of multiple pregnancies may be identified, fetal life confirmed, and gestational age estimated. Both the pregnant woman and the operator may be reassured by seeing that the fetus appears unaffected by the procedure. Ultrasound can be of particular help in demonstrating to parents who have previously had a malformed baby that their current fetus does not have the same defect.

Termination of pregnancy will be acceptable to many couples when the fetus has a lethal abnormality such as anencephaly, or a defect likely to result in major handicap such as spina bifida with hydrocephalus. Difficulties can arise when defects have less predictable sequelae, and also because diagnostic errors may occur. Prior consultation with surgical colleagues should help to reduce unnecessary elective early delivery (and the consequent morbidity resulting from iatrogenic immaturity) of babies with conditions that will not benefit from early surgery.

Ultrasound can, however, lead to a diagnosis of abnormality in a baby that is normally formed. This 'false positive' diagnosis is particularly tragic when it leads to the termination of a normal pregnancy.

Diagnosis of a malformation may help some parents prepare for the birth of an impaired child. On the other hand, some parents may suffer a prolonged and devastating upset through such information. Skilled counselling may be needed to help them plan ahead for the care of their child. Imparting information about important defects requires sensitivity and the availability of people who can be supportive.

2.4 Assessment of fetal growth

Almost 75 percent of babies born 'light-for-dates' can be identified by measurements of this parameter. For many years the biparietal diameter was the standard for ultrasound assessment of fetal growth.

Accurate measurement of the biparietal diameter may be difficult and sometimes impossible, especially during late pregnancy, when the fetal head is in a direct occipito-anterior or occipito-posterior position, or is low in the pelvis. It is also a relatively insensitive technique because of so-called 'brain-sparing'. Comparison of organ weights of 'light-for-dates' infants with those of controls of either similar birthweight or similar gestational age, shows that the organs most diminished in weight are the thymus, spleen, and liver. In contrast, brain weight is relatively much less reduced. Thus, in performing cephalometry, the ultrasonographer is measuring an index of the size of the fetal organ least affected by growth retardation.

Trunk measurements are better predictors of fetal size than head measurements. These have been generally adopted as the best single parameter, although there remains little published information on their serial use to assess growth rather than to assess size on a single measurement.

Measurement of total intrauterine volume was prompted by the fact that 'light-for-dates' babies tend also to have small placentae and less amniotic fluid. Total intrauterine volume predicts 'light-for-dates' babies with similar sensitivity and specificity to the much simpler trunk area, and offers no advantage over the simpler measurement. Alternative measurements, including femoral length and thigh circumference, have been proposed, but there are no indications that these measurements will prove to be especially useful.

'Light-for-dates' fetuses form a heterogeneous group within which individual fetal risk varies greatly. Attempts have been made to analyse patterns of growth in the hope of shedding light on the underlying pathogenesis and of providing an estimate of the risk to the individual fetus. 'Light-for-dates' fetuses can be divided into two groups: the first showing arrest of previously normal biparietal diameter growth; the second showing early departure from normal limits of biparietal diameter growth that continues until delivery. The first of these patterns has been attributed to 'utero-placental insufficiency', and the latter to low growth-potential. This latter group includes infants that are inherently abnormal (especially chromosomally abnormal), some that have suffered a major insult (for example, from rubella) during the critical period of organogenesis, and some that are small because of their genetic endowment. Comparative measurements of the fetal head and trunk have been suggested as a means to further differentiate these two groups. While there is a higher incidence of intrapartum fetal distress and operative delivery in the asymmetrical-growth group, the perinatal mortality and incidence of low Apgar scores are similar and high in both groups.

The significance of ultrasonically detected patterns of fetal growth requires further study, and seeking correlations with the results of Doppler studies (see later) would be of interest. Thus far, the available evidence indicates that trunk measurements are superior to head measurements in predicting 'light-for-dates' babies, but little is known about serial measurements, and particularly about their relationship to neonatal outcome.

2.5 *Examination of the placenta*

Ultrasound is the best available method for locating placental position. This is of particular importance prior to chorion villus sampling and amniocentesis, and in cases of antepartum haemorrhage, fetal malpresentation, or other clinical situations that suggest the possibility of placenta praevia. The placenta is easily visualized with ultrasound, although the woman must have a full bladder for the lower pole of the uterus to be satisfactorily visualized. The lower margins of posteriorly sited placentae are more difficult to identify than those of anterior placentae, both because of acoustic shadowing from the fetus and because of a less clearly defined anatomical reference point. The exact margins of the lower uterine segment cannot be identified ultrasonically, and therefore ultrasound cannot achieve 100 per cent accuracy in identifying or excluding placenta praevia.

The phenomenon of placental 'migration' is now well recognized: a placenta that appears low earlier in pregnancy may, with formation of the lower uterine segment, appear to have risen on repeat ultrasound examination and thus no longer seem praevia.

2.6 *Miscellaneous indications*

There is an extensive list of clinical situations in which ultrasound examination is considered useful. These include investigation of raised maternal serum alpha-fetoprotein, suspected multiple pregnancy, assessment of amniotic fluid volume, fetal presentation, suspected uterine abnormalities, location of an intrauterine contraceptive device, external cephalic version, and cervical cerclage.

3 Routine ultrasonography

The greatest controversy surrounding obstetrical ultrasound has been whether its use should be extended from specific indications to routine screening of all pregnant women, either early (usually 16–19 weeks, but sometimes earlier) or later in pregnancy (usually 32–36 weeks).

Most claims of benefit for routine scanning are based on the assumption that clinical action taken on the results of the examination improves clinical outcome. This assumption can only be tested adequately by randomized controlled trials, but few of these have been conducted. The six trials that have been conducted to date are of varying design and quality and have assessed a variety of scanning regimens; and not all have used the same measures of outcome. Nevertheless, they provide the best evidence that is currently available.

3.1 Routine early ultrasonography

It has been proposed that early scans performed at 16–20 weeks gestation may improve pregnancy outcome through clinical action prompted by earlier identification of multiple pregnancies or congenital malformations, or because of more accurate estimation of gestational age. If the screening examination is performed even earlier in pregnancy, some clinically unsuspected non-viable pregnancies, (for example, blighted ova and hydatidiform moles) may be detected. However, a satisfactory inspection of fetal anatomy to detect malformation cannot be performed before 16 weeks and if inspection of the heart is to be included, examination closer to 20 weeks may be necessary.

An early scan was evaluated as a component of the routine scanning regimen in three of the six trials of routine ultrasonography in pregnancy (in two of these, a routine late scan was also part of the experimental regimen). The information provided in an early scan led to a small reduction in the prevalence of undiagnosed twins at 26 weeks gestation and undiagnosed major fetal anomalies, but the differences were not statistically significant. Routine early scanning was, however, associated with a statistically significant reduction in the use of induction for so-called 'post-term' pregnancy. Furthermore, it is worth noting that in one trial, four of the infants in the control group who had been delivered following induction for 'post-term' pregnancy were judged to be preterm by paediatricians; and also, that infants in the routinely scanned group spent fewer days in special-care nursery because of hyperbilirubinaemia.

It is difficult to come to any firm conclusions about whether the overall effects of routine ultrasonography in early pregnancy on fetal diagnosis and obstetric care were reflected in improved outcomes overall, because the few differences that emerged from the trials could easily be a chance result.

3.2 *Routine late ultrasonography*

The main purpose of routine scanning in late pregnancy is to identify growth-retarded fetuses who may benefit from elective delivery. The randomized trials reveal no consistent pattern of effect on admission to hospital during pregnancy or on the use of elective delivery for indications other than 'post-term' pregnancy. There were no detectable effects on the risks of low Apgar score, admission to the special-care nursery, or perinatal mortality.

4 Doppler studies

Doppler ultrasound has been used for a number of years to identify and record fetal heart pulsation, and, in adults, to assess blood flow in compromised vessels. In 1977 the use of the technique to demonstrate blood velocity wave forms in the fetal umbilical artery was described. Early experience suggests that alterations in fetal umbilical blood flow may occur as an early event in conditions of fetal compromise. In theory, Doppler studies could provide important information on the pathophysiology of compromised pregnancies (especially of fetal growth retardation), and possibly provide a useful technique for evaluating fetal wellbeing in high-risk pregnancies.

Thus far only one controlled trial on the utility of Doppler ultrasound has been reported. No difference in the overall rate of elective delivery was observed, but the group for which the results had been reported were less likely to experience intrapartum fetal distress, and less likely to receive oxygen therapy and assisted ventilation during the neonatal period. All of these differences may simply reflect chance variations. There was no suggestion of any difference in low Apgar scores, or admission rates to the special-care nursery between the experimental and control groups. The available evidence does not, at the present time, support the use of Doppler ultrasound in clinical practice, other than in the context of well-designed trials.

5 Women's reactions to ultrasound in pregnancy

An ultrasound examination has the potential to be a fascinating and happy experience for prospective parents, but real or mistaken diagnosis of fetal abnormality using ultrasound can lead to psychological devastation. Women's reactions to ultrasonography during pregnancy have not received the systematic attention from researchers that they deserve.

A majority of the women interviewed in the available studies valued ultrasonography in early pregnancy because it confirmed the reality of the baby for them, and because the examination was often followed by a reduction in anxiety and an increase in confidence. A study conducted in the United States found that American women felt that nearly half the value of ultrasonography in an uncomplicated pregnancy pertained to uses outside the realm of medical decisions, such as knowing the sex of the child or having an early picture to show their children.

Women's views on the desirability of routine ultrasonography during pregnancy, in addition to being influenced by what is actually available, are also influenced by differing perceptions of the potential benefits, and by concerns about the possible adverse effects of ultrasound. The only generalization that can be made on the basis of the available research is that there is considerable variation in women's views about the indications for ultrasonography. The obvious implication for practice is that it is important for ultrasonographers to take this variation into account when dealing with individuals.

Another important message with practical implications is that the subjective experience of actually having a scan, even if the findings are normal, can be an unpleasant experience because of uncommunicativeness on the part of the ultrasonographer. In practice, some ultrasonographers, technicians in particular, may be put under professional constraints that limit them from communicating freely with the women they are examining. Whether it is as a result of these constraints, or for other reasons, uncommunicativeness can eliminate the potentially beneficial psychological effects of the examinations. The risk of this adverse effect is likely to be increased when the human resources available for ultrasonography are stretched, as they often are when ultrasonography is routinely performed on every pregnant woman.

6 Potential hazards of obstetric ultrasound

Any consideration of the use of diagnostic ultrasound in obstetrical practice must weigh potential benefits against potential risks. There has been surprisingly little well-organized research to evaluate possible adverse effects of ultrasound exposure on human fetuses. Two apparently well-designed and well-conducted case–control studies have sought a relationship between ultrasound exposure and childhood malignancy. Both were reassuring with one possible exception: neither study showed any difference in exposure between the cases and controls up to the age of five, but children dying of leukaemia or cancer over the age of five were more likely than controls to have been exposed to ultrasound as fetuses in one of the studies. This difference was not seen in the other, statistically more powerful study.

Evidence from cohort studies is very limited. In one such study, babies exposed to ultrasound as fetuses were more likely than controls to have abnormal grasp and tonic neck reflexes, but were comparable in respect of 122 other parameters for which associations were sought. In another study, many outcomes were examined and no association with ultrasound exposure was found for the majority of them. One potentially important exception concerned dyslexia, which was associated with exposure to ultrasound. This could either have been the result of chance (it was not statistically significant in conventional terms), or of bias from inadequate matching.

These two non-randomized studies and the randomized trials have been used to investigate whether or not the reduction in birthweight suggested by some animal studies was to be found in humans. The data are reassuring, providing no evidence that *in utero* exposure reduces birthweight.

The randomized controlled trials conducted to date have been far too small to have a reasonable chance of identifying an effect of ultrasound exposure on any rare adverse outcome.

7 Conclusions

The place of ultrasound for specific indications in pregnancy has been clearly established. The place, if any, for routine ultrasound has not as yet been determined. In view of the fact that its safety has not been convincingly established, such routine use should for the present be considered experimental, and should not be implemented outside of the context of randomized controlled trials.

13

Assessment of fetal wellbeing

This chapter is derived from the chapters by Adrian Grant and Diana Elbourne (28); Sophie Alexander, Rosalind Stanwell-Smith, Pierre Buekens, and Marc J. N. C. Keirse (29); and Patrick Mohide and Marc J. N. C. Keirse (30) in EFFECTIVE CARE IN PREGNANCY AND CHILDBIRTH.

1 Introduction

Two general assumptions underlie the contention that antenatal biochemical or biophysical monitoring is clinically useful: first, that these methods can detect or predict fetal compromise; and second, that with appropriate interpretation and action, they can reduce the frequency or severity of adverse perinatal events or prevent needless interventions.

A wide range of tests of fetal wellbeing have been introduced during the last fifty years, and have enjoyed waves of popularity. In some places the use of biochemical tests continues unabated; in others they have largely been replaced by biophysical tests of fetal wellbeing. Fetal movement counting by the mother has also been proposed and evaluated as a screening method with potential for improving perinatal outcomes.

Both biochemical tests (which primarily monitor the endocrine function of the feto-placental unit) and biophysical methods of monitoring (which provide indirect information about fetal neurological and neuromuscular function) have the theoretical ability to detect changes in fetal wellbeing that may occur over days or weeks. No known method of fetal assessment is likely to predict or prevent the consequences of sudden events, such as rupture of the membranes with cord prolapse or abruptio placentae.

2 Biochemical tests

2.1 Oestrogens

The enthusiasm for oestrogen assays that prevailed in the 1940s and 1950s was based on the observation that perinatal mortality rates were twice as high in women with low oestrogens as in the general population. However, the usefulness of the tests was marred by the facts that they were not sensitive enough to detect the majority of pregnancies destined to have an adverse outcome, and that a great many women with normal pregnancies falsely appeared to be at risk.

Among the many studies reported, there has been only one randomized controlled trial. In this trial knowledge of oestriol levels did not have any detectable effect on either perinatal mortality or the rate of elective delivery, either by caesarean section or by induction of labour. Similar conclusions were reached in studies in which pregnancy outcomes were compared within the same institution in two consecutive periods with and without the use of oestrogen assays. Thus, on the basis of the available studies, there is no evidence to suggest any benefit from oestrogen assays.

2.2 Human placental lactogen

Like oestrogens, human placental lactogen measurements have been utilized in the hope of predicting and possibly averting a variety of poor outcomes. The results are similar to those discussed for oestrogen assays.

There has been only one randomized intervention study of human placental lactogen measurement. In this trial human placental lactogen assays were performed at each visit on all women, but in half of them (the control group) the results were not reported to the clinician. In the experimental group abnormal values were reported promptly to a perinatology fellow. If the results of a repeat measurement were low and the fetus was considered to be mature, action was taken to expedite delivery.

The results of this trial suggest, on first inspection, that revealing the results of human placental lactogen measurements to a clinician armed with a predetermined intervention programme statistically significantly reduced fetal and perinatal mortality. These data, however, relate only to the 8 per cent (4 per cent in each group) of pregnancies that had abnormal human placental lactogen values. Data on the large majority of pregnancies (92 per cent) that did not belong to that category were not reported, and are no longer available.

Although the data of this trial are often cited to indicate that human placental lactogen measurements are beneficial for the surveillance of high-risk pregnancy, one cannot exclude the possibility that the benefits found in pregnancies with abnormal values were counterbalanced or outweighed by negative effects in pregnancies with normal values.

Despite the unsatisfactory evidence concerning their usefulness as a screening procedure or as a diagnostic test, human placental lactogen measurements have acquired great popularity. In part, this can be attributed to the infectious enthusiasm and optimism exuded by proponents of this test. In part, it relates to a serious misunderstanding of the available evidence.

2.3 Serum alpha-fetoprotein

The concentration of alpha-fetoprotein in maternal serum depends on the rate of its secretion by the fetal liver, and on its rate of escape from the fetal circulation to the maternal circulation. Although its measurement in the mother's serum was originally intended only for the purpose of screening for neural tube defects, it was later observed that women with a high level of alpha-fetoprotein and no neural tube defect were more likely to have an infant of low birthweight, and interest was generated in the assay as a predictor of fetal wellbeing.

The predictive value of the test is low. All except one of the studies from which test properties could be calculated showed that less than a third of the women with an abnormally high level of alpha-fetoprotein gave birth to a baby with low birthweight or low weight for gestational age. The usefulness of alpha-fetoprotein screening for conditions other than neural tube defects is poor.

An exception should be made for low alpha-fetoprotein levels. Lower alpha-fetoprotein concentrations are found in pregnancies in which the fetus is affected by Down's syndrome. While low alpha-fetoprotein concentrations can certainly not be considered as diagnostic for Down's syndrome, there is no doubt that the combination of maternal age and alpha-fetoprotein levels is more precise in estimating the likelihood of Down's syndrome than is maternal age alone.

2.4 Human chorionic gonadotrophin

Human chorionic gonadotrophin is a glycoprotein secreted in large quantities by the trophoblast. Its assay has mainly been used as a pregnancy test, and for assessment of bleeding or anomalies of early pregnancy such as threatened abortion, ectopic pregnancy, and molar pregnancy when ultrasound was not available. Where ultrasound is

available, there is no place for the use of human chorionic
gonadotrophin in established intrauterine pregnancy, whether early
or late.

2.5 *Other biochemical tests*

In addition to human placental lactogen and human chorionic gonadotrophin, which may be described as placental protein hormones,
several proteins of placental origin have been described since the
1970s and new ones are regularly being reported.

Placental proteins have never gained the popularity enjoyed by
oestrogens, human placental lactogen, alpha-fetoprotein, or human
chorionic gonadotrophin as markers for healthy pregnancy, nor has
there been much pressure to use placental protein measurements on
a large scale. It may be that there is some scope for further research in
the field of placental proteins, but there are no indications as yet that
any of these measurements are of current clinical use.

Various other hormones, enzymes, and other substances have
generated interest, although this interest has often been short-lived.
These include oxytocinase, alkaline phosphatase (thermostable and
leucocyte), and progestogens. These tests have waned in popularity.
The available studies do not present data in such a way that either
their predictive properties or their usefulness can be determined.

3 Biophysical tests

3.1 *Fetal movement counting*

Reduction or cessation of fetal movements may precede fetal death
by a day or more. In theory at least, recognition of this reduction,
followed by appropriate action to confirm jeopardy and expedite
delivery, could prevent fetal death. This is the basis for using counts
of fetal movements as a test of fetal wellbeing.

Not all late fetal deaths are even theoretically preventable in this
way. Some are not preceded by a reduction in fetal movements. For
others, there may be insufficient time between the reduction and fetal
death to allow clinical action.

Other late fetal deaths may be preceded by conditions that are
recognizable in their own right, such as pre-eclampsia, or intrauterine
growth retardation. In these cases fetal movement counting may be
theoretically useful as a supplement to other, hospital-based tests of
fetal wellbeing.

The cause of most antepartum late fetal deaths, however, is unknown. These deaths are unpredictable, and the extent to which they
can be prevented by current forms of antenatal care is therefore
limited. Screening by fetal movement counting, because it can be
performed each day, has theoretical advantages over other tests of

fetal wellbeing, all of which are either difficult or impossible to perform daily for practical reasons. The possibility that these unexplained deaths may be preventable is the basis for screening all pregnancies by fetal movement counting.

The average number of movements felt per hour in late pregnancy varies widely from woman to woman. Counts below 10, and counts above 1000 per 12 hours have been recorded for apparently healthy fetuses. In addition, a woman may experience wide normal variations from time to time within a single pregnancy.

There are four reasons for these normal variations. First, some fetuses are consistently vigorous and others consistently sluggish. Second, mothers differ widely in their ability to perceive movements; some notice nearly all of their baby's movements, others only a proportion, and some apparently none at all. Rates of perceived activity vary more than tenfold from one woman to another. Third, fetuses pass through active and quiet phases. Active phases of body movement on average last 40 minutes, while quiet phases, which are characterized by absent body and extremity movements, last an average of 23 minutes. Finally, a mother's perception of her baby's movements may vary. The majority of women are consistent over time in the proportion of movements that they feel and record, but about 25 per cent may show wide day-to-day variation. Both distraction and prolonged periods of counting reduce the proportion of movements perceived.

The fact that it is the mother rather than her attendants who assumes responsibility when fetal movements are being monitored is an attraction of this method of surveillance; but the attitudes to fetal movement counting of those providing antenatal care are also important. One study found significant differences in rates of kick-chart completion in groups of women supervised by different midwives. Unless the staff are convinced that fetal movement counting is useful they are unlikely to motivate women fully.

Demonstration that a reduction in fetal movements is predictive of antepartum late fetal death and of other measures of adverse outcome still leaves the two most crucial questions unanswered. First, does it predict adverse outcome at a time when it would be possible to avert or moderate the outcome? Even though there is often a delay between a reduction in movements and poor outcome recognized at delivery, it is possible that the pathological process may be too far advanced to be altered. Second, is there a suitable treatment available to effect this improvement? Early intervention prompted by a reduction in fetal movements might lead to the delivery of a baby who dies during labour or shortly after birth rather than in the antepartum period, or who survives with a severe handicap.

Only two randomized controlled trials have addressed the question of whether clinical actions taken on the basis of fetal movement counting improve fetal outcome. In the first of these there were 12 antepartum deaths of normally formed babies weighing more than 1500 g in the control group compared with only 3 in the counting group.

The striking difference in normally formed antepartum late fetal deaths observed in this trial must be somewhat qualified. After the onset of labour there were two more deaths in the counting group than in the control group (11 versus 9), so some part of the difference in antepartum deaths may simply represent a delay in the time of, rather the prevention of, death. The difference observed in the antepartum death rates is only just statistically significant. The other, as yet unreported, trial shows no clear difference between the counting and control groups.

The effects of formal fetal movement counting on the mother, both negative and positive, must be considered, as well as those on the fetus. Counting and acting on reduced movements is time-consuming for the mothers, and there is a possibility that it may induce stress and anxiety. In addition, health service resources that might be otherwise better employed are required to train women in the counting procedures and to respond to reports of reduced movements.

On the other hand, the formalized focusing of a mother on her fetus *in utero* may strengthen the mother–infant bond after delivery. The provision of a formal channel of communication between mothers and hospital personnel, combined with clear guidelines about when to make contact, may decrease stress and anxiety. Feedback to women of information about their fetuses has been shown in other contexts of antenatal care to reduce anxiety, to increase confidence and positive feelings towards the fetus, to enhance compliance with other health-related advice, to increase feelings of control, and to improve communication with staff. Some of these issues have been recently studied. Of the women surveyed, over half were reassured by filling in the chart, many equating fetal movements with fetal wellbeing. Almost a quarter of the women, however, were worried by formal counting. These worries were of two broad types: those resulting from lack of knowledge about normal variations in fetal movement patterns, and those caused by episodes of perceived reductions in movement.

Less than one in a thousand women might benefit from fetal movement counting in terms of prevention of late fetal death. The wider social, psychological, and economic implications, however, affect all women and must be taken into account.

3.2 Contraction stress testing

Continuous recording of fetal heart rate and uterine activity was first developed for use in labour, in an attempt to identify the fetus at risk of death or morbidity due to intrapartum asphyxia. Because many fetal deaths occur prior to the onset of labour, the stimulation of contractions with oxytocin for short periods of time was proposed, to allow observation of the fetal heart rate under labour-like conditions in pregnancies at risk.

This technique, which subsequently became known as the 'oxytocin challenge test' or 'contraction stress test', suffers from a number of disadvantages. It is time-consuming, requires an intravenous infusion, and has the potential to harm the fetus. Its use is contraindicated in some pregnancies at risk, for example when there is antepartum bleeding, placenta praevia, a history of preterm labour, or preterm rupture of membranes.

The nipple-stimulation stress test is similar in purpose to, and has been directly compared with the oxytocin challenge test. The pregnant woman is encouraged to stimulate her nipples with her fingers, palms, a warm, moist facecloth, or a heating pad, directly, or through her clothing. Contractions can be stimulated effectively; but the mechanism, previously assumed to be oxytocin release, remains unknown. The nipple-stimulation stress test has some of the same disadvantages as the oxytocin challenge test with the additional problem that, while stimulation is easily discontinued, there is a time-lag of more than three minutes between stimulation and peak uterine response. Excessive uterine activity occurs in over half the women who undergo this test, and this will result in fetal bradycardia in 7 to 14 per cent. Cases of severe uterine tetany associated with fetal heart rate abnormalities have also been reported. Because of these concerns, and because it offers no clear advantages over other techniques, the nipple-stimulation stress test should probably be relegated to the history books.

3.3 Non-stress testing

The evaluation of fetal heart rate patterns without the added stress of induced contractions was first proposed in 1969. This 'non-stress test' has been widely incorporated into antenatal care for both screening and diagnosis.

There is no universally accepted technique for performing non-stress antepartum testing. Various durations and frequencies of monitoring are used, and these can have a powerful influence on the predictive properties of the test. Additional manoeuvres, such as abdominal stimulation, sound stimulation, glucose infusions, postprandial repeat tests, and follow-up oxytocin challenge tests for suspected abnormal records, have been suggested or used.

A large number of factors may interfere with the interpretation of the non-stress test. Like the contraction stress test, the non-stress test requires sophisticated equipment, which may occasionally malfunction. Fetal and maternal movements may produce artifacts, since ultrasound detects movement rather than sound. During fetal rest periods, which not uncommonly last for more than thirty minutes, normal physiological reduction in heart rate variability may be confused with pathological change. Medications taken by the mother are often transferred to the fetus, and, particularly in the case of drugs with a sedative effect on the central nervous system, may in themselves produce heart rate patterns that can be interpreted as abnormal. Likewise the gestational age of the fetus has a strong influence on the frequency of false positive non-reactive tests, with 'abnormal' patterns being more frequently described in the preterm fetus. When all these factors are taken into consideration, as many as 10–15 per cent of all records may be unsatisfactory for interpretation.

A variety of methods for interpreting non-stress cardiotocograms have been described, all of which include evaluation of some or all of the following characteristics: baseline fetal heart rate; various interpretations of fetal heart rate variability; accelerations of fetal heart rate associated with spontaneous and/or stimulated movements of the fetus; and decelerations associated with spontaneous uterine contractions. The more complicated systems assign scores to some or all of these parameters, sometimes subsequently grouping the scores. The most commonly used method is to divide traces into reactive (normal) and non-reactive (abnormal), based on the presence or absence of adequate baseline heart rate variability and heart rate accelerations with fetal movement. Even when a fixed method is used, interpretation of a trace may vary when an individual observer reads the same trace at different times, or when the same trace is read by different observers.

Perinatal death, fetal distress, Apgar scores, cord pH, forms of neonatal morbidity, and combined assessments of these outcome events have all been used to evaluate the test. The non-stress test is a reasonably good predictor of adverse outcome when morbidities and mortalities are combined.

There are several real dangers in using the non-stress test to screen women in whom the likelihood of the fetus being in difficulty is small. Screening a group of women with a low probability of adverse outcome will result in a higher proportion of positive test results that are false positive. Intervention based on the results of a 'positive' non-stress test in a low-risk group of women will often do more harm than good.

In each of the four trials of non-stress testing that have been reported, fetal heart rate abnormalities during labour and perinatal deaths from causes other than malformations were *more* common in the groups in which clinicians had access to the test results ('revealed') than in the control ('concealed') groups. There was no demonstrable effect on caesarean section rates, the incidence of low Apgar scores, abnormal neonatal neurological signs, or admission to special-care nurseries.

3.4 Fetal biophysical profile

The 'biophysical profile' was derived from a study of serial ultrasound examinations and antenatal cardiotocography (non-stress test) in high-risk pregnancies. Combining five biophysical 'variables' considered to be of prognostic significance (fetal movement, tone, reactivity, breathing, and amniotic fluid volume) into a score reduced the frequency of false positive and false negative results compared to the non-stress test alone. An additional advantage of the biophysical profile over the non-stress test is that it permits assessment of the possibility of major congenital anomalies. This may be important as detection of a serious anomaly may, on occasion, help avoid the use of a caesarean section where the baby is clearly abnormal.

Only two controlled trials of biophysical profile testing have been performed. Both were conducted in women referred to units specializing in fetal biophysical assessment, and compared care based on biophysical score results with that based on non-stress test results, following a management protocol. In both studies the biophysical profile score was a better predictor of low five-minute Apgar scores than the non-stress test. The biophysical profile was both more sensitive and more specific in predicting overall abnormal outcome than the non-stress test.

Despite the better predictive value of the biophysical score than the non-stress test, its use did not result in any improvements in outcome for the baby. Outcomes measured included perinatal death, fetal distress in labour, low Apgar score, and low birthweight for gestational age.

4 Conclusions

Biochemical tests of fetal wellbeing are expensive and have a low predictive value for adverse outcome. While they have added immensely to knowledge of placental and fetal physiology, none of them have been shown to be clinically useful. Their use should be restricted to research, and they should not be employed in clinical practice.

Maternal monitoring of fetal movements is a simple and inexpensive test of fetal wellbeing that can be performed daily. If used, it should be used as a screening test, the results of which should prompt other, diagnostic tests, rather than more definitive obstetric intervention. The possibility of congenital malformation should be considered before delivery is expedited.

Biophysical tests are employed today with the same enthusiasm that characterized biochemical testing in the past. These tests have greatly increased our understanding of fetal behaviour and development, but their use has not been demonstrated to confer benefits in the care of an individual woman and her baby. For this reason, despite their widespread clinical use, biophysical tests of fetal wellbeing should be considered of experimental value only, rather than as validated clinical tools. They should be acknowledged as such, and, at the very least, further extension of their clinical use should be curtailed until or unless they can be demonstrated to be of benefit in improving the outcome for mother or baby.

The role of the non-stress test as either a screening or a diagnostic test seems questionable, because of its relatively high cost and poor predictive properties. The biophysical profile may have greater potential as a diagnostic test for women in whom there is a high risk of fetal problems, but the usefulness of this approach is still not established.

14

Suspected fetopelvic disproportion and abnormal lie

This chapter is derived from two chapters by G. Justus Hofmeyr (31, 42) in EFFECTIVE CARE IN PREGNANCY AND CHILDBIRTH.

1 Fetopelvic disproportion
2 Shoulder dystocia
3 Breech presentation
4 External cephalic version for breech presentation
5 Oblique and transverse lie
6 Conclusions

1 Fetopelvic disproportion

Fetopelvic disproportion exists when the capacity of the birth canal is insufficient for the safe vaginal delivery of the fetus. In the past, antenatal strategies to diagnose fetopelvic disproportion received considerable attention, with the objective of early induction of labour or delivery by planned caesarean section should disproportion be diagnosed. Attempts to predict the occurrence of fetopelvic disproportion have included measurement of maternal height and shoe size, and clinical and X-ray pelvimetry.

It is important to distinguish between the risk of disproportion related to the presenting fetal part and that related to a non-leading part of the fetus, because of the special hazards of obstructed labour to the partly born fetus, as in shoulder dystocia, or obstruction to the after-coming head in a breech presentation. Maternal height has limited value for predicting fetopelvic disproportion, although short mothers tend to have a higher rate of caesarean section. The statistical significance of correlations between maternal height or shoe size and cephalopelvic disproportion is of limited clinical use, because of the large overlap in the obstetrical outcome between women with small and large dimensions.

There is a reasonable correlation between clinical and radiological assessment of pelvic dimensions, but neither are particularly accurate in predicting the outcome of labour. The effects of clinical pelvimetry have not been evaluated by randomized studies.

The meaning of non-engagement of the fetal head near term as an indicator of cephalopelvic disproportion is not well established. In black primigravidae, in whom such non-engagement commonly occurs, it is associated with longer labours, but not with operative delivery or increased maternal or fetal morbidity. The most reliable predictor of pelvic adequacy remains the history of the uncomplicated birth of a baby of similar or greater birthweight than that estimated for the current pregnancy.

The widespread use of X-ray pelvimetry to predict cephalopelvic disproportion has come under critical scrutiny since the reports of an association between prenatal irradiation and childhood leukaemia. As a general principle, irradiation that is not likely to benefit mother or baby should be avoided. The use of ultrasound for pelvimetry has been reported, but it has not been widely adopted.

There is wide variation among individuals and institutions in the use of X-ray pelvimetry. Its utility has been questioned because of its poor predictive value as a screening test for cephalopelvic disproportion, and the infrequency with which the results influence management.

Two prospective randomized studies of X-ray pelvimetry failed to detect any clear evidence of benefit to either mother or baby. Both trials, and their combined results, show a substantial increase in the rate of caesarean section with the use of X-ray pelvimetry.

Neither X-ray nor clinical pelvimetry have been shown to predict cephalopelvic disproportion with sufficient accuracy to justify elective caesarean section for cephalic presentations. Cephalopelvic disproportion is best diagnosed by a carefully monitored trial of labour, and X-ray pelvimetry should seldom, if ever, be necessary.

Computed tomographic pelvimetry, which greatly reduces the radiation exposure to the fetus, has been found in two small studies to be easier to perform, and in the measurement of a model pelvis, probably more accurate than conventional X-ray pelvimetry.

2 Shoulder dystocia

Shoulder dystocia is an obstetric emergency associated with considerable risk of fetal trauma. If a high likelihood of the condition could be predicted antenatally this would enable prevention by caesarean section. Caesarean section has been suggested for diabetic women with fetal weight estimated to be above 4000 g, and for non-diabetic women with an estimated fetal weight above 4500 g and slow progress of labour. Such a policy has not been subjected to prospective evaluation, and even if fetal weight estimation were accurate, this would prevent only a small proportion of potential cases of shoulder dystocia, while the majority of the caesarean sections would be unnecessary. Almost half of the cases of shoulder dystocia occur in infants weighing less than 4000 g.

There is at present no reliable method of antenatal prediction of shoulder dystocia, and efforts to reduce the problem should be directed towards ensuring that birth attendants are skilled in the management of this condition. Recent reports of novel methods of management require further evaluation. These include squatting, symphysiotomy, and even pushing the head back up followed by caesarean section.

3 Breech presentation and external cephalic version

Breech presentation, although sometimes associated with uterine or fetal abnormalities, is usually simply an error of orientation that places a healthy mother and a healthy baby at risk. The risk to the mother is an increased likelihood of caesarean section, and to the fetus the hazards of breech delivery.

The rate of caesarean section for breech presentation has increased in recent years, varying from a low of 45 per cent in Norway to 93 per cent in Sweden. The risk to the mother of the immediate and long-term complications of caesarean section is thus a serious considera-tion. The increased risk, if any, to the baby from vaginal breech delivery is difficult to determine. Perinatal mortality, corrected for abnormalities which may have caused the malpresentation, is es-timated to be about four times that for cephalic presentation.

The prevalence of breech presentation decreases from about 15 per cent at 29 to 32 weeks' gestation to between 3 and 4 per cent at delivery. Spontaneous changes from breech to cephalic presentation occur with decreasing frequency during the third trimester.

Cephalopelvic disproportion is perilous in a breech presentation because of the risk of entrapment of the aftercoming head. Several recent studies have confirmed the safety of vaginal breech delivery in women carefully selected to exclude cephalopelvic disproportion using X-ray pelvimetry, and usually estimation of fetal weight, assess-ment of neck flexion, and exclusion of double footling presentation. Such studies in no way establish that X-ray pelvimetry contributes significantly to the selection of women for either vaginal or abdominal delivery. For this a randomized trial comparing women with and without pelvimetry would be required. No such trial has been carried out.

The rare condition of deflexion of the head with a breech presen-tation may add additional risk to vaginal delivery. Ultrasound ex-amination in early labour can lead to rapid diagnosis or exclusion of the condition.

There is no reason to expect that X-ray pelvimetry should be more accurately predictive of cephalopelvic disproportion for breech than for cephalic presentations. In breech presentations, however, it is usual to avoid vaginal delivery when pelvic dimensions are even slightly reduced, in an attempt to ensure exclusion of all potential cases of cephalopelvic disproportion. Careful clinical assessment of fetopelvic relationships should be possible even in advanced labour, with the use of betamimetics to temporarily delay the progress of labour if necessary.

4 External cephalic version for breech presentation

A great variety of techniques have been used to promote correction of breech presentation. A midwifery technique claimed to be effective is to ask the mother to lie supine, hips slightly elevated and hips and knees flexed, and to gently roll through 180 degrees from side to side for ten minutes, repeating this three times a day. Traditional midwives in Gazankulu, South Africa, attempt to correct abnormal presentations during labour by manually shaking the uterus while the mother is in the knee-elbow position on the floor.

Uncontrolled studies have suggested that use of the knee–chest position is associated with a high rate of spontaneous version and normal vaginal birth. The woman is instructed to kneel with her hips flexed slightly more than 90 degrees, but with her thighs not pressing against the abdomen, while her head, shoulders and upper chest lie flat on the mattress. This is done for 15 minutes every 2 waking hours for 5 days. The only controlled trial of this method that has been carried out showed a small and statistically insignificant therapeutic gain of less than 10 per cent. The effectiveness, if any, of the knee–chest position is yet to be confirmed by controlled investigation.

Before the use of tocolytic drugs, external cephalic version was almost always attempted before 36 weeks' gestation, because the procedure was rarely found to be successful after that time. The effectiveness of external cephalic version before term remains controversial. Three randomized controlled trials have failed to demonstrate any effect on the incidence of breech birth, caesarean section rates, or perinatal outcome; the 1 per cent fetal mortality rate associated with the procedure led to a decline in its use. Interest in external cephalic version for breech presentation was revived by a 1975 report that cephalic version could be achieved in the majority of cases after 37 weeks' gestation, provided that the uterus was relaxed with betamimetic agents.

There are fundamental differences between external cephalic version attempted before term and at term, and these two approaches must be considered separately. Delay of external cephalic version attempts until term allows time for a maximal number of spontaneous versions to take place and for any obstetrical complications that may require delivery by caesarean section to become apparent. Thus, by waiting until term, fewer unnecessary attempts at external cephalic version are required. At term complications of the version can be readily managed by prompt abdominal delivery of the mature infant.

Following successful external cephalic version, fewer reversions to the breech presentation occur.

The major disadvantage of delaying external cephalic version until term is that the opportunity to attempt external cephalic version may be missed in women whose membranes rupture or whose labour commences before term.

The three randomized trials of external cephalic version at term that have been published all show that the external cephalic version significantly reduces the incidence of breech presentation at birth, and that the rate of caesarean section may be halved.

External cephalic version during labour is worthy of consideration as an extension of the trend towards version later in pregnancy. Earlier reports have included occasional references to attempted external cephalic versions during labour, and success rates up to almost 75 per cent have been reported.

In theory this approach has several advantages. Maximum time would be allowed for spontaneous version to take place and for possible contraindications to external cephalic version to appear, thus limiting the number of attempts of versions that would be necessary. The risks of external cephalic version may be reduced further by performing the procedure in the labour ward, with continuous subsequent monitoring of the fetal condition until delivery. In cases assessed as unsuitable for vaginal breech birth, the external cephalic version may be attempted in the operating theatre, and in the event of failure followed immediately by caesarean section.

Because waiting for the onset of labour would involve the inconvenience of performing version as an emergency rather than as an elective procedure, it is unlikely that external cephalic version during labour will become a first-line approach for breech presentation. However, when breech presentation is encountered during labour prior to rupture of the membranes, the limited data available to date suggest that external cephalic version with tocolysis is a reasonable procedure to consider.

The risk of attempted external cephalic version to the mother is exceedingly small. It consists of the possibility of adverse effects from any of the drugs used to facilitate version and the hazards of placental abruption, a rare but recognized complication.

The small but real risks of external cephalic version to the fetus are related to its gestational age, and to the methods employed. The complication rate is greater when external cephalic version is attempted before 37 weeks' gestation, when general anaesthesia is employed, and when the placenta is situated anteriorly. Attempted external cephalic version must be recognized as an invasive procedure that involves some risk to the fetus. Provided that fetal wellbeing is confirmed and monitored, and provided that appropriate precautions are observed, the risk to the mature fetus appears to be very small.

5 Oblique and transverse lie

Breech presentation is an error of polarity in which the forces necessary to maintain a longitudinal lie of the fetus are intact. Oblique and transverse lies are the result of an entirely different situation, in that the fetus fails to adopt a longitudinal lie. They are associated with multiparity, abdominal laxity, uterine and fetal anomalies, shortening of the longitudinal axis of the uterus by fundal or low-lying placenta, and conditions that prevent the engagement of the presenting part, such as pelvic tumours and a small pelvic inlet.

Abnormal lie, particularly oblique lie, may be transitory and related to maternal position. Oblique lie is frequently erroneously diagnosed during ultrasound examination because of displacement of the presenting part by the over-distended maternal bladder.

When non-longitudinal lie is encountered after 32 weeks' gestation, underlying abnormalities should be sought. Further management options include antepartum attempts at external version, version at term followed by induction of labour, or expectant management with or without intrapartum attempted version if the abnormal lie persists.

The role of external version in the management of oblique and transverse lie has not been assessed in a randomized trial. A number of descriptive case series have been reported. With expectant management most cases of abnormal lie will revert to the longitudinal lie by the time of delivery. Less than 20 per cent of transverse lies observed after 37 weeks' gestation persist to delivery. Given the high spontaneous version rate and the unstable nature of the non-longitudinal lie, with a high probability of reversion following external cephalic version, there is no firm case for external version prior to labour or planned delivery. The risk of delaying intervention until the onset of labour is that cord prolapse or strong labour may occur prior to the woman's arrival at hospital.

Care of the woman with a transverse or oblique lie encountered during labour is more straightforward, as the choice lies between caesarean section and external version. A prospective but uncontrolled study of external version for transverse lie in labour showed a modest rate of success. There were no fetal or maternal complications associated with the procedure, though larger studies are needed to evaluate potential risks.

In the absence of controlled trials, the timing of intervention in pregnancies complicated by non-longitudinal lie must remain a matter of clinical judgement. The advantage of gaining fetal maturity, allowing time for spontaneous version to take place, and allowing labour to begin spontaneously must be weighed against the risk of membrane rupture or cord prolapse before the version can be attempted. Once labour has begun or the decision has been made to deliver the baby, attempted version in selected cases, with immediate recourse to caesarean section if necessary, is a reasonable option. Further evaluation of its place in modern obstetrics is required.

6 Conclusions

No reliable methods are available for accurate prediction of fetopelvic disproportion before labour. Labour is the best test of pelvic adequacy in cephalic presentations.

External cephalic version for breech presentation before term is not warranted. External cephalic version at term, on the other hand, substantially reduces the incidence of breech presentation at birth and caesarean section.

The place of pelvimetry in breech presentation has not been established and a trial determining its benefits, if any, is warranted if this common practice is continued.

15

Symptoms in pregnancy

This chapter is derived from the chapters by Michael Bracken, Murray Enkin, Hubert Campbell, and Iain Chalmers (32) and Elaine Wang and Fiona Smaill (34) in EFFECTIVE CARE IN PREGNANCY AND CHILDBIRTH.

1 Introduction

Although an uneventful pregnancy is generally considered to be a state of health rather than disease, it is frequently accompanied by symptoms that, at other times or in other circumstances, might be thought to be signs of illness. Nausea and vomiting, heartburn, constipation, leg cramps, and vaginitis are neither life-threatening nor in themselves hazardous to mother or baby. Nevertheless, they can be the cause of significant discomfort and unpleasantness, and their alleviation is an important aspect of antenatal care.

2 Nausea and vomiting

Nausea and vomiting are the most frequent, the most characteristic, and perhaps the most troublesome symptoms of early pregnancy. The aetiology of nausea in pregnancy is still unknown, and the variety of treatments that have been recommended reflect the multitude of theories as to the underlying cause. As might be expected in a self-limiting condition, uncontrolled trials have yielded rather spectacular, if spurious, results. In contrast to the results obtained in the uncontrolled trials, those from controlled trials have not been quite so impressive.

A number of trials have demonstrated a variety of antihistamines to be better than placebo. Simple antihistamines, although they some-times provoke troublesome side-effects such as drowsiness and blur-ring of vision, are generally considered to be safe during pregnancy. There have been no major epidemiological studies to look for teratogenic effects of antihistamines.

By far the most widely used drug used to treat nausea in pregnancy was, until recently, Debendox (marketed as Bendectin in the United States and Canada, and as Lenotan in some other countries). Indeed, Debendox was the most widely used prescription drug of any kind taken in pregnancy. In June 1983 Debendox was removed from the market as a direct result of litigation brought against the manufac-turers, claiming that the drug had caused congenital malformations in the offspring of women who had used it. The litigation was brought despite overwhelming evidence *against* Debendox being a teratogen, and has almost certainly led to an increased use of alternative medica-tions for treating nausea and vomiting, about which, for any single product, much less human research has been conducted.

Debendox, at the time of its recall, had been used by over 30 million women worldwide, and in many countries, between a quarter and a third of all pregnant women used Debendox. When Debendox was used to treat nausea it was usually in the first trimester, during embryologic development. Because of concern about the teratogenic risks of other drugs, Debendox was often the only prescription drug used in pregnancy. If we assume an overall congenital malformation incidence rate of 3.5 per cent at delivery, then exposure to Debendox will have occurred in over one million babies born with a congenital malformation purely by chance alone. In the inevitable search for what may have produced her child's malformations, it is not surpris-ing that many mothers implicated Debendox, and, perhaps prompted by over-eager lawyers, some chose to sue.

The three small placebo-controlled trials that have been published provide strong evidence that Debendox provided considerable relief for nausea and vomiting in pregnancy. In spite of the wide variety of populations studied and methods employed, there is widespread agreement among the nineteen epidemiologic studies of Debendox, that the drug is *not* associated with increased risk of congenital malformations in offspring. The abrupt withdrawal of Debendox from the market has provided a unique further test of its safety. Despite the reduction in use of Debendox, from use in about one-third of pregnancies to use in none, there has been no correlated reduction in any malformation group as judged by their incidence reports.

With the withdrawal of the most widely studied antiemetic, Debendox, from the market, nausea in pregnancy is being treated by antihistamines that appear to be efficacious, as evidenced by the early trials, but whose safety has not been as extensively studied.

3 Heartburn

Heartburn affects about two-thirds of all women at some stage of pregnancy. It is another so-called 'minor' disorder of pregnancy, but it causes more discomfort and distress than do many more serious conditions. It is commonly associated with eating, stooping, or lying down. The most clear-cut precipitating factor is posture.

Self-medication with proprietary antacids is the most commonly employed treatment. There appears to be little evidence of differences in efficacy between the various available preparations.

Other pharmacological approaches to the treatment of heartburn have shown beneficial effects in randomized trials. Prostigmine was found to be significantly more effective than placebo. Dilute (0.1 ml in 10 ml flavoured syrup) hydrochloric acid, which may counteract the effects of regurgitated bile on the stomach and oesophagus, was also found to be more effective than placebo. More importantly, women who had not obtained relief from their symptoms with alkali were likely to obtain relief from acid, and vice versa. In this way there was a 98 per cent probability that one or other of these treatments would be efficacious.

There does not appear to be any hazard from the occasional use of any of the agents discussed. Individuals should be allowed to choose among different preparations, since therapeutic compliance will be increased when the product is found to be palatable as well as effective. Of the available antacids, the magnesium salts would appear to be the safest option for longer-term use. In situations where simple and sensible measures such as avoiding fatty or spicy foods and minimizing bending or lying flat after eating have failed, the evidence suggests that alkalis should be prescribed initially. If symptoms fail to respond to alkalis, dilute hydrochloric acid or prostigmine may be tried.

4 Constipation

Constipation is a troublesome problem for many women during pregnancy, particularly during the last trimester. Women who are habitually constipated usually become more so during pregnancy. The frequency of constipation among pregnant women will reflect their dietary habits, fluid intake, and pattern of physical exercise. Management of constipation using physiological approaches (alterations in diet, fluid intake, or exercises) has been found in observational studies to bring relief in at least a third of cases; nevertheless laxatives are required by many women.

Laxatives are usually classified by their mode of action. Saline cathartics (magnesium, sodium, and potassium salts) and lubricants (such as mineral oils) are contraindicated in pregnancy, the former because of the danger of inducing electrolyte disturbances, the latter because they interfere with absorption of fat-soluble vitamins, tend to seep through the anal sphincter and cause pruritis, and occasionally cause lipoid pneumonia and paraffinomas.

Hydrophilic bulking agents (polysaccharide and/or cellulose derivatives) and detergent stool-softeners (the dioctylsulphosuccinates) are relatively free of adverse effects because they are inert and not absorbed.

A variety of laxatives operate by their irritant action on the intestine. These include the diphenylmethanes (for example, bisacodyl and phenolphthalein), the anthraquinones (aloe, cascara, and senna), and castor oil. These irritant laxatives are all absorbed systemically to some extent. Most of them probably cross the placenta, but there is little information about possible effects on the fetus. The most common maternal side-effects include cramping or griping and increased mucous secretion and excessive catharsis with resultant fluid loss. Chronic use can result in loss of normal bowel function and laxative dependence.

More recent interest has focused on using modest supplemental intake of dietary fibre to reduce constipation. In a randomized trial comparing dietary supplement with wheat or corn bran with no intervention, women in both fibre-supplemented groups increased their number of bowel movements (statistically significantly so in the corn-bran-supplemented group) and experienced less constipation than the untreated women.

In attempts to prevent and treat constipation in pregnancy, modification of the diet, including increasing dietary fibre and fluid intake, should be considered before resorting to laxatives. Both bulking agents and stool-softeners are safe for long-term use in pregnancy. If these preparations fail to relieve symptoms, irritant laxatives (for example, standardized senna or bisacodyl) should be used on a short-term basis. Saline cathartics and lubricant oils should not be used at all.

5 Vaginitis

5.1 *Candidiasis*

Vaginal candidiasis causes an intensely irritating, pruritic vaginal discharge, and is a frequent problem during pregnancy. The incidence in pregnant women has been estimated to be between two and ten times higher than in non-pregnant women. The condition is more difficult to eradicate in pregnant women, but the organism is usually soon cleared after delivery.

The clinical diagnosis of vaginal candidiasis is neither specific nor sensitive. Typical symptoms include an irritating vaginal discharge and pruritus. Examination reveals reddened mucosa of the labia minora, introitus, and lower third of the vagina, with white patches and a thin discharge containing white flakes.

Congenital candida infections affect infants of very low birthweight, and manifest with pneumonia and skin infections. These infections, however, are rare considering the high frequency of vaginal candidal carriage in pregnant women. In view of the low incidence of adverse effects on babies born to asymptomatic mothers, screening of pregnant women for candida is not indicated.

A variety of different agents as well as different dosages and frequencies of administration have been studied. A randomized comparison demonstrated the effectiveness of nystatin compared to hydrargaphen, but most recent trials have compared nystatin with imidazole preparations, and these have shown imidazoles to be more effective than nystatin. There is no evidence that a 14-day course of antifungal therapy is any more effective in curing candidiasis than a 7-day course, and at least some evidence to suggest that a 1–3 day course is sufficient.

The initial treatment of symptomatic vaginal candidiasis should consist of clotrimazole because of its proven superior efficacy over nystatin. Repeat courses may be required given the tendency of the infection to recur. No treatment is indicated in asymptomatic infection.

5.2 Trichomoniasis

The protozoan *Trichomonas vaginalis* is frequently isolated from vaginal secretions during pregnancy. Infection with trichomonas in pregnancy may cause severe symptomatic vaginitis in some women. Whether or not it can have adverse effects on the course of pregnancy or on the newborn is uncertain. Unsubstantiated comments have suggested that failure to treat severe trichomonas vaginitis leads to preterm delivery. One randomized controlled trial reported no statistically significant difference in birthweight or gestational age at delivery whether asymptomatic *Trichomonas vaginalis* infection was either treated with a single dose of metronidazole or left untreated. Colonization of the neonate following vaginal delivery appears to be uncommon.

As *Trichomonas vaginalis* is often associated with other sexually transmitted organisms of significance in pregnancy, these should be specifically sought when *Trichomonas vaginalis* is identified.

Up to 50 per cent of women with the organism are asymptomatic. Vaginal discharge is the most common complaint, but the classically described green frothy discharge is found in only a small proportion of women. Microscopic examination of a wet preparation of vaginal secretions is simple to perform and highly specific, but its sensitivity compared to culture may be as low as 50 per cent. To maximize the sensitivity of a wet preparation, a drop of vaginal discharge diluted in saline should be examined under the microscope immediately. Cooling the secretions results in loss of the characteristic jerky motility of the organism.

Culture is the optimal method to diagnose trichomonas, but the methodology is time-consuming and not generally available. Papanicolaou smears have been used to diagnose the disease, but the sensitivity of this method compared to culture is only 40 per cent.

Metronidazole is a highly effective treatment of infection with *Trichomonas vaginalis*. Both a single two-gram dose and an extended seven-day regimen of 250 mg three times a day are curative in more than 90 per cent of women. The only available double blind randomized comparison of single and multiple dose regimens of metronidazole showed no statistically significant advantage of the multiple-dose regimen. Because patient compliance is high with single-dose therapy, this regimen is preferred clinically. The sexual partner should be treated concomitantly with the woman.

Metronidazole readily crosses the placenta. Although it has been found to be carcinogenic in rodents and mutagenic for certain bacteria, there is no evidence for teratogenicity in humans after its administration to pregnant women. Most obstetricians, however, refrain from its use during the first trimester of pregnancy.

Clotrimazole, an antifungal agent, has been shown to be effective *in vitro* against *Trichomonas vaginalis*. It has promise as a local palliative treatment during pregnancy.

6 Leg cramps

Leg cramps (painful spasms of the calf muscles) are experienced to some extent by almost half of all pregnant women, particularly in the later months of pregnancy. The symptom tends to occur at night, and may recur repeatedly for weeks or months, causing considerable distress. The cause and mechanism of these cramps are still not clear. Sometimes based on rather astonishing analogies, unsupported hypotheses, and uncontrolled studies, a number of drugs have been widely prescribed for treatment and prophylaxis. Quinine, Benadryl, vitamin D, and dietary calcium were widely acclaimed to be of benefit on the basis of uncontrolled studies.

Sodium chloride tablets were demonstrated to be more effective than placebo, no treatment, or calcium lactate in one controlled trial, but these results have not been confirmed. The only two placebo-controlled trials failed to show any improvement in symptoms among women who took 1 g of calcium twice daily for three weeks.

Calcium salts are still widely prescribed for the syndrome of nocturnal calf cramps in pregnancy, despite the lack of evidence from controlled trials that they have any benefit beyond that of a placebo. Unfortunately no further trials of the efficacy of increased sodium intake appear to have been carried out. It is probable that the observed benefits may be restricted to women who are sodium-deficient. Massage and putting the affected muscles on the stretch is stated to afford relief during an attack, and these innocuous measures are surely worth trying.

7 Conclusions

Our review of the available methods for managing some of the symptoms commonly experienced during pregnancy indicates that often these will be amenable to relief by using simple and physiological approaches. Where medication is deemed to be necessary, simple antihistamines appear to be the drugs of choice in the management of nausea and vomiting, although no single product has been satisfactorily tested for efficacy in enough trials and few studies are available to inform us about possible teratogenic risks. Unfortunately, Debendox—the antinauseant for which efficacy and safety has been documented—is no longer available.

When symptoms of heartburn are troublesome, antacids should be taken, and dilute hydrochloric acid if these fail to bring relief. Bulking agents, if necessary combined with stool-softeners, should be used in the management of constipation; irritant laxatives (such as standardized senna) should be reserved for short-term use in refractory cases.

Symptoms of candidal vaginitis respond well to short courses of clotrimazole, which will often give relief from the symptoms of trichomonas vaginitis as well. Metronidazole, which is most effective for trichomonas, readily crosses the placenta, and probably should be withheld during the first trimester.

No pharmaceutical treatment for leg cramps has yet been firmly based on scientific evidence.

The so-called 'minor symptoms' of pregnancy have received little systematic study in clinical trials. Because of their wide prevalence, and the significant discomfort that they cause, this systematic study is urgently required.

16

Hypertension in pregnancy

This chapter is derived from the chapter by Rory Collins and Henk C. S. Wallenburg (33) in EFFECTIVE CARE IN PREGNANCY AND CHILDBIRTH.

1 Introduction

Two aetiologically distinct entities account for most hypertensive disorders in pregnancy: one is a pregnancy-induced disorder, and the other is associated with chronic hypertension. In this review, the pregnancy-induced disorder is referred to as 'pre-eclampsia' if the pregnancy-induced hypertension is accompanied by proteinuria.

The second pathological entity that accounts for most of the remaining hypertensive disease in pregnancy arises from chronic hypertension. In addition, a combination of the two pathological conditions may occur, and this is referred to as 'superimposed pre-eclampsia'.

The reported incidences of maternal and fetal complications of hypertensive disorders in pregnancy vary widely. These conditions may have devastating consequences for mother and baby. A number of medical and surgical regimens have therefore been tried for the prevention and treatment of pre-eclampsia and eclampsia. One author reports that women with eclampsia have been 'blistered, bled, purged, packed, lavaged, irrigated, punctured, starved, sedated, anaesthetized, paralyzed, tranquillized, rendered hypotensive, drowned, been given diuretics, had mastectomies, been dehydrated, forcibly delivered, and neglected'.

The role of diet and hospitalization for bed rest have been considered in other chapters of this book. This chapter assesses the available evidence about pharmacological approaches to either prevent or treat pregnancy-induced hypertension, pre-eclampsia, and eclampsia.

2 Mild or moderate pregnancy-induced hypertension and pre-eclampsia

Moderate pregnancy-induced hypertension carries little risk to the mother or the fetus, unless severe hypertension, pre-eclampsia, or eclampsia ensue. For this reason, the aim of pharmacological treatment of moderate hypertensive disease in pregnancy has been to defer or prevent the development of severe hypertensive disease. Methyldopa is the most widely used drug in women with mild to moderate pregnancy-induced hypertension, but beta-blockers, labetalol, and calcium channel blockers are rapidly being introduced into clinical practice. Although there are anecdotal reports in the literature on their use in women with mild to moderate hypertensive disease in pregnancy, there are no randomized controlled trials of sufficient size to allow reliable assessment of their effects on serious outcome measures, or on deterioration of the disease.

2.1 Diuretics

There is no good evidence that excessive water retention, or even frank oedema, defines a group of women at particular risk of developing pre-eclampsia. Nevertheless, many attempts have been made and, indeed, are still being made by some obstetricians and midwives to prevent retention of salt and water in pregnancy by prescribing diuretics or a rigidly sodium-free diet in the belief that this will prevent pre-eclampsia.

The effects of the prophylactic use of diuretics in pregnant women with normal blood-pressure (with or without oedema or excessive weight gain), and of their therapeutic use in moderate hypertension have been studied in 12 randomized trials. The results reflect the well-known ability of diuretics to reduce blood-pressure, rather than any improvement in substantive outcomes. When the data on proteinuric pre-eclampsia, or the risk of perinatal death are considered, there is no clear evidence of benefit. This may be because the treatment was ineffective, but it may also be because the numbers studied were too small to detect some modest but worthwhile benefit. Serious side-effects of diuretic treatment in pregnancy, which have been described in occasional case reports, were not observed in these trials, which included nearly 7000 women and their babies. This suggests that the putative maternal and fetal risks of diuretic administration may have been overstated, perhaps as a result of selective case reporting. Until data from larger studies are available, it will not be known whether any benefits outweigh any risks.

2.2 Antithrombotic and antiplatelet agents

Changes in the blood-clotting system are well documented in established pre-eclampsia. The extent of the clotting disorders appears to be related to the severity of the pre-eclampsia, and early activation of the clotting system may contribute to the pathology of pre-eclampsia. For these reasons, the use of anticoagulant or antiplatelet agents has been considered for the prevention of pre-eclampsia and intrauterine growth retardation.

Heparin has been used in uncontrolled studies involving single cases, or small series of patients. It requires subcutaneous (or intravenous) administration, making it an inconvenient form of treatment, and its use in severe cases may be associated with dangerous side-effects. Warfarin has also been used prophylactically in an attempt to prevent recurrent pre-eclampsia in multiparous women. Anecdotal reports of its use do not provide any evidence of maternal or fetal benefit, and there is some suggestion that it may have serious side-effects.

Aspirin is a widely practicable antiplatelet agent that has been shown to prevent thrombotic occlusion of arterio-venous shunts and coronary artery bypass grafts, and to reduce death and reinfarction in unstable angina and after myocardial infarction and cerebral ischaemic attacks.

Two randomized trials of antiplatelet prophylaxis using either aspirin or aspirin combined with dipyridamole have recently been reported. Although the number of women involved was small the results appear promising. Several further trials are now in progress to assess more reliably whether beneficial (or adverse) effects of low-dose aspirin in the prevention and treatment of pre-eclampsia exist. Until these studies have been completed it will remain unclear whether or not this form of treatment should be adopted in clinical practice.

2.3 Antihypertensive agents

The most widely used antihypertensive agent in pregnancy is still methyldopa, although other agents, such as beta-blockers, are also being used. There is clear evidence that the use of methyldopa in women with moderate hypertension substantially reduces the risk of the development of severe hypertension. However, as for diuretics, no significant effect on the incidence of proteinuria or perinatal death has been detected.

Clonidine is similar to methyldopa in most respects, but it has a more rapid onset of action (about 30 minutes), compared with 4 hours for methyldopa. In a small randomized, double blind trial comparing methyldopa with clonidine, there were no statistically significant differences observed in terms of maternal blood-pressure control, development of proteinuria, incidence of fetal growth retardation, or neonatal condition.

Beta-blockers are effective antihypertensive agents which reduce cardiac output. It is possible that in pregnancy a reduction in cardiac output would be an unfavourable effect, since adequate perfusion of the maternal and uteroplacental circulation depends on maintenance of the elevated cardiac output of pregnancy. Two beta-blockers (atenolol and metoprolol) and one combined alpha- and beta-blocker (labetalol) have been studied in randomized trials.

Beta-blockers reduce the risk of severe hypertension developing in women with early signs or symptoms of pre-eclampsia. Despite this, there is virtually no evidence of any effect on the development of proteinuria. Too few women have participated in controlled studies for any reliable conclusions to be drawn about the effects of beta-blockers on perinatal death, nor is there sufficient information to assess whether they have any serious adverse effects on pregnancy outcome or infant development.

Direct randomized comparisons of beta-blockers and methyldopa do not indicate any significant difference between them, either in terms of the development of severe hypertension or of proteinuria. In only two of the five relevant trials were any perinatal deaths observed. Although there were slightly fewer in the beta-blocker groups of both trials, this difference is consistent with chance.

The small numbers of women studied in adequately controlled trials of antihypertensive medication for both the prevention and treatment of moderate hypertensive disease preclude definitive conclusions about their effects, even in overviews of all related trials. It seems likely that antihypertensive treatment prevents the development of severe hypertension in pregnancy, and for that reason may reduce the number of hospital admissions and emergency deliveries. There is no clear evidence that antihypertensive treatment with any of the drugs available may defer or prevent the occurrence of proteinuric pre-eclampsia, or of associated problems such as fetal growth retardation and perinatal death. Nor is there good evidence about the safety of such treatments, in particular with respect to child development. At present there seems to be no reason to prefer any one of the tested beta-blockers, or to prefer labetalol to a pure beta-blocker, or indeed, to prefer beta-blockers to methyldopa.

3 Severe pre-eclampsia and eclampsia

Although treatment of hypertension does not strike at the basic disorder, it may still benefit the mother and fetus. One of the important objectives in cases of severe hypertension in pregnancy is to reduce blood-pressure in order to avoid hypertensive encephalopathy and cerebral haemorrhage. For this reason, the aim in treating severely hypertensive pregnant women is to keep the blood-pressure below dangerous levels (around 170/110 mm Hg) and to maintain adequate circulating blood volume.

3.1 *Antihypertensive agents*

Hydralazine is the antihypertensive drug used most commonly in women with severe pregnancy-induced hypertension and pre-eclampsia, followed closely by diazoxide and by veratrum alkaloids. Methyldopa is also used in the treatment of severe hypertensive disease in pregnancy, although it has the disadvantage of a relatively slow onset of action (about four hours), even when given intravenously. There is no evidence justifying any strong preference for one of the various drugs that are available for treating severe hypertension in pregnancy, although one study suggests that control can be more simply and more consistently achieved with labetalol.

There have been several recent reports of the treatment of moderate to severe pregnancy-induced hypertension with calcium channel blockers and with ketanserin (a specific serotonin receptor antagonist). Intravenous infusion of prostacyclin has also been used to reduce blood-pressure by producing vasodilatation. This lowers maternal blood-pressure effectively, but the blood-pressure returns to its previously elevated levels as soon as the prostacyclin infusion is interrupted. In these few uncontrolled studies no beneficial effects on fetal condition were apparent.

In clinical practice, therefore, the choice of drug should probably depend on the familiarity of an individual clinician with a particular drug. In general, maternal side-effects are not different from those in the non-pregnant state, and are listed in pharmacology texts. All drugs used to treat hypertension in pregnancy cross the placenta, and so may affect the fetus directly, by means of their action within the fetal circulation, or indirectly, by their effect on uteroplacental perfusion.

From what is known about direct and indirect adverse effects on fetus and neonate, hydralazine appears to be relatively safe. Labetalol may cause severe and long-lasting fetal and neonatal bradycardia, particularly after high doses. These effects may be clinically important in the presence of fetal and neonatal hypoxia. Diazoxide can provoke a precipitous fall in maternal arterial pressure, leading to a reduction in uteroplacental perfusion, especially in severely pre-eclamptic women in whom placental blood flow is already compromised. In addition, hyperglycaemia has been reported in the newborn after maternal treatment with diazoxide.

There is, as yet, little clinical information on the fetal or neonatal effects of maternal use of calcium antagonists. Various problems have been observed in the neonatal period following their use in uncontrolled studies, but these effects could not be definitely attributed to maternal drug treatment.

3.2 Plasma volume expansion

Women with severe pre-eclampsia before delivery often have a contracted circulating plasma volume, and this has led to recommendation that plasma volume should be expanded with non-crystalloid solutions such as dextran and salt-poor albumin in attempts to improve the maternal systemic and uteroplacental circulation. One randomized trial studied the effect of plasma volume expansion with hyperosmolar solutions (dextran 40 and plasminate) and found that volume expansion was associated with significant improvements in haemoconcentration and output of urine, and a trend towards a lowering of mean arterial pressure.

Some recent uncontrolled studies suggest that rapid replenishment of intravascular volume may result in decreased arterial blood-pressure in pregnant women with moderate third-trimester hypertension, or pre-eclampsia. Although blood-pressure was not restored to normal by volume expansion, these uncontrolled studies suggest that such treatment may be an effective adjunct to the administration of antihypertensive drugs, and by reducing the doses needed, might minimize the risks of maternal and neonatal side-effects.

It should be borne in mind, however, that intravascular volume expansion carries a serious risk of volume overload, which may lead to pulmonary and perhaps cerebral oedema in pre-eclamptic women in whom colloid osmotic pressure is usually low. Plasma volume expansion may be particularly dangerous after delivery, when venous volume tends to rise, so that it should not be applied without careful monitoring.

Further studies are clearly needed to define the place of plasma volume expansion, with or without additional antihypertensive treatment, in the management of women with severe pregnancy-induced hypertension.

3.3 Anticonvulsant agents

Anticonvulsant and sedative drugs are widely used in the management of eclampsia, as well as in pregnant women with severe hypertensive disease and pre-eclampsia, in an attempt to prevent the occurrence of eclamptic seizures. In the United States barbiturates are used in moderately severe pre-eclampsia, while parenteral magnesium sulphate is the treatment most usually used in fulminating pre-eclampsia and eclampsia. In contrast, magnesium sulphate is rarely used in Europe and Australia, the most frequent choice being diazepam, followed by barbiturates and chlormethiazole. In Sweden many doctors still use 'lytic cocktails' consisting of hydralazine, chlorpromazine, and pethidine, in addition to diazepam and, sometimes, chlormethiazole. No adequately controlled clinical trials on the use of anticonvulsant drugs in pregnancy are available. The current popularity of magnesium sulphate in the United States reflects experience with a regimen of intravenous and intramuscular administration of magnesium sulphate, intravenous hydralazine, and delivery within 48 hours.

Only a small amount of magnesium appears to cross the blood–brain barrier after intravenous administration of magnesium sulphate; it has little effect on blood-pressure and virtually no sedative effect.

Magnesium can attain life-threatening levels as a result of excessive dosage or diminished excretion (for example, due to renal failure). As overdose can cause death by cardiorespiratory arrest, women receiving magnesium sulphate must be closely monitored at all times, and calcium as an antidote should be readily available.

Magnesium readily crosses the placenta, and high magnesium concentrations in cord blood have been shown to be associated with depression of the baby.

The benzodiazepines chlordiazepoxide (Librium) and diazepam (Valium) were introduced in the treatment of eclampsia and severe pre-eclampsia in the late 1960s as an alternative to the 'lytic cocktails' popular at that time. Following intravenous administration to the mother, diazepam readily crosses the placenta to the fetus, and is very slowly metabolized and cleared in the neonate. Maternal administration of diazepam may lead to loss of beat-to-beat variability in the fetal heart rate, and thus interfere with the clinical interpretation of the cardiotocogram. Given in high doses during labour, diazepam causes delayed onset of respiration, apnea, hypotonia, impaired response to cold, and poor sucking in the newborn infant. These well-documented effects may last several days.

Chlormethiazole has been widely used as a sedative and anticonvulsant in the treatment of severe pre-eclampsia and eclampsia. It acts rapidly following intravenous administration, and its effectiveness has been described in various uncontrolled studies. Like the other anticonvulsants, chlormethiazole also crosses the placenta, but, in contrast to diazepam, it is rapidly excreted by the fetus and the newborn.

The ideal anticonvulsant for use in severe pre-eclampsia and eclampsia would be the one which is easiest to administer, is rapidly effective in arresting and preventing convulsions, has a wide safety limit for the mother, and is non-toxic and non-depressant to the baby.

All the drugs discussed above appear to have a reliable and rapid anticonvulsant effect, but they differ with regard to their adverse effects on the fetus and neonate. The search for the ideal anticonvulsant to be used in severe pre-eclampsia or eclampsia continues.

4 Conclusions

Pharmacological lowering of blood-pressure is the mainstay of the management of women with hypertensive disorders in pregnancy. There is some evidence to support the hypothesis that antihypertensive treatment (diuretics, beta-blockers, methyldopa) of women with mild or moderate pregnancy-induced hypertensive disorders will prevent severe hypertension developing, but no evidence of any effect on the occurrence of proteinuric pre-eclampsia or perinatal mortality. This may be either because there are no benefits in terms of the more important outcome measures or because the effects on severe pre-eclampsia could not be detected in the small trials published to date.

For treatment of severe hypertensive disease, hydralazine appears to be effective in lowering blood-pressure. Labetalol may produce a more controlled lowering of blood-pressure than hydralazine or diazoxide, but this possibility requires further study.

The use of anticonvulsants is widespread, not only in the treatment of eclampsia but also in the management of severe pre-eclampsia. The choice of drug has been determined by historical factors rather than by evidence from controlled comparisons.

The potential benefits of antiplatelet agents such as aspirin in both the prevention and treatment of pre-eclampsia deserve priority in further investigation. Similarly, in view of the promising effects of beta-blockers and methyldopa in preventing the development of severe hypertension (and in view of their widespread use by many doctors), there is an urgent need for them to be evaluated in further, large-scale trials.

The results of the small trials of plasma volume expansion conducted so far are promising. Further study might help to determine whether this would be a practicable and effective way of reducing the need for (or dose of) antihypertensive therapy in the treatment of severe pregnancy-induced hypertension. Current treatment of hypertensive disorders in pregnancy appears to be largely based on clinical experience fed by anecdotal reports, rather than on reliable evidence from properly controlled trials of sufficient size. Given the large numbers of women who develop hypertensive disease in pregnancy, multicentre collaborative studies involving *much* larger numbers of women than have so far been studied should be mounted in order to assess more reliably the effects of the various treatments that are used.

17

Infection in pregnancy

This chapter is derived from the chapter by Elaine Wang and Fiona Smaill (34) in EFFECTIVE CARE IN PREGNANCY AND CHILDBIRTH.

1 Introduction
2 Urinary tract infection
3 Syphilis
4 Gonorrhoea
5 Rubella
6 Genital mycoplasmas
7 Toxoplasmosis
8 Chlamydia
9 Herpes
10 Group B streptococcus
11 Acquired immunodeficiency syndrome (AIDS)

---

1 Introduction

Deaths from bacterial infection are rare in most parts of the developed world today, although in the past infection was a major cause of both maternal and perinatal death. Nevertheless, maternal infection and colonization with pathogenic organisms continue to cause problems for both mothers and babies. The prevalence of various forms of infection in pregnancy is higher in poorer women, and this fact may in part explain the greater frequency of adverse outcomes of pregnancy among these women.

In addition to bacteria, other organisms may lead to serious disease during pregnancy and the peripartum period. Such organisms include fungi, viruses, and protozoa. A number of organisms that are more difficult to culture, such as *Chlamydia trachomatis* and the genital mycoplasmas, have now been linked with disease in pregnancy and childbirth. In addition, pregnant women are subject to the same range of acute and chronic infections as non-pregnant women.

2 Urinary tract infection

Three to eight per cent of pregnant women harbour significant numbers of bacteria in their urine, usually without exhibiting any symptoms, and 15 to 45 per cent of untreated women with asymptomatic bacteriuria will develop symptomatic urinary tract infections (acute cystitis or pyelonephritis). Acute cystitis and acute pyelonephritis are found in approximately one per cent of pregnancies. Urinary tract infection is thus one of the most common medical complications of pregnancy.

Culture and colony count of a single voided specimen will detect 80 per cent of cases of asymptomatic infection. The predictive value of a culture result depends on the prevalence of infection in the population studied. Other, more economical, methods to screen for infection have been suggested. Semiautomated instruments to screen specimens for bacteriuria, the detection of urinary nitrites, and microscopic analysis of a clean catch spun urine, may have a role to play in identifying which urines should be cultured in the interests of cost-saving; but their sensitivity and specificity in pregnant women is not high enough to allow them to replace urine culture as an adequate screening test.

Recognition and treatment of asymptomatic bacteriuria in pregnancy will result in a substantially decreased risk of the development of acute pyelonephritis and its short-term consequences to both mother and fetus.

The postulated relationship of asymptomatic bacteriuria in pregnancy with increased fetal mortality, preterm delivery, intrauterine growth retardation, and low birthweight infants is more tenuous. The associations are present, but they are weak and controversial. Antibiotic treatment of bacteriuria in pregnancy has not been shown to reduce the risk of subsequent infection in the long term, but the only trial in which a follow-up was conducted is small.

The available evidence from controlled trials suggest that where an isolate is known to be susceptible, sulphonamides, nitrofurantoin, ampicillin, and the first-generation cephalosporins are equally effective in the treatment of asymptomatic bacteriuria.

The original approach to therapy for asymptomatic bacteriuria in pregnancy was continuous antibiotic therapy for the duration of pregnancy. Single-dose therapy for uncomplicated urinary tract infection in women who are not pregnant is well established, however, and trials suggest that this is effective for pregnant women as well. It has obvious advantages in terms of patient compliance, minimization of adverse effects, and financial savings.

Symptomatic lower-tract infection in pregnancy may also respond to single-dose treatment, but there are insufficient data for this treatment to be recommended. Regular follow-up urine cultures must be obtained; failures, relapses, and recurrences treated appropriately; and when infection recurs consideration must be given to continuous prophylactic therapy for the remainder of pregnancy. Recurrent infection during pregnancy may signify an underlying abnormality of the urinary tract; and these women should be evaluated radiographically postpartum.

Pyelonephritis is diagnosed clinically by the presence of fever, flank pain, and dysuria, together with a positive urine culture. Patients should be hospitalized and antibiotic therapy instituted parenterally after blood and urine cultures have been taken. Ampicillin or a first-generation cephalosporin is appropriate initial treatment, as infection is probably due to *Escherichia coli*. Where there is concern about antibiotic resistance or the patient is seriously ill, combination therapy with an aminoglycoside and ampicillin is appropriate. Careful monitoring of serum aminoglycoside levels throughout therapy is strongly recommended to minimize fetal exposure to the drug.

Women with acute pyelonephritis are at risk of relapse and recurrence of infection, but the only reported randomized trial of suppressive therapy for the remainder of pregnancy failed to detect any advantage over close surveillance with cultures.

3 Syphilis

Syphilis during pregnancy is particularly important because transmission of *Treponema pallidum* from mother to baby may result in the development of congenital syphilis, with tragic sequelae. The outcomes of such transmission may consist of abortion, preterm delivery, or perinatal death (20 per cent). Subclinical congenital infection with resulting handicap is not uncommon. Congenital syphilis can be largely prevented by identification and treatment of the infected mother during pregnancy. Transmission to the fetus occurs particularly during the second trimester, although it may occur during the first trimester as well.

Most infected women are asymptomatic, and can only be identified by serological screening. A programme of screening and treating those women found to be seropositive is cost-effective, despite the rarity of syphilis occurring in pregnancy, because effective treatment is available.

Treatment of mothers should consist of efficacious antibiotics, preferably a penicillin. Infants and sexual partners should be followed up, and treated if found to be infected.

Diagnosis of congenital syphilis is difficult because the clinical presentation is variable, and many babies are asymptomatic. Treat-

ment of infants is recommended when the adequacy of treatment of
the mother is unknown, or if the mother received treatment for the
first time during the pregnancy with a drug other than penicillin.

4 Gonorrhoea

Screening for gonorrhoea during pregnancy is worthwhile because of
the severe effects of infection on both the mother and her baby. It can
be accomplished by obtaining specimens for culture at the first antenatal visit. In populations deemed 'at risk', either on demographic
grounds or because of a history of sexually transmitted disease, repeat
cultures should be taken.

Culture remains the 'gold standard' for diagnosis of gonorrhoea
in a woman. The Gram stain is not sensitive enough for specimens
obtained from the female genital tract. Although the infection may be
asymptomatic in the mother, pregnancy appears to increase the
likelihood of both arthritis and systemic disease.

Oral treatment should consist of ampicillin or amoxycillin rather
than phenoxymethyl penicillin, which has been associated with
failures. Disseminated disease usually responds dramatically to the
administration of parenteral penicillin with an initial dose of ten
million units per day, reduced after clinical improvement has been
observed and continued for ten to fourteen days. If joint involvement
has occurred, a longer duration of therapy is indicated. Repeat endocervical and rectal cultures should be obtained, as penicillin-resistant gonococci are increasingly encountered.

The most common gonococcal infection in neonates is conjunctivitis. Gonococcal ophthalmia characteristically manifests itself
early, at two to five days. If left untreated, this infection may lead to
permanent corneal damage and even perforation of the eye.

Obviously the ideal method of preventing neonatal ophthalmia is
detection and early treatment of maternal disease, but if this has not
been carried out, or is unsuccessful, prophylaxis or treatment of the
neonate is essential. A reduction in incidence of ophthalmia
neonatorum from 10 per cent to 0.3 per cent was reported with the
use of silver nitrate prophylaxis. Its success has been so dramatic that
in 48 of 50 states in the United States prophylaxis for the prevention
of gonococcal conjunctivitis is required by law.

Cohort studies of tetracycline, erythromycin, and penicillin found
that these agents were more effective than silver nitrate. This conclusion cannot be accepted uncritically because allocation to treatment agents was not randomized, and the groups may not have been
comparable.

Because of the declining incidence of gonococcal ophthalmia, the
irritant effects of silver nitrate, and the recognition of the importance

of chlamydia, regimens which are also active against the latter organism are now acceptable as alternatives.

5 Rubella

Rubella is typically a mild childhood illness. Maternal infection, occurring early in pregnancy, can lead to fetal death, low birthweight for gestational age, deafness, cataracts, jaundice, purpura, hepatosplenomegaly, congenital heart disease, and mental retardation in the infant. The objective of rubella vaccination programmes is to prevent fetal infection and the congenital rubella syndrome.

The risk to the fetus of maternal infection decreases with increasing duration of pregnancy. In a recent prospective study, infants whose mothers had confirmed rubella at successive stages of pregnancy were followed for two years. No defects attributed to rubella were found in children infected after 16 weeks' gestation, while infants infected before the eleventh week had significant cardiac disease and deafness.

Two approaches to rubella vaccination have been used—universal vaccination and selective vaccination. In the United States, universal vaccination of young children to interrupt transmission has led to a significant decline in reported cases of rubella and the congenital rubella syndrome. A concerted effort over the last decade to vaccinate all susceptible adolescents and young adults has resulted in the lowest recorded incidence of the congenital rubella syndrome.

Selective immunization was adopted in the United Kingdom, and initially girls aged 11–14 were vaccinated. The programme was later extended to include seronegative women of childbearing age. Moderate epidemics continue to occur, with a peak incidence of 16 cases per 100 000 during 1983. In that same year 25 cases of the congenital rubella syndrome were registered and 419 pregnancies were aborted for rubella. A vaccination rate of close to 100 per cent will be needed if congenital infection is to be eliminated.

Following an attack of rubella, life-long protection against disease usually develops. Reinfections can occur, but the majority of these are asymptomatic and detected only by a booster response in specific rubella antibody. Vaccination produces an overall lower antibody response than natural infection, but protection against infection can be expected in almost all vaccinated women.

The diagnosis of rubella in a pregnant woman who has been exposed to or develops a rubella-like infection can frequently be difficult. The laboratory must be provided with a detailed history, as routine screening tests are inadequate and additional testing is required. False negative results can occur if the specimen is drawn too soon after onset of exposure. The pattern of antibody response to acute infection and reinfection will vary according to the test method used, and expert consultation may be required for interpretation of data.

Pregnant women should not be given rubella vaccine, but if a pregnant woman is vaccinated unknowingly or she becomes pregnant within three months after immunization, available data suggests that the risk of teratogenicity from live rubella vaccine is virtually non-existent. As rubella vaccine virus has been isolated from fetal tissue following induced abortion, the risk cannot be assumed to be zero, but receipt of rubella vaccine in pregnancy is not ordinarily an indication for interruption of pregnancy.

The most significant cost factors associated with rubella are related to the long-term sequelae of congenital rubella. The costs of the congenital rubella syndrome far outweigh that of vaccination of infants of both sexes, teenage girls, and postpartum women.

High immunization levels must be achieved and maintained, and all susceptible women of childbearing age should be identified and vaccinated. Prenatal screening should be carried out on all pregnant women without documented immunity, and vaccination given following delivery, miscarriage or termination of pregnancy. Where follow-up cannot be assured, rubella vaccination without prior serological testing may be preferable. One third to one half of current cases of the congenital rubella syndrome could be prevented if postpartum vaccination programmes were fully implemented.

Termination should be offered when maternal infection is diagnosed in the first 16 weeks of pregnancy. Routine use of immune serum globulin for post-exposure prophylaxis against rubella is not recommended, although it may have a role where maternal rubella occurs and termination of pregnancy is not an option.

6 Genital mycoplasmas

Genital mycoplasmas have been postulated as causative agents of recurrent abortion, chorioamnionitis, preterm delivery, low birthweight, stillbirth, and postpartum fever. As these organisms are found in the vaginal secretions of between 35 and 90 per cent of pregnant women, it is important to determine whether or not they are, in fact, pathogenic.

The suggestion that genital mycoplasmas might be a cause of pregnancy wastage has largely been based on case–control studies in which investigators obtained a higher rate of mycoplasma isolation from women who had the adverse outcomes in question than from pregnant women who did not have these abnormal outcomes. As is true of all such studies, other factors, both known and unknown, may have caused the adverse outcome, irrespective of the presence or absence of mycoplasma infection. For example, if such infections are simply markers for sexually transmitted disease in general, other organisms might be the actual causes. An increased prevalence of mycoplasma infection is associated with a number of factors associated with transmission of venereal diseases, including young age, non-white race, lower socioeconomic status, and greater sexual activity.

In the light of these uncertainties, it also remains uncertain whether or not there is any value in screening for these organisms, or in treatment if they are isolated. Although the organisms are sensitive to a number of antibiotics, only one randomized trial has examined the effects of treatment, and because of major methodological weaknesses, its results are uninterpretable.

7 Toxoplasmosis

Maternal infection with the protozoan parasite *Toxoplasma gondii* acquired during pregnancy may result in congenital infection of the infant, sometimes with serious sequelae. Individuals can be infected only once, so a woman who is immune prior to pregnancy is not at risk of transmitting the organism to her infant.

Clinical manifestations of congenital toxoplasmosis, which consist of chorioretinitis, recurrent seizures, hydrocephalus, and intracranial calcifications, may be present at birth or appear later.

The vast majority of infections are asymptomatic in the mother, although lymphadenopathy may occur. The method of identifying asymptomatic infection is by observing a high antibody level to *Toxoplasma gondii* in the serum.

Studies on congenital toxoplasmosis have relied on serological results to identify maternal infection. Both the prevalence of seropositivity (indicative of past exposure and immunity), and the risk of acquisition during pregnancy vary in different countries and even in different regions within the same country. This has been ascribed, at least in part, to different habits with respect to the handling and consumption of raw meat and the disposal of cat litter, both of which can be reservoirs of the organism. Routine screening for the condition is conducted in some countries (for example, France, Belgium, and Luxembourg) but not in many others, such as the United Kingdom or the Netherlands.

The risk of transmission of toxoplasmosis from mother to baby is dependent on the time in the pregnancy that the maternal infection occurs. In one major study the frequency of infection rose from 17 per cent in infants whose mothers were infected during the first trimester to 65 per cent in infants whose mothers acquired the infection in the third trimester. Although the incidence of transmission from mother to fetus, based on serology, was highest in third-trimester infections, transmission in the first-trimester was associated with more severe symptoms. Severe disease occurred in 14 per cent of first-trimester transmissions and in none of third trimester transmissions. Some of the early infections may result in spontaneous abortions. The high frequency of neonatal clinical disease after infections early in gestation has led French investigators to recommend termination of pregnancy where feasible, and an anti-protozoan drug, spiromycin, when termination is not possible.

When the prevalence of toxoplasmosis is low, the low pick-up would not justify the expense of a universal screening programme. A health education programme, advising pregnant woman against eating raw or undercooked meat, to wash their hands after its preparation, and to wear gloves when gardening or cleaning cat litter would be more cost-effective.

Much work is still necessary to determine the true frequency of infection and the sequelae of congenital toxoplasmosis. Neither spiromycin nor pyrimethamine-sulpha are very efficacious against this parasite, and the latter agent is associated with a high frequency of side-effects in pregnant women. Trials are needed of new anti-protozoan drugs with potentially better efficacy and safety. Such studies will require prolonged follow-up, as some of the sequelae of such infections may occur many years after birth.

8 Chlamydia

Maternal infection with *Chlamydia trachomatis* is important primarily because of the potential adverse effects of infection on the newborn infant. The condition is often asymptomatic in the mother, and may not be detected clinically, although some infected women may have a mucopurulent cervicitis, salpingitis, or the urethral syndrome.

The prevalence of *Chlamydia trachomatis* in pregnant women varies widely; estimates ranging from 2 per cent to nearly 40 per cent have been reported. Higher rates are found in young women, unmarried women, and black women, as well as women from lower socioeconomic groups and those attending inner-city antenatal clinics.

The newborn infant can acquire chlamydial infection through contact with infected maternal genital secretions at birth. Inclusion conjunctivitis will develop in 18 to 50 per cent of infants born to infected mothers, making *Chlamydia trachomatis* the most common cause of neonatal conjunctivitis. The estimated risk of an infant born to an infected mother developing chlamydial pneumonia ranges from 3 to 18 per cent.

The diagnosis of maternal *Chlamydia trachomatis* infection is made either by culture of the organism from an endocervical specimen or by the identification of chlamydial antigens directly in endocervical smears. The detection of chlamydial antibodies has no role in routine diagnosis, and the sensitivity of cytological methods is low. Tissue culture is considered to be the gold standard for diagnosis. Commercial kits using immunofluorescent staining or enzyme immunoassay are available, and the sensitivity of these tests ranges from 70 to 100 per cent.

If the prevalence of maternal infection exceeds 6 per cent, it is cost-effective to screen for chlamydia using cell-culture techniques, and treat the women infected. When less expensive diagnostic tests become available screening may be justified at lower prevalence rates.

There have been no randomized controlled trials to guide care for women colonized with *Chlamydia trachomatis* during pregnancy. Tetracycline is contraindicated because of its hepatotoxicity in pregnancy. Erythromycin is generally considered to be the drug of choice, but the optimal dose, duration, and timing of antibiotic therapy have not been established. A cohort study, using as controls women who refused therapy, showed a significantly lower prevalence of chlamydial infection in infants born of infected mothers treated with erythromycin 250 mg (base) four times daily for seven days at the thirty-sixth week of pregnancy.

The natural history of *Chlamydia trachomatis* infections in pregnancy is inadequately known, and the role of the organism in the adverse outcomes of pregnancy remains to be resolved. Well-designed trials are required to clarify the usefulness of screening for and treating this condition. As erythromycin is not completely effective in eradicating infection, and as some women do not tolerate the drug, trials of effective alternatives are needed.

9 Herpes

Herpes simplex infection of the newborn, acquired from the mother, is a rare, but potentially serious condition, occurring in between 1 in 2500 and 1 in 10 000 births. Its clinical presentation varies widely, from asymptomatic, through involvement of only the skin, to involvement of the eye or nervous system, or widespread dissemination.

The risk of transmission from mother to baby at the time of birth is high in primary herpes infections, but the risk of transmission from a mother with recurrent genital herpes is very low, estimated to be a maximum of 8 per cent even in women who are shedding herpes virus at the time of delivery.

Suggestive clinical findings are present in only half the women who show cytological evidence of disease, and cytological smears lead to the diagnosis of *Herpes simplex* in less than half the lesions from which the virus can be cultured. Serology is of value only when paired sera of initial infections are available. Thus only evidence from cultures or from electron microscopic examination of specimens is adequate to exclude the disease. On the other hand, the presence of

characteristic cytological findings allows the condition to be diagnosed with confidence.

A recently published study addresses the natural history of *Herpes simplex* colonization in women. Four hundred and fourteen pregnant women with a history of recurrent genital herpes underwent regular sampling for herpes virus cultures during late pregnancy. Only one of 17 asymptomatic women with positive antepartum cultures had herpes virus recovered at the time of delivery, and she had a herpetic lesion at that time. Furthermore, none of the five asymptomatic mother–infant pairs who were shedding herpes virus at the time of delivery, had positive antepartum cultures, despite repeated sampling during the four weeks prior to delivery, the most recent previous cultures being taken one to ten days prior to delivery. Asymptomatic excretors even in the week prior to delivery were not the same women as asymptomatic excretors at the time of delivery. Twenty per cent of women with lesions or a prodrome did shed herpes virus.

Thus clinical assessment remains the best criterion for identifying women who are shedding virus at the time of delivery, and repeated cultures in asymptomatic women are relatively useless. An economic analysis comparing a screening policy that included viral culture or cytology during the last four to eight weeks of pregnancy versus using only a weekly history and physical examination found that the cost per case averted through screening would be approximately $1.8 million.

There have been no randomized trials to evaluate clinical policies for care of women with herpes in pregnancy, and the evidence on which recommended policy is based is weak indeed.

Caesarean section should be carried out if there is clinical evidence of active disease and viral shedding cannot be ruled out by electron microscopy, and if the membranes have not been ruptured for more than four to six hours.

Further studies are needed to develop practical and rapid detection methods to determine the presence of *Herpes simplex* shedding at the time of delivery. Randomized trials of the efficacy of acyclovir (or any other antiviral agent) in reducing the risk of transmission to the baby are required.

10 Group B streptococcus

Group B streptococcus has become the most frequent cause of over-whelming sepsis in neonates. The early, and most serious, form of infection is characterized by rapid onset of respiratory distress, sepsis, and shock. The likelihood of disease, which occurs in one to two per cent of colonized babies, is directly related to the number of sites colonized and the density of colonization. Infants with birthweights of less than 2500 grams have a much higher overall infection rate than infants weighing 2500 grams or more.

Attempts to prevent disease by giving antibiotics to either all babies or those considered to be at high risk have proved disappointing. Although the available data suggest that infant sepsis with group B streptococcus can be reduced with antibiotic prophylaxis given to the baby, such prophylaxis in the neonate is accompanied by an increase in sepsis with penicillin-resistant organisms, and this results in a higher rate of deaths from infection in the neonates given antibiotics.

Since attempts at prophylaxis after the baby has been delivered may be too late, attention has focused on studies of the effectiveness of antepartum and intrapartum antibiotics.

Based on the available data, a course of antibiotics given during pregnancy results in only a temporary eradication of group B streptococcal carriage, with no detectable effects on infant colonization or sepsis with group B streptococcus. On the other hand, treating colonized women with either oral ampicillin or erythromycin from the thirty-eighth week of gestation right through to delivery will significantly reduce both maternal and infant colonization at delivery.

It thus appears that treatment during pregnancy, unless continued into labour, has only a transient effect on the vaginal flora, and will not influence the rate of infant sepsis. It is quite likely, then, that screening during pregnancy and treating carriers would not eliminate the transmission of group B streptococcal disease.

Identification of carriage in the intrapartum period may be the ideal method of screening, as more than half the infants born to mothers who are carriers during labour will be colonized with group B streptococcus.

Four randomized controlled trials have demonstrated a major reduction in group B streptococcus colonization in infants born to mothers treated intrapartum with antibiotics compared with infants of control mothers. Even more importantly, infant sepsis with group B streptococcus was reduced in the treated groups in the three trials that reported sepsis rates. The available data also show a reduction in neonatal deaths from infection in the treated group.

As intrapartum prophylaxis of colonized pregnant women offers the possibility of reducing the incidence of infant sepsis, rapid methods for screening women in preterm labour are desirable. A number of such methods of rapid diagnosis of colonization are currently under development. A cost-effectiveness evaluation incorporating such diagnostic techniques with chemoprophylaxis is required.

11 Acquired immunodeficiency syndrome *(AIDS)*

Acquired immunodeficiency syndrome has recently been identified as a major health problem, characterized by defects in the immune system, with attendant susceptibility to infections by opportunistic micro-organisms and specific tumours.

Despite the introduction of some promising chemotherapeutic agents, including interferon and azidothymidine, almost no one survives for longer than three years after developing the disease.

Paediatric acquired immunodeficiency syndrome was first recognized in 1982, and numerous case series have been reported since. The virus may be transmitted *in utero* and has been associated with characteristic dysmorphic features in the newborn. The condition may present with recurrent bacterial infections and sepsis, persistent or recurrent thrush, and failure to thrive. Many of the infants are born preterm or small for gestational age, although this may be due to associated maternal risk factors. Later symptoms include lymphadenopathy, hepatosplenomegaly, chronic or recurrent diarrhoea, chronic pneumonitis, and salivary gland enlargement.

The organism in adults is usually transmitted sexually, but is also transmitted through infected blood and blood products, or the sharing of needles among infected drug users. In paediatric cases, transmission from mother to infant may occur *in utero*, during delivery, or through breast milk. Studies have reported transmission rates from mother to baby of 30–65 per cent.

Both asymptomatic and symptomatic women may transmit the infection to their infants. In one study, disease developed in mothers up to four years after the birth of the affected infant. Thus, all women who belong to a risk group should be offered screening, not just those who are symptomatic. In addition, women who have had one affected infant may have subsequent infected infants.

There is no proven efficacious treatment for acquired immunodeficiency syndrome. Clinical trials are currently being conducted to study a number of investigational drugs in both adults and children.

18

Rhesus isoimmunization

This chapter is derived from the chapter by Jack Bennebroek Gravenhorst (35) in EFFECTIVE CARE IN PREGNANCY AND CHILDBIRTH.

1 Introduction
2 Prevention of isoimmunization
    2.1 *After delivery*
    2.2 *During pregnancy*
3 Diagnosis of isoimmunization
4 Treatment of isoimmunization
5 Conclusions

1 Introduction

Isoimmunization against Rhesus antigens, which may result in haemolytic disease of the fetus and newborn, was once a major cause of perinatal mortality, neonatal morbidity, and long-term disability and mental handicap. The condition is rarely seen today.

The reduction in the frequency of Rhesus isoimmunization is sometimes credited entirely to modern programmes of immunoprotection. The discovery, introduction, and utilization of anti-D gammaglobulin has been one of the major obstetrical achievements of the past quarter-century. It should not be forgotten, however, that a large part of this reduction is the result of an increased proportion of one- and two-child families, in which the condition is unlikely to occur.

2 Prevention of isoimmunization

The effectiveness of anti-D immunoglobulin in the prevention of Rhesus isoimmunization has been demonstrated in a number of trials conducted in different countries. The question is not whether or not women at risk of Rhesus immunization should receive anti-D immunoglobulin, but which women should receive such prophylaxis, at what times, and in what doses.

There is a risk of isoimmunization in any situation in which Rhesus-positive red blood cells enter the circulation of a Rhesus negative woman. The degree of this risk will vary with the amount of Rhesus antigen to which she is exposed.

2.1 *After delivery*

The most common time for Rhesus-positive fetal cells to enter the mother's circulation is at delivery of a Rhesus-positive baby. Without the administration of anti-D immunoglobulin, Rhesus negative women who give birth to a Rhesus-positive baby have a 7.5 per cent risk of developing Rhesus antibodies within six months of delivery, and a much larger risk (17.5 per cent) of showing evidence of sensitization in a subsequent pregnancy. With postpartum administration of anti-D immunoglobulin, this risk is reduced to 0.2 per cent.

ABO incompatibility, commonly believed to confer significant protection against the development of Rhesus antibody formation, does not confer enough protection for it to be relevant in guiding clinical practice.

It is reasonably well established that 20 micrograms of anti-D immunoglobulin will neutralize the antigenicity of 1 ml of Rhesus-positive red cells, or 2 ml of whole blood. Hence, the usually administered dose of 300 micrograms is sufficient to protect against a feto–maternal bleed of 30 ml. Smaller doses might be given in the interests of economy, but in this case the amount of feto–maternal transfusion must be assessed. The relative cost effectiveness of giving a smaller dose of anti-D immunoglobulin along with assessment of the amount of feto–maternal transfusion, compared with routine administration of a higher dose, will depend on local circumstances and the relative costs of anti-D immunoglobulin and of laboratory tests.

Feto–maternal haemorrhages of more than 30 ml can occur after even an uneventful delivery in about 0.5 per cent of deliveries, and these require larger doses of anti-D immunoglobulin to prevent immunization. After traumatic deliveries, Caesarean section, and manual removal of the placenta, the risk of a large feto–maternal haemorrhage is increased. For this reason, counts of fetal cells in maternal blood have become routine after delivery in some centres, to determine whether a larger dose of anti-D immunoglobulin should be given.

The best time to administer the anti-D immunoglobulin would be as soon as possible after delivery, but immediate administration is not practical in view of the time required to determine the blood group of the baby. From the trials that have been conducted it would appear that an interval of up to 72 hours is compatible with effective prophylaxis.

2.2 *During pregnancy*

A small proportion of women develop Rhesus antibodies during their first pregnancy; most such immunizations take place after 28 weeks of gestation. For this reason the antenatal administration of anti-D immunoglobulin has been proposed. Doses of 200 to 300 micrograms of anti-D immunoglobulin given at 28 or 34 weeks to all unsensitized Rhesus-negative women, and a further dose administered after delivery to all women giving birth to a Rhesus–positive child, will further reduce the remaining incidence of Rhesus–isoimmunization from 0.2 to 0.06 per cent. The costs of such a programme are high, and insufficient supplies of anti-D immunoglobulin limit its use in this manner.

Feto–maternal haemorrhage has been documented as a consequence of chorion villus sampling, amniocentesis, placentocentesis, and fetoscopy. Abdominal trauma, placenta praevia, placental abruption, or any form of uterine bleeding may occasionally cause feto-maternal transfusion. This may sometimes be suspected on the basis of the findings at cardiotocography prompted by these conditions. Feto-maternal transfusion may also occur without any obvious cause. Unexplained fetal or intrapartum death, or the birth of a pale, distressed baby should raise the possibility that a feto-maternal transfusion has occurred.

Placental trauma associated with either spontaneous or induced abortion can also cause feto–maternal bleeding. The incidence of feto–maternal bleeding in spontaneous abortion has been estimated at about 6 to 7 per cent during the first trimester of pregnancy. In the second trimester, incidences of 20 per cent and more have been reported.

Up to 13 weeks of pregnancy a dose of 50 to 75 micrograms after termination of pregnancy or miscarriage is sufficient to ensure adequate protection. In the second trimester the standard postpartum dose of 200 to 300 micrograms is recommended.

3 Diagnosis of isoimmunization

All women should have routine assessment of their Rhesus status in early pregnancy. Women who are Rhesus (D)-negative should be further screened for the presence of antibodies. The other Rhesus antigens are far less immunogenic, but occasionally can cause serious clinical problems. Anti-Kell, anti-Kidd, anti-Duffy, and some of the more rare antigens can also on occasion cause haemolytic disease in the fetus and newborn. For this reason, many centres screen all pregnant women for other blood-group antibodies, in addition to the Rhesus status.

The presence of antibodies indicates that the fetus may become affected if it carries the antigen to which the antibodies were formed; it does not indicate whether the fetus carries the antigen. For this reason it is helpful to determine whether the woman's partner is homozygous or heterozygous for the antigen. If the father is homozygous, the fetus will always carry the antigen; if the father is heterozygous, there is a 50 per cent risk that it will carry the antigen. Zygosity of the Rhesus (D) antigen cannot be determined with certainty, but it can be estimated with a probability ranging between 80 and 96 per cent.

The level of an antibody titre does not always predict the presence or severity of disease, although in a first affected pregnancy there is a reasonable correlation between the antibody titre and the severity of disease. The major prognostic determinant of the severity of disease is the past obstetric history. The severity of the disease in previous pregnancies, in combination with serial antibody titres, will give a reasonably accurate assessment of the severity of the haemolytic disease in the current pregnancy about 95 per cent of the time. They will not, however, give sufficient precision to determine the optimal time for intervention. For this, amniocentesis and spectrophotometric analysis of haemoglobin degradation products (bilirubin) in the amniotic fluid are required. This must be repeated at regular intervals, depending upon the level and change in the level of amniotic fluid bilirubin. The timing of intervention will depend primarily on this level.

4 Treatment of isoimmunization

Pre-emptive delivery, before the fetus is too severely affected to be effectively treated by postnatal therapy, remains the mainstay of treatment for established isoimmunization. When the pregnancy cannot be carried to a stage of fetal maturity that would allow delivery of an infant who can be successfully treated by the currently available methods of intensive neonatal care, intrauterine transfusion is the treatment of choice.

By infusing Rhesus (D)-negative packed cells into the fetal circulation, fetal anaemia can be corrected and delivery may be postponed to a more advanced stage in pregnancy. The procedure can be started as early as 21 to 22 weeks of gestation, and can be repeated if necessary.

Other treatments that have been used include plasmapheresis from early pregnancy onward, immuno-suppression with promethazine, and desensitization by oral administration of Rhesus (D) red blood cells. The value of these methods has not been evaluated in controlled trials.

5 Conclusions

Haemolytic disease of the fetus and newborn, while by no means the frequent problem that it once was, remains a problem that requires constant vigilance and attention to prophylactic care. Although effective prophylaxis is available it must be properly used.

Postpartum prophylaxis with anti-D immunoglobulin is of over riding importance. Anti-D immunoglobulin should also be administered to all Rh-negative women during pregnancy when there is an increased risk of feto-maternal bleeding. Routine use at 28 weeks of pregnancy for all Rh-negative women is of value as well, but the costs of such a programme are high.

Situations in which Rhesus immunization does occur have become sufficiently rare, and its treatment is sufficiently complex, to warrant regionalization of care for these women and babies.

Research to adequately evaluate less invasive methods of treating established haemolytic disease of the fetus is still required.

19

Diabetes in pregnancy

This chapter is derived from the chapter by David J. S. Hunter (36) in EFFECTIVE CARE IN PREGNANCY AND CHILDBIRTH.

1 Introduction
2 Prepregnancy counselling and assessment
3 General care during pregnancy
4 Diabetic control
5 Care for labour and delivery
6 Care after birth
7 Conclusions

---

1 Introduction

Although there is general consensus on the impact of overt diabetes in pregnancy, the significance and appropriate management of lesser degrees of hyperglycaemia is widely debated. Diabetes is a disturbance of multiple metabolic pathways rather than of glucose metabolism alone, although the effects on carbohydrate metabolism are the most apparent. Generally accepted criteria for a diagnosis of diabetes in the presence of symptoms (polyuria, polydipsia, ketoacidosis) are random venous plasma glucose levels greater than 11 mmol/l (200 mg/dl) or fasting levels of greater than 8 mmol/l (140 mg/dl).

Normal values for plasma glucose values are defined as less than 8 mmol/l on a random sample, and less than 6 mmol/l fasting. Values between the normal and those of diabetes are considered to be 'equivocal', and evaluation with a glucose challenge is recommended (75 grams taken orally after an overnight fast). Values over 11 mmol/l two hours post-challenge are taken to be diagnostic of diabetes, and those between 8 and 11 mmol/l are termed 'impaired glucose tolerance'.

Perinatal mortality in pregnancy associated with diabetes has dropped tenfold in the last four decades, compared with a fourfold to fivefold drop in the general population. At the present time perinatal mortality rates are reported that are not significantly different from those of the population at large.

A number of factors have played a part in this remarkable improvement. These include, among others, increasing acceptance by physicians of the importance of tight control of diabetes; the introduction of programmes to achieve this control; the development of home glucose monitoring to facilitate such programmes; gradual trends towards prolongation of pregnancy; and advances in neonatal care. It is clear that meticulous care throughout pregnancy and childbirth is required.

2 Pre-pregnancy counselling and assessment

Increasingly, women with diabetes wish to discuss the implications of pregnancy before they conceive. While preconception clinics may fulfil an important role, the provision of adequate preconceptional care and advice does not depend on such specialized clinics. All who care for diabetic women should be aware of, and prepared to discuss, the significance of pregnancy to the diabetic woman; the risks to the fetus and neonate as well as to herself; the importance of tight control of the diabetes just before and during pregnancy; and the need for accurate estimation of the date of conception.

Since diabetes is a chronic and progressive disease, the advice may need to include a discussion of the fact that postponement of pregnancy until a later age may worsen the prognosis.

The risks to the fetus are significant. Diabetes is associated with an increased incidence of congenital anomalies, up to three times as great as for the infants of non-diabetic mothers. Although no information is available from randomized trials, cohort studies suggest that tight control of the diabetes immediately before conception can reduce this risk significantly.

Macrosomia is still more common in the infants of diabetic mothers than in those of non-diabetic mothers, even with the best diabetic control currently available. Diabetes is not typically associated with intrauterine growth retardation unless the diabetes is complicated by microvascular disease, in particular nephropathy. Women with vascular complications of diabetes will need particularly careful counselling.

Nephropathy without significant hypertension and a normal serum creatinine is not associated with a poor fetal outcome. The prognosis worsens in the presence of hypertension or impaired renal function. Renal disease that does not cause symptoms in non-pregnant individuals can jeopardize pregnancy outcome in some women. Although the majority of women with renal disease do not experience a deterioration of renal function during pregnancy, some women do suffer significant deterioration that does not improve after delivery.

There is also concern about the effect of pregnancy on women with proliferative retinopathy. Pregnancy appears to be associated with a deterioration in the condition. Cohort studies comparing pregnant and non-pregnant women with diabetic retinopathy, however, show that with intensive laser treatment throughout pregnancy visual acuity can be maintained, and the prognosis is no worse than for the non-pregnant woman.

The risk of preterm delivery in diabetic women relates mainly to the widespread policy of elective delivery before term, and can be minimized by reconsideration of that policy.

Diabetic women contemplating pregnancy will be reassured to learn that there is no good evidence of any long-term adverse effects of their diabetes on the development or intelligence of the offspring, and that the risk of their children developing juvenile diabetes is in the order of 2 per cent or less.

3 General care during pregnancy

The first few weeks of pregnancy are a period of readjustment, and many women require re-education about their diabetes and its control. Rotation of insulin injection sites, the interaction of diet and exercise, and the dietary requirements of pregnancy may be unfamiliar to many women. Specialist care in and for pregnancy should start as early as possible. When the gestational age is in doubt, it should be estimated precisely as soon as possible by pregnancy tests and/or early ultrasound.

Hypoglycaemia can be troublesome at this stage, and control of the diabetes may be difficult to achieve because of poor motivation, nausea and vomiting, or changes in the hormonal milieu. Considerable education is needed to resist over-treatment of impending hypoglycaemic reactions. Glucose or sugar should be avoided; milk or a light snack, which can be repeated if necessary, are most appropriate. All diabetic women should be provided with glucagon for emergency situations.

In addition to routine prenatal assessment, obstetric care at this time should include assessment of renal function in diabetic women who have hypertension or proteinuria, and retinoscopy, particularly in women who have had diabetes for more than ten years. Urine cultures should be repeated regularly in those with nephropathy. Detailed ultrasound at approximately eighteen weeks is recommended because of the increased risk of congenital anomaly, particularly of cardiac anomaly or neural tube defect.

A diabetic woman without nephropathy or retinopathy, and with no other complications of pregnancy, usually experiences an uneventful second trimester. The educational and readjustment processes are hopefully complete as far as possible, and unless there is a risk of compromised fetal growth or early pre-eclampsia there is little need for intensive obstetric supervision at this time.

Women with associated hypertension may need to be followed closely, and, if necessary, treated with hypotensive drugs. Serial uric acid estimations and assessment of renal function can be particularly useful in following these pregnancies.

4 Diabetic control

The aim of diabetic control is to establish normal levels of blood glucose, both fasting and before and after meals. Blood glucose levels can be effectively monitored and controlled by the woman at home, provided that she has readily available advice and support, predominantly through telephone contact.

The dose and type of insulin needed may require careful and frequent adjustment. Insulin may have to be given more frequently than before pregnancy, occasionally requiring three or even four injections a day. Pumps for continuous subcutaneous infusion of insulin are now available, but are expensive and complex to use. Trials have shown no benefits for continuous infusion over conventional insulin administration, either in terms of metabolic control or of adverse pregnancy outcome. Despite the importance of the subject, to date the benefits and drawbacks of tight control of diabetes in pregnancy have been assessed in only one randomized trial. This trial compared the effects of very tight control (aiming to keep blood sugar levels below 5.6 mmol/l), tight control (blood sugar levels between 5.6 and 6.7 mmol/l) and moderate control (blood sugar levels between 6.7 and 8.9 mmol/l).

Best results were obtained with tight, rather than either very tight or moderate control. Very tight control was associated with episodes of hypoglycaemia, and conferred no benefits in other pregnancy outcomes compared to tight control. On the other hand, a policy of only moderate control, in which blood sugar levels were allowed to rise up to 8.9 mmol/l, is associated with a higher incidence of macrosomia, urinary tract infection, and Caesarean section, and a trend towards an increase in hypertension, preterm labour, respiratory distress syndrome, and perinatal mortality.

This evidence confirms the conclusion from observational studies that keeping blood sugars within a well-controlled range is better than either too strict or too lenient a regimen.

5 Care for labour and delivery

Elective preterm delivery has long been one of the classical management strategies applied in diabetic pregnancy, based on an observation in one influential study that the stillbirth rate rose above the neonatal death rate after 36 weeks of gestation. Other cohort studies have shown, however, that this observation was flawed, and that pre-emptive delivery does not result in an improvement in perinatal mortality. There is no valid reason to terminate an otherwise uncomplicated pregnancy in a diabetic woman before term, and probably not before the expected date of delivery.

Assessment of pulmonary maturity has until recently been considered a prerequisite for planned delivery of the diabetic woman. There is increasing evidence to suggest that in well-controlled diabetics, the lecithin–sphingomyelin ratio reflects the same degree of pulmonary surfactant production, and therefore the same risk of hyaline membrane disease, as in non-diabetics. The infants of poorly controlled diabetic mothers may have a disturbance in the development of pulmonary maturity. The problem will probably become less important as delivery is delayed to a later gestational age, and as elective caesarean section is used less frequently.

Although caesarean section in diabetic women, as in all women, should only be performed for obstetrical indications, caesarean section rates tend to be much higher for diabetic women than for the general population. There seems to be little justification for this.

As blood glucose levels can be controlled confidently throughout labour with a glucose infusion with insulin added, the only increased hazard of vaginal delivery in diabetic women is that of birth trauma to the infant, particularly brachial plexus injury secondary to macrosomia and shoulder dystocia. Rather than resort too readily to caesarean section to avoid this hazard, it is probably wiser to advise caution in managing the labour and delivery of a diabetic woman with a suspected large infant.

6 Care after birth

After birth, all insulin therapy should cease with delivery of the placenta, and thereafter insulin requirements should be recalibrated according to blood glucose levels.

Family planning is an important consideration. There is no contraindication to the use of low-dose oral contraceptives, particularly in young, non-obese, non-hypertensive, non-smoking diabetics. The development of headaches or hypertension is an indication to change to alternative methods. The intrauterine device has until recently been a reasonable alternative, but adverse publicity, along with concern over its effectiveness in diabetics, is making it less acceptable. Barrier methods also provide a reasonable alternative. For all women, the risk of future pregnancy must be carefully weighed against the risk of the proposed method of contraception.

In general, sterilization, if required, is better not performed at the time of caesarean section if this can be avoided, in view of the increased risk that the newborn may have still undiagnosed cardiac anomalies. If necessary, the procedure can easily be performed by laparoscopy within the next few months.

Women with nephropathy or retinopathy should be counselled carefully about limiting family size.

7 Conclusions

One can only admire the fortitude with which diabetic women cope with their disease, and the way in which they rise to the added challenge of pregnancy and parenthood. Their care should be individualized, so that disruption will be minimized and care tailored to meet the circumstances of each woman.

There is considerable evidence to suggest that pregnancy in diabetic women should be managed with fewer obstetric interventions than are currently practised. Specialized care and collaboration among various disciplines will achieve the best results, but good perinatal outcome is not confined to tertiary care centres. The majority of diabetic women should be treated as normal pregnant women, with the one major addition of careful control of blood glucose levels. Tight, rather than either very tight or moderate, control is required.

Allowing pregnancy to continue for its normal duration, associated with a decreased need to assess pulmonary maturity and the judicious use of caesarean section, may further reduce both neonatal and maternal morbidity, and may allow pregnant women with diabetes to feel more like their non-diabetic counterparts.

Much has been achieved in improving the care for, and the outcome of, pregnancies in diabetic women without resort to randomized clinical trials. The lack of controlled studies, however, has resulted in a blurring of the contributions made by the various components of care, and in doubts about the utility of some. The need continues for well-designed trials to assess the value both of current treatments and of suggestions for their improvement. In addition, better survey data on the diabetic population are still needed, as data that refer only to those women who attend tertiary care centres can be seriously misleading. Population-based survey data may highlight deficiencies in the system of care and lead to improvements.

Bleeding in the latter half of pregnancy

This chapter is derived from the chapter by Robert Fraser and Robert Watson (37) in EFFECTIVE CARE IN PREGNANCY AND CHILDBIRTH.

1 Introduction

Bleeding in the second half of pregnancy is no longer a common cause of maternal death in the industrialized world, but it continues to be a major cause of perinatal mortality, and of both maternal and infant morbidity. Approximately half the women who present with bleeding in the second half of pregnancy are eventually found to have either placental abruption or placenta praevia. No firm diagnosis can be made in the other half.

2 Placental abruption

Placental abruption, or retroplacental haemorrhage, is a contributor to perinatal mortality among normally formed fetuses. Although maternal mortality is fortunately rare now, maternal morbidity in the forms of haemorrhage, shock, disseminated intravascular coagulation, and renal failure is sufficiently frequent to justify intensive treatment of those affected.

The frequency which placental abruption is diagnosed will vary with the criteria used for the diagnosis. The perinatal mortality rate with confirmed abruption is high, often over 300 per 1000. More than half the perinatal losses are due to fetal death before the mother arrives in hospital. Neonatal deaths are principally related to the complications of preterm delivery. Amongst surviving infants, rates of respiratory distress, patent ductus arteriosus, low Apgar scores, and anaemia are more common than in unselected hospital series.

2.1 Clinical presentation

Abruption may occur at any stage of gestation. The diagnosis should be considered in any pregnant woman with abdominal pain, with or without bleeding. Mild cases may not be clinically obvious.

In severe abruption there may be heavy vaginal bleeding, or evidence of increasing abdominal girth if the blood is retained within the uterus. Uterine hypertonus is a common physical sign in the more severe grades of abruption, particularly when the fetus has died. In these cases the woman is usually in severe pain, and may be shocked as a result of hypovolaemia. Absence of clotting may be obvious in the vaginal blood loss. Other signs of clotting defects may be bleeding from the gums or venepuncture sites, or haematuria.

The amount of blood loss may not be obvious—some may have been lost before admission, and large volumes of blood may be retained in the uterus. Clinical signs of hypovolaemia may be masked by increased peripheral resistance. Cerebral and cardiac perfusion may be preserved, although renal blood flow is jeopardized. This will become manifest by oliguria.

Ultrasound examination of the uterus and contents, when available, has an important role in the differential diagnosis of antepartum haemorrhage. Most important is its ability to localize the placenta. A low-lying placenta brings placenta praevia into the differential diagnosis, while a posterior placenta might make the diagnosis of abruption more likely in a woman with back pain. The diagnosis of retroplacental haematoma by ultrasound is not always straightforward.

2.2 Treatment

In suspected mild abruption the symptoms may resolve, and if there has been bleeding this may cease, with the fetal condition apparently satisfactory. It may be impossible to confirm the diagnosis. In this case, the woman may safely be allowed home after a period of observation, as for a woman with bleeding of unknown origin.

In moderate and severe abruption, maternal resuscitation and analgesia are priorities. Restoration of the circulating volume and emptying the uterus are the cornerstones of treatment. The use of whole blood has become traditional in volume replacement in these women. It is likely, however, that a crystalloid infusion to precede the blood would be beneficial. It is probably best to use fresh frozen plasma, at the rate of 1 unit for every 4–6 units of bank red cells transfused, to replenish labile clotting factors. No systematic attempts have been made to study alternatives to blood transfusion in this condition. Plasma substitutes such as plasma protein, dextran, gelatin, and starch may produce adverse reactions, and dextran in particular can interfere with platelet function *in vivo* and cross-matching *in vitro*.

A clotting defect should be sought, although defects of clinical significance are rare when there is a live fetus. The process of disseminated intravascular coagulation usually starts to resolve after delivery.

When the fetus is alive, a decision about delivery in its interest should be made in the light of its estimated maturity. In former years the usual policy was vaginal delivery at all reasonable costs, because the newborn prognosis was so poor. More recently, policy has shifted to earlier resort to caesarean section in the fetal interest, and improved survival of the preterm newborn has often resulted. A recent series suggests, however, that an attempt to deliver vaginally, inducing or augmenting labour with oxytocin when necessary, and using continuous electronic fetal heart rate monitoring, may result in a 50 per cent reduction in the caesarean section rate without a significant increase in the risk of perinatal mortality.

In severe abruption when the fetus is dead, vaginal delivery should be planned, except where there is an obvious obstetrical indication for caesarean section, such as transverse lie. Labour should be induced or augmented if needed, using oxytocin, or prostaglandins if there is no satisfactory response to oxytocin. Caesarean section is required in the rare cases in which uterine contractions can not be stimulated, or when clinical shock associated with haemorrhage has been uncontrollable. Coagulation defects are common in this situation, and the maternal risks are considerable.

When caesarean section in a woman with disseminated intravascular coagulation is judged to be inevitable, it should be undertaken after close consultation with the anaesthetist and a haematologist. Volume replacement and transfusions of whole blood, frozen plasma, and specific coagulation factors should be given before and during the surgical procedure.

A well-equipped hospital should be able to provide adequate emergency treatment for the mother, and will usually be able to achieve safe delivery of a fetus that is alive on admission. Survival of such liveborn infants will depend on the quality of neonatal care. Advances in the management of abruption would be more likely to occur if some means of predicting abruption could be developed.

3 Placenta praevia

Placenta praevia is defined as a placenta which is situated wholly or partially in the lower uterine segment. The overall prevalence of the condition is slightly over 0.5 per cent. The major cause of both mortality and morbidity is haemorrhage; prevention and effective treatment of haemorrhage has reduced the gravity of the condition. With modern care a perinatal mortality rate of 50 to 60 per 1000 is now attainable.

3.1 *Clinical presentation*

Although it is well recognized that a small proportion of women with placenta praevia do not bleed until the onset of labour, less than 2 per cent of cases of placenta praevia present in this way. Painless vaginal bleeding in the absence of labour is the most common presentation. Some form of fetal malpresentation (transverse, oblique, or unstable lie, and breech presentation) is found in approximately one third of cases. In cephalic presentation the presenting part is invariably high, and is often displaced slightly from the midline.

All placentae praeviae are asymptomatic prior to the first onset of bleeding. With routine ultrasound scanning in the early second trimester approximately 5 to 6 per cent of placentae are found to be low lying. Over 90 per cent of cases of asymptomatic placenta praevia diagnosed by ultrasound in the early second trimester remain asymptomatic and become normally situated subsequently. Women with low or cervical placental implantation found early in gestation should be rescanned between 30 and 32 weeks' gestation. Any asymptomatic women found to still have a low-lying placenta on ultrasound after 32 weeks should be managed as if they have a symptomatic placenta praevia, by expectant conservative management.

3.2 *Treatment*

A digital examination is absolutely contraindicated when there is any possibility of placenta praevia, except in the operating room when termination of pregnancy is forced by bleeding or labour, or when the pregnancy has reached an adequate gestation for safe termination. The really dangerous haemorrhage is often the one that has been provoked by ill-advised obstetrical interference, such as digital examination of the cervical canal at or very shortly after the time of the warning haemorrhage. Rectal examination is even more dangerous than vaginal examination.

If bleeding is less severe or has stopped, confirmation of the diagnosis by ultrasound should be performed at the earliest opportunity. The early and accurate diagnosis of placenta praevia is imperative to spare those women with a normally implanted placenta the economic, emotional, and social expense of conservative care, with possibly long-term hospitalization.

The primary object of expectant conservative management is to reduce the number of preterm births by allowing the pregnancy to continue until the baby has grown to a size and age that will give it a reasonable chance of survival. This form of management usually requires that the woman must remain in a fully equipped and staffed maternity hospital from the time of diagnosis until delivery, because of the risks to both mother and fetus from further major haemorrhage. Some clinicians have adopted a policy of permitting selected women to return home as part of expectant management. Many women sent home require readmission to hospital for significant maternal bleeding, but no maternal deaths and no significant differences in perinatal outcome compared to those kept in hospital have been reported.

Preterm birth continues to be a major problem even when expectant management is used. During the period of expectant management maternal and fetal wellbeing should be monitored. The mother should not be allowed to become anaemic, and her haemoglobin should be maintained at a normal level by haematinics or, if necessary, by transfusion.

With every episode of bleeding, the Rhesus-negative woman should have a Kleihauer test performed for the presence of fetal cells, and be given prophylactic immune anti-D if fetal cells are present.

The optimal timing for delivery remains controversial. Although expectant management until 37 weeks is most generally accepted, some clinicians have recommended elective preterm delivery after 34 weeks when amniocentesis has confirmed pulmonary maturity. No controlled trials to evaluate either approach have been reported.

3.3 *Delivery*

There is almost no indication for vaginal delivery for women with even marginal placenta praevia whose babies have attained a viable age. The hazards of vaginal delivery include profuse maternal haemorrhage, malpresentation, cord accidents, placental separation, fetal haemorrhage, and dystocia resulting from a posterior placental implantation. If the fetus is previable, malformed, or dead, vaginal delivery may occasionally be appropriate.

With improved ultrasound diagnosis many authorities suggest elective caesarean section without prior digital confirmation. This approach has considerable merit, since digital examination may cause serious haemorrhage. Digital examination in the operating theatre does have a place, where ultrasound is not available, when the ultrasound appearances are equivocal, or the clinical signs of placenta praevia are not confirmed by ultrasound. If digital examination is indicated, it should be carried out only in the operating room, with the staff scrubbed and prepared for immediate caesarean section should catastrophic haemorrhage be provoked.

4 Bleeding of uncertain origin

Haemorrhage of undetermined or uncertain origin is the most common type of antepartum haemorrhage. Although in some cases the cause of bleeding later becomes clear, in the majority no cause can be demonstrated. The importance of this subgroup lies in its frequency, in the clinical problems it presents in diagnosis and management, and in the associated high fetal loss.

Haemorrhage of uncertain origin is a collective clinical category, and must include minor but unrecognized cases of all specific types of antepartum haemorrhage—localized abruption, marginal haemorrhage, cervical and vaginal lesions, and excessive show.

The clinical presentation of bleeding of unknown origin is painless antepartum haemorrhage without the signs associated with placenta praevia. In the majority of cases the blood loss is not of an extent to cause serious concern, and usually it settles spontaneously. The most serious threat to the fetus is preterm labour and delivery.

The management of painless antepartum haemorrhage depends primarily on the gestational age of the fetus at the time of the initial bleed. An ultrasound examination for placental localization should be performed as soon as possible, and if placenta praevia is diagnosed or cannot be excluded, then management should follow the plan already discussed for placenta praevia. When the placenta is clearly defined in the upper segment the woman should be allowed home after a period of rest and observation in hospital, provided that she has no recurrence of bleeding. The risk to the fetus in such cases is preterm delivery, and the great majority of perinatal deaths are due to preterm delivery occurring within seven to ten days of the initial haemorrhage. After the bleeding has settled, and before discharge from hospital, both a speculum examination to exclude a local cause for the bleeding and a digital examination to exclude advanced cervical dilatation should be performed.

If a policy of expectant management is adopted, fetal wellbeing should be monitored. Although frequently recommended, routine induction of labour at 38 weeks should not be performed, and women should be allowed to go into spontaneous labour.

5 Conclusions

Bleeding in the second half of pregnancy constitutes a possibly life-threatening condition. All professionals who care for women during pregnancy and childbirth must be aware of the causes and prognosis of such bleeding, and have a clear plan in mind for its differential diagnosis and management.

21

Maintaining pregnancy and promoting fetal growth

This chapter is derived from the chapters by Peter A. Goldstein, Henry Sachs, and Thomas C. Chalmers (38); Caroline Crowther and Iain Chalmers (39); Adrian Grant (40); and G. Justus Hofmeyr (41) in EFFECTIVE CARE IN PREGNANCY AND CHILDBIRTH.

1 Introduction

The desire to prevent an adverse outcome of pregnancy is fundamental to all aspects of antenatal care, and is responsible for most of the components of that care. It is not surprising that a number of interventions have been proposed and used when the risk of an adverse outcome appears to be increased above normal. Chief among these interventions has been the use of various hormones, the prescription of bed rest (either at home or in hospital), and the operation of cervical cerclage. Other measures, no longer popular, include abdominal decompression. Whether, or when, these measures should be used depends on an assessment of their effects, both beneficial and unwanted.

2 Hormone administration for the maintenance of pregnancy

Over the last fifty years, hormones have been given to pregnant women in attempts to prevent miscarriage, fetal death, preterm delivery, and other adverse outcomes of pregnancy. Studies in the mid–1930s suggested a link between hormonal abnormalities and complications of pregnancy. The conclusion that inadequate hormone secretion meant that hormones had to be administered as drugs is a classic example of the danger of applying pathophysiological reasoning to clinical practice without appropriate evaluation.

2.1 *Diethylstilboestrol*

The synthetic hormone, diethylstilboestrol, was administered to pregnant women on a wide scale for over thirty years. Based on animal studies and uncontrolled observations in humans, it was thought that it would be effective in preventing a variety of adverse outcomes. Although this hypothesis was supported by studies using observational data, five studies with contemporary controls did not substantiate the postulated positive effects. The frequencies of miscarriage, stillbirth, neonatal death, all of these outcomes combined, and 'premature' delivery (less than 38 weeks' gestation or birthweight less than 2500 grams) in women given diethylstilboestrol were no different from those in untreated control women.

The long-term adverse effects of the use of diethylstilboestrol in pregnancy that were later reported could have been minimized if more attention had been paid to the results of the randomized trials showing the drug to be ineffective.

2.2 *Progestogens*

Progestogens are prescribed in attempts to maintain pregnancy in between 3 and 25 per cent of all pregnancies in different countries. There is no evidence from the available data to suggest that progestogens reduce the risk of miscarriage, stillbirth, or neonatal death. There is some suggestive evidence, though, that the risk of 'prematurity' may be reduced.

Although the progestogen follow-up studies have been largely anecdotal and uncontrolled, there have been suggestions from some studies that fetal exposure to the drug may increase the risk of oesophageal atresia, cardiac, neurological, neural tube and other major malformations, and female masculinization, or 'tomboyishness' in girls. Other studies, however, have failed to detect these adverse effects, and so the safety of progestogens, like their postulated benefits, remains an open question.

2.3 *Human chorionic gonadotrophin*

Data from the two controlled trials that have examined the effects of human chorionic gonadotrophin on the risk of miscarriage in women with a past history of repeated early pregnancy loss, suggest that this treatment may be effective.

The results of these trials must be interpreted with caution, however, because of the small number of women studied. These studies must be replicated on a larger scale before any recommendation can be made about the use of human chorionic gonadotrophin in practice.

3 Bed rest and hospitalization

Bed rest is a common prescription for women whose pregnancies are complicated by a number of conditions, including bleeding, multiple pregnancy, pre-eclampsia, fetal growth retardation, and threatened preterm delivery. Women with such pregnancy complications either may be advised to rest in bed at home or they may be admitted to hospital, to facilitate bed rest and to permit closer investigation and surveillance of their pregnancies.

The extent to which women are advised to rest in bed at home or in hospital varies considerably, but such advice is very common in some places. The intervention is not innocuous. Both confinement to bed at home and hospitalization during pregnancy may result in financial and social costs for pregnant women and their families. Antenatal hospitalization is often a disruptive and stressful experience, and adoption of this policy has involved substantial costs to the health services.

3.1 *Threatened miscarriage*

The only reported attempt to undertake any form of controlled evaluation of the effectiveness of bed rest in the management of threatened miscarriage was made over thirty years ago. The results of this study gave no support to the view that a policy of advising bed rest reduces the risk of miscarriage after bleeding occurs in early pregnancy.

Bed rest is sometimes advised for many days if spotting or bleeding is persistent, and this may cause considerable family disruption. Yet in a substantial proportion of these pregnancies the fetus is already dead, so no amount of bed rest is likely to be helpful. The presence of a non-viable pregnancy can now be demonstrated by ultrasound. Since there is no valid basis for advising bed rest, the preferences of individual women should be the deciding factor in whether or not they should rest in bed.

3.2 *Multiple pregnancy*

Prolonged bed rest in twin pregnancy, aimed at increasing the duration of gestation, improving fetal growth, and decreasing perinatal mortality, has been advocated for over half a century. There is still no consensus as to when bed rest should be started or discontinued, nor whether rest should be in hospital or at home. In several countries it is common practice to admit women with a multiple pregnancy to hospital for rest for varying periods between 29 and 36 weeks of gestation.

The policy of routine hospitalization of women with twin pregnancies for bed rest has only recently been evaluated in controlled trials. There is some suggestion from these trials that routine hospitalization may result in a decreased risk of the mother developing hypertension, and a reduced incidence of low-birthweight babies. The differences are small and they could have arisen by chance. In other respects the data suggest that routine hospitalization of women with twin pregnancies may have adverse effects. The risk of (spontaneous) preterm birth and very-low-birthweight babies appears to be *increased* by routine hospitalization. The data on infant morbidity and mortality provide no support for the policy: no differences were detected in the incidence of depressed Apgar score, admission to the special-care nursery, or perinatal mortality.

Some obstetricians have suggested applying the policy of hospitalization for bed rest in multiple pregnancy only to women deemed to be at higher than average risk of complications. Although this more conservative advice is possibly justified, there is remarkably little good evidence to support it. Only two such selective policies have been evaluated in randomized trials. Although the comparisons between the hospitalized and control groups in women who either have triplet pregnancies or show evidence of cervical dilatation tended to suggest beneficial effects of routine hospitalization, the differences observed could easily reflect the play of chance, and they do not provide a basis for widespread adoption of the policy.

3.3 *Hypertension*

The effectiveness of bed rest for non-proteinuric hypertension has been evaluated in two controlled trials. Unfortunately, no clear picture on the value of the policy emerges. One of the trials suggests that hospitalization may have a beneficial effect on the evolution of pre-eclampsia, while the other tends to suggest the opposite. There are also contrasting patterns of preterm delivery in the two trials.

When proteinuria develops in addition to hypertension in pregnancy, the risks for both mother and fetus are substantially increased. Admission to hospital is then considered necessary for evaluation and increased surveillance to detect any deterioration in maternal or fetal condition as soon as possible. Whether the hospitalization should be linked with strict rest in bed is less clear.

4 Cervical cerclage to prolong pregnancy

In normal pregnancy the uterine cervix is thought to assume a sphincter-like function to retain the contents of the uterus. A congenital or traumatically-acquired weakness of the cervix, or the unusual physiological circumstance of multiple pregnancy, are factors that may render the cervix incapable of performing this function as efficiently as usual. Belief in such 'incompetence' of the cervix is the basis for performing the operation of cervical cerclage.

4.1 Diagnosis of 'cervical incompetence'

There is no good diagnostic test for 'cervical incompetence'. The decision to insert a cervical suture is most commonly based on past obstetric history, and, to a lesser extent, on clinical assessment of the cervix during pregnancy. The history most suggestive of 'cervical incompetence' is that of one or more second-trimester miscarriages or preterm deliveries, with little evidence of uterine contractions.

The diagnosis of 'cervical incompetence' may be made on the basis of a single vaginal examination, or on serial clinical assessments of the cervix that suggest dilatation. Other symptoms, such as mucous vaginal discharge, lower abdominal discomfort and a bearing-down sensation, or signs, such as visualization of the membranes bulging through the cervix, are either very uncommon, or may appear too late to be helpful in prevention of miscarriage.

Ultrasound visualization of the cervix in early pregnancy may allow a more objective assessment of the cervical dilatation, but its usefulness is controversial. Similarly, methods to assess the cervical compliance and resistance between pregnancies with intracervical balloons or graduated dilators still require appropriate evaluation.

4.2 Effects of cervical cerclage

There is considerable variation in the frequency with which cervical cerclage is performed. In part, this wide variation reflects the difficulties in making a definite diagnosis of 'cervical incompetence'; but it is also an expression of the lack of satisfactory evidence on the potential benefit and harm of the operation.

Four randomized controlled trials of cerclage have been published to date. At the time of writing, a multicentre, multinational, randomized controlled trial is still in progress, but interim results are available. The trials show decreases in the incidence of preterm delivery and of delivery before 33 weeks, and there is a statistically significant decrease in the combined rate of miscarriage and perinatal death when the operation is done for the indication of previous second-trimester miscarriage or preterm delivery.

Data from the trials show that the use of cerclage is associated with more intensive management, including more frequent antenatal admission to hospital, increased use of oral tocolytics, induction of labour, and caesarean section. Cervical cerclage can have adverse effects. Cervical trauma and difficulties in removing the stitch may occur, and puerperal pyrexia may be another consequence of the operation.

The usefulness of cervical cerclage is likely to depend on the indications for the operation. The beneficial effect of the operation is most likely to be a shift in the time of delivery of the few cases with true 'cervical incompetence' from the second trimester to a time in gestation at which survival of the baby is more likely. On the basis of the evidence currently available, the operation will prevent one delivery before 33 weeks about every 20 times it is used among women who have had previous second-trimester miscarriages or preterm deliveries.

There is so far no evidence to justify the use of the operation in other circumstances, such as after cervical surgery, or in twin pregnancies.

5 Abdominal decompression

Suboptimal maternal blood flow to the placenta is hypothesized to be an important cause of both impaired fetal growth and pregnancy-induced hypertension, but there are no well-validated methods for increasing uteroplacental circulation. The concept that repeated brief decompression of the abdominal region may increase the flow of blood to the placenta has intrigued a number of enthusiasts, but has not found acceptance in mainstream obstetrical practice.

Abdominal decompression was first used during the first stage of labour to relieve the resistance of the abdominal wall musculature to the forward movement of the contracting uterus. The observation of unanticipated effects such as relief of pain, shortening of the duration of labour, and improved fetal oxygenation prompted further investigation of the effects of abdominal decompression on outcome in normal and abnormal pregnancies.

On the whole, the few physiological studies of abdominal decompression have been poorly controlled and documented. The available data suggest that the technique may reduce intrauterine pressure, increase maternal placental blood flow, and increase fetal movements and fetal heart rate accelerations and variability.

It may be important to assess whether or not abdominal decompression affects uteroplacental blood flow. The advent of blood velocity measurement with ultrasound using the Doppler effect offers an opportunity to assess this more rigorously.

5.1 Prophylaxis in normal pregnancy

Information about the effects of using abdominal decompression prophylactically in normal pregnancies is available from two controlled trials. The rate of admission to hospital for pre-eclampsia was similar for women who received or did not receive prophylactic decompression. None of the available data suggest that prophylactic abdominal decompression affects duration of gestation or birthweight. They give no support to suggestions that prophylactic abdominal decompression has a beneficial effect on the condition of the infant at birth. The incidence of depressed Apgar score is similar whether or not decompression is used.

One carefully controlled trial studied the effects of abdominal decompression on child development. Although the developmental scores were very slightly higher in the study group at 28 days and at 3 years of age, the differences were neither clinically nor statistically significant.

5.2 Treatment of the compromised fetus

In contrast to the lack of evidence that prophylactic abdominal decompression in normal pregnancies has any beneficial effects, there is some evidence to suggest that the technique may have a place in the management of pregnancies in which the fetus is likely to be compromised.

Abdominal decompression appears to slow the progression of pre-eclampsia. In addition, in one trial, abdominal decompression was associated with a statistically significantly faster weekly growth in the fetal biparietal diameter. These differences between experimental and control groups were reflected in somewhat less use of induction of labour for 'placental insufficiency' and less fetal distress during labour in the women who had received decompression.

Observer bias and possibly reporting bias may account for some or all of the putative effects of abdominal decompression noted above. The assessment of birthweight is less subject to large observer biases. Abdominal decompression was associated with a substantial reduction in the incidence of low birthweight, and an increase in mean birthweight (2800 g versus 2296 g) in two of the three trials that have been conducted. The available data suggest a reduction in the incidence both of depressed Apgar score and of perinatal mortality.

The studies are thus suggestive of a beneficial effect of abdominal decompression on fetuses with impaired growth, but their methodological shortcomings limit the confidence that one can place in their conclusions.

6 Conclusions

In the present state of knowledge, hormone administration of any type in pregnancy should be used only within controlled clinical trials until the ratio of benefits to hazards has been more clearly established. Future trials should involve only those pregnancies in which ultrasonography has confirmed that the fetus is alive.

Hospitalization during pregnancy is costly and disruptive for many families. Discussion with individual women will make it clear that a prescription for rest, either at home or in hospital, would sometimes   welcome. As there is no strong evidence that this is likely to have harmful effects, women's views should be taken into account. By the same token women with bleeding in early pregnancy, uncomplicated multiple pregnancy, or non-albuminuric hypertension should not be coerced into resting in bed at home, or into being hospitalized against their better judgement. There is currently no good evidence to support such recommendations.

Unlike many clinical interventions, cervical cerclage has the paradoxical potential both to prevent and to cause early delivery. The balance between these two effects is likely to depend on the inherent risk of early delivery as a result of 'cervical incompetence' in the women treated. Taking this consideration and the other recognized adverse effects of the operation into account, it seems sensible to limit the use of the operation to women with a high likelihood of benefit. Current evidence suggests that increasing numbers of previous second-trimester miscarriages or preterm deliveries constitute the firmest basis for cervical cerclage. There is currently no good evidence to support the use of this operation on the basis of previous surgery to the cervix, multiple pregnancy, or other indications.

There is some evidence that abdominal decompression may be of value in certain abnormal states of pregnancy, but the studies reported to date are not of sufficient methodological quality to support its use except within the context of further, methodologically sounder, controlled trials. Nevertheless, there are so few options for managing the compromised fetus other than elective delivery that it is important to subject abdominal decompression to further evaluation. Doppler blood flow measurement may offer an opportunity to assess its effect on uteroplacental and fetal blood flow.

22

Promoting pulmonary maturity

This chapter is derived from the chapter by Patricia Crowley (45) in EFFECTIVE CARE IN PREGNANCY AND CHILDBIRTH.

1 Introduction

Respiratory distress syndrome is the commonest complication of preterm birth, affecting over 50 per cent of babies born before 34 weeks' gestation. It is a significant cause of death and severe morbidity in preterm infants.

A number of agents can promote fetal lung maturation and thereby reduce the risk of respiratory distress syndrome in the neonate. Only three of these have been evaluated in controlled trials: corticosteroids, ambroxol, and thyroid-releasing hormone administered in combination with corticosteroids.

Of these, only corticosteroids have been evaluated thoroughly enough for the findings to be applicable to clinical practice.

2 Benefits of antenatal corticosteroid administration

2.1 *Respiratory distress syndrome*

Controlled trials of antenatal administration of corticosteroids that pass through the placenta to the fetus show a statistically significant decrease in the incidence of respiratory distress syndrome. The magnitude of this effect is largest if more than 24 hours and less than 7 days have elapsed between commencement of treatment and delivery. Analyses based on data from all the reported trials show that among both babies born within 24 hours and babies born more than 7 days after starting treatment, there is also a reduction in the incidence of respiratory distress.

Although there is a widespread view that corticosteroids are ineffective at very early gestational ages, the data show that among babies born at less than 31 weeks' gestation, corticosteroid administration is followed by a similar reduction in the risk of respiratory distress to that observed for preterm babies as a whole. Similarly, although respiratory distress is uncommon among babies born after 34 weeks' gestation, the reduction of risk is similar to that found at earlier gestational ages. Analyses based on all the available data on outcome by infant gender do not support the view that gender modifies the effects of antenatal corticosteroid administration.

2.2 *Other neonatal morbidity and mortality*

Corticosteroids reduce the risk not only of respiratory morbidity, but also of other serious forms of neonatal morbidity, such as periventricular haemorrhage. This effect is likely to be related to the reduced risk of respiratory distress, although it might also reflect an effect of corticosteroids on the periventricular vasculature.

A similar effect has also been observed on the incidence of necrotizing enterocolitis. As with periventricular haemorrhage, this benefit probably arises secondarily to the reduction in respiratory distress syndrome and the need for mechanical ventilation; but a more direct drug effect on the gastrointestinal tract or its vasculature may also be involved.

Not surprisingly these marked reductions in serious forms of neonatal morbidity have been reflected in a substantial reduction in the risk of early neonatal mortality. This reduction in neonatal mortality was not accompanied by any increase in the risk of fetal death, so it represents a decrease in overall perinatal mortality.

An important secondary benefit of corticosteroids has been a reduction in the duration and cost of neonatal hospital stay.

3 Potential risks of antenatal corticosteroid administration

3.1 *Risks to the mother*

Instances of pulmonary oedema have been reported in pregnant women receiving a combination of corticosteroids and labour-inhibiting drugs. It is difficult to estimate the magnitude of this risk, or to differentiate the separate effects of corticosteroids and the labour inhibiting drugs.

Infection is another potential risk of antenatal corticosteroid administration. Trials reporting the incidence of maternal infection provide no strong evidence of either an increase or a decrease in the risk of infection.

Other pharmacological effects of corticosteroid administration in adults relate to long-term treatment, and they provide few grounds for concern when corticosteroids are used for a period of 24–48 hours to promote fetal maturation.

3.2 Risks to the baby

Evidence concerning potential risks of steroid therapy are available from four sources: animal studies, corticosteroid treatment for maternal disease, corticosteroid treatment in the neonate, and follow-up data from the trials of antenatal corticosteroid administration for the prevention of neonatal morbidity and mortality.

The animal studies do not reflect the doses and conditions of human antenatal corticosteroid administration; they merely indicate areas that should be examined very carefully in humans.

Human fetuses may be exposed to corticosteroids throughout pregnancy if their mothers are receiving long-term steroid therapy for ulcerative colitis, asthma, rheumatoid arthritis, or other conditions. A review of the literature shows no striking excess over expectation for any adverse outcomes.

Human neonates have been exposed to corticosteroids in unsuccessful attempts to prevent retrolental fibroplasia and to treat respiratory distress syndrome. In one of the three relevant trials infection was more common in the infants exposed to steroids; in the other two trials infection was more common among those who had received placebo. None of the observed differences were statistically significant.

It should be emphasized that the doses of corticosteroid used in these attempts to prevent retrolental fibroplasia and to treat respiratory distress syndrome were up to five times higher than the equivalent dose of betamethasone recommended for antenatal use. These differences in dose of corticosteroids between human neonatal and antenatal administration make it impossible to reach firm conclusions on the long-term effects of antenatal therapy on the basis of data from neonatal treatments.

The immunosuppressive effects of corticosteroid therapy could, in theory, result in an increased susceptibility to infection or to a delay in its recognition. There is no evidence that corticosteroid therapy results in an increased risk of perinatal infection.

The most reliable evidence about the long-term effects of antenatal corticosteroid therapy comes from follow-up of children whose mothers had been treated in the randomized trials. Three follow-up studies have been published. Because of the reduced neonatal mortality rate in corticosteroid-treated babies, survivors from the corticosteroid groups had a lower mean gestational age at delivery than survivors from the control group; despite this, neurological and intellectual functions, if anything, are better in the corticosteroid-treated group than in the controls. This is plausible in the light of the complications that sometimes accompany both respiratory distress and its treatment.

4 Effects in elective preterm delivery

Elective preterm delivery differs from spontaneous preterm birth in at least four main ways. First, the timing of elective preterm delivery can be controlled, thus securing the delay required to gain maximum benefit from corticosteroid administration. Second, caesarean section, which predisposes to respiratory distress, is the most common route of delivery in this group of babies. Third, elective preterm delivery usually takes place somewhat later in gestation than spontaneous preterm delivery, so that the absolute risk of respiratory distress is usually lower. Finally, elective preterm delivery is often undertaken for conditions such as severe hypertension, Rhesus isoimmunization, or diabetes, in which corticosteroid administration may have unwanted effects.

4.1 Hypertensive disease

Hypertensive disorders in pregnancy constitute one of the major indications for elective preterm delivery. There was a statistically significantly increased risk of fetal death associated with corticosteroid use in the 90 women with pre-eclampsia studied in the first reported trial. All 12 deaths occurred in women with proteinuria of more than 2 grams per day for more than 14 days, a severity of disease that was not found in any of the placebo-treated women. There were no fetal deaths of babies of a similar number of hypertensive women in the other trials from which data are available to address this issue. A consistent adverse effect of corticosteroids would have resulted in an increased incidence of stillbirth overall, but this did not occur.

Even in the absence of any adverse effect of corticosteroids in women with pre-eclampsia, the clinician may be faced with the possible risks of postponing delivery for the few hours required to achieve a useful effect of corticosteroid administration. In some cases this delay may constitute an unacceptable risk of eclampsia or cerebral haemorrhage in the mother.

4.2 Intrauterine growth retardation

Intrauterine growth retardation, like hypertensive disease in pregnancy, is a common indication for elective preterm delivery.

Moreover, the two conditions often coexist. The lungs of fetuses with growth retardation in the absence of maternal hypertension may have accelerated maturation, but there might still be benefit from corticosteroid administration.

A potential disadvantage of antenatal corticosteroid therapy with intrauterine growth retardation is the risk of neonatal hypoglycaemia, which is an important complication in growth-retarded infants. One trial reported 11 cases of neonatal hypoglycaemia among 75 corticosteroid-treated babies compared with 5 in 71 controls. Without information from other trials it is difficult to know whether this is anything more than a chance difference.

4.3 Diabetes mellitus

Maternal diabetes mellitus may predispose to the development of respiratory distress syndrome. The results of the randomized trials do not clarify whether or not the use of corticosteroids is of benefit in preterm delivery of diabetic women, as only 35 such women were included in the trials.

While the efficacy of antenatal corticosteroids in pregnancies complicated by diabetes mellitus is unknown, the potential side-effects should be a source of concern. Fetal hyperinsulinism may or may not cause cortisol resistance in the fetal lung. Administration of corticosteroids causes insulin resistance in the diabetic. Loss of diabetic control is to be expected with the doses of corticosteroids administered to promote fetal pulmonary maturation. Therefore, antenatal corticosteroid therapy in the diabetic woman would require exceptionally close supervision, possibly with continuous intravenous insulin and frequent blood glucose estimation. Failure to maintain control can result either in ketoacidosis, which carries a high perinatal mortality rate, or in a state of fetal hyperinsulinism, which would increase the likelihood of failure to respond to corticosteroid therapy. Corticosteroid administration, if used at all in diabetic women, should be used with great caution, as it may well do more harm than good.

4.4 Rhesus isoimmunization

Elective preterm delivery plays an important role in the management of Rhesus isoimmunization. Unlike other conditions associated with chronic intra-uterine stress, Rhesus disease is not thought to provoke an acceleration of pulmonary maturation. While there is a trend towards a reduction in perinatal mortality and in the incidence of respiratory distress syndrome in steroid-treated infants compared with controls, the numbers reported in the trials are too small to provide any secure estimates of the likely effects.

There are no specific contraindications to the administration of corticosteroids in women with Rhesus isoimmunization. The fact that amniocentesis for bilirubin spectrophotometry is an essential part of the management of Rhesus isoimmunization provides an opportunity for the estimation of lung maturity. When the lecithin--sphingomyelin ratio is less than 2.0 and there is a high risk of intrauterine death, early delivery, following the use of corticosteroids, may be worth considering as an alternative to intrauterine transfusions.

As corticosteroids may result in an artefactual drop in optical density they should not be administered until a commitment to delivery has been made.

5 Conclusions

Antenatal treatment with 24 mg betamethasone, or 24 mg dexamethasone, or 2 g hydrocortisone, is associated with a significant reduction in the risks of neonatal respiratory distress. This reduction is of the order of 40 to 60 per cent, is independent of gender, and applies to babies born at all gestational ages at which respiratory distress syndrome may occur. While the most dramatic benefit is seen in babies delivered more than 24 hours and less than seven days after commencement of therapy, babies delivered before or after this optimum period also appear to benefit. This reduction in the risk of respiratory distress is accompanied by reductions in periventricular haemorrhage and necrotizing enterocolitis. These reductions in morbidity are reflected both in a reduced mortality rate, and in the cost and duration of neonatal care.

These benefits are achieved without any detectable increase in the risk of maternal, fetal, or neonatal infection. Antenatal corticosteroid administration does not increase the risk of stillbirth.

Of other agents tested, ambroxol is of interest because it may be as effective as corticosteroids. The main disadvantage is the five-day period required to complete therapy. There is some evidence from comparisons of corticosteroids and thyroid-releasing hormone with corticosteroids used alone that the combined treatment may be superior to corticosteroids used alone. The randomized comparisons that are currently being conducted should provide valuable information.

23

Preterm labour

This chapter is derived from the chapter by Marc J. N. C. Keirse, Adrian Grant and James F. King (44) in EFFECTIVE CARE IN PREGNANCY AND CHILDBIRTH.

1 Introduction

Preterm labour differs little from labour at term, except that it occurs too early. Judging whether preterm labour has or has not commenced is difficult. One cannot adopt an expectant attitude and observe for signs of progress. The more advanced labour is, the more difficult it is to stop.

A number of drugs and other interventions have been used in attempts to suppress uterine contractions. Assessment of the effects of these treatments is impossible without controlled comparisons. It is difficult to differentiate between true and false labour; in many instances, apparently progressive preterm labour stops, irrespective of whether any treatment is instituted. Suppression of uterine contractility does not necessarily mean that delivery will be postponed to an extent that is clinically useful, or that the outcome for the infant will be improved. Finally, any drug or treatment that is powerful enough to suppress uterine contractions effectively may have other effects on the mother or the baby, some of which may be undesirable.

2 Betamimetic drugs

Betamimetics are used more extensively than any of the other labour-inhibiting agents that are employed to suppress uterine contractions preterm. A variety of betamimetics have been introduced in the hope of developing agents that would have a maximum effect on uterine relaxant effect, with minimal effect on the heart or other body organs. They have been used in attempts to prevent preterm labour, as therapy to inhibit established preterm labour, and for maintenance therapy after labour has been inhibited.

2.1 *Prophylaxis*

Many clinicians prescribe betamimetic drugs to prevent uterine contractions in women who, for one reason or another, are considered to be at increased risk of preterm labour. Trials of prophylactic betamimetics, both in multiple pregnancy and in women with singleton pregnancies believed to be at high risk, have failed to detect any evidence of reduced risk of preterm delivery, low birthweight, or perinatal mortality.

2.2 *Inhibition of active preterm labour*

Only three of the many betamimetic agents available have ever been compared with a control group that received either no active treatment or placebo for inhibition of preterm labour. Some of the drugs that are widely used, such as salbutamol or fenoterol, have never been tested. The majority of the controlled trials studied ritodrine.

The data from these trials show that betamimetics reduce both the proportion of deliveries that occur within the first 24 hours or 48 hours after beginning treatment, and the incidence of preterm delivery. No decrease in perinatal mortality or serious morbidity, such as respiratory distress syndrome, has been detected. This apparent lack of effect of betamimetic drug treatment on the important adverse outcomes may be due to the inclusion in these trials of too many women in whom postponement of delivery and prolongation of pregnancy were unlikely to confer any further benefit to the baby. It may also be due to direct or indirect adverse effects of the drug treatment, including prolongation of pregnancy when this is contrary to the best interests of the baby.

Several randomized trials have compared one betamimetic drug with another. None of the studies has been large enough to have had a chance of detecting or excluding important differences in the outcomes that really matter. Nor has any of the trials shown any clear differences in serious maternal outcomes, such as pulmonary oedema. Taken together, the trials comparing different betamimetic agents show no reason to prefer one agent over another.

2.3 Unwanted effects

The most frequently observed symptoms associated with beta-mimetic use are palpitations, tremor, nausea, and vomiting. Headache, vague uneasiness, thirst, nervousness, and restlessness may occur. Chest discomfort and shortness of breath should alert those providing care to the possibility of pulmonary congestion.

The placebo-controlled trials do not suggest that betamimetic drug treatment frequently poses great hazards to either mother or baby. It must be kept in mind, however, that all of the trials together provide information on less than 500 betamimetic-treated women. This is probably less than 1 per cent of the number of women who annually receive treatment with one of these agents. The likelihood that rare but serious adverse effects of betamimetic drugs, if they exist, would have been uncovered by any one of these trials is small. Other data in the literature indicate that these drugs are not harmless.

Pulmonary oedema is a well-recognized complication of betamimetics used in preterm labour. In the absence of underlying heart disease most cases are due to aggressive intravenous hydration and to the neglect of signs of a fluid accumulation. It is safer to administer betamimetic drugs in a small volume of fluid with the use of a perfusion pump than to rely on intravenous infusion of dilute solutions of the drug.

Many of the cases of pulmonary oedema have been observed in women with twin pregnancies. Plasma volume expansion is larger in women with multiple pregnancies, so these women are at greater risk of developing pulmonary oedema during treatment with betamimetics.

Myocardial ischaemia has been described as the other main, but rare, complication of betamimetic drug treatment. Betamimetic drug administration in pregnancy results in a marked increase in cardiac output, of the same order as that observed in moderate exercise. The additional work imposed on the myocardium may be too much for women with pre-existing cardiac disease. These women should not be given betamimetic drug treatment, as the hazards for them are likely to be greater than any possible benefits that might be derived.

The most common, and dose-related, side-effect observed in all betamimetic treated women is an increase in heart rate. Only rarely will effective labour-inhibition be achieved with maternal heart rates below 100 beats per minute. Heart rates of 130 to 140 beats per minute, on the other hand, should preclude further increases in the dose of betamimetics administered.

Clinically significant hypotension is less frequently encountered with currently used betamimetic drugs, such as ritodrine and ter-butaline; but the problem has not been eliminated. All betamimetic agents show a clear tendency to lower diastolic blood-pressure, but this is usually accompanied by an increase in systolic blood-pressure, with the effect of a net increase in pulse pressure.

Other drugs, including calcium antagonists (verapamil) and beta–1 blockers (atenolol, metoprolol) have been tried as adjuncts to betamimetics in attempts to reduce the cardiovascular side-effects. The use of these agents has not been shown to achieve the desired effects in these circumstances, and the available data do not justify their use.

All betamimetic agents influence carbohydrate metabolism. Blood sugar levels increase by about 40 per cent, and there is an increase in insulin secretion. In women with diabetes the rise in glucose levels is even more pronounced. Thus a woman with well-controlled diabetes is likely to become deregulated when betamimetics are administered. This applies even more forcibly when betamimetics are combined with corticosteroids, which also have diabetogenic effects.

There is no doubt that betamimetic agents cross the placenta. Stimulation of beta receptors in the fetus evokes roughly the same effects as it does in the mother. The cardiovascular effects result in fetal tachycardia, although this is usually less pronounced than it is in the mother. Since the metabolic effects in mother and fetus may result in hypoglycaemia and hyperinsulinism after birth, assessment of blood sugar levels is advisable in infants born during or shortly after use of betamimetics to inhibit labour.

A few studies have compared long-term outcomes between infants whose mothers had received betamimetic drugs and infants whose mothers had not received such treatment. All of these studies have been rather small, and the control groups have been variously constructed. No long-term ill effects have been observed.

2.4 *Maintenance of labour inhibition*

Placebo-controlled trials of betamimetics given orally to maintain labour-inhibition after uterine contractions had been arrested by intravenous therapy, suggest that such treatment will reduce the risk of recurrent preterm labour, but this has not been shown to lead to a reduction in the incidence of preterm delivery. No effect on the incidence of perinatal death or respiratory distress syndrome was detected in the trials of oral maintenance of labour-inhibition, but a total of only 250 women participated in these trials.

3 Inhibitors of prostaglandin synthesis

There is substantial evidence that prostaglandins are of crucial importance in the initiation and maintenance of human labour. Suppression of prostaglandin synthesis is therefore a logical approach to the inhibition of preterm labour. Several agents with widely different chemical structures inhibit prostaglandin synthesis. Those that have been used to treat preterm labour include naproxen, flufenamic acid, and aspirin; but the most widely used has been indomethacin.

All of these drugs act by inhibiting the activity of an enzyme necessary for the synthesis of prostaglandin, but the inhibition of the enzyme is not always achieved in the same way. Aspirin, for example, causes an irreversible inhibition of the enzyme, whereas indomethacin results in a competitive and reversible inhibition.

All prostaglandin-synthesis inhibitors are effective inhibitors of myometrial contractility, both during and outside pregnancy. They are more effective in this respect than any of the betamimetic drugs. No case has been reported in which a betamimetic drug resulted in suppression of uterine contractility after inhibition of prostaglandin synthesis had failed; the reverse has been observed repeatedly. Trials of indomethacin show clearly that this drug reduces the frequency of delivery within 48 hours and within 7–10 days of beginning treatment, the frequency of preterm birth, and low birthweight. There is a trend, not statistically significant, towards a reduction in the incidence of perinatal death and respiratory distress syndrome.

Only a few reports on the use of naproxen, flufenamic acid, and aspirin have appeared in the literature. These drugs have not been as widely used as indomethacin, and there have been no controlled trials of their use.

Inhibitors of prostaglandin synthesis are not innocuous. The most serious potential maternal side-effects are peptic ulceration, gastrointestinal and other bleeding, thrombocytopenia, and allergic reactions. Gastrointestinal irritation is common with the use of prostaglandin-synthesis inhibitors, and it can occur irrespective of the route of administration. With indomethacin it is less frequent with rectal than with oral administration, and, as the drug is equally well absorbed with both routes of administration, the rectal route offers some advantage. Nausea, vomiting, dyspepsia, diarrhoea, and allergic rashes have all been observed in women treated, even briefly, with prostaglandin-synthesis inhibitors in preterm labour. Headache and dizziness may occur at the very start of treatment.

Signs of infection may be masked by administration of prostaglandin-synthesis inhibitors, and this may hamper or postpone the diagnosis of incipient intrauterine infection if it occurs. The prolongation of bleeding time seen with prostaglandin-synthesis inhibitors may be important, especially when epidural anaesthesia is considered.

Prostaglandin-synthesis inhibitors cross from the mother to the fetus, and may influence several fetal functions. Apart from a prolonged bleeding time, which is a constant feature in infants born with detectable levels of such drugs, knowledge of effects in human fetuses and neonates is based on case reports. The most consistent observations relate to the cardiopulmonary circulation, renal function, and coagulation.

The major worries about the use of these drugs for the inhibition of preterm labour relate to constriction of the ductus arteriosus. This probably has little effect on fetal oxygenation in the short term, but if prolonged will result in changes similar to those seen in persistent pulmonary hypertension in the newborn. Several reports have linked persistent pulmonary hypertension to the prenatal use of prostaglandin-synthesis inhibitors.

Indomethacin treatment may reduce both fetal and neonatal renal function. The effect is dose-related and appears to be transient. Several reports have noted impaired renal function in fetuses and in the neonates at birth following administration of prostaglandin-synthesis inhibitors to the mother. Long-term maternal treatment may influence fetal urine output enough to alter amniotic fluid volume, although other mechanisms may also be involved in the reduction of amniotic fluid volume that is occasionally seen during indomethacin treatment. There is no evidence, however, that the use of this drug in preterm labour leads to permanent impairment of renal function in the infant.

Inhibitors of prostaglandin synthesis all inhibit platelet aggregation and prolong bleeding time. They do so in the mother, in the fetus, and in the neonate at birth. Since neonates, and particularly preterm neonates, eliminate these drugs far less efficiently than their mothers, these effects will be of longer duration in the baby than in the mother. Salicylates are particularly troublesome, as their effects are not reversible.

Indomethacin may be a useful drug for obtaining sufficient delay of delivery to improve infant outcome. More and better controlled data will be needed before an adequate assessment of its usefulness in care for preterm labour can be made.

The lasting effect of salicylates on platelet function and the large doses required to arrest uterine contractions preclude the use of these drugs for preterm labour.

4 Ethanol

Ethanol, for a long time one of the main labour-inhibiting drugs, is now only of historical interest. It is less efficacious than other drug treatments and has serious side-effects in both mothers and babies.

5 Progestogens

Progestational agents have been used prophylactically to prolong pregnancy in women who were judged to be at increased risk of miscarriage or preterm birth, or who had experienced a threat of miscarriage.

There is an indication from placebo-controlled trials that regular intramuscular injections of 17α-hydroxyprogesterone caproate may reduce the incidence of preterm labour and preterm delivery in women considered to be at high risk of preterm labour. Thus far, these effects have not been accompanied by a detectable decrease in either perinatal mortality or morbidity. The findings are encouraging enough, however, to warrant further study. It would probably be useful if further studies were directed at evaluating a form of administration that does not require intramuscular administration.

Only one controlled trial of progesterone in established preterm labour has been reported. No labour-inhibiting effects were detected.

6 Magnesium sulphate

The effects of routine magnesium supplementation on a number of adverse pregnancy outcomes, including preterm labour, have been studied in one controlled trial. Unfortunately, the method of allocation used has considerable potential for bias. The results of the trial suggest a statistically significant reduction in the incidence of *hospitalization* for preterm labour. No statistically significant differences were observed in any of those outcomes (such as the incidence of preterm delivery or of delivery of a low-birthweight infant) that are less likely to be influenced by prior knowledge of treatment allocation, although they tend to favour the supplemented group. Better designed trials are needed to clarify whether the benefits suggested by this trial are real.

Magnesium sulphate has also been used for inhibition of preterm labour, although no placebo-controlled trials in established preterm labour have been reported. Comparisons with betamimetics have not detected any differential effects in arresting labour.

The combination of ritodrine and magnesium sulphate results in a higher incidence of serious side-effects than ritodrine alone. Pulmonary oedema has been reported in association with magnesium sulphate and corticosteroid administration in preterm labour. As magnesium is primarily excreted by the kidney, hypermagnesaemia can occur if renal function is impaired. This may lead to impaired reflexes, respiratory depression, alteration in myocardial conduction, cardiac arrest, and death. Regular examination of the knee-jerk reflex is said to offer protection against such complications, since these reflexes disappear at less elevated magnesium levels than those that cause respiratory depression and cardiac conduction defects.

Magnesium levels in the fetus closely parallel those in the mother. Infants born during or shortly after treatment are reported to be drowsy; they have reduced muscle tone and low calcium levels, and may need three or four days to eliminate the excess magnesium.

Although magnesium sulphate may be efficacious for arresting uterine contractions in women who are not actually in preterm labour, it has no demonstrated advantages over betamimetics in established preterm labour, and it can have serious side-effects.

7 Other drug treatments

7.1 Calcium antagonists

'Calcium channel blockers', or 'calcium antagonists' include a wide range of different and apparently unrelated compounds, some of which, such as verapamil and nifedipine, have been used in the treatment of ischaemic heart disease and arterial hypertension, and have also been used for the treatment of hypertension in pregnancy.

Apart from trials in which calcium antagonists were used mainly to supplement labour-inhibiting treatment with betamimetic drugs, there has been only one trial on the use of one of these agents in preterm labour. This compared nifedipine with intravenous ritodrine. Thus far, there are not enough data on any of these agents to justify their use outside the context of well designed and carefully monitored randomized trials.

7.2 Diazoxide

Diazoxide is a powerful antihypertensive agent. Its use in women in labour was found to be associated with a marked inhibition of uterine contractions, and it was thus applied to the treatment of preterm labour. It shares a large number of the properties of the betamimetic drugs both on the cardiovascular system and on carbohydrate metabolism.

No controlled trials of this drug in preterm labour have been reported, although it is said to be the principal tocolytic agent in at least a few centres in North America. The available evidence does not justify the use of diazoxide for the inhibition of preterm labour.

7.3 Antimicrobial agents

Subclinical infection and bacterial colonization may cause preterm labour with or without prior rupture of the membranes. A wealth of data in support of these suggestions has, for many years, been described in various epidemiological, microbiological, and histological associations between preterm birth and infections of the reproductive tract. The hypothesis that antibiotic therapy might be of benefit in the care of women in preterm labour is thus attractive.

Only one trial has so far tested this hypothesis. Enteric-coated erythromycin was given orally for 7 days to women who were in preterm labour before 34 weeks of gestation, and who were also being treated with terbutaline or magnesium sulphate, in a placebo-controlled trial. The authors concluded that the addition of erythromycin to their standard labour-inhibiting regimen resulted in a greater prolongation of pregnancy and a lower rate of preterm delivery, but only in women with cervical dilatation at the beginning of treatment.

These conclusions were based on a subgroup analysis of 17 of the 58 women entered into trial. The potential for bias in the selection of the subgroup is so large that this study can only be seen as hypothesis-generating. In provides no clear evidence on potential harm or benefit of the treatment.

8 Conclusions

There is currently no evidence that the prophylactic use of oral betamimetic agents does more good than harm. Because long-term treatment with these agents cannot be assumed to be free from adverse effects on the baby, they should not be used outside the context of controlled trials. There is reasonable evidence, however, that oral maintenance treatment after inhibition of active preterm labour with intravenous betamimetics reduces the frequency of recurrent preterm labour, and the need for repeated hospitalization and intravenous treatment with betamimetic agents. This use of oral betamimetics would thus seem to be worth while.

At present, only two categories of drugs merit consideration for the inhibition of preterm labour: betamimetic agents and inhibitors of prostaglandin synthesis. All the others are either obsolete or in an experimental stage. There is no longer a place for ethanol or progesterone in the treatment of preterm labour. Oxytocin analogues and calcium antagonists have been insufficiently studied to assess whether they have any beneficial effect. Other drugs, such as magnesium sulphate or diazoxide, should not be used in attempts to inhibit preterm labour because of their potential for serious side-effects. If they are used at all, they should only be permitted within the context of adequately controlled trials to assess whether their claimed benefits exist, and if so, whether these outweigh their known adverse effects.

This does not imply that the evidence in favour of either the betamimetic agents or the inhibitors of prostaglandin synthesis is beyond reproach. On the contrary, there are many flaws in the evidence available, particularly with regard to prostaglandin-synthesis inhibitors.

Both betamimetics and prostaglandin-synthesis inhibitors are effective in postponing delivery. There is no evidence that the use of these drugs, *per se*, reduces infant morbidity. They can be useful, however, when the time that is gained before delivery is used to implement effective measures. Such measures could include transfer of the mother to a centre with adequate facilities for intensive perinatal and neonatal care, the administration of corticosteroids to reduce neonatal morbidity, or judicious use of 'expectant management' in the period of gestation in which the infant's chances of intact survival are very poor.

Treatment with these powerful drugs may be dangerous for the mother and can occasionally result in maternal death. The potential benefits of betamimetics weighed against the risk of adverse effects does not justify their use in women with cardiac disease, hyperthyroidism, or diabetes. If labour needs to be inhibited in these women, prostaglandin-synthesis inhibitors are the logical choice. In all other women, betamimetic drugs are currently the drugs of choice, since the available data on prostaglandin-synthesis inhibitors are not yet sufficient.

Prostaglandin-synthesis inhibitors are more powerful inhibitors of uterine contractions than the betamimetic agents. There are too few data from controlled comparisons, either with no treatment or with other drug treatments, to recommend them as a first-line approach in the inhibition of preterm labour. Their potential hazards, weighed against potential benefits, do not justify the use of any of these agents in the doses that are necessary to inhibit uterine contractions for any longer than is necessary (two or three days). The available evidence does not justify the use of aspirin and other salicylates (in the large doses that are required) for inhibition of preterm labour.

The placebo-controlled trials of labour-inhibiting agents in active preterm labour have clearly demonstrated that many women treated with labour-inhibiting drugs do not require such treatment. The trials have also demonstrated that, in many other women, these drugs are ineffective in delaying delivery to any useful extent. Future research should focus on methods of distinguishing more clearly these two categories of women, so that women and babies are not exposed to treatments which are unlikely to benefit them.

Prelabour rupture of the membranes

This chapter is derived from the chapters by Marc J. N. C. Keirse, Arne Ohlsson, Pieter E. Treffers, and Humphrey H. H. Kanhai (43); and John Grant and Marc J. N. C. Keirse (64) in EFFECTIVE CARE IN PREGNANCY AND CHILDBIRTH.

1 Introduction

Prelabour rupture of the membranes is defined as spontaneous rupture of the membranes before the onset of regular uterine contractions. It is often referred to as 'premature rupture of the membranes', but 'prelabour rupture' is a more precise and appropriate expression, because of the diverse connotations of the word 'premature'. When this condition occurs before 37 weeks it is referred to as 'prelabour rupture of the membranes preterm'; at or after 37 weeks, as 'prelabour rupture at term'. The distinction, while arbitrary, is important both for prognosis and for care.

2 Diagnosis

2.1 *Ruptured membranes*

The diagnosis of rupture of the membranes is in many instances obvious from the sudden gush of clear amniotic fluid from the vagina and its continued dribbling thereafter. If the rupture has occurred recently, it will often be possible to collect some fluid by sitting the woman on a suitable receptacle. Alternatively, it may be possible to obtain a sample from a pool of amniotic fluid in the posterior fornix on speculum examination.

If the rupture has occurred some hours previously and most of the fluid has escaped from the vagina, it may be difficult or impossible to establish or confirm the diagnosis with any degree of confidence. In these circumstances, much depends on taking a careful history from the woman. Information can be obtained as to when and how the gush of fluid occurred; whether anything like it has ever happened before; approximately how much fluid was lost; what the colour was like; whether it smelled of anything; and whether there was anything else remarkable. The latter question may elicit a comment on the presence of white or greasy particles.

If fluid is available, differentiation between amniotic fluid and urine or vaginal secretions is essential, and is usually not difficult. Amniotic fluid contains protein, while urine usually does not, and this may readily be determined with a dip stick. When amniotic fluid is put on a glass slide and allowed to dry, it will assume a typical fern-like pattern when viewed under the microscope; urine will show no such pattern. The pH of urine will usually be acidic; that of amniotic fluid will be higher, at 7.1 to 7.3. Vernix particles or meconium, if present, are diagnostic of amniotic fluid.

The nitrazine test is probably the most widely used test for differentiating liquor amnii from other body fluids, but it has a false-positive rate of about 15 per cent. For this reason an additional test, usually microscopic observation of ferning, is worth while. The fern test is less likely to produce false positive results, although it has a higher rate of false negatives.

The ultrasound finding of oligohydramnios is strong confirmatory evidence of prelabour rupture of membranes when there is a history of sudden release of fluid.

It is not clear whether or not high (hindwater) rupture of the membranes should be considered as clinically distinct from low rupture. There is little information about how these two types of rupture can be differentiated, or whether or not they warrant different forms of care. In the absence of such data, the only practical approach is to consider them as equivalent.

2.2 Vaginal examination

It is likely that vaginal examinations can introduce or increase the risk of intrauterine infection, although no controlled comparisons have been conducted to substantiate or refute this belief. The only reason to perform a vaginal examination would be to obtain information that would be useful in determining further care, and that cannot be obtained in a less invasive way. There is probably little benefit to be derived from performing both digital and speculum examinations. The information that can be obtained by speculum examination, which may include visualization of amniotic fluid 'pooling' in the posterior fornix, collection of some of that fluid for nitrazine test, microscopic examination for ferning, or phosphatidylglycerol determination, and the collection of material for culture or screening for group B streptococci, is likely to be superior to that obtained by digital examination. On the other hand, speculum examination is likely to be more unpleasant for the mother than digital examination, and is unlikely to provide much useful information if the membranes have been ruptured for some time. Unfortunately no controlled comparisons have been conducted to establish the benefit, if any, of either digital or speculum examination.

2.3 Assessing the risk of infection

Any woman with prelabour rupture of the membranes should be assessed for signs of intrauterine infection. These include fever, maternal and fetal tachycardia, and leucocytosis. If any one of these is accompanied by a tender uterus and foul-smelling liquor there will be no doubt about the diagnosis. Uterine tenderness and fetid discharge are, however, late signs of intrauterine infection.

The earliest clinical signs of intra-amniotic infection are fetal tachycardia and a slight elevation of maternal temperature, but both these signs are rather non-specific. A few years ago, there were hopes that the estimation of C-reactive protein in the maternal circulation might be reasonably reliable as an early sign of intrauterine infection, but these hopes have not materialized; nor has the value (if any) of using C-reactive protein estimation ever been assessed in controlled comparisons.

Although intrauterine infection may on occasion precede rupture of the membranes, the main risk is infection ascending from the vagina into the uterine cavity. Information on the presence of pathogens may therefore be useful, particularly about those organisms that are responsible for the majority of fetal infections, such as the group B streptococci, *Escherichia coli*, and *Bacteroides*. Intrapartum antibiotic treatment of mothers carrying group B streptococci in the vagina reduces the incidence of neonatal sepsis and neonatal death from infection.

Amniocentesis has been advocated to assess the risk of infection particularly in the preterm period. There are problems, however, with the use of amniocentesis. These include: failure to obtain amniotic fluid in a significant proportion of cases; the invasiveness and risks associated with the procedure itself; and, most importantly, the lack of a strong correlation between the results of diagnostic tests applied to the liquor and the development of fetal infection. Bacteria are not found in all women with clinical signs of intra-amniotic infection, nor are they always absent in women without signs of infection. Some studies have suggested that white cells in the amniotic fluid are more predictive of infectious morbidity than bacteria, but this has not been confirmed by others.

There has been only one controlled trial to assess the value of amniocentesis for fetal maturity tests and detection of intrauterine infection by Gram stain and culture after prelabour rupture of the membranes preterm. The use of amniocentesis did not reduce the proportion of women delivered because of clinical amnionitis or the number of perinatal deaths. It did result in a reduced frequency of abnormal fetal heart patterns in labour and a reduction in the average number of days that the infants remained in hospital after the mother had been discharged. On the whole, there is inadequate evidence to judge whether the use of amniocentesis in women with prelabour rupture of the membranes preterm confers more benefit than harm on mother and baby.

A number of observational studies suggest that fetal breathing movements and gross body movements cease when intra-amniotic infection develops. These changes in fetal behaviour may prove to be as reliable for the detection of intrauterine infection as the more invasive technique of amniocentesis, but they too require further assessment.

2.4 *Assessing the risk of fetal immaturity*

Assessing the risk of fetal immaturity largely depends on a careful assessment of gestational age and on ascertainment of any such assessments made earlier in pregnancy. There will usually be little difficulty in identifying either fetuses who are profoundly immature or those who are clearly close to term. In between these two categories, and most typically between 26 and 34 weeks of gestation, weighing the risk of relative immaturity is considerably more difficult.

Pulmonary maturity, as determined by analysis of amniotic fluid, is associated with a decreased risk of mortality and morbidity from respiratory disorders, but does not necessarily imply that other hazards associated with preterm birth, most notably periventricular haemorrhage, will be avoided.

3 Prelabour rupture of the membranes preterm

3.1 *Risks*

The most serious, and most common, consequence of prelabour rupture of the membranes preterm is preterm delivery. The risk associated with this is directly related to the gestational age and maturity of the fetus. At the extreme lower end of the gestational age range, improvement in perinatal outcome will depend entirely on maintaining the pregnancy. At the other end of the preterm gestational age range, care policies should differ little, if at all, from those that apply after rupture of the membranes at term. Prelabour rupture of membranes at gestational ages between these two extremes (roughly between 26 and 34 weeks) presents one of the greatest dilemmas in obstetrical care.

Infectious morbidity, mostly due to ascending intrauterine infection, is the second most important hazard for the baby. This risk too is greater at lower gestational ages, possibly because of the relative immaturity of antibacterial defense mechanisms, as well as development of the bacteriostatic properties of amniotic fluid with advancing gestational age.

In addition to these two main risks, other hazards of prelabour rupture of the membranes before term include pulmonary hypoplasia and various deformities associated with persistent oligohydramnios; placental abruption; umbilical cord complications, either immediately or when labour supervenes; and the mechanical difficulties (if caesarean section becomes necessary) of delivering a baby from a uterus that contains little, if any, amniotic fluid, and has a poorly developed lower segment.

3.2 *Care before the onset of labour*

The first decision in the care of a woman with prelabour rupture of the membranes preterm is whether the primary objective should be to effect delivery, or to prolong pregnancy.

Most women with prelabour rupture of the membranes in the preterm period will deliver within a week of the rupture.

Preterm delivery is *the* main consequence of prelabour rupture of the membranes preterm. Where adequate facilities for intensive perinatal and neonatal care are lacking, the most effective form of care is referral to a centre where such facilities are readily available. It is possible that leakage will stop and that amniotic fluid will accumulate again; this, however, is the exception rather than the rule.

Four forms of care for women whose membranes ruptured

preterm, and in whom there is no evidence of either uterine contractions or infection, have been evaluated in controlled comparisons. These are: prophylactic antibiotics; prophylactic tocolytics; corticosteroids to promote fetal pulmonary maturity; and induction of labour. Some of the controlled comparisons have evaluated combinations of these interventions.

3.2.1 *Prophylactic antibiotics*   Controlled trials of the use of prophylactic antibiotics after prelabour rupture of the membranes and before the onset of labour show no reduction in the incidence of maternal infection before delivery, or of neonatal infection after birth. Neonatal pneumonia, a more reliable indicator of intrauterine infection than other neonatal infections, occurred equally frequently with or without antibiotic prophylaxis.

The only statistically significant effect of antibiotic prophylaxis found was a decreased incidence of maternal infectious morbidity postpartum. It is quite possible that a similar reduction of postpartum morbidity might have been achieved with antibiotic treatment starting at, instead of before, labour or delivery.

3.2.2 *Prophylactic tocolytics*   The question of whether the administration of tocolytic drugs might improve outcome in women not in labour after prelabour rupture of the membranes preterm has been addressed in two small studies utilizing oral ritodrine. There was no difference in the proportion of women who delivered within 10 days, and the number of women involved was too small to assess the influence, if any, on neonatal infection, respiratory distress syndrome, or perinatal mortality.

These data, and data from other placebo-controlled trials on the prophylactic use of betamimetic drugs in women without ruptured membranes, offer no support for suggestions that prophylactic tocolysis before the onset of uterine contractions is worth while in women with prelabour rupture of the membranes.

3.2.3 *Corticosteroid administration*   There is justified concern that corticosteroids might be both superfluous and hazardous in women with prelabour rupture of the membranes. Rupture of the membranes *per se* may enhance fetal pulmonary maturity, and this enhancement might be sufficient to make the use of corticosteroids unnecessary. As corticosteroids have immunosuppressive effects, administering them to women with prelabour rupture of the membranes might both increase susceptibility to intrauterine infection and mask early signs of infection, thereby causing a delay in its diagnosis.

An overview of the randomized trials from which data on the effects of corticosteroid administration to women with preterm prelabour rupture of the membranes are available gives a clear-cut response to these concerns. Irrespective of any effects that prelabour rupture of the membranes itself may have on fetal pulmonary maturity, the incidence of respiratory distress syndrome was reduced by corticosteroid administration. The incidence of neonatal infection was not statistically significantly higher in the corticosteroid-treated group than in the control group.

While the data suggest that corticosteroid administration may be more likely to increase than to decrease the incidence of neonatal infection, that effect is probably smaller than the benefit derived in terms of a lower incidence of respiratory distress. Whether the possibility of an increased risk of perinatal infections should lead to concomitant antibiotic treatment cannot be assessed from the data that are currently available. This is certainly worth considering and investigating in further controlled comparisons.

3.2.4 *Induction of labour* Two controlled comparisons have been reported in which women with demonstrated fetal pulmonary maturity, or who had received corticosteroids, were assigned either to an 'active' policy intended to effect delivery, or to a control policy in which no such measures were taken. The results of these two trials show no protective effect of the more active policy in respect of either maternal sepsis or infant outcome measures, such as neonatal infection, neonatal sepsis, respiratory distress syndrome, intracranial haemorrhage, and perinatal death from causes other than congenital malformations. On the whole the tendency is for most outcomes to be less favourable in the group with pre-emptive delivery.

3.2.5 *Surveillance* Most women will go into labour within hours or a few days after rupture of the membranes. In some women, however, labour will be delayed much longer. Among these women will be some in whom the diagnosis of ruptured membranes was made erroneously, and some in whom a high leak may have sealed over.

Provided that mother and fetus are well at the initial assessments, the main concerns in the first few days after rupture of the membranes centre on detecting the onset of infection or of uterine contractions. This can be accomplished by regular assessments of maternal temperature and pulse, uterine contractility, and fetal heart rate. It is not clear whether regular determinations of leucocyte counts add anything to this surveillance. Variation in leucocyte counts can be quite large, particularly when the influences of labour or corticosteroid administration are added.

Other elements of surveillance are guided by the other complications which are known to occur more frequently after prelabour rupture of the membranes. These are primarily related to compression or prolapse of the umbilical cord, placental abruption, and the development of fetal deformities and lung hypoplasia.

Prolapse of the umbilical cord is a well-recognized complication of prelabour rupture of the membranes. It may occur either at the time of membrane rupture or later with the onset of labour. Any change in an apparently stable situation, such as a resuming loss of liquor or the onset of uterine contractions, should alert the caregiver to this possibility. Cardiotocography and a careful ultrasound examination may be useful in these circumstances.

Compression of the umbilical cord may occur due to the loss of the protective effect of amniotic fluid. The risk of local increases in pressure escalates with the onset of uterine contractions, and the incidence of severe fetal heart rate decelerations is directly related to the degree of oligohydramnios.

The risk of placental abruption should be considered whenever blood loss or abdominal pain occur in a woman with ruptured membranes preterm.

Prolonged rupture of the membranes with oligohydramnios for several weeks may lead to the development of a spectrum of fetal postural and compression abnormalities. Pulmonary hypoplasia, the most dreaded of these complications, becomes the rule rather than the exception when oligohydramnios has been severe enough and of long enough duration to cause positional deformities. It is not clear whether the presence of fetal breathing movements may indicate that lung growth is preserved; the reported observational studies have yielded conflicting results.

Renewed accumulation of amniotic fluid may imply that the woman can return home with a reasonable degree of safety; although this has never been assessed in a controlled comparison.

3.3 Care after the onset of labour

The onset of uterine contractions may be the result of intrauterine infection. If this is the case, labour should be allowed to proceed to delivery as swiftly as possible in the interests of both mother and fetus, irrespective of the latter's degree of maturity. Decisions about the method of delivery and whether caesarean section will be necessary, should differ little from those for other preterm deliveries.

Whether or not antibiotics should be administered at once in these circumstances has not been addressed by controlled studies. Both clinical common sense and data from studies that have compared intrapartum with immediate postpartum antibiotic treatment for intra-amniotic infection tend to support the use of antibiotic treatment as soon as a clinical diagnosis of intrauterine infection is reached. When there is suggestive evidence, on the basis of either gestational age or fetal lung maturity tests, that fetal pulmonary maturity is adequate, preterm labour should probably be allowed to proceed to preterm delivery. Considerations such as the anticipated duration of neonatal hospitalization, infant–mother separation, and the costs of neonatal care, should be less influential than the probability that the risk of infection is likely to be increased if other care options are chosen.

When the fetus is so immature as to have no chance of extrauterine survival, attempts to prolong pregnancy should depend not only on what might be gained in terms of infant outcome, but even more on the maternal risks and the opinions of the parents.

The controlled trials that have compared tocolysis with no tocolysis in preterm labour following prelabour rupture of the membranes show no statistically significant differences in any of the outcome measures examined. These include delay of delivery, recurrence of preterm labour, preterm delivery, birthweight, mortality, and respiratory morbidity.

There is no evidence that tocolytic agents, *per se*, improve perinatal outcome. In the absence of evidence to the contrary, tocolytic drugs should be used in the same way irrespective of whether or not the membranes are ruptured; that is, only when the inhibition of labour permits the implementation of other measures that are known to be effective in improving outcome for the preterm infant, such as administration of corticosteroids, or transfer of the mother to a centre with adequate facilities for preterm delivery and care of the preterm infant.

Decelerations of the fetal heart rate during preterm labour occur more frequently if the membranes have ruptured before the onset of labour. Many of the abnormal fetal heart rate patterns are suggestive of umbilical cord compression, and may well be due to the loss of the protective effect of amniotic fluid. The relative merits and hazards of using amnioinfusion during labour in women with prelabour rupture of the membranes preterm have been assessed in only one controlled trial. The authors reported a statistically significant reduction in the number of mild, moderate, and severe variable decelerations per hour in the infused group as compared with the control group. The number of women who experienced such decelerations is not reported, but 7 women in the control group underwent caesarean section because of fetal distress, compared with only one in the amnioinfusion group. Umbilical blood pH values at birth were statistically significantly higher in the infused group than in the control group. The procedure did not produce a detectable increase in the incidence of endometritis postpartum. Although the only outcomes that were influenced to a statistically significant extent were the mean number of decelerations and the average umbilical pH (which may or may not explain the difference in caesarean section rates), this study warrants replication.

4 Prelabour rupture of the membranes at term

Most women with prelabour rupture of membranes at term will go into labour soon after the membranes rupture. Almost 70 per cent of these women will deliver within 24 hours, and almost 90 per cent will do so within 48 hours. A remarkably constant 2 to 5 per cent will be undelivered after 72 hours, and almost the same proportion will remain undelivered after 7 days. These women probably represent a high-risk group, with serious underlying dystocia. It is possible that these women may have a deficiency in prostaglandin production or in their prostanoid biosynthesis pathway, and that this is responsible not only for their failure to go into spontaneous labour, but also for the frequently observed poor progress in cervical dilatation with oxytocin induction of labour.

The main concerns related to prelabour rupture of membranes occurring at term are maternal and neonatal infection and an increased incidence of caesarean section. The increased proportion of caesarean sections may be because induction of labour fails to achieve sufficient progress in cervical dilatation, because of decelerations of the fetal heart rate, (possibly related to lack of liquor and cord compression), or because of underlying dystocia (which may have been the cause of the prelabour rupture of the membranes).

Infection, both maternal and neonatal, has been the main complication to worry obstetricians. Reports in the 1950s showed that prelabour rupture of the membranes at term was associated with maternal and fetal or neonatal infection, and a high risk of maternal and perinatal mortality. A controlled trial conducted at that time showed that antibiotics in labour resulted in a statistically significant reduction in perinatal mortality, but two subsequent trials conducted in the 1960s failed to show this effect.

The prognosis of prelabour rupture of the membranes at term has changed considerably in the second half of this century. Data collected over long periods, some of which include women who delivered more than twenty years ago, are of questionable relevance to current obstetric practice. The maternal deaths mostly occurred in women with prolonged, severe intrauterine infection, who often had inadequate antibiotic therapy judged by today's standards, if they had received any care at all before becoming moribund. Maternal mortality is almost never found in more recently conducted studies of prelabour rupture of the membranes at term, and perinatal death from infection has also become a rarity.

4.1 *Induction of labour or expectant care?*

The widespread practice of early induction of labour when a diagnosis of prelabour rupture of membranes at term was made arose from concern about maternal and fetal infection. The controlled trials that have compared this policy to an expectant policy were subject to possible biases in allocation, and their results cannot be considered conclusive. They are, however, the best evidence available.

Data from these trials suggest that active management leads to significant increases in the use of caesarean section for delivery, and in the rate of maternal pelvic infection. The increased incidence of maternal infection in the induced group may have been due to the larger number of caesarean sections and the threefold higher number of vaginal examinations in women in the induced groups than in the control groups. The overall rate of serious neonatal infection in the trials was very low (less than 1 per cent), and no differential neonatal effects of the two policies were detected.

None of the trials specifically addressed the questions of the length of labour, analgesia, and the degree of discomfort experienced by the woman, but in some trials the duration of labour could be estimated from the data given. The interval from time of membrane rupture to delivery was reduced from an average of about 30 hours to about 24 hours by a policy of induction, but the duration of labour averaged 15 hours in the induced group versus 6 hours in the group with expectant care.

The evidence thus suggests that a policy of induction of labour for prelabour rupture of the membranes at term exposes the mother not only to a higher risk of caesarean section and infectious morbidity, but also to a longer and probably less comfortable labour, without any demonstrable benefit.

4.2 Prophylactic antibiotics

The two controlled trials of prophylactic antibiotics conducted in the 1960s together involved more than 2000 women with prelabour rupture of the membranes at variable gestational ages, most of whom were at term. These trials utilized antibiotic treatments that would no longer be used. Although they failed to show any effect on the incidence of fetal and neonatal infection, a statistically significant reduction in the incidence of infectious maternal morbidity postpartum was observed after antibiotic prophylaxis. In some centres this has led to the adoption of policies involving routine administration of antibiotics *after* delivery to women with prolonged rupture of the membranes. Although the utility of this approach has not been addressed in randomized comparisons, it would be worth assessing which women without overt signs of infection might benefit from postpartum antibiotic prophylaxis.

One small randomized trial has addressed the question of whether prophylactic antibiotics should be given to the baby after birth in women with prolonged prelabour rupture of membranes, some of whom were at term. There was some support for the idea that prophylactic antibiotics reduced the risk of infection, but the trial requires replication on a larger sample, with blind assessment of infant outcomes.

5 Conclusions

Any woman with a history suggestive of prelabour rupture of the membranes should be assessed as soon as possible. Attention should be directed to whether the membranes are indeed ruptured; to a careful review of the menstrual history and assessment of gestational age; to possible signs of incipient or established infection; to signs of fetal distress due to cord compression or prolapse; and to signs of uterine contractions.

For the woman who is not in labour, is not infected, and shows no evidence of fetal distress or other fetal or maternal pathology, continuation of the pregnancy is more likely to be beneficial than harmful. The limited evidence that is available suggests that measures to effect delivery do more harm than good.   In view of the frequency with which preterm delivery will follow prelabour rupture of the membranes in the preterm period, corticosteroids should be administered if there is no evidence of sufficient pulmonary maturity. Whether corticosteroid treatment should be combined routinely with antibiotic treatment cannot be determined on the basis of the available evidence. On balance, combining antibiotics with corticosteroids is likely to do more good than harm; such a policy is probably worth adopting and certainly worth investigating in a controlled manner.

In populations with a high prevalence of group B streptococci carriers, either screening for the organism or routine antibiotic treatment should be adopted as standard care. In all other populations, an initial culture should be part of the care provided after prelabour rupture of the membranes preterm. Since the main risk is ascending infection, there is no justification for amniocentesis in order to obtain culture data directly from within the uterus.

There is no evidence that the prophylactic use of betamimetic agents before uterine contractions begin is of any value in preventing the onset of labour.

By contrast with uncomplicated prelabour rupture of the membranes preterm, if there are signs of intrauterine infection antibiotic treatment should be started and delivery effected. These objectives should be pursued with adequately intensive surveillance and the presence of a skilled neonatologist at birth.

Except for the special circumstances mentioned above, there is little evidence that the onset of preterm labour after rupture of the membranes requires forms of care that are distinctly different from those normally required in preterm labour. Due consideration should be given, however, to the possibility that the initiation of labour may have resulted from intrauterine infection, and that it may entail an increased risk of cord prolapse.

There is no evidence to support a policy of labour-induction for prelabour rupture of the membranes at term. Induction should not be used for this purpose other than in the context of appropriately sized, properly randomized trials, in which maternal and infant morbidity is assessed by observers who are unaware of the allocated group.

25

Post-term pregnancy: induction or surveillance?

This chapter is derived from the chapters by Leiv S. Bakketeig and Per Bergsjø (46); and Patricia Crowley (47) in EFFECTIVE CARE IN PREG-NANCY AND CHILDBIRTH.

1 Introduction
2 Risks in post-term pregnancy
3 Effects of elective delivery
   3.1 *Effects on the mother*
   3.2 *Perinatal morbidity*
   3.3 *Perinatal death*
4 Surveillance
5 Conclusions

1 Introduction

The reported frequency of post-term pregnancy varies from 4 to 14 per cent, depending on the nature of the population surveyed, the criteria used for assessment of gestational age, and the proportion of women who undergo elective delivery. Not only does the incidence vary, but contradictory findings and conclusions with regard to the fetal risks have led to opposing views concerning management.

The difficulty of determining the incidence and significance of post-term pregnancy is compounded by variations in the way it is defined, which have ranged from 41 weeks to 43 weeks. Semantic problems have also contributed to the confusion. The terms 'post-term', 'prolonged', 'post-dates', and 'post-mature' are all listed as synonymous in the International Classification of Diseases, yet nuances of meaning remain, and the terms are laden with different evaluative overtones.

The name 'post-maturity' has also been given to a clinical syndrome in the infant with a hierarchy of features ranging from evidence of loss of subcutaneous fat and dry cracked skin, through meconium staining and birth asphyxia, to respiratory distress, convulsions, and fetal death. Confusion is bound to arise when a clearly pathological syndrome is described by a word that is also used to make a simple statement about the chronological duration of a pregnancy.

2 Risks in post-term pregnancy

Perinatal mortality is increased in post-term pregnancy. The proportion of babies with congenital malformations is higher among post-term deliveries than among deliveries at term, and this accounts for about 25 per cent of the excess mortality risk. Prolonged pregnancy is associated with an increased risk of intrapartum and neonatal death but not of antepartum death. The risk thus increases with the onset of labour. A high prevalence of meconium-stained amniotic fluid is an outstanding feature among the intrapartum and asphyxial neonatal deaths. The incidence of early neonatal seizures, a marker of perinatal asphyxia, is between two and five times increased in infants born after 41 weeks.

3 Effects of elective delivery

Obstetricians have for many years expressed irreconcilably different opinions on the place of induction of labour for post-term pregnancy. The results of even large studies using observational data shed little light on the question, because of inherent selection biases and the influence of both time and other aspects of care on outcome. The best evidence for the value of routine induction at term comes from randomized trials.

Trials that examine the effects of induction at or about 40 weeks address the risks and benefits of pre-empting post-term pregnancy, while those which deal with management at 42 weeks address the risks and benefits of alternative ways of managing post-term pregnancy when it has already occurred.

3.1 Effects on the mother

No data is available on women's views with regard to induction after 42 weeks' gestation. Before this time, women have been found to be much more likely to refuse a policy of routine induction for post-term pregnancy than one of expectant management.

Policies of active induction of labour do not show any effect on the use of epidural analgesia. This is somewhat surprising, as women who have labour induced are in the labour ward throughout labour, and during daylight hours—both factors that might be expected to increase their opportunity to avail themselves of an epidural service.

Active induction policies are not associated with an increased use of caesarean delivery. This challenges a widely held belief that there is an inherent association between elective delivery and an increased risk of caesarean section. This may reflect characteristics of the women who participated in these trials, for example, the 'ripeness' of their cervices.

3.2 Perinatal morbidity

Elective delivery, either at term or after 42 weeks, reduces the risk of meconium-stained fluid. No other effects, good or bad, have been established. There is no evidence that active induction policies affect the risk of fetal heart rate abnormalities during labour, either when all trials are considered together, or when routine induction at term and routine induction at 42 weeks are considered separately. The incidence of depressed Apgar score does not appear to be affected by active induction policies.

During the 1970s there were several reports of an association between elective induction of labour and unintended preterm delivery followed by respiratory distress and other neonatal morbidity. By the 1980s, this had become less of a problem, because of greater awareness of the dangers of elective induction of labour without firm grounds for being certain about the duration of gestation. No cases of iatrogenic respiratory distress syndrome are reported in the randomized trials of elective delivery, but it must be remembered that well-documented fetal maturity was one of the entry criteria for all of them.

No consistent effect of elective induction on the incidence of neonatal jaundice has been demonstrated in the available trials.

Another, more common outcome of great importance to parents is admission of their baby to special-care nurseries. This has only been reported in one trial, which showed that more babies born after a policy of active induction were admitted to a special-care nursery than after more conservative management. As a number of conditions requiring admission to paediatric units might be altered by elective delivery, including suspected perinatal asphyxia, meconium inhalation, neonatal jaundice, and neonatal respiratory distress syndrome, this measure of outcome should be incorporated in future trials.

3.3 Perinatal death

Eight perinatal deaths occurred among the almost 3500 women randomized in the reported trials of elective delivery in post-term pregnancy. This small number makes any conclusion about the effect of active induction policies on the risk of perinatal death impossible. Since the risk of antepartum death ceases by definition at the onset of labour, induction of labour must be associated with a small but finite reduction in the risk of antepartum fetal death. This saving could be offset by an increased risk of intrapartum or neonatal death following induction of labour, but the available data do not permit any confident conclusions about this.

4 Surveillance

In all the randomized trials of elective delivery at 42 weeks some form of fetal surveillance was used in the conservatively managed arm of the trial. This surveillance usually involves consultations at 2–3 day intervals after 42 weeks, and varies from the mildly intrusive use of ultrasound or cardiotocography, to the highly invasive procedures of amnioscopy or amniocentesis. There is some evidence that these tests can detect pregnancies in which there is 'something wrong', but less evidence that their use improves outcome.

5 Conclusions

Prolonged pregnancy, in most cases, probably represents a variant of normal, and is associated with a good outcome, regardless of the form of care given. In a minority of cases there is an increased risk of perinatal death and early neonatal convulsions.

There is no justification for a policy of delivering babies electively after 280 days in order to prevent post-term pregnancy altogether. The randomized trials show only one benefit from such a policy—a reduction in the incidence of meconium-stained amniotic fluid; and many women find induction unacceptable.

The options of elective versus selective delivery at 290–294 days must be assessed in the light of available evidence from the randomized trials and women's views. The central issue of perinatal mortality and neonatal seizures remains unanswered because insufficient numbers of pregnancies have been studied. The limited evidence available suggests that, at 42 weeks, an equal proportion of women request and refuse elective delivery.

Faced with such finely balanced evidence, there are only two ways of caring for women with post-term pregnancies which can be classified as effective care. The first is to enroll all women with prolonged pregnancies in a large multicentre trial of elective versus selective delivery to assess which policy was better judged in terms of perinatal death and morbidity. Such a trial could also be used to assess the effects of these policies on the incidence of caesarean section and instrumental delivery. Further evidence of women's views about elective delivery should be sought either in the context of the kind of

trial outlined above, or by incorporating an arm in which women made their own choice between elective and selective induction.
  The alternative option is to discuss the currently available evidence with women, and allow them to decide between elective and selective induction.

------------------------------ 26 ------------------------------

Fetal death

This chapter is derived from the chapter by Marc J. N. C. Keirse and Humphrey H. H. Kanhai (65) in EFFECTIVE CARE IN PREGNANCY AND CHILDBIRTH.

1 Introduction

The interval between a diagnosis of antepartum death and delivery is a time of great distress. When this diagnosis has been made and confirmed by ultrasound examination, women require the time and opportunity to adjust to it. Rushed decisions are unnecessary. Women should be made aware of the options available to them, and given time to consider these options and to decide what they want. They must be allowed the time to grieve, and to make decisions in an environment in which they feel secure. Most women will want to return home, even if only for a brief period. It is important to remember to ask the woman how she arrived at the hospital or clinic for the ultrasound examination. She should not have to drive at such a time, or go home unescorted.

2 Choosing between active and expectant care

From the physical standpoint, given appropriate means to induce labour after fetal death, there are no overwhelming benefits or hazards for induction of labour over expectant care. The advantages and the disadvantages of both these approaches relate almost exclusively to their emotional and psychological effects. The woman herself is the best judge of these, and she is the one who should make the choice. Her caregivers should assist her by providing her with the information she needs in order to make an informed choice, and ensuring that whatever option she chooses is implemented with as little psychological and physical discomfort as possible.

It is wrong to assume that all women desire the most rapid method of delivery when their baby has died *in utero*. For some women, learning of the death is the worst moment; carrying the dead fetus still permits them a feeling of closeness to the baby, which will be lost once delivery occurs. A decision by the caregiver to induce labour, if made with little consultation or input by the woman and her partner, may be seen by the parents as a way of compensating for guilt, or as the search for a quick solution.

Many women, on the other hand, are anxious to deliver the baby as quickly as possible. Some may even suggest that this should be done by caesarean section. Discussing the facts and alternatives with the woman and her partner conveys compassion and understanding. Often it will help to defuse initial feelings of anger, suspicion, inadequacy, and guilt, which are typically felt by all, caregivers and women alike, after the sad diagnosis is made.

The main advantage of the expectant option is the absence of any need for intervention. The woman can stay at home, and she will avoid procedures that might turn out to be less effective and more risky than anticipated.

The disadvantages of expectant care are mainly psychological, and relate to the unpredictable and usually long time during which the woman may have to carry the dead baby. Sometimes, she or her relatives may be under the impression that the baby may rot inside her and exude toxins that can poison her. It is important to attempt to dispel such fears, although this may not always be successful.

The only physical hazard of the expectant policy relates to a possible increase in the risk of disturbances in blood coagulation. These are most likely to occur when fetal death has been caused by placental abruption. Disorders of coagulation in association with other causes of fetal death are rare. The hypofibrinogenaemia that is held responsible for these disorders occurs very slowly and is rarely clinically significant in the first four to five weeks after fetal death. By the time that clinically significant alterations in coagulation mechanisms have occurred, the chances are that delivery will have supervened.

The only advantage of an active policy to effect delivery in the care of women with a dead fetus is that it offers the option of ending a pregnancy that has lost its purpose. The disadvantages of an active policy relate to the means through which it is effected. If induction of labour is considered, the efficacy and safety of the method selected will be the most influential factor in considering the relative merits of the policy.

3 Choice of methods for inducing labour

Before prostaglandins became available, attempts to induce labour after fetal death with oestrogen administration, intra-amniotic injection of hypertonic solutions, and high doses of oxytocin sometimes turned into iatrogenic nightmares. Instead of diminishing emotional anguish, the procedure aggravated it, leaving the woman exasperated and exhausted after every failed attempt to induce labour.

The availability of prostaglandins dramatically changed the prospects for inducing labour after intrauterine fetal death. Cumulative clinical experience with the administration of prostaglandins for this indication showed the overwhelming superiority of prostaglandins compared with previously available methods. Successful induction (vaginal delivery following a single course of treatment) was achieved in 95 per cent of cases or more, irrespective of the prostaglandin used and the dose in which it was administered.

In the absence of controlled comparisons between the various dose regimens and routes of administration of prostaglandins for inducing labour after fetal death, guidance must be obtained from a careful assessment of whatever other evidence is available. Intravenous administration, although undoubtedly efficacious, has now largely been superseded because of a relatively high incidence of side-effects compared to local routes. Experience with intra-amniotic administration has been limited and was mostly gathered in the early days of clinical prostaglandin research. When the fetus has died it is often difficult to identify a clear amniotic pool in which to administer the drug, or to obtain a sample of clear fluid to guarantee that the right compartment has been found. This, and postmortem changes in the fetal membranes that render the degree of absorption of the drug into the myometrium and into the maternal circulation unpredictable, mean that intra-amniotic administration is probably not suitable.

Vaginal administration of PGE_2, usually in the form of 20 mg suppositories, is probably the most widely used approach nowadays because of its convenience and ease of administration. Its effect, however, depends on its absorption into the circulation; hence there is a high rate of undesirable side-effects.

Extra-amniotic administration of natural prostaglandins, either by continuous infusion or by administration in a viscous gel, appears to produce the lowest incidence of systemic side-effects. The method requires insertion of a catheter into the extra-amniotic space, which in addition to being bothersome for the woman and limiting her freedom of movement during labour, carries a risk of introducing infection. It requires some experience in order to avoid rupture of the membranes and premature expulsion of the catheter. These complications occur in a sizable minority of cases.

When intrauterine fetal death occurs in late pregnancy it is usually possible to induce labour with any of the prostaglandin regimens that are employed for other inductions. Methods with which one is thoroughly accustomed tend to perform better than those that are only rarely needed and require careful study before being applied. This is of little help, however, at the earlier gestational ages when the sensitivity of the uterus to prostaglandins is much lower than it is at term. At these stages of pregnancy the choice between the various routes for administering natural prostaglandins is not easy. Despite their efficacy, they all have several drawbacks.

Structurally modified prostaglandin analogues have been synthesized in the hope that they might overcome some of the drawbacks of the natural compounds. These analogues are not suitable for induction of labour with a live fetus because of the possible toxic effects of their metabolites on infant development, and because of the longer-lasting effect that makes them more prone to cause uterine hyperstimulation, which may be hazardous to a live fetus. For induction of labour after fetal death, however, they offer a number of potential advantages. Their longer duration of action results in less need for continuous administration, thus permitting intermittent doses and alternative routes of administration.

Results obtained with the PGE_2 analogue, sulprostone, appear to be superior to those obtained with the $PGF_{2\alpha}$ analogues, although no formal comparisons between the drugs have been reported. Sulprostone, although suitable for both intravenous and intramuscular administration, is probably best administered intravenously. A multicentre trial comparing a continuous intravenous infusion of 1 µg sulprostrone per minute with 3 µg per minute showed a statistically significant lower incidence of both vomiting and diarrhoea with the lower dose regimen, with no lengthening of the induction to delivery interval, increased incidence of placental retention, or excessive bleeding.

4 Conclusions

In the case of fetal death, the decision whether or not to induce labour should be made on psychological or social grounds, and the woman herself is the best judge of these. Should induction be chosen, this should be implemented with the use of a prostaglandin or a prostaglandin analogue. In the later weeks of pregnancy the most effective method is likely to be the method of which the caregiver has adequate experience from inducing labour in other pregnancies. Earlier in gestation, prostaglandin analogues (sulprostone in particular), if available, constitute the treatment of choice. Where such compounds are not available, a natural prostaglandin can be used by any one of a variety of routes, none of which will be ideal.

The introduction of natural prostaglandins and prostaglandin analogues for inducing labour after fetal death represented an important advance over the very unsatisfactory options that were previously available. Although this judgement could be made confidently without carefully controlled trials, it is necessary (and obviously feasible) to mount multicentre randomized trials to assess the relative merits of different prostaglandins and prostaglandin analogues in this situation.

27

Care of the bereaved

This chapter is derived from the chapter by Gillian Forrest (85) in EFFECTIVE CARE IN PREGNANCY AND CHILDBIRTH.

----

1 Introduction

There have been great changes in attitude towards perinatal death and childhood illness and impairment over the past few decades. Improvements in perinatal and infant mortality rates have been accompanied by ever-increasing expectations by parents that their children will be born safely and survive. When things do go wrong it comes as a great shock. Many parents suffer not only a sense of the loss of the healthy baby they had anticipated, but also the loss of their faith in modern medicine and doctors. It is often similarly shattering for the caregivers to witness the apparent failure of their skills.

To compound the difficulties further, in industrialized societies we have lost our day-to-day familiarity with death and bereavement, and the mourning rituals that used to play an important part in meeting the psychological needs of the bereaved. We have thus become poorly equipped to cope with this tragic situation.

The two components of normal grief are the 'pangs of grief', (episodes of restlessness, angry pining, and anxiety), set against a background disturbance, consisting of chronic low mood, loss of purpose in life, social withdrawal, impaired memory and concentration, and disturbances of appetite and sleep. These symptoms occur as bereaved people go through the process of coming to terms with the reality of their loss, and of psychologically withdrawing from their relationships with those who have died, in order to continue with their own lives in a positive manner. This process may take months or years to complete. A successful outcome depends on the personalities and life experiences of the people concerned; the circumstances of the death; the relationship with the dead person; and on the effectiveness of the supportive network surrounding bereaved people.

A number of generalizations can be made about the needs of people coping with loss: they are in a state of intense emotional turmoil, which temporarily overthrows their normal coping strategies; having an object to mourn—a body—facilitates grief work as the bereaved are thereby confronted with the painful reality of their loss; escaping confrontation with the painfulness of the loss (not attending the funeral, never speaking of the dead person, or never revisiting the place of death) hinders rather than helps mourning; in trying to cope, the bereaved seek facts as anchor points of reality, although any information offered to them while they are shocked and numb, will need to be repeated later; and recovery from bereavement is marked by a gradual return to a normal pattern of life, free of depression or anxiety and with a regained capacity for enjoyment.

2 Perinatal bereavement

2.1 Perinatal death

Grief after perinatal death is not different from that following the death of any loved person. There are, however, some special features to be considered.

Anxiety and anger are frequent, with blame being directed at the staff, other members of the family, or at one's self, as guilt. This may be due in part to the suddenness of the death, and is probably compounded when there is no 'scientific' explanation for what has gone wrong. Parents desperately seek for a cause of the baby's death. It is clearly easier for those who have an explanation, such as malformations or extreme immaturity.

'Empty arms' is another common and distressing symptom after the phase of numbness has passed. Mothers are frequently tormented by hearing their dead baby cry. Some bereaved parents experience negative feelings towards other babies and are fearful of losing control, while others long to hold a baby—any baby—however painful this might be. Many mothers do not expect to lactate once the baby has died, and find the fact that they do upsetting. Most mothers experience a great loss of self-esteem, a sense of being failures, both as women and as wives.

Most young parents will not have been bereaved before, and have difficulties coping with the complicated registration and funeral procedures. Many are unprepared for the emotional turmoil of their grief reaction, and feel they should be 'over it' after a few weeks. This view may be reinforced by well-meaning friends, relatives, and even medical practitioners, who may advise the couple to go ahead with another pregnancy long before they have recovered sufficiently from their loss. There is evidence that fathers recover from their grief more quickly than mothers. This in itself may lead to problems with their relationship, particularly if the couple are not used to sharing their feelings, or if one of them is blaming the other for the baby's death. Sexual and marital difficulties are common, although it is hard to separate any specific effect of perinatal bereavement from the loss of libido that accompanies many forms of bereavement.

Another difficult area is the reaction of other young children in the family to the loss of the baby. They may be confused about what has happened to the baby, and even feel responsible for the disappearance. Behavioural changes are common; they may take the form of over-activity, naughtiness, regression, and school problems, as well as emotional problems. These reactions are usually fairly short-lived (a few weeks or months) unless the emotional state of the parents is such that there is an absence of normal warmth in family relationships for an extended period, or unless serious difficulties develop in the relationships between the mother and her living children.

It may be particularly difficult to work through one's grief when a baby is stillborn. There is no real object to mourn. The baby has never lived outside the womb and there are no memories to help. The problems are accentuated if the stillborn baby is rapidly removed from the delivery room before the parents have a chance to see or hold him or her, and if the hospital, for whatever reason, takes over the funeral arrangements without involving the parents.

Long-term follow-up studies show that a significant proportion, up to a fifth of women interviewed, still suffer from serious psychological symptoms for years after losing a baby. Although it is not possible to identify with great confidence those most at risk of developing problems, the most frequently reported markers are not seeing or holding the baby, having an unsupportive partner or social network, and embarking immediately on another pregnancy.

There may be problems with parental relationships when babies have been conceived too quickly after a loss. If the dead child has been incompletely mourned before the start of a new pregnancy, mourning may be postponed until after the delivery of the baby, when it can reappear as 'postpartum depression'. The new baby's identity can become confused with that of the idealized baby, causing great emotional problems. The new child may never be able to live up to the parents' expectations, and may become the focus of any unresolved anger that the parents have as a result of their loss. The survivor of a twin pregnancy may be involved in similar problems if the dead twin is not properly mourned at the time.

2.2 *Illness and impairment*

The reaction of parents to a newborn baby who is gravely ill or impaired is a form of grief reaction to the loss of the healthy child that the parents had expected. The initial phase is marked by shock and panic ('I can't look after a handicapped child'); denial ('He's not my baby'); grief; guilt; and anger. This is followed by a phase of bargaining ('I will look after him if he can be taught to be clean and dry'); and finally acceptance, when parents cope with the reality of the situation. Some parents fail to adapt and remain in a state of chronic sorrow. It is important for staff to form an effective alliance with the parents, on which plans for care can be based.

In addition to a grief reaction, most parents of ill or impaired babies suffer high levels of anxiety, which appear to be increased by contact with the baby. This does not mean that separation of mother and baby is to be recommended.

Apart from the emotional stress of the situation, parents have the physical and financial stress of visiting their baby in hospital, particularly if the baby has recurrent medical crises, and needs care over a long period of time. Some parents withdraw emotionally and physically from their baby before the medical staff have given up hope of the baby's survival. This is termed 'anticipatory mourning' and can be precipitated by giving an excessively gloomy prognosis, or even by a casual remark indicating a possible bad prognosis. It carries with it a risk of rejection if the baby does eventually survive.

3 Care by the hospital

The maternity unit staff have a vital role to play in the care of bereaved parents. A programme of care should encourage the parents to see, hold, and name their baby, and to hold a funeral. Arrangements should be made for them to see senior obstetric and paediatric staff to discuss what went wrong; obtain genetic and obstetric counselling; and receive the autopsy results. Providing informed, compassionate care will significantly facilitate the recovery process after a perinatal death.

Effective care for most families can and should be provided by the maternity unit staff. These professionals are in the ideal position to help bereaved families by facilitating the establishment of normal grieving from the start, thus preventing abnormal reactions. Special bereavement counselling services are not often required.

3.1 Immediate and early care

For mourning to begin, parents must be enabled to overcome their fear of death and dying, so that they can experience the painful reality of their loss. This involves encouraging them to have as much contact as possible with their baby, both before and after death. It is particularly important for parents of a stillborn baby to see, hold, and name their baby.

When an intrauterine death is suspected, the fears for the baby's condition should not be denied, but shared with the parents, together if at all possible. If the mother is at the clinic, efforts should be made to contact her partner or a friend, so that she is not left to travel home alone and unsupported. The technicians in the ultrasound scanning room have an important role to play when the confirmatory scan is done. They need to be sympathetic to the situation and to allow the mother to be accompanied by anyone she chooses.

Most women are frightened at the prospect of delivering a dead baby, as well as shocked by their loss. It helps if staff take time to explain carefully what will happen, that adequate pain relief will be available, and what the baby will look like at delivery. This is usually successful in overcoming any reluctance that the parents may have about seeing or holding their baby. It may help to show a malformed or macerated baby to the parents wrapped up at first.

A few parents will not be able to cope with seeing and holding the baby at the time of delivery. A photograph should be taken and kept in the medical notes for possible use later, and further opportunities for seeing the baby should be offered to parents over the next few days, as they often change their minds. Photographs and other mementos of the baby are important, as they provide tangible evidence of the reality of the baby's existence and loss. They should be available for parents as keepsakes, if they wish.

When the baby lives long enough to be transferred to a neonatal unit, it is again important for staff to keep parents as fully informed as possible about the baby's condition, and to encourage them to share in the care. Photographs of the baby are helpful, particularly for fathers to keep at home, or if the mother is too unwell to visit the unit. In a randomized trial of the use of routine polaroid photographs of sick neonates in the first week of life, there was a significant increase in visiting by the parents of the photographed babies, compared with the non-photographed group.

When the baby's condition is known to be terminal, it is important to involve the parents in the decision to cease life support, and then to let them take their dying baby in their arms, if at all possible, free of all equipment that has been necessary until then. In describing this, authors quote parents saying such things as, 'It was all I could do for her to hold her in my arms as she died'. Feelings of guilt about removing the baby from the life-support system have not been reported.

Many parents like to help with the laying out of the baby's body, and this should be encouraged. Often they have selected special clothes or toys to be placed in the coffin with the baby. Facilitating the parents' contact with the reality of the death of their baby in these ways will facilitate their grief reaction. They will need privacy to express their grief, and this should be provided, however busy the unit happens to be.

The choice of site for the aftercare of the mother is important, as mothers differ in their requirements at this time. Some want to be on their own, far away from the sound of babies crying; others long to return to familiar faces on the ward. It is helpful if as much flexibility as possible is offered to them, and if, at least for the first night, partners are allowed to remain with them. Ideally, the hospital should provide a couch in the mother's room so that the parents can share their grief together. Lactation and help with its suppression is an important issue for the mother whose baby has died. If the mother is physically fit to return home immediately, and wishes to do so, it is important to ensure that she has a supportive network of family, friends, and professionals before discharging her.

3.2 *Autopsy*

Consent for an autopsy and chromosome studies should always be requested after a perinatal death. These investigations may provide information about the cause of death, help parents with their grief, and assist the planning of future pregnancies. Most parents agree to an autopsy, although it is often a painful decision for them. Having consented, parents cherish great hopes that the results will provide answers to their questions about why the baby died. It is important that they receive the results in a form that makes sense to them. The best person to do this would be a senior member of staff who can interpret the pathological findings.

3.3 *Death registration and funeral arrangements*

Knowledge of the legal procedures required when a baby dies or is stillborn is fundamental to good care. It is necessary to be familiar with the registration and funeral arrangements operating in one's own locality, as these are often complicated and baffling for parents still suffering from the shock of their baby's death. Religious practices vary greatly as well, and an awareness of these and sensitivity to the wishes of individual parents is crucial. The funeral may involve considerable expense; helping those in financial straits, and encouraging them to attend besides, are therapeutic aspects of care.

Many units have prepared leaflets outlining their own procedures and giving helpful advice on various aspects of losing a baby. These can be helpful for parents.

3.4 *Communication*

Good care hinges around good communication. Parents frequently comment on communication failures when describing their experiences. Staff must give bereaved parents opportunities to talk about the loss of their baby, and even more importantly, listen sympathetically to their expressions of grief. The senior obstetric or paediatric staff must help parents with their search for a cause of death and create opportunities for discussing this with them.

Seeing both parents together helps to strengthen their relationship as they share the experience of their baby's loss, and prevents misunderstandings and inconsistencies in explanation. Arranging for the same caregivers to attend regularly to the parents also helps this. Any information given in the first few days of the loss will probably need to be repeated later, as the initial shock of the bereavement passes. A follow-up interview a few weeks later seems to be the best way of overcoming this difficulty.

Good communication between professionals about the loss of the baby is necessary to prevent painful situations, such as a member of staff being unaware that the baby has died, and breezily asking the mother when she is to be delivered. The primary care team should be informed about the baby's loss immediately, so that they can make contact with the family as soon as, or even before, the mother is discharged. Parents may want the support of their own religious adviser, and the hospital should check on this and contact him or her if required.

3.5 *Follow-up*

Most mothers will be discharged home within a few days of their baby's death, still too shocked by it to grasp properly what has happened and why. Careful and supportive follow-up is extremely important. Parents should be able to contact the staff who cared for them by telephone after they leave the hospital. Some units are able to offer home visits by their social worker. An appointment should be made for both parents to see a senior member of staff two to six weeks later, as soon as the chromosome studies and autopsy results are available, and some form of perinatal mortality conference has taken place.

The timing of the next pregnancy is important. This will inevitably be an extremely anxious time, and the mother will need extra support during pregnancy and in the first few months after delivery.

4 Care in the community

4.1 *Health professionals*

The general practitioner, health visitor, and other primary health care workers form the professional supportive network once the mother has been discharged home. These professionals can help by continuing to facilitate the expression of emotion, informing parents about the symptoms of bereavement, and putting them in touch with any local support groups for parents who have lost a child.

The general practitioner can watch for signs of pathological grief reactions, and refer the parents for specialist help if necessary. These pathological reactions can take the form of an inhibited reaction, with no sign of any sense of loss, or a prolonged reaction, with unremitting symptoms of depression or severe anxiety, or the appearance of psychosomatic illness. There may be drug or alcohol abuse.

Unremitting anger is another feature of a pathological grief reaction, and general practitioners may need to deal with anger focused on the maternity unit. To do so, they must have good relationships with the obstetric and paediatric staff, and be fully informed about the course of events which led to the baby's loss. The parents may blame the general practitioner too, of course. When this happens, it is essential that he or she meets with the family as soon as possible so that they can ventilate their feelings, and, hopefully, re-establish their relationship. Many parents remain angry simply because they were denied any compassionate response to their situation: no one said 'I'm so sorry your baby died.'

The general practitioner or health visitor will probably be the person to whom the family will turn to for help in coping with the reactions of their other children to the baby's death. Parents may need help to allow their children to ventilate their feelings about so painful a subject. It must be remembered that young children will use play as a vehicle for doing so. Explaining death to children under five years of age is difficult because they are not yet able to grasp the concept. Even simple statements like 'The baby's gone' will be interpreted literally and lead to questions about where the baby has gone, and when a visit can be made. The parents will need to add more information as the child's capacity for understanding develops.

4.2 Self-help groups

Self-help can be effective in providing the right kind of support for parents facing many different kinds of problems, and perinatal bereavement is no exception. It is important, though, that the people running the group have recovered sufficiently from their own loss to be able to help others (two years is the usual time required) and that they have access to professionals for help and advice as and when necessary. Parents can benefit from sharing their experiences together, from discovering that they are not alone in their suffering, and from learning that time does help to heal the wounds. Not everyone can cope with group support, and it is unwise to rely on a local self-help group to meet the needs of all bereaved families. While it is invaluable to give parents the telephone number or address of a local contact, this should not replace follow-up by the hospital and general practitioner.

5 The role of specialist counsellors

Prevention of abnormal (pathological) grief reactions through appropriate care is not always successful. About one in five families will show pathological reactions. These reactions are likely to be accompanied by problems in family relationships. The help of specialist counsellors trained in grief work will be needed in these situations, either to advise other colleagues giving care, or to take over responsibility for care themselves.

The treatment required is often protracted, and antidepressant drugs and psychiatric surveillance may be necessary for severe depressive symptoms. Child and family psychiatrists may be particularly helpful in dealing with the relationship problems within families. Specialist counsellors can also try and promote normal grieving in parents most at risk of pathological reactions.

Specialist counsellors can also be useful in supporting the staff of the unit (through regular staff meetings, case discussions, or training sessions) and can offer help and advice to self-help groups. The training of staff in the care of families who lose their baby, or who are faced with a baby with a severe impairment, deserves as much emphasis as the development of their technical expertise.

6 Conclusions

Much can be done to help a bereaved family cope with their loss and recover from their grief. The extent to which this is accomplished will depend on the importance that is attached to training in this area, and on the attitudes of individual professionals, both in the maternity unit and in the community.

The practical aspects of death registration and funeral arrangements for babies should receive careful attention. Time must be spent, listening as well as talking, with parents whose baby has died or is impaired. The senior members of staff need to play a central role in caring for the parents, sharing their experience and expertise with more junior caregivers. The primary health care team must accept the role of monitoring and supporting the parents during the ongoing bereavement process.

The provision of adequate support will almost certainly lead to improved rapport with grieving families. It will help professionals to cope better with their own grief, because they feel more able to help. Most importantly, it will help families to emerge from their grief able to resume normal functioning, with positive attitudes towards the professionals who shared the loss of their baby.

28

Social and professional support in childbirth

This chapter is derived from the chapters by Cornelis Naaktgeboren (48) and Marc J. N. C. Keirse, Murray Enkin, and Judith Lumley (49) in EFFECTIVE CARE IN PREGNANCY AND CHILDBIRTH.

1 Introduction
2 Nature of support in childbirth
3 The birth environment: implications for support
4 Men during labour and at birth
5 Other support people
6 Controlled trials of support in labour
7 Conclusions

1 Introduction

Support during childbirth can be provided by the professionals who are responsible for the clinical care of the woman in labour; by professionals specifically designated to provide support rather than clinical care; or by the woman's partner, family, or friends. Controlled studies thus far have examined only the contribution of the second group, a person specifically designated to provide social, but not clinical, support in labour. Insights into the nature and value of support by other professional and non-professional people have been gleaned from data from observational studies.

2 Nature of support in childbirth

A central feature of support in childbirth is the promise that the labouring woman will not, at any time, be left alone. Support in the controlled studies was defined as physical contact (for example, rubbing the mother's back and holding her hands), conversation, and the presence of a friendly companion whom the mother had not met before.

Mere physical presence is not enough. Labouring women's companions should provide emotional support. This may include walking with her, holding her hand, and maintaining eye contact. It also involves ensuring that she understands clearly the purpose of every procedure and the result of every examination and that she is kept informed of progress, with regular updating of the time at which her baby is expected to be born.

Other descriptions of the support role mention advocacy as well as explanation, physical comfort and encouragement. Advocacy, which is particularly associated with plans and expectations before labour, is a common component of partners' and labour companions' supportive activities.

The separation of support from other functions of caregiving is slightly artificial. Many of the people involved in pregnancy and childbirth care provide, as a part of their role, some or all the components of the support described above. The caregivers often combine support with assessment and diagnosis. Autonomous midwives, for example, would be involved with physical comforting, explanation and encouragement, and information and feedback. Traditionally, and at least in theory, they would 'be there' all the time. The advocacy part of support would apply whenever complications developed and a doctor was called in.

In hospital settings the separation of support from management may be far greater, with doctors and midwives (or nurses) carrying out tasks of a technical nature. Among the professionals there is even more splitting of functions, with control and decision-making vested in the obstetrician, while the midwife is either restricted to monitoring and assessment, or loses this role to fetal-heart-rate and uterine-activity monitors. The loss of diagnostic and decision-making roles does not necessarily free the midwife to provide emotional and psychological support, since her time can be taken up with caring for the equipment and assisting the physician.

When caregivers do not or cannot provide consistent support during labour, then support develops into a separate issue. Either it becomes the province of family and friends, or it becomes a problem to be dealt with by the institution.

3 The birth environment: implications for support

Developments in obstetrical care over the past seventy-five years have resulted in the mother's isolation during labour. For perhaps a third of that time, this distressing feature of the birth environment was not apparent in several countries. The subjective experiences of labour and birth were submerged by twilight sleep and general anaesthesia. While women were unconscious, questions of psychological support were irrelevant. When the natural childbirth movement redefined the experience of giving birth as potentially positive, aspects of the birth environment took on a new significance.

There are many features of the contemporary birth environment that may increase its stressfulness: the unfamiliarity of the place and most of the people in it; the routine use of procedures such as insertion of intravenous lines, restriction of fluids and foods, shaving the perineum, enemas, regular vaginal examinations, restriction of movement, fetal monitoring, augmentation of labour, and epidural anaesthesia; and, increasingly, the high probability of an operative outcome. Many people believe that fear, pain, and anxiety are increased by the mechanized, clinical environment and the unknown attendants, with adverse effects on the progress of labour. Observational studies suggest that more intensive care may have adverse effects on low-risk mothers and infants.

Women appreciate a constantly available companion in labour. The perception of isolation and the reality of being left alone, even momentarily, are often compounded by the intermittent appearance and disappearance of large numbers of unknown people: obstetricians, midwives, nurses, and medical, nursing or midwifery students. One commentator has dubbed them 'masked intruders'. A Canadian study found that women giving birth in hospital encountered an average of 6.4 unfamiliar professionals during labour (range 3–14). Another survey reported that one low-risk mother having her first child in a teaching hospital was attended by 16 people during six hours of labour, but was still left alone most of the time.

Where there are extremes of isolation, overcrowding, use of painful procedures, a rapidly changing cast of professional staff, and no familiar person, it is not too fanciful to compare the state of the labouring woman with that of the absolutely terrified pregnant monkeys so often cited in relation to psychological stress and fetal asphyxia. How common these extreme situations are we do not know; but wherever they exist, the provision for a friendly companion chosen by the labouring woman to be with her is likely to improve her wellbeing.

The hospital environment, with its separation of family members and rigid procedures, is one of the factors believed to cause the high intervention rates during labour seen in many industrialized societies. Yet the opening up of labour wards, first to fathers and then to other support people, has been associated in time with a staggering increase in caesarean birth and other interventions. These facts are difficult to reconcile, indicating that the assumption that rigid policies in the birth environment lead to an increased resort to major interventions is not necessarily correct.

4 Men during labour and at birth

The arrival of men as husbands and partners into labour and birth is a relatively recent phenomenon. The reclaiming of birth by women as a positive experience has meant that the exclusion of a woman's sexual partner and father of the baby is widely seen as incongruous.

In the decades when natural childbirth and psychoprophylaxis were not well understood or accepted, partners were expected to reinforce what had been taught in childbirth education classes, and if necessary to act as advocates.

Another reason for partners' presence in labour wards has been to fill the gaps in care. The women planning a hospital birth in the Canadian study cited earlier rarely expected to have a nurse with them throughout labour. They felt the nurses would be too busy, or they saw them as unwelcome strangers, or viewed the nurse's role as purely technical in nature. They intended to rely on their partners for support, assistance with breathing techniques, and comfort measures. Recognizing that labouring women require psychological support, and realizing that nurses have little time to give it, hospitals have increasingly permitted and encouraged husbands to assume active roles in the care of their wives during labour.

In many countries in the industrialized world the presence of women's partners during labour has, within twenty years, gone from being occasionally permitted to being normative and virtually universal. Unfortunately, studies of the impact of the father's presence on labour and birth have been limited by small sample sizes and self-selection. Research in the 1970s, when the presence of fathers was relatively unusual, studied groups where the presence of fathers in labour or at birth was associated with higher social class, attendance at childbirth education classes, and preference for non-medicated birth.

Some doubts have been expressed about handing over the supportive role to fathers. One concern relates to whether they are equipped for tasks that were formerly the responsibility of an experienced and professionally trained person. Other questions relate to the way in which the father's presence might influence the labouring woman. It has been suggested that some support people, the woman's partner being no exception, can interfere with the normal progress of labour by their effects on the woman. When there are major tensions in the couple's relationship, practical and emotional support in labour may be difficult to provide or to accept.

In some settings husbands are unable to provide effective support in the conventional labour ward. Occasionally a husband is co-opted by the midwife to confirm her statements or to add his encouragement to hers, but is generally considered to be a marginal figure. Sometimes they are treated as children might be; given a 'pretend' role in the birth (for example, allowed to cut the cord) and referred to as if they were spoilt babies unaware of the real world of women's lives. These dismissive attitudes co-exist uneasily with ideas of father involvement and family togetherness.

An important mechanism by which the partner's presence may

influence the outcome of labour can be a change in the behaviour of the physician, since the frequency of interventions in labour is much more related to differences in caregiver policies than to differences between labouring women. Cartoonists have often portrayed the males in labour rooms either talking to each other and ignoring the woman, or jointly engrossed in the output from a machine. Perhaps the interaction of the physician with the partner in some way promotes a different pattern of care, which may include more rather than less intervention. We do not know.

There has been almost no research on the support actually provided by husbands and partners. Also unresearched are the expectations that women bring to labour about the support that they will have and that they will need. These expectations were compared in two matched groups of women planning home and hospital birth. Women in the home group expected their partners to be more helpful during labour than did those in the hospital group. Ironically, the latter women had much lower expectations of support from professional caregivers as well.

Several surveys using retrospective interviews have asked women to rate the quality of the support provided during labour and birth. The results are remarkably similar in very different settings, with partners almost uniformly rated very highly and mostly higher than midwives.

A recent study of pain in labour found that all primiparae had someone with them throughout labour (98 per cent had the baby's father). The presence of a labour partner who provided specific encouragement in pain-control techniques, *not* just a reassuring presence and emotional support, was associated with lower epidural rates and with fewer women describing panic, exhaustion, or overwhelming pain, although pain ratings in the two groups were not different. Self-selection presents a problem in the interpretation and generalizability of the results of such studies.

5 Other support people

Apart from institutionally employed support persons, midwives, and partners, two other categories of people are currently providing support in labour: other family members and friends, and paid professional companions usually named 'coaches' or 'monitrices'. Hospitals vary greatly in the extent to which they permit these other support people in labour wards.

In alternative birth settings it is customary for several people to be present for at least some of the time. The freedom to choose who will be present, and when, is often a factor in a woman's choice to give birth outside hospital. It would be unwise to assume, though, that the presence of several people will provide additional support. Family and friends, like husbands and partners, may be there to share in the experience rather than to provide support.

To some extent, the move to have additional family support arose from disillusionment with what the husband could provide, especially when the labour was a long one. (Professional support persons and student midwives, after all, work shifts rather than 24 hours a day.) Family and friend support is particularly appropriate where support is seen in terms of physical comfort, being there, maintaining eye contact, and encouragement. When coping with labour is seen more in terms of utilizing learned skills, such as controlled breathing patterns and relaxation, then the chosen additional support person is likely to be a professional.

Just as the role of support persons arose from the splitting of care into management and support, so the role of the labour coach comes from the splitting of education from care. Once education for childbirth becomes a separate activity, those responsible for care and management in labour may not know the constituents of that antenatal education, and may be unwilling or unable to support labouring women in the use of the skills that they have learned. They may belittle the usefulness of the education programme, at the same time complaining about the unreal expectations that it has created.

The potential for territorial rivalries over the provision of support is great indeed. When a labour coach is recruited as an advocate for the labouring woman, rivalries with other staff, especially with midwives, are almost inevitable, and the intended support may end up as a casualty of the conflict. One can legitimately ask if, given the constraints posed by institutional norms and policies, an employee of the hospital can provide the same quality of support and advocacy that a professional 'outsider' can. On the other hand, the presence of an outsider can pose a threat to the institution, which may have a negative influence on the quality of care received by the labouring woman.

Studies of the impact of professional support persons on childbirth outcomes and on the role of the husband/partner during labour are currently being carried out.

6 Controlled trials of support in labour

Only three controlled studies are available; all emanate from the same group, although they have been conducted in two different countries, Guatemala and the United States. The support persons ('doulas') employed in the Guatemalan studies were single and childless, highly trained research workers who had obtained more advanced training and degrees before joining the support project. They were similar to the pregnant women in ethnicity, culture, and language, but they were better educated.

The findings in these trials are consistent. The presence of a supportive companion during labour was associated with a striking reduction in the length of labour, with a consequent reduction in the rate of augmentation of labour with oxytocics. Fetal passage of meconium during labour was reduced; and this, together with the effect of the supportive companions on uterine action, resulted in fewer instrumental deliveries and caesarean sections. Low Apgar scores were also less common among the babies born to mothers who had companions, but this difference could be a reflection of chance.

The main questions about these randomized controlled trials are the mechanisms of action and the generalizability of the results. Since these are pragmatic trials, it might be thought that the mechanisms are irrelevant; but an understanding of these mechanisms may have important implications for generalizing the findings to other settings. The investigators believe that the most important factor is a reduction in fear, pain, and anxiety when women have a supportive companion, and they link these possible changes with effects of catecholamines on uterine contractions and uterine and placental blood flow.

Two other randomized trials have shown a shortening of labour in women assigned to different forms of care from the standard one: 'Leboyer delivery' and a birth room. These suggest that the length of labour may be readily influenced by a variety of factors. Whether it is the nature of the change or its novelty that is most important is not clear. Since assignment to the intervention programme in these trials was always apparent to all members of staff, it is possible that it affected interaction with the woman and decision-making.

The benefits demonstrated in the 'doula' trials may be specifically related to an adverse birth environment. The routines at the Guatemalan hospital where the trials were carried out were established in the 1950s, and were based on North American practices of that era. The setting in these studies, with 56–60 deliveries a day, an open observation ward for early labour, and 'hospital policies which did not permit any family member, friend or a continuous nurse caretaker to be present' sounds as if it might indeed be conducive to fear, pain, and anxiety. By contrast, birth in Guatemala had been until that time something which occurred at home, with women assisted by the mother's mother, the father's mother, and a village midwife. Thus women in the study would have been the first generation to labour alone and to give birth among strangers and in the presence of men. Given this information, and the accounts by the research team of the overcrowded and hectic labour and delivery wards in the two papers, it seems possible that the environment might well have been particularly stressful.

The generalizability of the results of these trials must be seriously questioned, in part because of the special features of the environments in which they were carried out, and in part because of the special characteristics of the support persons, which are unlikely to be reflected in other categories of support persons such as partners, midwives, and others.

7 Conclusions

Given the difficulties of generalizing from the few available randomized trials and the present state of collective ignorance, an interim conclusion might be that it is inappropriate for hospitals to take it upon themselves to exclude any category of support person from labour and birth. Where women have strong preferences for who should be with them at this time, these should be respected.

There is a very real possibility that an interaction which is beneficial to most people may have the reverse effect on some. Sensitivity to the possible negative effects of any support policy for a minority of those who are exposed to it is essential. The presence of husbands during labour, once grudgingly permitted, is now normative; yet, observations of father-attendance suggest that in some settings neither active support nor supportive companionship is manifested.

In settings where there is currently no continuous support or caregiving, there is an opportunity to implement changes within the context of randomized trials that might answer some of the vexing questions that remain unanswered. What is important in providing effective support? Is it enough to be there, or is it necessary to provide encouragement or physical comfort? What is the relationship between supporters and caregivers? Is it better for the support person to be a stranger than to be familiar, to be a peer or a professional? The results of the available studies provide important evidence, but the main lesson from them is that a lot remains to be learned.

29

Hospital policies and admission practices

This chapter is derived from the chapters by Iain Chalmers, Jo Garcia and Shirley Post (50); and by Sally Garforth and Jo Garcia (51) in EFFECTIVE CARE IN PREGNANCY AND CHILDBIRTH.

1 Introduction

Most births now take place in hospitals. Like other large institutions, hospitals (and the professionals working within them) depend on rules and routines for efficient functioning—and it is probably essential that they continue to do so. Professionals need a structure within which to do their work, and this structure necessarily involves working rules and at least some routines. This applies whether the professional is working independently or within an institution. Those who work in institutions are more likely to have to work within a framework of rules intended to serve the interests of other people working in and using the institution. Change can be slow because familiar rules and routines are comforting, and because it takes time to develop and agree on new policies—time that may be seen as better spent providing clinical care.

The marked variations that exist in the types of care women receive depend more on which maternity unit a woman happens to attend, and which professional she consults, than on her individual needs or preferences. These differences in practice are often so dramatic that they can not possibly be explained by differences in medical indications or by the preferences of the women attending the different hospitals.

2 First impression

A woman entering a hospital in labour may have experienced months or even years of anticipation, fear, and uncertainty about childbirth, all focused on the moment when she will walk past the 'point of no return' through the doors into the labour ward. This is the time when she feels, and is, at her most vulnerable. It is a woman in physical and emotional turmoil who needs to be welcomed into a strange environment and given comfort and care.

The midwife or labour-room nurse may have an entirely different set of priorities. Her main concerns are probably to discover what stage of labour the woman is in, and to reassure herself that the mother and baby are well. She will also have record-keeping tasks, and sometimes may be responsible for other women in labour. Providing appropriate care for each individual woman, with her own distinct needs, is a daunting task.

Various recommendations for changes in admission practices have been made because of a recognition that women are probably anxious, if not actually frightened, when they enter the hospital in labour. It is important that caregivers welcome and support mothers and their companions from the moment of arrival. Caregivers should introduce themselves, and give information about who else the mother might meet and be cared for by during labour. This is common courtesy, and should be universal. Although rarely practised, it would be helpful if midwives or nurses also asked women how they wish to be addressed.

Admission in labour provides an opportunity for discussion of a woman's requests and plans for (and worries and concerns about) labour and delivery. The time of admission also provides an opportunity for midwives and nurses to inform and reassure women, as they explain the various examinations and procedures that are being carried out.

The support of a partner or some other companion may be particularly important to a woman in labour at the time of admission to hospital. Surveys show that only a small proportion of women prefer not to have anyone with them at admission. Most women interviewed expressed pleasure and relief when their partner could stay, and disappointment when he was unable to do so, whether because he was at work or looking after other children, or excluded as the result of a hospital regulation.

A woman is usually asked to undress when she first arrives in labour. If this is done insensitively it can be a humiliating experience for her. Many women prefer the option of bringing a comfortable nightdress from home rather than having to wear a hospital gown; this gives them a little more dignity and individuality. Provision for privacy in admission rooms is important. This privacy is sometimes lacking, often involving curtains and screens of various designs, rather than a door that can be closed.

3 Clinical assessment

The 'diagnosis' of labour has received relatively little research attention, and some important practical questions remain unanswered. Different patterns of care can influence the timing of admission. The advice given to a woman antenatally about the onset of labour, and what she is told over the telephone when she calls in, will influence her decision on when to come into hospital. Once she comes into hospital her experience will depend on hospital policies and on the decisions made by her caregivers. If she is judged not to be in labour she may be sent home or to another hospital ward. There is little evidence about the effects of this process or the consequences of differing policies.

The main clinical tasks at admission are to assess a woman's progress in labour, and her condition and that of her baby, and to make decisions about care. In carrying out these tasks caregivers have various means at their disposal, including a discussion with the woman about her history and symptoms, and obstetric records; observation of her temperature, blood-pressure, and general condition; abdominal palpation and vaginal examination; and some form of monitoring of the fetal heart. An explanation of why these are necessary is not always given, and sometimes women are given no indication of the results. An explanation of what is being done is not sufficient; it is equally important to let a woman know why it is being done. Most women want to be involved in decisions about their care.

4 Preparation procedures

Admission to hospital in labour has often involved the routine use of bowel preparation with enemas or suppositories, and the shaving of some or all of the pubic and perineal area. A bath or shower is often part of the process as well.

4.1 Enemas

The routine use of bowel preparation has been recommended to allow the fetal head to descend; to stimulate contractions and thereby shorten labour; and to reduce contamination at delivery, and so to minimize infection rates for the mother and the baby. The practice is not without risk. Cases of rectal irritation, colitis, gangrene, and anaphylactic shock have all been reported.

Two randomized controlled trials have been mounted to evaluate the effects of routinely giving women enemas on admission to hospital in labour. The available evidence suggests that the rate of faecal soiling is unaffected during the first stage of labour, but reduced during the second stage. The soiling in the control groups was mainly slight, and easier to remove than soiling in the enema groups. No effects on the duration of labour or on neonatal or perineal wound infection have been detected.

Of the women who had enemas or suppositories, a small number were pleased or had requested this; half of the remainder either did not mind or were prepared to have whatever was necessary, while the other half expressed negative feelings, such as embarrassment, discomfort, or reluctance. The majority of women who did not have an enema were pleased or relieved not to, but some did not have strong views.

4.2 *Pubic shaving*

The stated purpose of routine predelivery shaving has been to lessen the risk of infection and, presumably, to make suturing easier and safer. As early as 1922 a controlled trial provided evidence that challenged these assumptions. That trial, and the only other controlled trial to examine this practice, were unable to detect any protective effect of perineal shaving in respect of puerperal febrile morbidity, a finding which was supported by the results of a non-randomized cohort comparison. Other writers have drawn attention to the disadvantages in terms of discomfort as the hair grows back, as well as the minor abrasions caused by shaving.

5 Conclusions

Hospital routines are necessary for efficient functioning.   The challenge faced by professionals working in maternity units is firstly to maintain and introduce only those routines and rules that have been shown, on balance, to do more good than harm, and secondly, to apply those routines flexibly and in a way that takes the needs of each individual childbearing woman into account.

The presence of a companion during admission, when they may be in most need of support, is important to many women. The presence of the companion or companions that women choose should be encouraged and facilitated.

Because admission is a time when women may be particularly vulnerable, caregivers should pay attention to ways of maintaining women's dignity. Maternity units should consider possible ways of providing more privacy and of treating women more as adults, for example, in styles of address and introductions by staff. Abandoning the traditional hospital gown is a step towards this goal.

Women appreciate the efforts that midwives and other caregivers make to inform and consult them about their progress in labour and the care they are to receive. When choices about care are offered to women, caregivers should present those choices in a manner that allows women to ask for what they want, and discuss their uncertainties.

There is no justification for continuing to administer enemas routinely, or for perineal shaving.

Controlled trials are required, to evaluate not only the effects of routine hospital policies and practices, but also methods of implementing changes when these practices are ineffective, inefficient, or counterproductive.

30

Nutrition and position in labour

This chapter is derived from the chapters by Claire Johnson, Marc J. N. C. Keirse, Murray Enkin and Iain Chalmers (52); and Joyce Roberts (55) in EFFECTIVE CARE IN PREGNANCY AND CHILDBIRTH.

1 Introduction
2 Nutrition
  2.1 *Risks of aspiration*
  2.2 *Measures to reduce gastric volume and acidity*
    2.2.1 *Restriction of oral intake*
    2.2.2 *Pharmacological approaches*
3 Maternal position during first stage of labour
  3.1 *Effects on blood flow and uterine contractility*
  3.2 *Effects on the mother and the baby*
4 Conclusions

---

1 Introduction

That food and drink should be withheld once labour has commenced is almost universally accepted in current hospital care. A small minority hold equally strongly that except for women at high risk of needing general anaesthesia the benefits of allowing women any nourishment they wish far outweigh the possible benefits of more restrictive policies. Equally strong opinions are held about whether women should, or should not be confined to bed during labour.

These contrasting opinions are expressed in practice, and it is therefore pertinent to examine the evidence on which they are based.

2 Nutrition

Surveys of labour ward policies in both England and the United States

show that most units prohibit all solid foods. Almost 50 per cent of
the responding units allowed no oral intake except ice chips; most of
the remainder allowed only sips of clear fluids; and only about one in
ten units allowed women to drink as much fluid as they desired. None
of the hospitals surveyed in the United States permitted women to eat
and drink as they wished.

For many women these restrictions do not present a problem. Most
women do not want to eat during labour, particularly during its later
phases. For those who do want to eat, however, enforced hunger
during the first stage of labour can be a highly unpleasant experience.
Why then are such restrictive policies employed when some women
so obviously find them distressing? The explanation lies in the
widespread concern that eating and drinking during labour will put
women at an increased and unacceptable risk of aspiration of gastric
contents following regurgitation.

2.1 Risks of aspiration

This concern is real, and serious. The risk of aspiration is, however,
almost entirely associated with the use of general anaesthesia. The
degree of risk therefore relates directly to the frequency with which
general anaesthesia accompanies childbirth, and to the care and skill
with which the anaesthetic is administered.

Policies that restrict oral intake during labour have the objective of
reducing the risk of regurgitation and inhalation of gastric contents.
Aspiration of food particles of sufficient size to obstruct a main stem
or segmental bronchus may result in atelectasis distal to the obstruction, possibly with severe hypoxaemia as a consequence. Even in the
absence of particulate matter, gastric aspirate, if sufficiently acidic,
will cause chemical burns in the airways, resulting in disruption and
necrosis of the bronchial, bronchiolar, and alveolar lining. It is this
syndrome of acid aspiration in particular, described by Mendelson
over forty years ago, that constitutes the greatest risk in pregnant
women who undergo general anaesthesia.

The absolute level of the risk of aspiration has always been low,
and is now very low. It is clear that aspiration of gastric contents plays
a very small role, in both absolute and relative terms, as a cause of
maternal death. It does remain, however, a cause of unquantified
maternal morbidity in women who aspirate gastric contents, but do
not die.

Over the years a number of specific measures have been introduced in attempts to avoid aspiration. It has been pointed out
repeatedly that failure to apply proper anaesthetic technique is the
major reason that deaths from aspiration of gastric contents still occur.

Whether or not aspiration problems could be completely abolished
if proper anaesthetic technique were to be employed at all times

remains uncertain. It is clear, however, that most of these problems could be prevented by a combination of decreasing the frequency of procedures that require anaesthesia (particularly caesarean section), the use of regional anaesthesia whenever feasible, and meticulous attention to safe anaesthetic technique.

2.2 Measures to reduce gastric volume and acidity

Measures to reduce the volume and to increase the pH of gastric contents cannot compensate for inadequate anaesthetic technique. Such measures are, however, widely used.

2.2.1 Restriction of oral intake

Fasting, with the aim of ensuring an empty stomach, is the most commonly used measure aimed at reducing the volume of the gastric contents. Fasting during labour does not have the desired effect of ensuring an empty stomach, and to quote the conclusions of one study 'the myth of considering the time interval between the last meal and either delivery or the onset of labour as a guide to gastric content volume should now be laid firmly to rest'. There is no guarantee that withholding food and drink during labour will ensure that the stomach will be empty in the event that general anesthesia should become necessary. No time interval between the last meal and the onset of labour guarantees a stomach volume of less than 100 ml.

The use of a low-residue, low-fat diet with the aim of providing palatable, attractive, small meals at frequent intervals is a reasonable alternative to fasting. Such a diet could consist of tea, fruit juice, lightly cooked eggs, crisp toast and butter, plain biscuits, clear broth, and cooked fruits. One major textbook on obstetrical anaesthesia stated that 'Those women and they form the great majority of the patient population who are unlikely to require general anaesthesia, are classified as 'low risk', and may be offered the prepared diet at any appropriate time during labour'.

Nor can fasting during labour be relied on to lower the acidity of the gastric contents. One author commented provocatively 'Is it not intriguing that, in England and Wales, the number of maternal deaths from acid-aspiration apparently rose only after the institution of severe dietary restriction in labour, amounting in most units almost to starvation?'

Restricting food and drink during labour may result in dehydration and ketosis. Whether the degree of ketosis that occurs in some women during labour is a harmless physiological state or a pathological condition that interferes with uterine action is uncertain. There has been no research published about the nutritional needs of the labouring woman. For some women, these are likely to be similar to those of an individual engaged in strenuous athletic activity.

The most common response to the problem of ketosis in maternity units where eating during labour is prohibited is the use of intravenous infusion of glucose and fluid. The effects of this practice should be carefully weighed against those of the alternative course of allowing women to eat and drink as they desire.

The maternal effects of intravenous infusion of carbohydrate--containing solutions during labour have been evaluated in a number of controlled trials. The rise in mean serum glucose levels appears to be accompanied by a rise in maternal insulin levels and a reduction in mean levels of 3-hydroxybutyrate. The available data show no consistent direction of effect on either maternal pH or lactate levels.

Infusion of carbohydrate-containing solutions to the mother results not only in an increase in plasma glucose levels in the baby but may also result in a decrease in umbilical arterial blood pH. Hyperinsulinism in the fetus can occur when women receive more than 25 g glucose intravenously during labour. This can result in neonatal hypoglycaemia and raised levels of blood lactate. Furthermore, the excessive use of salt-free intravenous solutions can result in serious hyponatraemia in both the mother and the fetus.

The use of intravenous infusion of glucose and fluids to combat ketosis and dehydration in the mother may thus have potentially serious unwanted effects on the baby. These potential hazards might be obviated by the more physiological approach of using the oral route for supplying calories and fluids during labour.

2.2.2 *Pharmacological approaches* The frequency of unpredictably large volumes and equally unpredictable low pH values of the gastric contents, whether women fast or do not fast during labour, has led to the deployment of a number of agents in an attempt both to lower the gastric volume and to decrease the gastric acidity of labouring women.

An increase in the rate of gastric emptying can be achieved with both cimetidine and metoclopramide, and this results in quite striking decreases in gastric volume, as shown in controlled comparisons of cimetidine and antacids.

The stomach contents can be emptied mechanically with a stomach tube, or vomiting can be induced with apomorphine pre-operatively. A comparison of these two methods for women in labour who required a general anaesthetic showed no statistically significant difference in the mean gastric aspirate during operation. The majority of the women having the stomach tube passed found it 'very unpleasant', whereas the majority of those receiving apomorphine found the procedure only 'slightly unpleasant'. It should be noted that neither method guarantees that the stomach will be empty.

The results of controlled trials have shown that gastric pH can be raised prior to delivery by the use of aluminium hydroxide, magnesium trisilicate, sodium citrate, metoclopramide, and the hydrogen ion antagonist cimetidine. Randomized comparisons between different agents have provided no evidence that any particular agent or class of agents influences gastric pH prior to delivery any more effectively than other agents or classes of agents.

The effectiveness of these agents in raising gastric pH, however, does not necessarily mean that they will have an effect on the incidence or severity of Mendelson's syndrome. Although from 1966 onward there has been a movement towards the routine administration of alkalis to all women in labour, cases of Mendelson's syndrome still occur in women who have had a full regimen of antacid treatment.

3 Maternal position during first stage of labour

Interest in maternal position during the first stage of labour has existed throughout the twentieth century, but until recently there has been relatively little well-controlled research to assess the validity of the various strongly held opinions. At the present time recumbency continues to be a policy in many maternity units, and is required by many of the professionals who provide care during labour. The available data cast doubt on the wisdom of this policy.

3.1 *Effects on blood flow and uterine contractility*

The supine and sitting positions result in a significant reduction in cardiac output. The compression of the lower aorta is not relieved even when the compression of the inferior vena cava is partially relieved by the contracting uterus and by engagement and descent of the fetus into the pelvis. The supine position is associated with a greater decline in femoral than in brachial arterial pressure, which does not occur with the lateral position or when the uterus is tilted to the left. This observation suggests that the supine recumbent position can compromise uterine blood flow during labour.

Contraction intensity is consistently reduced, and contraction frequency often increased, when the labouring woman sits or lies supine after being upright. Standing and lateral recumbency are associated with greater contraction intensity. The efficiency of the contractions (their ability to accomplish cervical dilatation) is also increased by standing and by the lateral position.

The results of several studies suggest that the supine position can adversely affect both the condition of the fetus and the progression of labour, by interference with the uterine blood supply and by compromising the efficiency of uterine contractions. Frequent changes of maternal position may be a way of avoiding the adverse effects of supine recumbency. No evidence derived from controlled studies suggests that the supine position should be encouraged.

3.2 *Effects on the mother and the baby*

The results of controlled trials show that women who were asked to stand, walk, or sit upright during labour had, on the average, shorter labours than women asked to remain in a supine position. Trials in which an upright position was compared with lying on the side showed no striking differences in the length of labour.

In the only trial in which labour was found to be longer in the ambulant than in the non-ambulant group, women in the recumbent group were permitted to get up if they desired and women in the ambulant group were allowed to rest in bed 'whenever they wanted'. Women in the upright group preferred to recline in bed as labour progressed, often at about 5–6 centimetres dilatation.

As might be expected from the shorter labours, women allocated to an upright posture used less narcotic analgesics or epidural anaesthesia, and received fewer oxytocics to augment labour. In part this may because it is easier to administer such drugs to women who are lying in bed. The available data provide no evidence of a consistent effect of position during the first stage of labour on the likelihood of instrumental delivery.

Similarly, there is no consistency of the findings with respect to the condition of the baby. Only one trial reported significantly lower incidences of fetal heart rate abnormalities and depressed Apgar scores associated with an upright position. Other investigators, some of whom used telemetry in conjunction with ambulation, did not detect differences in fetal heart rate patterns or Apgar scores. No information is available about the effect of position during the first stage of labour on more substantive indicators of the babies' wellbeing.

4 Conclusions

No presently known measures can ensure that a labouring woman's stomach is empty, or that her gastric juices will have a pH greater than 2.5. Enforced fasting in labour, the use of antacids, or pre-anaesthetic mechanical or chemical emptying of the stomach are only partially effective. All of these have unpleasant consequences, and are potentially hazardous to the mother and possibly her baby.

The syndrome of aspiration of gastric contents under general anaesthesia is rare but serious. It is wise to avoid general anaesthesia for delivery whenever possible, and to use a proper anaesthetic technique with meticulous attention to the known safeguards when general anaesthesia must be used.

Professional requirements that women remain supine during the first stage of labour are less widespread than they used to be, but they still exist. The available evidence suggests that this policy compromises effective uterine activity, prolongs labour, and leads to an increased use of oxytocics to augment contractions.

31

Monitoring the fetus during labour

This chapter is derived from the chapters by Adrian Grant (54) and Robert Bryce, Fiona Stanley, and Eve Blair (76) in EFFECTIVE CARE IN PREGNANCY AND CHILDBIRTH.

---

1 Introduction

The aim of monitoring the fetus during labour is to identify fetal problems which, if uncorrected, might cause death or short-term or long-term morbidity. In theory at least, it should then be possible to avert the adverse outcomes by appropriate and timely treatment.

A variety of methods of monitoring fetal wellbeing have been evaluated in randomized trials. These trials have generated consistent evidence about the effects of alternative methods of monitoring on fetal and maternal outcome, but controversy still remains about how monitoring should be performed and about the appropriate response to an 'abnormal' result.

2 Clinical methods of fetal monitoring during labour

2.1 *Intermittent auscultation of the fetal heart*

Intermittent auscultation of the fetal heart had become the predominant method of monitoring the fetus during labour by the start of the twentieth century. Although some authorities felt that changes in fetal heart rate during contractions might give an earlier warning sign, auscultation was usually performed between contractions. The criteria for 'fetal distress' were a fetal heart rate above 160 or below 100–120, an irregular heart beat, or the passage of fresh meconium. Despite a trend during the 1970s and early 1980s to replace intermittent auscultation by continuous electronic monitoring, intermittent auscultation continues to be widely used.

2.2 *Assessment of the amniotic fluid*

Passage of meconium is associated with an increased risk of intrapartum stillbirth, neonatal death, and various measures of neonatal morbidity, such as low Apgar score or lowered acid–base status. Part, but by no means all, of this association is explained by respiratory problems due to meconium aspiration.

Thick meconium recognized at the onset of labour carries the worst prognosis, and is associated with a five- to sevenfold increased risk of perinatal death. Thick, undiluted meconium also reflects reduced amniotic fluid volume at the onset of labour, which in itself is a significant risk factor. Slight staining of the liquor at the onset of labour probably carries a small increase in risk, but this has been disputed.

Meconium-staining of the fluid at the onset of labour reflects events that occurred prior to the onset of labour. It may be a sign of impaired placental function that exposes the fetus to the risk of hypoxia during labour. Passage of meconium for the first time after the onset of labour is less common, and it seems to carry an associated risk intermediate between heavy and light early passage of meconium. Whatever the degree or time of passage of meconium, the risks associated are increased if fetal heart rate abnormalities are also present.

Because of these associations between liquor status and adverse outcomes, routine assessment of the amniotic fluid in early labour, if necessary by amnioscopy or artificial rupture of the membranes, has been recommended as a screening test for identifying fetuses at increased risk. Unfortunately, no controlled evaluation of such a policy has been reported.

3 Continuous assessment of the fetal heart

The development in 1960 of an electrode that could be attached to the fetal scalp led to a rapid growth in research into the relationship between fetal heart rate changes and events during labour. Various fetal heart rate changes were deemed to indicate 'fetal distress'. Although tachycardia (abnormally rapid fetal heart rate) and bradycardia (abnormally slow fetal heart rate) were classical signs of 'fetal distress', a distinction could be made between constant or 'baseline' bradycardias, which were almost invariably associated with good fetal outcome, and bradycardias which represented a change in rate from a previously higher level. Late fetal heart rate decelerations, which were thought to be due to uteroplacental insufficiency, and variable decelerations, which were ascribed to umbilical cord compression, could be differentiated.

Continuous electronic fetal heart monitoring during labour is now most commonly achieved either 'externally' by Doppler ultrasound, or 'internally' by electrocardiography. Doppler ultrasound provides the most reliable method for monitoring the fetal heart rate during late pregnancy and for external monitoring of the fetal heart rate during labour. Ultrasound fetal heart rate monitors are satisfactory for determining the fetal heart rate, but give a poorer impression of fetal heart rate variability than those which use electrocardiographic and phonocardiographic recording. Additional problems are that a maternal heart rate may occasionally be counted in error (which may lead to an inappropriate diagnosis of fetal distress), and that when the fetus or mother moves the signal may be lost or artefactual, necessitating frequent repositioning of the transducer.

External monitoring is usually employed during early labour, particularly before the membranes have ruptured. In many centres internal monitoring is preferred later in labour because it provides a more reliable trace and allows the mother greater freedom of movement.

4 Fetal scalp blood acid–base assessment

The technique of sampling blood from the fetal scalp for assessment of the acid–base status during labour was first described in the early 1960s. A scalpel or stylette is passed through the cervix to make a small incision in the fetal scalp. A sample of blood is then collected in a capillary tube and analysed to determine its acid–base status. The technique has changed little since it was first described, and remains somewhat cumbersome and time-consuming.

5 Current approaches to fetal monitoring

The two broad approaches to fetal monitoring currently practised are, first, the use of electronic monitoring in as high a proportion of women as possible, and second, its use restricted to women whose pregnancies are deemed to be at high risk.

There is no question that continuous electronic fetal heart rate monitoring provides more information than intermittent auscultation with a fetal stethoscope. Listening for a minute every fifteen minutes between contractions, as is commonly employed with intermittent auscultation during the first stage of labour, samples the fetal heart rate for only about 7 per cent of the time, and provides relatively little information about the relationship between changes in the fetal heart rate and uterine contractions, or about fetal heart rate variability. The question is whether the increased information provided by continuous electronic monitoring during labour leads to any improvement in outcome.

Although continuous electronic fetal heart monitoring gives a substantially more accurate measurement of the fetal heart rate, the interpretation of fetal heart rate traces is open to great variation. Tracings are often interpreted differently, not only by different obstetricians, but also by the same obstetrician at a later time. The problem with electronic fetal heart monitoring is not with its ability to measure, but in its interpretation.

6 Comparison of auscultation and electronic fetal monitoring

6.1 *Effects on the mother*

Nine randomized controlled trials comparing different methods of intrapartum fetal heart rate monitoring, involving over 17 000 women, have been reported. Operative delivery rates were higher in all the intensively monitored groups, with a typical increase of about one third, regardless of whether fetal blood pH estimate was available. With the use of fetal pH assessment, the *type* of operative delivery was modified, with less of an increase in the use of caesarean delivery, and greater use of instrumental vaginal delivery. The higher operative delivery rates in the electronically monitored groups are reflected in somewhat higher rates of maternal infection postpartum.

One concern about the use of continuous electronic monitoring (without telemetry) has been the possibility that it prolongs labour by restricting women's movement. In those trials for which data are available, the results suggest that this is not the case. Neither is there any clear effect of the fetal monitoring method on the use of epidural analgesia.

6.2 *Effects on the fetus and neonate*

The 61 perinatal deaths that occurred among the 17 000 births in the trials of electronic fetal heart monitoring with fetal pH estimation when indicated were evenly distributed between the electronically monitored and control groups, but because of the small number of deaths a differential effect can not be ruled out. Only nine of the deaths occurred during labour. There is a suggestion in the largest trial that continuous monitoring was associated with fewer deaths due to 'asphyxia' and more due to 'trauma'. This observation is based on small numbers of deaths, but it is plausible given the extra forceps deliveries in the electronically monitored group and the known association between forceps delivery and intracranial trauma.

There is no evidence that intensive fetal heart rate monitoring, with or without fetal pH estimation, reduces the risk of low Apgar score, or the rates of admission to special-care nurseries.

The one measure of neonatal outcome that does seem to be improved by more intensive intrapartum monitoring is neonatal seizures. This effect seems to be restricted to electronic fetal monitoring backed by fetal pH estimation, and the odds of neonatal seizures appear to be reduced by about half. A secondary analysis of the largest trial suggested that the reduced risk of neonatal seizures was limited to labours that were induced or augmented with oxytocin, or that were prolonged. No effect was seen in preterm babies, and so the estimated protective effect is even greater in the term babies.

The finding of a 50 per cent reduction in the risk of neonatal seizures associated with continuous monitoring of the fetal heart and fetal acid–base estimation is potentially very important: between a quarter and a third of babies who suffer neonatal seizures die, and a further quarter to a third are seriously impaired in childhood. Based on the follow-up data available, however, the neonatal seizures prevented by intensive monitoring do not appear to be those associated with long-term impairment. No difference was found in the incidence of major neurological impairment between the electronically monitored and intermittently auscultated groups, and this finding is consistent with other evidence.

Neonatal infection was uncommon in all the trials, but there is no evidence to suggest that intensive monitoring increased this risk. The data are insufficient to explore differences between types of electrode in this respect.

6.3 *Maternal opinions*

Most studies of women's opinions of intrapartum fetal monitoring have been uncontrolled surveys of their views. These surveys suggest that continuous monitoring is acceptable to most women, but that it can also have important adverse consequences for some.

Many women interviewed in these surveys reported that continuous monitoring and recording of the fetal heart rate was reassuring because it demonstrated that the baby was alive, and provided the information that caregivers need during labour. These feelings are enhanced if women are given a clear view of the monitor during labour. Women at relatively high risk of problems during labour, and those most knowledgeable about continuous monitoring, seem most likely to be reassured. Detailed information given just prior to the start of labour, however, appears to have little positive effect on women's perceptions of intrapartum monitoring.

Continuous electronic monitoring of the fetal heart rate can generate anxiety in a number of ways that cannot be predicted in advance for individual women. Some women interviewed in the surveys reported discomfort and restriction of movement, or worries that an electrode would damage the baby's scalp. Others found the monitor a distraction that interfered with their relationships with caregivers and/or companion in labour.

The trace may become worrying, and this may be particularly disquieting if there is uncertainty about the significance of the 'abnormality' amongst those giving care. It may be of poor quality or even artefactual, or the monitor itself may malfunction, sometimes repeatedly. An external abdominal transducer may become displaced or a scalp electrode detached. These problems are not uncommon events in a labour ward, particularly if there is a policy of universal electronic monitoring.

How much weight should be given to the various maternal views of electronic fetal heart rate monitoring revealed in these uncontrolled surveys? A subsample of 200 women who took part in the large trial conducted in Dublin were interviewed after delivery. No difference between the trial groups was detected in respect of the proportions of women who reported 'worries or anxieties' during labour, or that labour had been 'unpleasant'. Electronic monitoring appeared to increase the chances of a woman's being left alone during labour, but nearly all women interviewed reported that they were able to get in touch with a nurse or doctor at any time. In line with the observational studies, more women in the continuously monitored group felt 'too restricted' during labour.

7 Other methods of fetal monitoring and diagnosis in labour

7.1 Intrapartum fetal stimulation tests

Fetal heart rate acceleration is commonly accepted as an indicator of fetal wellbeing in antepartum non-stress testing. These accelerations in a non-stress test are commonly associated with fetal movements or uterine contractions, but may be evoked by other stimuli such as sound. The observations that fetal heart rate acceleration sometimes coincided with fetal scalp blood sampling, and that scalp blood pH tended to be normal if an acceleration occurred, prompted a prospective study using 'firm digital pressure on the head followed by a gentle pinch of the scalp with an atraumatic clamp'. Response (by fetal heart rate acceleration) to either of these stimuli was associated with a scalp blood pH of greater than or equal to 7.19. Of the fetuses which showed no response, about 40 per cent had pH estimations below 7.19. A study using sound stimulation by an 'electronic artificial larynx' placed over the fetal head had broadly similar results. Fetal heart rate acceleration in response to sound stimulation was associated with fetal pH values greater than 7.25.

These studies require replication. If their results are confirmed, fetal stimulation tests could be very useful. They could reduce the need for scalp blood sampling, or be used as an alternative when scalp sampling is either not available or technically impossible. On the basis of currently available evidence a non-reactive stimulation test should be followed by fetal scalp blood acid–base estimation.

7.2 The admission test

Intrapartum fetal distress commonly reflects problems which predate the onset of labour. For this reason there is a strong case for careful risk assessment at the beginning of labour.

A short (15–20 minute) period of external electronic fetal heart monitoring on admission in labour has been recommended as a screening test for women who otherwise are deemed to be at low risk. The rationale for this practice is that it would identify a subgroup of fetuses who would benefit from more intensive monitoring, and might identify major fetal problems that would be missed by intermittent auscultation.

The acoustic stimulation test mentioned above also appears to be useful as a basis for further categorizing the group with equivocal admission tests. In one study the minority with an abnormal acoustic stimulation test were at high risk of developing fetal distress.

A screening test on admission in labour used as a basis for deciding on selective intensive monitoring is attractive in principle because it should identify the 'prevalent' cases of fetal distress in fetuses which embark on labour in an already compromised state. The results of one study suggest that the admission test would improve the predictive properties of monitoring in this way. This study does not, however, evaluate the other two components of monitoring that must be fulfilled if the policy is to be effective: whether the test is interpreted accurately, and whether it is acted on appropriately when it is used in clinical practice. These questions can only be addressed satisfactorily in randomized controlled trials.

Other methods of fetal monitoring in labour, including fetal electrocardiography, fetal encephalography, and continuous biochemical monitoring, are currently under investigation. They are still fraught with technical difficulties, have been used on only a small number of fetuses, and their utility, if any, remains to be determined.

8 Conservative management of fetal distress

The most common treatment for intrapartum fetal distress, diagnosed by persistent fetal heart rate abnormalities or depressed fetal scalp blood pH, is prompt delivery. Many fetal heart rate abnormalities, however, will resolve with simple conservative measures, such as a change in maternal position (to relieve aorto-caval compression and pressure on the umbilical cord); discontinuation of oxytocin administration to increase utero-placental blood flow; and maternal oxygen administration (to improve oxygen transport to the placenta).

Maternal hypotension often follows the induction of epidural anaesthesia, with consequent fetal heart rate abnormalities. Preloading with intravenous fluids has been shown in a well-conducted trial to counteract the relative hypovolaemia that follows epidural block, and to substantially reduce the frequency of fetal heart rate abnormalities.

Intravenous betamimetics are a useful treatment for 'buying time' when persistent fetal heart rate abnormalities indicate elective delivery. In a randomized controlled trial involving 20 labours characterized by both ominous fetal heart rate changes and a fetal scalp blood pH of less than 7.25, 10 of the 11 treated with intravenous terbutaline showed improvement in the heart rate pattern, compared with none in the control group. At birth, the babies were less likely to be acidotic and to have low Apgar scores. This short-term improvement could be very useful in places where facilities for emergency caesarean section are not immediately available, or to allow time to set up regional anaesthesia. The improvement in the trace pattern is sometimes sustained. In these circumstances, labour can be allowed to continue without further intervention.

Another temporizing manoeuvre, amnioinfusion to correct oligohydramnios, has been described as a measure to deal with variable deceleration patterns, a fetal heart rate abnormality often considered to be due to cord compression. Saline is infused through an intrauterine catheter into the uterine cavity, either until the variable decelerations have resolved, or until 800 ml have been infused. In a randomized controlled trial involving almost a hundred women, variable decelerations persisted in less than half of the amnioinfusion group compared with almost all in the control group. Neonatal outcome was similar in the two groups.

A third approach to the conservative treatment of persistent fetal distress has been to 'treat' the fetus to prevent any adverse effects. Piracetam, a derivative of gamma-aminobenzoic acid, is thought to promote the metabolism of the brain cells when they are hypoxic. It has been evaluated in a single placebo-controlled trial. The results suggest that piracetam treatment reduces the need for caesarean section, and improves neonatal outcome as judged by the Apgar score and neonatal 'respiratory problems, and signs of hypoxia'.

9 Conclusions

Amniotic fluid which is sparse or contains meconium is associated with an increased risk of perinatal mortality and morbidity. The status of the liquor when the membranes have ruptured spontaneously should be assessed early in labour and the presence of meconium or low liquor volume should prompt more intensive fetal surveillance. Whether or not routine amnioscopy or artificial rupture of the membranes to assess the liquor is justified is not clear from the available evidence.

Evidence from the randomized comparisons of different methods of fetal heart rate monitoring, particularly the large trial conducted in Dublin, suggests that intrapartum death is equally effectively prevented by either intermittent auscultation or continuous electronic fetal heart rate monitoring, provided that importance is attached to the prompt recognition of intrapartum fetal heart rate abnormalities, whatever the monitoring policy adopted. (During the two years of the Dublin trial, for example, the intrapartum death rate was lower than in the preceding and following years.)

The reliability of intermittent auscultation may be increased by the use of hand-held ultrasound monitors when heart sounds are difficult to hear with a conventional stethoscope. There are arguments for always using these devices, partly because they may cause less maternal discomfort than a stethoscope. Compliance with intermittent auscultation should be straightforward if a caregiver has responsibility for only one woman during labour. Such individualized attention is likely to have other benefits for a woman, and it is to be deplored that current staffing and other policies for intrapartum care in many delivery wards make this ideal impossible to meet. The implication is that auscultation may not be performed as frequently or regularly as it should be to provide safe fetal monitoring.

The complexity of continuous electronic monitoring makes it susceptible to technical and mechanical failures. Machine maintenance and replacement and in-service training of personnel are therefore important. Electronic fetal monitoring may also provide suboptimal surveillance if it reduces the frequency with which the caregiver formally checks the fetal heart rate. A fetal heart monitor should be an adjunct to, not a substitute for, personal care.

The wide variation in the interpretation of continuous fetal heart rate records, even amongst 'experts', demonstrates that this is a major problem with current methods of continuous monitoring. The evidence suggests that not only false positives (false alarms) but also false negatives are reduced by the use of fetal blood sampling as an adjunct to fetal heart rate monitoring. Despite its practical problems, fetal acid–base assessment is, on the basis of current evidence, an essential adjunct to fetal heart rate monitoring, and should be much more widely used during the second stage as well as the first stage of labour.

The policy implications of the review of the randomized comparisons of continuous electronic monitoring and intermittent auscultation will depend on the importance that the reader attaches to the observed reduction in the risk of neonatal seizures. Limited follow-up of the children in the Dublin trial who suffered neonatal seizures suggests that the neonatal seizures which are potentially preventable by more intensive monitoring, are *not* associated with long-term problems. Nevertheless, some people will consider that neonatal seizures are sufficiently important in their own right for their prevention to form the basis for current policy. On this basis, there is a good case for using more intensive monitoring when labour ceases to be 'physiological', for example, during induction or augmentation of labour if labour is prolonged, if there is meconium-staining of the liquor, or with multiple pregnancy.

For the majority of labours for which no such indications apply, the current evidence suggests that more intensive monitoring increases obstetric intervention with no clear benefit for the fetus. Regular auscultation by a personal attendant, as used in the randomized trials, therefore seems to be the policy of choice in these labours. Such a policy will be difficult to reimplement in the many hospitals whose current policy is universal electronic monitoring. Firstly, individualized care during labour is often perceived as not possible; and secondly, midwives and others have lost the ability and confidence to monitor labour by intermittent auscultation.

The choice of technique for fetal heart monitoring has much wider ramifications than the direct effects on the physical health of fetus and mother. Depending on the prevailing system of care for women during childbirth, it may influence the roles and relationships of those involved. With intermittent auscultation the midwife is the centre of caregiving, with the obstetrician playing a consultative role when the midwife is worried that there may be problems. In contrast, use of continuous electronic monitoring changes the delivery room into an intensive care unit. The midwife takes on a more technical role, with obstetricians becoming more centrally involved in routine care. The presence of a monitor may also change the relationships between the woman and her partner on the one hand, and the woman, midwife, and doctor on the other. These wider implications must be recognized.

Monitoring the progress of labour

This chapter is derived from the chapter by Caroline Crowther, Murray Enkin, Marc J. N. C. Keirse, and Ian Brown (53) in EFFECTIVE CARE IN PREGNANCY AND CHILDBIRTH

1 Introduction

Labour, the culmination of pregnancy, is a special time both emotionally and physically for each woman. It is a time of intense physical activity, stress, and pain, and it may prove to be a time of overt or hidden danger. The care that a woman receives during labour should not only help her to cope with the effort, stress, and pain, but should minimize or remove the danger as well.

The purpose of monitoring progress in labour is to recognize incipient problems, so that their development into serious problems may be prevented. Prolonged labour is strongly associated with several adverse outcomes. It can lead to maternal exhaustion, perinatal asphyxia, and even death. Thus the anticipation of prolonged labour cannot be considered a trivial issue, as inefficient uterine action can be corrected and some adverse outcomes can be prevented. This monitoring must be carried out with thought and consideration, rather than as an unthinking routine or a procrustean attempt to make all women fit predetermined criteria of so-called normality.

2 Recognition of the onset of labour

The diagnosis of labour is usually a self-diagnosis made by the woman on the basis of painful, regular contractions. Sometimes she will make the diagnosis after a show of mucus or blood, or after rupture of the membranes. On admission to hospital the diagnosis of labour may, or may not, be confirmed by the professional staff.

One of the most important decisions in care in labour is to recognize whether or not labour has started. True labour must be differentiated from false labour. The clinical diagnosis of active labour is easy when 'pains' plus progress in cervical dilatation are present. To confirm or deny the diagnosis of labour in a patient self-admitted as 'in labour' is much more difficult when the cervix is uneffaced and closed.

Labour is, by definition, the presence of regular uterine contractions, leading to progressive effacement and dilatation of the cervix, and ultimately to the delivery of the baby. While there is no difficulty in confirming the presence of labour when it is strong and well established, the diagnosis is never as clear-cut as this definition would suggest. The time of onset of labour is not always precisely known, and at least two assessments are required to establish whether or not progressive effacement and dilatation of the cervix is occurring.

In spite of the difficulties in establishing reliably that labour has started, the most convenient and most used marker of the onset of labour (although an arbitrary rather than a biologically correct starting point), is the time when the woman is admitted to hospital in labour. This serves as a semi-objective surrogate index of the onset of labour, and is a practical starting point from which subsequent progress can be monitored.

The point in labour at which a woman presents herself for admission to hospital will vary from woman to woman. Several factors may influence her decision about when to go to the hospital, including the way she feels, her expectations of labour, her anxiety about arriving too early or too late, and any complications that may have arisen. It will also depend on the advice that she has been given as to how and when she should recognize herself to be in labour and when to come to the hospital, which in turn will depend on the admission policy of each maternity unit.

All of these factors will affect when a woman is admitted to hospital, and hence the apparent length of her labour. The timing of hospital admission may have important consequences for the progress of labour. Studies show that although the women who come to hospital early have a shorter total length of labour than those admitted in more advanced labour, they have more diagnoses of 'difficult labour' recorded, and receive more intrapartum interventions and more caesarean sections. They also have a longer postpartum hospital stay than women who are admitted later in labour.

It is unlikely that any universal 'best' time for hospital admission in labour will be determined. For most women, the 'best' time is when they feel that they would be happier or more comfortable in hospital.

3 Condition of the mother

The physical and mental state, and the comfort and wellbeing of the woman must be just as carefully monitored during labour as the progress of contractions or the state of the cervix. The possible causes of symptoms such as nausea, dyspnoea, or dizziness should be fully assessed, and treatment provided if necessary. Fear can be allayed and stress alleviated by the presence of companions and competent, caring staff. The intensity of pain she experiences will determine her need for, and the timing of, pain relief.

Adequate attention must be paid to her general condition, and in most circumstances this will include, at least, assessment of her blood-pressure, pulse, and temperature. Although such assessments have become traditional, there is little agreement as to how frequently they should be performed. The value, if any, of frequent assessments of pulse and blood-pressure in normal labour to screen for problems such as intrapartum pre-eclampsia is unknown. It is likely to be small. In the presence of known or suspected abnormality (such as antepartum or intrapartum haemorrhage, or pre-eclampsia), such assessments 'should be made as frequently as necessary, or even continuously, rather than being dictated by the regulations of a rigid scheme that is applied to all women. It is questionable whether any useful purpose is served by routine repeated observations of these parameters in healthy women in apparently normal labour.

4 Uterine contractions

Labour is initiated, and progress maintained, by the contractions of the uterus. Almost always the woman herself is aware of the contractions, their frequency, their duration, and their strength. These parameters can be confirmed by abdominal palpation. Self-report by the woman, supplemented by abdominal examination when required, is quite sufficient to monitor the contractions adequately in most situations.

Abdominal palpation cannot, however, accurately quantify the changes in uterine pressure resulting from the contraction, and this constraint also applies to the record of uterine contractions made by an external tocodynamometer. It may provide an accurate record of the frequency, and, to a lesser extent, of the duration of contractions; but not of their intensity. The latter information can be important when progress in labour is slow, and augmentation of the strength of contractions is considered.

No study has demonstrated improvements in the outcome of labour by the use of more sophisticated measurements of uterine activity. If labour progress is considered abnormal because the cervix does not adequately efface or dilate, the precise information on uterine activity that can be obtained from intrauterine pressure recording may enable better evaluation of the problem, and may provide a means of monitoring changes in uterine activity in response to treatment. Although theoretically reasonable, these postulated benefits have not been demonstrated by prospective controlled trials.

5 Cervical dilatation

The rate of dilatation of the cervix is the most exact measure of the progress of labour. Cervical dilatation is usually estimated in centimetres, from 0 cm when closed to 10 cm at full dilatation. Assessment of cervical dilatation is not, however, as precise as one would like to believe. To our knowledge, no studies of either inter-observer or intra-observer variation have been reported, but personal experience has shown substantial variations in estimates by different observers in the same situation, and even by the same observer on repeat examination.   There is no clear guidance from the literature as to the most accurate time to assess the dilatation in relation to a contraction, but consistency of the time of observation is probably important when assessing progress.

Cervical dilatation and effacement can be assessed directly by vaginal examination or indirectly by rectal examination. Rectal examinations were advocated toward the end of the nineteenth century in the belief that, unlike vaginal examinations, they did not cause contamination of the genital tract. Several studies comparing vaginal and rectal examinations were made in the United States from the mid-1950s to the 1960s. All showed a similar incidence of puerperal infection whether rectal or vaginal examinations were employed during labour. Women's preference for vaginal rather than rectal examinations was clearly demonstrated in a randomized clinical trial.

On the basis of these studies, vaginal examinations have become standard practice for the assessment of cervical dilatation during labour, although a few units have continued the use of rectal examination for assessment. Overall, the available evidence suggests that rectal examinations have no place in monitoring the progress of labour.

In many units masks are worn when vaginal examinations are performed, but there is no evidence that they are of any benefit. In view of the fact that masks have not been shown to be of value during vaginal surgery or in the delivery room it is highly unlikely that any infections are prevented by this practice.

The recommended frequency of vaginal examinations to assess the progress of cervical dilatation varies greatly among units and in the literature. This variation illustrates the lack of consensus for the optimal timing of vaginal examinations in labour. Like all assessments in labour, it would seem most sensible that the number and timing of vaginal examinations should be frequent enough to permit adequate assessment of progress and to detect any problems promptly, but no more frequent than is necessary to accomplish this end.

6 Descent of the presenting part

If the head is presenting, its relationship to the brim of the pelvis can be determined by abdominal or vaginal examination. Descent can be estimated abdominally by determining the amount of the baby's head that is still above the pelvic brim. Abdominal assessment avoids the need for vaginal examination, and is not influenced by the presence of a caput succedaneum or moulding. On vaginal examination the level of the presenting part can be related to the ischial spines. Moulding of the fetal head, an important observation in following the progress of labour if cephalopelvic disproportion is suspected, can also be determined by vaginal examination. Given the additional information that can be obtained, it would seem reasonable that both methods of examination should be carried out before operative delivery is undertaken.

7 Normal labour

Normal labour can be defined either in terms of the total length of labour, or as a rate of progress of cervical dilatation (usually expressed in cm per hour). The latter measure is clinically more useful, as the total length of labour can only be known in retrospect.

A rate of 1 cm per hour in the active phase of labour is commonly accepted as the cut-off between normal and abnormal labour. The validity of this can certainly be challenged. Many women who show slower rates of cervical dilatation proceed to normal and uneventful delivery. A rate of 0.5 cm per hour may be more appropriate as a lower limit for defining normal progress; but this too should be interpreted with discretion, in the context of the woman's total wellbeing.

8 Recording the progress of labour

When monitoring the progress of labour, recording the findings is almost as important as making the assessments. The primary reasons for doing so are to make the degree of progress readily apparent, so that problems will be recognized early, and to facilitate transfer of information to other caregivers. Several methods of recording measures of progress are in current use.

A time-based diary of events permits a detailed documentation of all important maternal and fetal assessments, but the recording and inspection of such a record can be tedious. It is often difficult to follow, particularly when labour is prolonged or when there is a change of staff. A more structured representation of events and progress can facilitate early recognition of potentially correctable problems.

The partogram, a structured graphical representation of the progress of labour, has been adopted in many units throughout the world. In addition to the graph depicting cervical dilatation in relation to time, space can be provided for notes on the frequency of contractions, medications, the fetal heart rate, and other important events. With the use of a partogram the progress of labour can be seen at a glance on one sheet of paper, failure to progress can be readily recognized, and the writing of lengthy descriptions can be avoided. It is simple to use, a practical teaching aid, and is an efficient means of exchange of technical information about labour progress between teams of caregivers.

9 Conclusions

The wellbeing of the mother as well as that of the fetus must be carefully monitored during labour. This monitoring does not necessarily require the use of special equipment, but it always requires careful and individualized observation.

Monitoring the progress of labour requires more than the assessment of uterine contractions and cervical dilatation. The rate of progress must be considered in the context of the woman's total wellbeing, rather than as simply a physical phenomenon. A dilatation rate of 1 cm per hour in a woman who is having strong contractions and is in severe distress is far more worrying than a rate of 0.3 cm per hour in a woman who is comfortable, walking around, drinking cups of tea, and chatting with her companions.

Vaginal rather than rectal examination should be used to assess the progress of labour, but no more often than is deemed necessary. Slow progress should alert one to the possibility of abnormal labour, but should not automatically result in intervention.

33

Prolonged labour

This chapter is derived from the chapters by Caroline Crowther, Murray Enkin, Marc J. N. C. Keirse, and Ian Brown (53); and Marc J. N. C. Keirse (58) in EFFECTIVE CARE IN PREGNANCY AND CHILDBIRTH.

1 Introduction

Slow progress in labour does not necessarily mean abnormal labour or the presence of a problem. It should, however, alert to the potential or possibility of a problem. Slow progress in the first stage of labour can occur in either the latent or the active phase.

2 Prolonged labour

2.1 *Prolonged latent phase*

The latent phase of labour, from the start of uterine contractions until progressive effacement and dilatation of the cervix commences, is poorly understood. As this phase usually starts before the woman is admitted to hospital, the precise time of onset is often difficult to determine. The duration of the latent phase varies so greatly from woman to woman that a normal range is virtually impossible to define.

According to some studies, a prolonged latent phase is not associated with increased perinatal morbidity, mortality, or other adverse outcome. Other studies have shown a significantly higher incidence of caesarean section and lower 5-minute Apgar scores in both primigravidae and multigravidae with a prolonged latent phase. Whether these adverse effects were due to the underlying condition or were the result of a treatment policy of amniotomy and oxytocin stimulation is uncertain.

One of the major problems in care is differentiating between a prolonged latent phase and false labour. Unfortunately, this distinction can only be made in retrospect. It has been suggested that, if no progress in effacement or cervical dilatation occurs within 4 hours after admission, the woman should be given 100 mg pethidine for analgesia and sedation. If at 8 hours she is still in the latent phase with no progress, amniotomy and oxytocin is advised. No trials of this approach have been carried out. There is an urgent need for controlled studies about this common, distressing, and poorly understood problem in labour, its aetiology, its significance, and the best policy of care.

2.2 Prolonged active phase

Slow progress or failure to progress in the active phase of labour has been defined either as an overall measurement (for example, longer than 'x' hours), or as a rate related measurement (for example, a rate of cervical dilatation of less than 'y' cm per hour). It should be noted that the commonly cited 12-hour duration of the active phase is roughly equivalent to a rate of 0.5 cm per hour, half as fast as the 1 cm per hour that is also commonly used.

Deviation from this arbitrarily defined 'normal' rate of dilatation is an indication for consideration rather than for intervention.

Cephalopelvic disproportion must be considered when progress in labour is slow. Efficient uterine action must be assured, as otherwise cephalopelvic disproportion cannot be excluded. If gross cephalopelvic disproportion or marked moulding of the fetal skull is present, a caesarean section is necessary.

3 Treatment of prolonged labour

Protracted labour has been recognized as a problem for centuries, and a bewildering variety of treatments have been proposed to correct the condition. The assumption underlying all these treatments is that in some way 'inadequate' progress is bad, and that 'something should be done about it'. In recent decades proposed remedies have included homoeopathic medications, various spasmolytic drugs, sparteine sulphate, oestrogens, relaxin, caulophyllum, dimenhydrate, nipple stimulation, intracervical injections of hyaluronidase, vibration of the cervix, and acupuncture. The most commonly used measures today are amniotomy and intravenous oxytocin infusion.

Many factors can influence myometrial contractility and the progress of labour. Consideration of these factors suggests a number of measures that can help to prevent prolonged labour, and obviate much of the need for augmentation. The presence of a supportive companion, and ambulation during labour, have been shown to result in shorter labours and a lesser use of oxytocics. Less well documented, but generally known to those who provide care in labour, is the observation that uterine contractility tends to subside when a women is taken from home to the hospital. More often than not, allowing her and her companion(s) the necessary time to settle in and feel at home in the new environment will do more good than a cascade of interventions aimed at procuring so-called 'adequate progress'.

When more active intervention is required, this may consist of measures to increase the power of the uterine contractions, or to reduce the degree of resistance to cervical dilatation and descent of the presenting part.

3.1 Increasing uterine contractility

There is a close relationship between low levels of uterine contractility and slow progress in labour. Treatments to increase uterine contractility may be based either on increasing the endogenous production of prostaglandins by amniotomy, or the administration of uterine stimulants, such as exogenous oxytocin or prostaglandins.

3.1.1 *Amniotomy*   Artificial rupture of the membranes has been used to augment labour for decades, but whether the procedure confers more benefit than harm is still undetermined. Increases in uterine activity following amniotomy have been demonstrated by the use of intrauterine pressure measurements before and after amniotomy, and data from the few trials that have addressed the subject indicate that labours progress more quickly if the membranes are ruptured than if they are left intact.

None of the reported studies specifically addressed the question of whether or not amniotomy is effective in augmenting slow or prolonged labour, and to the best of our knowledge this issue has never been addressed in a randomized controlled trial. Given the evidence that is available from the controlled trials in spontaneous labour, and from the data on induction of labour, it is highly likely that amniotomy would enhance progress in prolonged labour as well.

The effects of amniotomy during spontaneous labour on other labour and delivery outcomes, such as use of oxytocics to augment labour, malrotation of the fetal head to occipito-lateral or occipito-posterior positions, and operative delivery, have been reported in only two controlled trials; the small amount of data does not allow firm conclusions to be reached about the effects of amniotomy on any of these outcomes.

A variety of adverse effects of amniotomy have been postulated. It has been suggested that increased pressure differentials around the fetal skull, combined with a reduction in amniotic fluid volume after amniotomy, predispose to fetal skull deformity, an increased incidence of early decelerations in fetal heart rate, and acidosis of the infant at birth. Unfortunately, the studies that purport to show these harmful effects of amniotomy on the fetus and neonate are subject to considerable selection bias, and do not permit an adequate assessment of the effects of amniotomy during labour on fetal or neonatal wellbeing.

Only one of the randomized trials reported thus far provides unbiased estimates of the effects of amniotomy during spontaneous labour on fetal and neonatal outcomes. From the data provided in this study there is no evidence of any significant effect, but the number of women included in the trial was so small that only dramatic differences would have been uncovered.

3.1.2 *Oxytocin* Intravenous infusion of synthetic oxytocin, usually after either spontaneous or artificial rupture of the membranes, is the most widely applied treatment to expedite labour when progress is deemed to be inadequate. Despite this, there is very little evidence about the effects of oxytocin from controlled trials.

Only three controlled trials provide data on the length of labour when intravenous oxytocin infusion was used to expedite labour in cases of poor progress, and only two of these show a shorter mean duration in women allocated to early oxytocin augmentation compared with controls. In the third trial, in which women in the control group were encouraged to get up and to move around, stand, or sit as they wished, the mean duration of labour was slightly shorter in the control group than in the augmented group.

The available data on the rate of cervical dilatation show a similar pattern, with a trend towards a slightly faster rate of dilatation when oxytocin was compared with recumbent controls, but a slower rate than controls when ambulation was prescribed in the control group.

In each of the controlled trials a high proportion of the women assigned to be controls ultimately received oxytocin for subsequent failure of adequate progress in labour (as defined by the authors). These studies thus indicate that many women who are not primarily treated with oxytocin for inadequate progress will still require an oxytocin infusion before delivery.

Active management of labour with liberal use of amniotomy and oxytocin augmentation has been reputed to be instrumental in achieving low caesarean section rates. This may well be the case, but it has not been not demonstrated by the results of the published trials. Unfortunately, the total number of women included in these trials is too small to give a clear indication of the effect of oxytocin augmentation on the caesarean section rate. For the same reason, the effects of labour augmentation on instrumental vaginal delivery are still undetermined.

Neither Apgar scores nor the incidence of admission to a special-care nursery were detectably different between oxytocin augmentation and control groups in the trials that reported on these outcomes. No other categorical data on infant outcomes are available from controlled trials.

Only one of the studies sought women's views on the augmentation procedures. Over half of the women asked about their opinion on the oxytocin treatment said that it was unpleasant and indicated that they would like to try without the drug when next giving birth. Over 80 per cent felt that it had increased the amount of pain that they had experienced, whereas less than 20 per cent of the women in the ambulant group felt that walking about had increased their pain.

From the data available thus far, it does not appear that liberal use of oxytocin augmentation in labour is of benefit to the women and babies so treated. This does not imply that there is no place for oxytocin augmentation in slow progress of labour. It does suggest, however, that other simple measures, such as allowing the woman freedom to move around, and to eat and drink as she pleases, may be at least as effective and certainly more pleasant for a sizeable proportion of women considered to be in need of augmentation of labour.

Situations will undoubtedly remain in which pharmacological augmentation will be necessary to correct inadequate uterine activity, in order to prevent maternal exhaustion and risks of fetal and maternal infection. Logic would dictate that, in such circumstances, the smallest effective drug dose should be given, in the most effective manner. As individual sensitivity to oxytocin varies greatly from woman to woman, oxytocin titration by means of an intravenous infusion is the treatment of choice. It is less clear, however, what the initial dose should be, how large the increments should be, and at what interval they should be implemented. Few data are available to answer these questions. Insufficient doses will result in an unacceptably long time to achieve an adequate response, while excessive doses will result in hyperstimulation.

Slow progress in cervical dilatation is not necessarily due to subnormal levels of uterine activity. The level of activity that is needed both to ensure adequate progress and to avoid hyperstimulation has not yet been established. A major additional factor in the rate of progress of labour is the amount of resistance that must be overcome.

3.2 *Influencing resistance*

Between a third and a half of women with slow progress in labour have levels of uterine activity usually judged to be adequate. One way to overcome this would be the use of high doses of oxytocin, to augment uterine activity to levels well in excess of those encountered during normal spontaneous labour. A more logical approach would be to reduce resistance.

Three methods to influence resistance directly or indirectly in order to accelerate cervical dilatation have been tested in controlled trials: the use of intravenous or intramuscular porcine relaxin; local cervical injections of hyalouronidase; and cervical vibration. The trials did not demonstrate any advantage from the use of these modalities. Observational studies, however, have suggested that vibration may be useful when cervical dilatation is not achieved despite satisfactory uterine activity and the absence of cephalopelvic disproportion, and that it appears to be safe. Evaluation awaits a controlled trial of adequate size.

Despite the fact that their use would seem reasonable, measures to reduce soft-tissue resistance have not been adequately explored.

4 Conclusions

Attention devoted to the prevention of prolonged labour is at least as worth while as the attention which is usually devoted to its cure. Measures that have been demonstrated to be effective include allowing women to move about as they please and the provision of friendly support. Both of these may be seen as characteristics of a welcoming environment without unnecessary prohibitions and restrictions.

Slow progress or lack of progress in the first stage of labour does not necessarily result from a lower level of uterine contractility than that seen in normally progressing labours. It may be due to a higher resistance in the soft parts of the birth canal or to cephalo-pelvic disproportion. It will often be necessary to ensure that adequate uterine contractility exists, if necessary by oxytocic stimulation, in order to differentiate these dissimilar mechanisms.

Approximately half of the women judged to have slow labour or poor progress in cervical dilatation will progress equally well whether or not oxytocic drugs are administered. When augmentation becomes necessary, the first approach should be to rupture the membranes. The data that are available suggest that amniotomy will shorten the length of spontaneous labour, and that it may forestall the need for oxytocin infusion in some of these women. The combination of amniotomy with oxytocin may provide a better stimulation of labour than oxytocin alone.

There is no evidence that high and rapidly escalating doses of oxytocin confer any advantage over a more moderate approach in which small doses are increased at half-hourly intervals in response to uterine contractility. The risks of hyperstimulation and increased pain are greater with larger doses of oxytocin.

Other methods for augmenting uterine activity, including the use of prostaglandins, are certainly worth considering, but they have been inadequately explored up to the present time.

In view of the importance of labour progress and the amount of discomfort that slow progress can provoke in the woman, the fetus, and the caregivers, it is important that the many suggested guidelines for care should be substantiated by solid research evidence.

34

Control of pain in labour

This chapter is derived from the chapters by Penny Simkin (56) and Kay Dickersin (57) in EFFECTIVE CARE IN PREGNANCY AND CHILDBIRTH.

1 Non-pharmacological methods

The study of pain transmission and its modulation have produced many exciting findings in the past twenty-five years, and many of these are being applied today in a variety of non-pharmacological approaches to relieve the pain of childbirth. Some of these are a revival of traditional methods, some are newly developed. They can be usefully classified as: techniques that reduce painful stimuli; techniques that activate peripheral sensory receptors; and techniques that enhance descending inhibitory neural pathways. Many of these techniques are taught in antenatal childbirth preparation classes.

1.1 Techniques that reduce painful stimuli

The most obvious solution to the problem of pain is to avoid or reduce the stimuli that cause it. In labour the painful stimuli arise from the uterine contractions or from pressure exerted by the presenting part of the fetus, and cannot be avoided. Techniques to reduce these painful stimuli are at least theoretically possible. This is the designated purpose of various maternal positions, movement, counterpressure, and abdominal decompression.

1.1.1 Maternal movement and position changes
Labouring women find that they experience less pain in some positions than in others, and if left to their own devices, will usually select those positions that are most comfortable to them. Many labouring women today tend to be restricted to bed, either because of cultural expectations, or because of obstetrical practices such as electronic fetal monitoring, intravenous hydration, and medications that render movement out of bed difficult or unsafe.

Despite these restraints, women seem to prefer freedom of movement when it is allowed. Given freedom to assume any position in or out of bed during the course of their labour, without interference or instruction by attendant personnel, labouring women spontaneously adopt upright postures such as sitting, standing, and walking, often tending to return to a recumbent position in advanced labour.

When the mother changes positions, she alters relationships between gravity, the uterine contractions, the fetus, and her pelvis, which may enhance the progress of labour and reduce pain. For example, pressure of the fetal head against the sacroiliac joint may be relieved if the mother moves from a semirecumbent to a 'hands and knees' posture. The effects of maternal position on perceived pain are influenced by a number of factors including fetal size, position, head size and shape, size and shape of the maternal pelvis, and the strength of the uterine contractions. Knowing this, experienced caregivers place trust in the mother's ability to find pain-reducing positions. They try not to restrict women, and encourage them to seek comfort, suggesting possible positions and trusting their judgment.

1.1.2 Counterpressure
Counterpressure consists of steady strong force applied to a spot on the low back during contractions, using one's fist, the 'heel' of the hand, or a firm object. While there are no controlled trials of its effectiveness, it appears to alleviate back pain in some labouring women. It seems to be most effective when a

woman suffers extreme back pain, possibly related to an occiput posterior position.

1.1.3 *Abdominal decompression* Abdominal decompression was introduced in the mid–1950s as a non-pharmacological method for shortening labour and reducing labour pain. It has now largely disappeared from use, partly because of the lack of good evidence that it is beneficial, but also because the decompression apparatus is cumbersome, constrictive, noisy, and uncomfortable.

1.2 *Techniques that activate peripheral sensory receptors*

1.2.1 *Superficial heat and cold* Superficial heat is generated from hot or warm objects, such as hot water bottles, hot moist towels, electric heating pads, heated silica gel packs, warm blankets, baths, and showers. Superficial cold can come from ice bags, blocks of ice, frozen silica gel packs, and towels soaked in cool or ice water.

In addition to possible direct effects on pain perception, several well-known physiological responses elicited by heat and cold indirectly result in pain relief. The therapeutic use of heat and cold, because of their widespread empirical acceptance and low incidence of harmful effects when used reasonably (that is, at temperatures that cause neither burns nor frost damage), have not been evaluated in randomized controlled trials. Observational evidence suggests that they may be effective. The use of hot compresses applied to the low abdomen, groin, or perineum, a warm blanket over the entire body, or ice packs on the low back, anus, or perineum, relieve pain in labour for some women.

As comfort measures, heat and cold are widely accepted, if not fully understood. Because they provide only partial relief from labour pain, they might at best be considered only as an adjunct to other measures.

1.2.2 *Hydrotherapy: baths and showers* Although they are a common household remedy for numerous ailments such as aches and pains, sores and burns, fatigue and tension, baths and showers are not available to many women labouring in hospitals. Most obstetrical units have few such facilities because they were designed and built when women were routinely confined to bed and sufficiently drugged to make bathing impossible. While that remains the case to a large extent today, some new birthing facilities provide bath tubs and showers for labouring women.

The healing and pain-relieving properties of water—hot or cold, flowing or still, sprayed or poured—have been hailed over the centuries. The efficacy of hydrotherapy in reducing labour pain has not been evaluated scientifically. The degree to which showers, baths, or immersion can reduce pain awareness in labour is unknown, although the published observational and cohort studies suggest that it might produce substantial benefits.

Resistance to the idea of immersion in water is prompted by concerns about its safety. There is concern that, if the membranes are ruptured, bacteria in bath water may enter the vagina and uterus, increasing the likelihood of infection. A further concern arises over the comparative inconvenience of monitoring maternal vital signs, contractions, and fetal heart tones with a woman immersed in water or a shower. Although such monitoring is possible, it is less convenient for the staff. The possibility exists that the mother will be unable or unwilling to leave the bath at the time of birth. This has happened on a few occasions, with no detectable untoward effects on mother or baby.

Hyperthermia, another potential risk, can be prevented by periodic checking of maternal vital signs and taking appropriate action.

Controlled trials would be highly desirable, comparing morbidity, length of labour, analgesic use, numbers and types of interventions, and patient satisfaction in groups using and not using hydrotherapy.

1.2.3 *Touch and massage* The use of touch in various forms conveys pain-reducing messages, depending on the quality and circumstances of the touch. A hand placed on a painful spot, a pat of reassurance, stroking hair or a cheek in an affectionate gesture, a tight embrace, or more formal purposeful massage techniques—all communicate to the receiver a message of caring, of wanting to be with and help her. The object of massage is to make people feel better, or to relieve pain and facilitate relaxation.

Massage takes the form of light or firm stroking, vibration, kneading, deep circular pressure, continual steady pressure, and joint manipulation. It can be carried out by using fingertips, entire hands, or various devices which roll, vibrate, or apply pressure. In theory, the various forms of massage stimulate different sensory receptors. When discontinued, the woman's awareness of her pain increases. In addition, the phenomenon of adaptation may diminish the pain-relieving effects of massage over a period of time. Therefore use of intermittent massage, or variation in the type of stroke and location of the touch, may prolong the pain-reducing effects.

None of the touch or massage techniques has been subjected to careful scientific investigation. The apparently harmless intervention is well received by labouring women and easily discontinued if they wish; therefore it seems unlikely to occupy a high priority in anyone's list of research questions.

1.2.4 *Acupuncture and acupressure* Acupuncture consists of the insertion of strategically placed needles in any of more than 365 points along the twelve 'meridians' of the body. Today it is combined with an electrical current, which is believed to augment the pain-relieving effect. The technique of obstetrical acupuncture varies among practitioners in terms of the selection of points, size of needle and method of insertion. Acupuncture appears to block both sensory and emotional components of pain, but the mechanism is poorly understood.

Acupuncture during labour has not been well studied, and no controlled trials have been published, despite indications that it might provide good analgesia. Descriptive studies of acupuncture for relief of pain in labour have given little useful information. The techniques involved in the use of acupuncture are complex and time-consuming, and the use of multiple needles attached to electrical stimulators is inconvenient and immobilizing to the woman.

Acupressure has been called 'acupuncture without needles'. The technique, also called *shiatsu*, involves the application of pressure or deep massage to the traditional acupuncture points, with thumb, fingertip, fingernail, or palm of hand. There are no published reports of its effects, either anecdotal or scientific. Acupressure is easy to learn and can be applied by a non-professional companion of the labouring woman. Formal evaluation of its effectiveness would be worth while to establish its place (if any) as a comfort measure for labour.

1.2.5 *Transcutaneous electrical nerve stimulation (TENS)* Transcutaneous electrical nerve stimulation (TENS) is a non-invasive and easy-to-use method of pain management, which can be discontinued quickly if necessary. Used originally for the relief of chronic pain, trauma, and postsurgical pain, transcutaneous electrical nerve stimulation has recently been introduced for pain relief in labour.

The transcutaneous electrical nerve stimulation unit consists of a portable, hand-held box containing a battery-powered generator of electrical impulses. A low-voltage electric current is transmitted to the skin using surface electrodes, and this results in a 'buzzing' or tingling sensation. The labouring woman may vary the intensity, pulse frequency, and patterns of stimulation, so that she can increase, decrease, or pulse the sensations as she wishes.

Safety concerns have focused on theoretically possible effects of high-intensity transcutaneous electrical nerve stimulation on the fetus's heart function, especially when electrodes are placed on the low abdomen close to the fetus. Further concerns arise in regard to interference with electronic fetal monitor tracings. Though no untoward effects on the fetus have been reported, there has been only one investigation of the fetal safety aspects of transcutaneous electrical nerve stimulation. In 15 births, the investigators established a limit or maximum current density level at 0.5 microamperes per square millimetre when transcutaneous electrical nerve stimulation was used in the suprapubic region. No adverse fetal effects were detected. Less concern has been raised when electrodes are placed only on the back, which is where they have been placed in most studies.

Transcutaneous electrical nerve stimulation for childbirth pain has been subjected to more controlled trials than any of the other modalities of non-pharmacological pain relief. Unfortunately, the results of the trials still remain inconclusive. Overviews of the trials suggest paradoxical conclusions: the effect of transcutaneous nerve stimulation is to actually increase, rather than decrease the incidence of reported intense pain, yet it is favourably assessed by the women who use it. Although the use of transcutaneous nerve stimulation decreases the likelihood of epidural anaesthesia, it has no obvious effect on the use of other forms of analgesia.

1.3 Techniques that enhance descending inhibitory pathways

1.3.1 *Attention focusing and distraction* Many methods for coping with pain involve the conscious participation of the individual in attention-focusing or mind-diverting activities, designed to 'take one's mind off the pain'.

Attention focusing may be accomplished by deliberate intentional activities on the part of the labouring woman. Examples include patterned breathing, attention to verbal coaching, visualization and self-hypnosis, performing familiar tasks (such as grooming and eating), and concentration on a visual, auditory, tactile, or other stimulus.

Distraction may be a more passive form of attention-focusing, with stimuli from the environment (television or a walk out of doors) or from other people drawing a woman's attention away from her pain. It does not require as much mental concentration as deliberate attention focusing measures, and is probably ineffective when pain is severe. Attention-focusing and distraction are usually used in combination with other strategies.

1.3.2 *Hypnosis* Hypnosis was introduced into obstetrics in the early nineteenth century, and has been used in various ways ever since. It is defined as 'a temporarily altered state of consciousness, in which the individual has increased suggestibility'. Under hypnosis a person demonstrates physical and mental relaxation, increased focus of concentration, ability to modify perception, and ability to control normally uncontrollable physiological responses, such as blood-pressure, blood flow, and heart rate.

Hypnosis is used in two ways to control pain perception in childbirth: self-hypnosis and post-hypnotic suggestion. Most hypnotherapists teach self-hypnosis, so that women may enter a trance during labour and reduce awareness of painful sensations. Among the techniques used are: relaxation; visualization (helping the woman imagine a pleasant, safe scene and placing herself there, symbolizing her pain as an object that can be discarded, or picturing herself as in control or free of pain); distraction (focusing on something other than the pain); glove anaesthesia (through suggestion, creating a feeling of numbness in one of her hands, and then spreading that numbness wherever she wishes by placing her numb hand on the desired places of her body). The woman is taught to induce these techniques herself; only rarely do hypnotherapists accompany their clients in labour.

Other therapists rely almost completely on post-hypnotic suggestion. These hypnotherapists do not teach their clients to enter a hypnotic state routinely during labour, because they will not need to. Most, they claim, will be comfortable as a result of the effectiveness of the post-hypnotic suggestions. Exceptions to this are circumstances such as forceps delivery or episiotomy and repair, under which it would be necessary to go into a trance.

To date, only one randomized trial of hypnosis in labour has been reported. There was no difference in analgesia use between the experimental and control groups. The mean duration of pregnancy and the mean duration of labour were both statistically significantly longer in the hypnosis group.

Hypnosis appears to have lost its popularity among obstetricians by the early 1970s, probably because of the development of better methods of anaesthesia and the amount of time required for adequate hypnosis preparation.

1.3.3 Music and audioanalgesia Music and audioanalgesia are used to control pain in numerous situations, including dental work, postoperative pain, the treatment of burns, and occasionally in childbirth. Many childbirth educators use music in antenatal classes to create a peaceful and relaxing environment, and also advocate it for use during labour as an aid to relaxation.

Audioanalgesia for pain relief in obstetrics consists of the use of soothing music between contractions combined with 'white sound', the volume of which is controlled by the labouring woman, during contractions.

The only published randomized placebo-controlled trial of audioanalgesia noted a trend towards better pain relief in the audioanalgesia group, but the effect was confined to primigravidae, and was not statistically significant. As the 'placebo' consisted of a lower intensity of white sound, which might have had pain-relieving qualities in itself, a true benefit of the audioanalgesia might have been masked.

A number of other investigators found decreased use of analgesic medication and reports of pain from the use of audioanalgesia in non-randomized cohort studies. These results, though equivocal, merit further trials.

The interest in audioanalgesia or white sound for labour pain has faded, while the use of music has elicited a modest degree of interest, especially among childbearing women, childbirth educators, and a few care providers. The pleasing qualities of music may offer an added dimension beyond the distraction brought about by white sound. Music from a tape recorder or record-player creates a pleasant and relaxing ambience; or if the mother uses earphones, music blocks out disturbing, distracting, or unpleasant sounds. When carefully chosen, music may be used to reinforce rhythmic breathing patterns and massage strokes, or to facilitate visualizations and induction of hypnosis. Thus, music may have the potential to reduce stress and to enhance other pain-relieving measures. Music may also elicit more relaxed and positive behaviour from the staff and from the woman's chosen companions.

The few small studies of the pain-relieving effects of music in labour have found positive effects. These small studies of childbirth pain, when combined with findings of the effects of music or auditory stimulation on other types of pain (for example, post-operative pain, dental pain, pain associated with burn therapy) suggest that music has the capacity to reduce pain, at least in some women. Its efficacy, however, seems to depend on the degree of prior education, preparation, and accommodation to the personal musical tastes of each woman.

2 Pharmacological control of pain in labour

Pharmacological control of pain in childbirth has a long history. The use of opiates was mentioned in early Chinese writings; the drinking of wine was noted in the Persian literature; and wine, beer, and brandy were commonly self-administered in Europe during the Middle Ages. Various concoctions and potions have been used over time, some inhaled, some swallowed, and some applied to the labouring woman's skin.

There have been more clinical trials of pharmacological pain relief during labour and childbirth than of any other intervention in the perinatal field. The benefits of pain relief are obvious, but the possible adverse effects on the mother or infant have received little attention in this research. The clinically important question is 'what method will achieve an acceptable degree of pain relief while least compromising the health of the mother and child?'

2.1 *Systemic agents*

2.1.1 *Narcotics* Systemic narcotics can generally provide reasonable pain relief. Both maternal and perinatal depression are associated with their use. The effect is dose-related; thus the amount of analgesia achievable is limited by the side-effects of the drug. These maternal side-effects include orthostatic hypotension, nausea, vomiting, dizziness, and a decrease in gastric motility.

There is ample evidence that narcotics cross the placenta, and this may result in neonatal depression. Trial data have shown lower Apgar scores and more neonatal behavioural abnormalities in babies of mothers receiving narcotic analgesia in labour than in babies of mothers who received a placebo.

A randomized controlled comparison of self-administered intravenous pethidine with midwife-administered intramuscular pethidine showed a trend towards increased pain relief and a lower total dose of pethidine in the women who controlled the administration of the drug themselves. Apgar scores were similar in the two groups. These data suggest that self-administered intravenous pethidine is preferable to intramuscular pethidine.

Narcotic antagonists (Naloxone, nalorphine, or levallorphan) have been administered together with a narcotic to counteract the depressant effects of narcotics, either with each dose of narcotic, or ten to fifteen minutes before delivery. Although the rationale is to provide analgesia with minimal respiratory depression, this does not make sense. Antagonists also reverse the effects of pain relief. There is a role for administration of narcotic antagonists (Naloxon in particular) to neonates depressed by narcotics.

2.1.2 *Sedatives and tranquillizers* Many clinicians feel that the use of a tranquillizer, especially in early labour, is helpful in reducing the woman's anxiety and in promoting sleep.

The barbiturates (secobarbital, pentobarbital, and amobarbital) are no longer popular for use in obstetrics, both because they have no analgesic properties and because they may have a profound depressant effect on the newborn. They are still used in the early latent phase of labour for their sedative effect.

The phenothiazine derivatives (promethazine, propiomazine, chlorpromazine, promazine, and prochlorperazine) are, with the benzodiazepines diazepam and droperidol, the major tranquillizers currently used in obstetrics. They are often administered intramuscularly or intravenously in combination with narcotics. Known for their antiemetic as well as sedative properties, the phenothiazines do not appear to cause neonatal depression.

Diazepam (a benzodiazepine) causes neonatal respiratory depression, hypotonia and lethargy, and hypothermia.

2.2 Inhalation analgesia

The use of inhalation analgesia has been decreasing in recent years, primarily because it does not offer reliable or complete pain relief. In addition, side-effects of nausea and vomiting, as well as the possibility of aspiration of gastric contents in cases of accidental overdose, decrease the usefulness of the method. Concern about possible long-term effects of exposure to inhalation agents on medical and nursing personnel has also resulted in decreased use.

Advantages of inhalation analgesia are that the mother remains awake and in control of the analgesia; that neither uterine activity nor 'bearing down' during the second stage is affected; that the duration of effect is short and thus better control is possible; and that clinically obvious side-effects on the mother or fetus have not been noted.

The most commonly used agent is nitrous oxide, usually in a 50 per cent concentration in 50 per cent oxygen. Trials comparing 50 per cent and 70 per cent nitrous oxide administration showed no significant differences in pain relief in normal labours. Other inhalation analgesic agents (methoxyflurane, enflurane, isoflurane, trichloroethylene) have also been employed, but their use has been curtailed or eliminated because of potential toxicity.

2.3 Regional analgesia

Over the past twenty years techniques of regional analgesia have emerged as the major approach to pain relief in obstetrics, not only for labour, but for operative vaginal deliveries and for caesarean section as well. There are many reasons for the popularity of regional anaesthesia. The most important are that it is more effective in relieving pain than other agents, and that the mother remains conscious.

2.3.1 Epidural anaesthesia Trials comparing epidural block to narcotic analgesia show that epidural is associated with a longer duration of effective analgesia, with prolongation of the second stage of labour, and with an increase in instrumental deliveries. The increased risk of instrumental delivery associated with epidural block may well be reduced by careful timing of top-up doses and a liberal attitude to the length of the second stage of labour.

A trial comparing regular top-ups of epidural analgesia at 90-minute intervals with top-up on maternal demand showed that episodes of severe pain were reported by only 4 per cent of the women who received regular top-ups, compared with over 30 per cent of the women who had top-ups on demand. Either moderate or severe pain was experienced by 14 per cent of the women in the regular top-up group, compared to 86 per cent in the demand group.

A well designed double blind trial compared the effect of continuing administration of bupivicaine by continuous infusion after 8 cm dilatation, with administration of a saline placebo. The continued bupivicaine had no effect on the adequacy of analgesia for the remainder of the first stage, but did result in more adequate analgesia in the second stage. The use of continued bupivicaine resulted in prolongation of the second stage. Instrumental delivery was used for over half the women with bupivicaine compared to just over a quarter of the women who received saline. Thus the use of epidural anaesthesia after 8 cm dilatation can result in both prolongation of the second stage and increased use of instrumental vaginal delivery.

Epidural analgesia can be administered either by continuous administration with an infusion device or by intermittent 'top-up' doses by way of an indwelling catheter. Recently, a trial comparing the two methods has been completed. Mothers who were administered the continuous infusion block received almost twice as high a dose of bupivicaine as the mothers who had top-ups. Their labour was longer on the average, and they were significantly more likely to require outlet forceps. Although there was a trend indicating greater pain relief with the continuous infusion, the difference was not statistically significant.

Numerous trials have compared dosages of various anaesthetic agents. The effort spent on these trials is disproportionate to their value, in view of the relative importance of the safety and efficacy of the method itself compared to the effects of specific drugs or dosage regimens.

A recent development in regional anaesthesia is epidural administration of narcotics. Their use appears to potentiate the analgesic effect of epidural bupivicaine. Unwanted effects of epidural narcotics include pruritis, urinary retention, and delayed respiratory depression in the mother.

Reported maternal complications of epidural analgesia, rare as they may be, include: dural puncture; hypotension; nausea and vomiting; shivering; prolonged labour; increased use of operative delivery; neurological complications; bladder dysfunction; headache; backache; toxic drug reactions; respiratory insufficiency; and even maternal death. The fetus may also suffer complications as a result of maternal effects (for example, hypotension) or direct drug toxicity.

2.3.2 *Other routes of regional analgesia*

Caudal block is rarely used today. It requires a larger dose of the anaesthetic agent; results in more blocked neural segments; and the spread of the anaesthetic is less easily controlled than with the usual form of epidural analgesia. Failures occur in 5 to 10 per cent of cases. It is possible for the anaesthetist to miss the caudal canal and insert the needle into the baby's scalp, which can be lethal when the anaesthetic is administered. The only advantage of the caudal approach over the usual lumbar epidural technique is the decreased likelihood of a dural tap.

Paracervical block provides adequate analgesia, and has the advantage that it can be administered by the obstetrician, thus avoiding the need for anaesthetic personnel. This form of analgesia was popular in the 1950s and 1960s, but has fallen out of favour because of reports of fetal bradycardia, acidosis, and fetal death associated with its use.

Spinal anaesthesia is mainly used for the second stage of labour, although there has been recent interest in intrathecal opiates, which appear to give excellent analgesia for the first stage of labour. A high proportion of the mothers develop side-effects of pruritis, nausea and vomiting, and urinary retention. Delayed respiratory depression is the most serious side-effect.

3 Conclusions

Non-pharmacological techniques cannot match epidural analgesia for analgesic effectiveness, but they are likely to have fewer harmful side-effects. All that need be said about them is that they seem to help some women. Many of them require time and effort to accomplish, and their effectiveness is unpredictable.

Satisfaction in childbirth is not necessarily contingent upon the absence of pain. Many women are willing to experience pain in childbirth, but do not want the pain to overwhelm them. For those women whose goals for childbirth include the use of self-help measures to manage pain with minimal drug use, and for those who have little or no access to pharmacological methods of pain relief, many of the non-pharmacological methods are useful alternatives.

Systemic narcotics can reduce pain in labour, although they do not provide as effective analgesia as epidural block. Their use in effective doses is limited by their side-effects of maternal drowsiness, nausea and vomiting, and neonatal depression, with resultant lowered Apgar scores. These effects, plus their effect in delaying gastric emptying, must be kept in mind, particularly if general anaesthesia might be required for delivery.

Self-administered intravenous narcotics appear to give better pain relief with lower doses than does intermittent use of narcotics.

Barbiturates have no analgesic effect. Their sedative effect may occasionally be useful in early labour, but their significant depressant effect must be kept in mind. Diazepam can result in neonatal respiratory depression, hypotonia, and hypothermia. Inhalation agents, such as 50 per cent nitrous oxide in oxygen, are only moderately effective analgesics, but are simple to use, have a short duration of action, and are under the control of the mother. No major side-effects have been noted.

Epidural block produces the most effective pain relief of any of the available analgesic agents, and allows the woman to be awake and aware. It results in increased use of instrumental vaginal delivery, but this effect may be minimized by allowing a longer duration for the second stage of labour.

Epidural analgesia should be administered as regularly scheduled top-ups. This method gives more effective pain relief than do top-ups on maternal demand. Continuation of the epidural after 8 cm dilatation does not confer better analgesia for the first stage of labour; it does result in less pain during the second stage, but also in increased use of instrumental delivery. Continuous infusion of the anaesthetic agent results in the need for a higher total dose of anaesthetic, prolongation of labour, and increased use of instrumental delivery. It does not appear to confer any advantage over scheduled top-ups.

Serious side-effects of epidural block can occur, but they are relatively rare, considering the widespread use of this form of analgesia.

Consideration of the needs of each individual labouring woman, along with knowledge of the analgesic effectiveness and the adverse side-effects of each form of analgesia, will help her to achieve the optimum balance for her.

35

The second stage of labour

This chapter is derived from the chapter by Jennifer Sleep, Joyce Roberts and Iain Chalmers (66) in EFFECTIVE CARE IN PREGNANCY AND CHILDBIRTH.

1 Introduction

In some respects it is undesirable to separate consideration of care during the second stage from care during the first stage of labour. Nevertheless, the second stage is a period during which the whole tempo and nature of activities surrounding labour tend to change. It is a time when women may become vulnerable and dependent on the influence of those who assist them. Discussion about aspects of care is not easy at this time, and this leaves the caregiver with even more than usual responsibility to safeguard the interests of the mother and baby.

2 Diagnosis of the onset of the second stage of labour

By definition, the second stage of labour, which ends with the birth of the baby, begins when the cervix is fully dilated. This 'anatomical' onset may or may not coincide with the onset of the expulsion phase, when the mother begins to feel the urge to bear down. In some women, the urge to bear down occurs before the cervix is fully dilated; for others this urge may not come until well after full cervical dilation is achieved.

The mother herself may signal the transition into the expulsive phase in words, by action, by a change in the expression on her face, or in the way she may squeeze her companion's hand. If the presenting part is visible at the introitus, full dilatation is easily confirmed. If the mother feels that she wishes to start pushing when the progress of labour gives reason to believe that the cervix may not be fully dilated, cervical dilatation should be checked by vaginal examination. If the cervix is only 6 or 7 cm dilated, the woman should be asked to find the position in which she feels most comfortable and try to resist the urge to push; an epidural may be given if necessary. If there is only a rim of cervix left and the woman has an irresistible urge to push, she may feel better doing so, and it is unlikely that any harm will come from this spontaneous pushing before full dilatation, as long as she does not exhaust herself.

When an epidural anaesthetic has been administered for pain relief in labour, maternal bearing-down efforts are reduced, delayed, or abolished. Because the woman is usually in a supine or semi-recumbent position, abdominal palpation is a satisfactory way of gauging descent of the presenting part. Full dilatation can be tentatively diagnosed in this way, and confirmed either by the appearance of the presenting part at the vulva or by vaginal examination.

3 Pushing during the second stage of labour

In a study of healthy nulliparous women who had received no formal childbirth education and were allowed to push spontaneously without any directions from those caring for them, three to five relatively brief (four- to six-second) bearing-down efforts were made with each contraction. The number of bearing-down efforts per contraction increased as the second stage progressed, and most were accompanied by the release of air. The minority of bearing-down efforts that were not accompanied by the release of air were accompanied by very brief periods of breath holding (lasting less than six seconds). Despite this pattern of breathing, the average length of the second stage of labour was 45 minutes, and did not exceed 95 minutes for any of the 31 women studied.

The duration of breath holding (less than six seconds) in the women who spontaneously used this technique contrasts with the 10–30 second duration which is widely advocated for sustained, directed bearing-down efforts. Although sustained bearing-down efforts accompanied by breath holding result in shorter second stages of labour, the wisdom of the commonly given advice to make these efforts can be questioned. In addition to respiratory-induced alterations in heart rate and stroke volume, maternal bearing-down efforts, particularly when the mother is in a supine position, are associated with compression of the distal aorta and reduced blood flow to the uterus and lower extremities. In combination with sustained maternal breath holding, these effects may compromise fetal oxygenation.

In all three of the published controlled trials comparing different approaches to bearing down in which cord umbilical arterial pH assessments were available, mean cord umbilical arterial pH was lower in the group in which sustained or early bearing down had been encouraged. Sustained bearing-down efforts also appear to predispose to abnormalities of the fetal heart rate and depressed Apgar score.

In women with epidural anaesthesia, rotational forceps deliveries tend to be more common among women who have been encouraged to bear down relatively early. There is no evidence that a policy of early bearing down has any compensating advantages for either the mother or the baby.

Despite the limitations of the available evidence, a consistent pattern emerges. The widespread policy of directing women to use sustained and early bearing-down efforts may well result in a modest decrease in the duration of the second stage, but this does not appear to confer any benefit; indeed it seems to compromise maternal–fetal gas exchange.

4 Position during the second stage of labour

The use of upright positions such as standing, sitting on a specially designed chair, or squatting for delivery is common in many cultures. Yet in institutions women have been expected to adopt recumbent positions for delivery. Constraining women to adopt positions that they find awkward or uncomfortable can only be justified if there is good evidence that the policy has important advantages for the health of either the mother or her baby.

Upright posture has been compared with the recumbent position during delivery in several trials. In most of these, either specially designed obstetric chairs or a back rest or wedge were used to support the upright position.

The mean duration of the second stage of labour was found to be shorter with the upright position in most of the trials. There is no evidence, however, that posture during the second stage of labour affects the incidence of either operative delivery or perineal trauma/episiotomy.

Women using birth chairs during the second stage of labour are at increased risk of postpartum haemorrhage. This tendency to postpartum haemorrhage is likely to arise from perineal trauma exacerbated by obstructed venous return. Excessive perineal oedema and haemorrhoids have been observed in women who are upright in birth chairs for extended periods of time.

Abnormal fetal heart rate patterns are less frequently observed, and mean umbilical arterial pH is higher in babies born to women who use the upright position for delivery. These effects may be due to the avoidance of the aortocaval compression associated with recumbency. This alteration in fetal acid–base status was also observed in two trials comparing the effects of the supine position with a 15-degree left lateral tilt. Babies whose mothers had adopted the supine position had lower umbilical cord arterial pH values than those whose mothers had been placed in a left lateral tilt. The available data also suggest that an upright position during the second stage of labour leads to a reduced incidence of depressed Apgar score.

Without exception, more mothers in the groups that used the upright position during the second stage of labour expressed a positive response about the position. The perceived advantages included less pain and less backache. A majority of women wished to use a birth chair or upright position for a subsequent birth.

Evidence that intra-abdominal pressure can be increased effectively in the squatting position, along with radiological reports of an increased sagittal diameter of the pelvic outlet in the squatting position, has resulted in renewed interest in the potential advantages of squatting for birth. Adoption of the squatting position for excretion, resting, and other reasons is not common in industrialized societies, and many people find it uncomfortable. The relative merits and possible disadvantages of the squatting position for birth have not yet been systematically explored.

5 Duration of the second stage

The second stage of labour has been considered to be a time of particular risk to the fetus for well over a century. Echoes of this view exist today in the widespread policies of imposing arbitrary limits on the length of the second stage.

Statistical associations have been demonstrated between a prolonged second stage of labour and obviously undesirable outcomes such as infant mortality, postpartum haemorrhage, puerperal febrile morbidity, and neonatal seizures, as well as with outcomes of less certain significance relating to the acid–base status of the baby at birth. On their own, these associations are not sufficient justification for concluding that the length of the second stage of labour, *per se*, is the crucial variable.

Curtailing the length of the second stage of labour by active pushing or operative delivery can modify the decline in fetal pH that tends to occur over the course of labour. However, without some evidence that this policy has a beneficial effect on important outcomes, the maternal trauma and occasional fetal trauma resulting from the increased surgical interference can hardly be justified.

Decisions about curtailing the second stage of labour should be based on the same principles of monitoring the wellbeing of mother and baby that apply during the first stage of labour. If the mother's condition is satisfactory, the baby's condition is satisfactory, and there is evidence that progress is occurring with descent of the presenting part, there are no grounds for intervention.

Maternal exhaustion can occur at any time during labour, but is more likely to occur during the second stage, when the extra effort of pushing is added to the stress of the contractions. If the mother is not unduly distressed, and is not actively pushing (particularly when she has epidural analgesia), there is no reason to think that the second stage is any more likely to cause exhaustion than the first stage.

Monitoring the fetal heart using intermittent auscultation may on occasions pose difficulties, as it is sometimes hard to find the fetal heart when the baby moves down into the pelvis. It can be frustrating and uncomfortable for a woman to have people continually trying to listen to her baby's heart, or to have to change her position in order to facilitate fetal auscultation. In these circumstances, electronic fetal monitoring is often more comfortable and less disruptive for the woman.

Failure of the presenting part to descend may be due to inadequate or incoordinate uterine contractions; to malposition or malpresentation of the baby; or to cephalopelvic disproportion. The cause of this failure to progress must be diagnosed and appropriately treated. Malpresentation, or minor degrees of cephalopelvic disproportion, may sometimes be overcome by encouraging the mother to vary her position. Intravenous oxytocin can be used if contractions are inadequate. Instrumental or manual manipulation, or sometimes caesarean section, may be necessary.

6 Care of the perineum

Reducing the risk of perineal trauma is important, because the consequent discomfort can dominate the experience of early motherhood and result in significant disability during the months and years that follow. This risk can be minimized by intervening to expedite delivery only on the basis of clear maternal or fetal indications rather than 'because of the clock', and by the use of the vacuum extractor rather than forceps when instrumental delivery is required.

Perineal damage may occur either from spontaneous lacerations or from episiotomy. Although some individual accoucheurs appear to be particularly skilful in assisting delivery in a way that minimizes perineal trauma, in most hospitals at least two-thirds of all women giving birth for the first time sustain trauma sufficient to require suturing.

6.1 Guarding and massaging the perineum

The practice of guarding the perineum, with the birth attendant's hand held against the perineum during contractions, is widespread. It is believed that this practice supports the tissues sufficiently to reduce the risk of spontaneous trauma. The practice would seem logical if combined with gentle pressure applied to the fetal head to control the speed of crowning, as this is the time that the perineal tissues are most at risk of spontaneous damage. Unfortunately there have been no formal evaluations of the alternative strategies.

'Ironing out' or massaging the perineum as the second stage of labour advances, sometimes with an emollient such as olive oil or the application of a hot pad, are also designed to stretch the tissues and reduce the risk of trauma. These techniques have enthusiastic advocates, as well as detractors. The latter suggest that touch may be a disruptive distraction and that the increase in vascularity and oedema in tissues that are already at risk of trauma is counterproductive. Neither of these diametrically opposed opinions can be supported with evidence from controlled comparisons.

6.2 *Episiotomy*

If monitoring during the second stage of labour suggests that either the fetus or the mother has become distressed during the second stage of labour, or that progress has ceased, it may be necessary to hasten delivery either by instrumental delivery or by episiotomy.

Like any surgical procedure, episiotomy carries a number of risks: excessive blood loss, haematoma formation, and infection. Trauma involving the anal sphincter and rectal mucosa may lead to rectovaginal fistulae, loss of rectal tone, and perineal abscess formation.

All the case reports of serious complications of episiotomy relate to clinical practice in North America, where midline incisions are preferred to the mediolateral approach used in the United Kingdom. The two operations have been compared in only one controlled trial. The perineum was significantly less bruised in the women who had the midline operation. On the other hand, third-degree lacerations occurred in almost a quarter of the women in the midline episiotomy group, and in less than ten per cent of those in the mediolateral group. The amount of pain experienced was similar in the two groups, as was the proportion of women requiring analgesics.

Women in the midline episiotomy group began intercourse significantly earlier than those who had a mediolateral incision. At follow-up, the investigators judged the cosmetic appearance and texture of the scar to be somewhat better following the midline operation. Well-controlled research to assess the short- and long-term advantages and disadvantages of midline and mediolateral episiotomies is long overdue.

Episiotomies are sometimes performed using scissors, sometimes with a scalpel. Those who favour scissors maintain that they are less likely to damage the presenting part of the baby and more likely to promote haemostasis in the wound edges, because of their crushing as well as cutting action. Those who favour the scalpel say that it minimizes trauma, and is thus followed by better healing of the perineal wound. There are no data on which to base any judgements about the validity of these claims.

6.3 Liberal use of episiotomy

The most common cause of perineal damage is episiotomy, which is carried out on between 50 and 90 per cent of women giving birth to their first child. Although this extensive use of episiotomy has been questioned, the prevailing view appears to be that the policy is justified.

Liberal use of an operation with the risks described above, however rare these may be, could only be justified by evidence that it confers worthwhile benefits if used frequently. There are three postulated benefits of a liberal use of episiotomy. These are: first, prevention of damage to the anal sphincter and rectal mucosa (third- and fourth-degree lacerations), and easier repair and better healing than with a spontaneous tear; second, prevention of trauma to the fetal head; and third, prevention of serious damage to the muscles of the pelvic floor. A substantial review of the literature was unable to uncover any evidence to support these postulated benefits of liberal use of episiotomy.

Liberal use of episiotomy is associated with higher overall rates of perineal trauma. There is no evidence that this policy reduces the risk of serious perineal or vaginal trauma. Where data from randomized trials are available, women allocated to either a liberal or restricted use of episiotomy experienced a comparable amount of perineal pain at ten days and three months postpartum. Women allocated to liberal use of episiotomy resumed intercourse somewhat later than those who had experienced restricted use of the operation; but the proportions of women experiencing pain on intercourse three months and three years after delivery was almost identical.

There is no evidence to support the suggestion that liberal use of episiotomy minimizes trauma to the fetal head. Data from the randomized trials show similar distributions of Apgar scores and rates of admission to the special-care nursery.

The question of whether stress incontinence is caused or aggravated by vaginal delivery remains controversial. A long-held belief is that injury to the pelvic floor muscles, or to their nerve supply or to the interconnecting fascia, is an inevitable consequence of vaginal delivery, particularly if the delivery is difficult. This in turn, it is argued, may cause genital prolapse and stress incontinence.

A frequent claim in support of liberal use of episiotomy is that it prevents pelvic relaxation during delivery and thereby prevents urinary incontinence and genital prolapse. If the intention really were to protect the pelvic floor, a much more extensive incision than is usual would almost certainly be required.

Liberal and restricted use of episiotomy are associated with contrasting patterns of trauma: liberal use is associated with a lower frequency of anterior vaginal and labial tears. This raises the possibility that episiotomy may have a more specific protective effect on the tissues around the bladder neck. There is no good evidence, however, that more liberal use of episiotomy is protective against urinary stress incontinence. In the three years of a comparison of liberal with restricted use of episiotomy follow-up rates and severity of incontinence were almost identical in the two trial groups.

7 Delivery

Women may choose a variety of positions for delivery if they are encouraged to discover for themselves which is most comfortable for them. Accoucheurs should be sensitive to these differences among women. There is no justification for requiring, or actively encouraging, a supine position during delivery. Women who choose to lie down for delivery often appear to find a lateral position comfortable.

The woman will depend on the midwife's guidance to moderate her pushing effort to allow an unhurried, gentle delivery of the head. This can be achieved by interspersing short pushing efforts with periods of panting, thus giving the tissues time to relax and stretch under pressure. Using this approach, several contractions may occur before the head crowns and is delivered.

After delivery of the head, the shoulders rotate internally. If the umbilical cord is tightly wound around the baby's neck, it may be possible to loosen it, then loop it over the baby's head. If necessary, it can be clamped and severed. Once rotation is complete, the shoulders are delivered one at a time to reduce the risk of perineal trauma. When the mother is in the semi-recumbent position, the anterior shoulder may deliver first; in the squatting or kneeling position, the posterior shoulder may be released first. The mother may then wish to grasp her baby and complete the rest of the delivery herself.

Difficulty with delivery of the shoulders is rare following spontaneous delivery of the head, but if the baby has felt large on abdominal palpation, the accoucheur should be alert for and prepared to deal with shoulder dystocia. It is important that delivery of the shoulders should not be attempted until they have rotated into the antero-posterior axis. Posterior traction on the head, combined with the mother's expulsive efforts, is usually sufficient to effect delivery of the anterior shoulder. The accoucheur should be aware of techniques to overcome the problem of shoulder dystocia on the rare occasions in which it does occur. These include wide abduction of the mother's thighs and complete flexion of her hips; manual rotation of the posterior shoulder anteriorly; and, if necessary, sustained pressure exerted by an assistant directly above the pubic bone.

8 Conclusions

There are no data to support a policy of directed pushing during the second stage of labour, and some evidence to suggest that it may be harmful. The practice should be abandoned. Similarly, there is no evidence to justify restricting women to a supine position during the second stage of labour. With some reservations, the data tend to support the use of upright positions. There is a tendency for recumbency to lengthen the second stage of labour, to reduce the incidence of spontaneous births, to increase the incidence of abnormal fetal heart rate patterns, and to reduce umbilical cord blood pH. Although some birth attendants report that upright positions sometimes caused them inconvenience, there has been a consistently positive response from the women who have used an upright position for birth. On the other hand, at least some of the birthing chairs that have been introduced during recent years appear to predispose to perineal oedema and venous engorgement, which, in conjunction with perineal trauma, can result in the loss of substantial amounts of blood. Use of a birthing chair is not, however, the only way of adopting an upright position during labour. The mother should be encouraged to use the position that she prefers.

There is no evidence to suggest that, when the second stage of labour is progressing and the condition of both mother and fetus is satisfactory, the imposition of any upper arbitrary limit on its duration is justified. Such limits should be discarded.

There is no evidence to support the practice of 'ironing out' or massaging the perineum, or to support claims that liberal use of episiotomy reduces the risk of severe perineal trauma, improves perineal healing, prevents fetal trauma, or reduces the risk of urinary stress incontinence after delivery. Episiotomy should be used only to relieve fetal or maternal distress, or to achieve adequate progress when it is the perineum that is responsible for lack of progress.

36

The third stage of labour

This chapter is derived from the chapter by Walter Prendiville and Diana Elbourne (67) in EFFECTIVE CARE IN PREGNANCY AND CHILDBIRTH.

1 Introduction

After the excitement of giving birth to a baby, the delivery of the placenta (the third stage of labour) is somewhat anticlimactic. This period is, however, a time of great potential hazard. Postpartum haemorrhage remains an important cause of both maternal morbidity and maternal mortality. Retained placenta can necessitate manual removal; and inversion of the uterus, while rare, can be frightening and life-threatening. The effects of care during this period can have important consequences.

2 Active management of the third stage

Active management of the third stage of labour, including *prophylactic* use of oxytocic drugs, early clamping and division of the umbilical cord, and controlled cord traction for delivery of the placenta, has been widely adopted as a measure to prevent postpartum haemorrhage and retained placenta.

    The value of this policy has recently been called into question, both by professionals and by childbearing women, who have suggested that it may interfere with physiological processes to the detriment of mother or baby.

2.1 *Effects of routine prophylactic use of oxytocics*

While few would dispute the contribution of oxytocic drugs in the treatment of postpartum haemorrhage, the routine, prophylactic administration of these drugs to reduce the risk of postpartum haemorrhage has not been so universally accepted. During the 1940s several uncontrolled reports claimed a beneficial effect of routine administration of ergometrine for the management of the third stage of labour. Later investigators reported advantages from combining ergometrine with oxytocin (Syntometrine). The value of the combined preparation was claimed to lie in the rapid effect of the oxytocin and the sustained effect of ergometrine.

Nine trials, including a total of well over 4000 women, have compared women who did or did not receive prophylactic oxytocic preparations. The available data suggest that routine administration of oxytocics results in an important reduction in the risk of postpartum haemorrhage.

The effect of prophylactic oxytocics on retention of the placenta is far from clear. There is some suggestion, from limited data, that routine administration of oxytocics reduces the risk of retained placenta, but this finding might easily reflect either selective presentation of outcome data or the play of chance.

A statistically significant hypertensive effect of oxytocics was demonstrated in the studies that provided information about hypertension as a potential side-effect. More general data on blood-pressure from other studies also suggest that the prophylactic use of oxytocics leads to a rise in blood-pressure.

The advantages of prophylactic oxytocics must be weighed against the rare but serious morbidity that sometimes has been associated with their administration. Maternal deaths from cardiac arrest and intracerebral haemorrhage have been attributed to ergometrine, as have non-fatal instances of cardiac arrest and myocardial infarction, postpartum eclampsia, and pulmonary oedema. Because these events are so rare, the available randomized trials cannot provide useful estimates of the extent to which they may be attributed to oxytocic administration.

Other rare but definite adverse consequences of routine oxytocic administration include intrauterine asphyxia of an undiagnosed second twin, and neonatal convulsions in a baby mistakenly injected with an oxytocic instead of prophylactic vitamin K.

In principle, randomized trials should be able to provide useful information about adverse effects which are less serious but more commonly encountered, such as nausea and vomiting, and headache.

Little usable information is available from the trials. Apart from the investigation of hypertensive effects, there were few systematic attempts to quantify side-effects. In view of the fact that ergometrine is known to lower serum prolactin levels, it is unfortunate that none of the trials has investigated whether or not it interferes with breastfeeding.

On balance, however, the evidence suggests that the benefits of routine oxytocic administration outweigh the likely risks.

2.2 *Comparisons of different oxytocics*

From the trials in which oxytocin has been compared with ergot alkaloids, there is no evidence that these two kinds of oxytocics differ greatly in their effects on the incidence of postpartum haemorrhage. The use of oxytocin was associated with a trend towards less postpartum haemorrhage, and was less likely than ergot alkaloids to lead to a delay in placental delivery, or to a rise in blood-pressure. None of these differences achieved statistical significance.

There is no suggestion of a difference in the effect of Syntometrine and ergot alkaloids on the rate of postpartum haemorrhage. Syntometrine is somewhat less likely than ergot alkaloids to be associated with a prolonged third stage. In the only trial that considered effects on blood-pressure, Syntometrine was less likely than ergometrine to be associated with a 20 mm Hg elevation of diastolic blood-pressure.

Syntometrine has been compared with oxytocin in a number of trials, but data on postpartum haemorrhage are available from only two. These suggest that Syntometrine reduces the risk of postpartum haemorrhage more effectively than oxytocin used alone. Other studies have shown a lower mean blood loss with Syntometrine than with oxytocin, although one trial, which presented no data on postpartum haemorrhage as such, reported that oxytocin was superior in this respect.

2.3 *Early clamping and division of the umbilical cord*

Active management of the third stage of labour usually entails clamping and dividing the umbilical cord relatively early, before beginning controlled cord traction. It has been suggested that pre-empting physiological equilibration of the blood volume within the feto-placental unit in this way predisposes to retained placenta, postpartum haemorrhage, feto–maternal transfusion, and a variety of unwanted effects in the neonate, respiratory distress in particular. Delayed cord clamping results in a placental transfusion to the baby varying between 20 per cent and 50 per cent of neonatal blood volume, depending on when the cord is clamped, and at what level the baby is held before clamping.

Early cord clamping leads to heavier placentae and a higher

residual placental blood volume, but the clinical relevance of these observations is not clear. The duration of the third stage is reduced by the use of early cord clamping. The time of cord clamping does not appear to influence the frequency of postpartum haemorrhage.

Allowing free bleeding from the placental end of the cord is associated with a reduced risk of feto-maternal transfusion, which may be important with regard to isoimmunization.

Early cord clamping results in lower haemoglobin values and haematocrits in the newborn, but these effects are minimal at six weeks of age and undetectable at six months after birth. Neonatal bilirubin levels are lower in the babies born after early cord clamping. It is difficult to draw relevant information from the trials about the effect on clinical jaundice. No detectable differences were noted in the trials that reported on this.

2.4 Controlled cord traction

Use of controlled cord traction involves traction on the cord while maintaining counter-pressure upwards on the lower segment of the uterus, using a hand placed on the lower abdomen. There have been two controlled trials in which controlled cord traction has been compared with a less active approach, one of which sometimes entailed use of fundal pressure. Controlled cord traction was associated with a lower mean blood loss and shorter third stages, but the trials provide insufficient data to warrant any firm conclusions about its effects on either postpartum haemorrhage or manual removal of the placenta. One of the two investigators noted that the umbilical cord had ruptured in 3 per cent of the women managed with controlled cord traction, but that women were more likely to find fundal pressure uncomfortable.

2.5 Active versus expectant management of the third stage

The effects of prophylactic oxytocics, early clamping of the cord, and controlled cord traction were considered separately in the controlled trials from which the above conclusions were drawn. Active management of the third stage (including all three of those elements) has been compared to physiological management (no prophylactic oxytocics, cord clamping after placental delivery, no cord traction, and maternal effort aided by gravity) in a recently published randomized controlled trial involving almost 1200 women.

Women allocated to active management had less blood loss, fewer blood transfusions, shorter third stages and less need for therapeutic oxytocics, but were more likely to vomit than those allocated to 'physiological' management.

In terms of neonatal effects, the increased placental transfusion associated with expectant management resulted in a higher mean birthweight and a higher neonatal haematocrit, as well as an increase in the incidence of jaundice and the need for phototherapy.

3 Complications of the third stage

3.1 Postpartum haemorrhage

The care for a woman with postpartum haemorrhage depends on a rapid but careful assessment of the cause, and prompt arrest of the bleeding before the situation becomes critical. If the source of the bleeding is traumatic, this will require surgical repair; if it is due to uterine atony, contraction of the uterus must be achieved by ensuring that the uterus is empty and well-contracted by massage and the use of oxytocics.

Oxytocin and ergometrine have been the traditional first-line approaches for achieving contraction of the uterus when the haemorrhage is due to uterine atony. Since numerous reports of the superior haemostatic effect of prostaglandins have appeared, these agents should be the first line of approach in severe postpartum haemorrhage due to uterine atony. Although the superiority of prostaglandins for arresting postpartum haemorrhage has not been demonstrated in controlled trials, their dramatic effect when all other measures have failed suggest that these drugs are worth trying. Injection of prostaglandins into the myometrium may obviate the need for uterine packing, internal iliac artery ligation, or even hysterectomy.

3.2 Retained placenta

The conventional treatment for retained placenta is manual removal following digital separation of the placenta from the uterine wall, usually under either general anaesthesia or epidural block. Other methods have been proposed, but to date none have been found to be effective.

Three well-controlled trials have compared the effects of oxytocin with saline injected into the umbilical vein on the incidence of retained placenta and prolonged third stage. No benefit of oxytocin (or saline) was demonstrated.

Waiting 60 minutes before resorting to manual removal will almost halve the number of women who will require manual removal with its attendant anaesthetic risks. In the absence of bleeding, this is a more effective approach than embarking on manual removal too early.

3.3 Inversion of the uterus

Inversion of the uterus is now very rare. It may occur as a result of excessive cord traction in the presence of a relaxed uterus, vigorous fundal pressure, or exceptionally high intra-abdominal pressure as a result of coughing or vomiting. Inappropriate cord traction without counter-pressure to prevent fundal descent is said to result in the occasional case of uterine inversion. Treatment involves replacement of the inversion.

4 Conclusions

The routine use of oxytocic drugs in the third stage of labour will result in a reduced risk of postpartum haemorrhage, in the order of 30 to 40 per cent. This advantage must be weighed against the relatively small risk of hypertension and the disadvantages attending the routine use of injections.

The evidence available provides no support for the continued prophylactic use of ergometrine. This drug offers no advantage over oxytocin in reducing blood loss, and it is associated with a greater risk of hypertension and vomiting.

Early cord clamping reduces the length of the third stage of labour. The available evidence does not reveal any effect upon blood loss or postpartum haemorrhage. In Rhesus-negative women it should be avoided because it increases the risk of feto–maternal transfusion. As a package, the active management of labour is superior to 'physiological' or expectant management by virtue of its significant protective effect in terms of postpartum haemorrhage.

In the presence of severe intractable postpartum haemorrhage it is worth trying prostaglandin therapy, but which preparation, dose, or route of administration is unclear.

37

Repair of perineal trauma

This chapter is derived from the chapter by Adrian Grant (68) in EFFEC-TIVE CARE IN PREGNANCY AND CHILDBIRTH.

1 Introduction

As many as 70 per cent of women in the developed world are likely to require repair of perineal trauma following childbirth. The majority of these women experience perineal pain or discomfort in the immediate postpartum period. Even three months later as many as 20 per cent still have problems, such as pain during intercourse which can be related to perineal trauma and its repair.

In addition to the nature and extent of the trauma, the technique of repair and the choice of suture material are likely to have a bearing on the extent of morbidity associated with perineal trauma. A wide variety of techniques and suture materials are in current use, and there is clearly no consensus as to which are most effective. Data from controlled studies may help to clarify the choices.

2 Technique of perineal repair

Perineal trauma is most commonly repaired in 'layers'. The three stages are repair of the vagina, repair of the deeper perineal tissues, and closure of the skin. The vaginal trauma may be repaired with a continuous suture or (less commonly) with interrupted sutures. In theory a continuous stitch might 'concertina' the vagina, and for this reason a locking stitch is usually recommended.

The deeper perineal injuries are usually closed with interrupted sutures, but sometimes continuous 'running' sutures are used. The skin is commonly closed with interrupted transcutaneous sutures; alternatively, a continuous subcuticular suture using an absorbable material may be used. An alternative approach, to simply appose the deeper tissues with 'a few catgut sutures', has been claimed to result in satisfactory healing with minimal discomfort. No controlled studies have compared any of these techniques.

Continuous subcuticular suture has been compared with inter-rupted transcutaneous suturing techniques for closure of the perineal skin in four randomized trials. The continuous subcuticular technique was associated with fewer short-term problems. The women whose perineal trauma was repaired with continuous subcuticular sutures experienced less pain, and used less analgesia in the immediate postpartum period. No substantial differences between the two tech-niques were found in respect of long-term pain or pain during inter-course.

3 Choice of absorbable suture material

The absorbable materials most commonly used for perineal closure are polyglycolic acid (Dexon, Vicryl) and chromic catgut. The controlled trials that have been carried out comparing these materials show clearly that the use of polyglycolic acid sutures results in less short-term pain and less use of analgesia than chromic catgut. In the one trial that included an adequate follow-up after discharge from hospital, both perineal pain and pain during intercourse were equally common in the two groups three months after delivery.

Removal of some suture material was required more frequently with the use of polyglycolic acid sutures. This was particularly marked in the first ten days, but persisted up to three months postpartum. The commonest reasons given were 'irritation' and 'tightness'. The number of cases requiring resuturing was small, but this occurred more frequently with the use of catgut than with the use of a polyglycolic acid suture.

In summary, the evidence suggests that polyglycolic acid sutures cause less pain in the immediate postpartum period, but may cause irritation sufficient to lead to the removal of some sutures in an important minority of cases.

Polyglycolic acid sutures cause less tissue reaction than do chromic catgut. This may explain why their use is associated with less pain in the immediate postpartum period. Another suggested explanation for the trial findings is that they reflect differences in the tightness of the stitches rather than differences in the materials *per se*.

The only other published trial of two absorbable materials com-pared glycerol-impregnated catgut with chromic catgut, both materials being used for all layers. The use of glycerol-impregnated catgut was associated both with more pain ten days after delivery and with an increased prevalence of pain during intercourse three months postpartum. The increased prevalence of pain during intercourse persisted, it being reported nearly twice as commonly three years after delivery by women sutured with glycerol-impregnated catgut. On the basis of this trial, glycerol-impregnated catgut sutures should not be used for repair of perineal trauma.

4 Skin closure

Absorbable sutures (Dexon) have been compared with non-absorbable skin sutures (silk, nylon, or Supramid) in six controlled trials. The groups repaired with absorbable sutures generally had less pain and used less analgesia in the first few days after delivery. No clear effects have been noted on longer-term morbidity.

Polyamide sutures, such as nylon or Supramid, would be expected to cause less pain than silk because they cause less tissue reaction and pass easily through the tissues. Handling and knotting polyamides is less easy, however. They tend to be stiff and have a 'memory', and they thus require three or four throws in a knot. The handling properties of silk, on the other hand, are probably the best of all suture materials, and it knots easily and securely. These latter characteristics almost certainly explain silk's continuing popularity for perineal repair, despite the fact that it results in increased discomfort.

5 Who should perform the repair?

It seems likely that the skills of the operator are as important, if not more important, than the materials and techniques used. There is, however, little research evidence on the effects of skill on symptoms associated with perineal repair. Experience does not necessarily result in a better outcome—the same mistakes may be made with increasing confidence. There is an urgent need for this to be clarified in respect of the repair of perineal trauma.

Perineal repairs are often delegated to a junior obstetrician or a medical student. Training is likely to have an important effect on the outcome of perineal repair, but has been a neglected area for research. The usual approach is still 'see three, do three, and now you are on your own!' Video recordings have been introduced in some places to supplement this, and apparatuses on which to practise suturing are becoming available. Ideally, the usefulness of these developments should also be carefully assessed before they are introduced widely.

6 Conclusions

On the basis of currently available evidence, polyglycolic acid sutures (Dexon or Vicryl) should be chosen for both the deep layers and the skin. Questions still remain about the long-term implications of this policy, but the available evidence is reassuring. The relatively frequent need to remove polyglycolic acid material in the puerperium because of irritation indicates either that this material is not ideal, or that the stitches were tied too tightly.

A continuous subcuticular stitch appears to be preferable to interrupted transcutaneous sutures, particularly for the experienced operator; but the easier, interrupted technique may cause fewer problems in the hands of the inexperienced or novice operator. Whichever material is chosen for the skin, polyglycolic acid appears to be the material of choice for the deeper tissues.

38

Instrumental vaginal delivery

This chapter is derived from the chapter by Aldo Vacca and Marc J. N. C. Keirse (71) in EFFECTIVE CARE IN PREGNANCY AND CHILDBIRTH.

1 Introduction

When there is a valid indication for expediting the birth of the baby, instrumental vaginal delivery rather than caesarean section may be selected on the basis of a number of factors. These include the condition of the fetus and mother, progress in labour, dilatation of the cervix, the station of the presenting part, position and moulding of the fetal head, comfort, morale, and co-operation of the mother, experience and attitudes of the operator, and the availability of the necessary equipment.

Few indications for instrumental delivery are absolute, and there are considerable regional and international differences in the rate of instrumental deliveries. In the English-speaking world, in general, forceps is the preferred instrument, and adequate familiarity with the vacuum extractor is rare. The situation is the reverse in many European countries, where the use of forceps is uncommon.

2 Conditions for instrumental delivery

The operator is a major determinant of the success or failure of instrumental delivery. Unfavourable results are almost always caused by the user's unfamiliarity with either the instrument or the basic rules governing its use.

A fully dilated cervix is a prerequisite for instrumental vaginal delivery. Moreover, use of oxytocin may be better than premature instrumental delivery for the treatment of delay in the second stage of labour before the baby's head reaches the pelvic floor. The station and degree of moulding of the head must be carefully assessed, and the position accurately known.

The common indications for instrumental delivery, such as fetal distress or delay in the second stage of labour, can also create anxiety in the mother and her partner. Some of this anxiety can be relieved by keeping them fully informed of the reasons for the procedures being undertaken.

Effective and appropriate analgesia should be provided before instrumental delivery is commenced. Less pain relief is needed, as a rule, for vacuum extraction than for forceps delivery. Vacuum extraction or outlet forceps delivery can usually be accomplished comfortably with local infiltration of the perineum or pudendal nerve block. Rotational forceps deliveries often require a more profound form of anaesthesia, such as epidural or spinal block.

The total force exerted on the fetal head during instrumental delivery will depend on the duration of the procedure and on the number and strength of pulls. Some descent of the head should occur with each pull. No descent with traction on a correctly positioned instrument should be regarded by the operator as a reason to abandon the procedure in favour of caesarean section.

3 Equipment and techniques

3.1 *Forceps*

Since the introduction of forceps, numerous modifications have been made in attempts to improve their efficiency and safety. Forceps can be grouped on a functional basis into those whose primary function is to exert traction and those whose primary function is to correct malposition. No controlled trials of the use of different types of forceps have been reported.

3.2 *Vacuum extraction*

Various modifications of the vacuum extractor have been made in attempts to increase manoeuverability of the cup in order to achieve a more correct application on the fetal head.

All the vacuum cups are satisfactory for outlet and non-rotational midpelvic operations. Operators would be well advised first to develop confidence in outlet and non-rotational midpelvic procedures; the basic technique is similar in all positions of the occiput, and experience gained with non-rotational procedures will prove invaluable when the more difficult rotational operations are attempted. The few trials that have been carried out comparing the various rigid cup designs to one another have not demonstrated any differences in outcome.

The risk of injury to the infant is directly related to the number of pulls with the vacuum extractor. Sudden cup detachments are often associated with injury to the scalp of the infant.

4 Comparison of vacuum extraction and forceps

4.1 *Efficiency*

The mean time between the decision to deliver and delivery itself is similar for forceps and vacuum extraction, although the range of the decision-to-delivery interval is greater for forceps. This is at least in part due to the time required to institute the more complex forms of analgesia needed for forceps delivery.

There is a consistently higher failure rate for vacuum extraction than for forceps, but this is not reflected in any difference in the use of caesarean section to accomplish delivery.

4.2 *Effects on the mother*

General and regional anaesthesia are more likely to be used with forceps than with vacuum extraction. In spite of the use of these more powerful forms of pain relief, women in controlled comparisons of forceps and vacuum extraction are more likely to report having experienced moderate or severe pain if they had been allocated to forceps delivery. Women allocated to forceps delivery were also more likely to sustain significant injury to the genital tract.

4.3 *Effects on the infant*

Apgar scores of infants allocated to forceps delivery tend to be lower than those of babies allocated to vacuum extraction. Vacuum extraction is more likely to cause cephalhaematoma than forceps, but forceps are more likely to cause other kinds of scalp and facial injuries. Mild neonatal jaundice is more common in babies delivered by vacuum extraction. There is not enough evidence available to assess whether vacuum extraction is more likely than forceps delivery to be followed by jaundice of a degree that gives rise to medical or maternal concern.

There is not enough information available to judge the relative effects of the two instruments on the risk of perinatal death or the long-term condition of the infants. In the only follow-up study of cohorts randomized to the two instruments, the incidence of problems was similar in the vacuum and forceps groups, but the numbers of infants studied was too small to exclude anything other than very dramatic differential effects of the two instruments.

5 Conclusions

Forceps delivery and vacuum extraction are to a large extent interchangeable procedures. The available evidence indicates, however, that the use of forceps is more likely to result in severe maternal injury, and is more dependent on the use of more complex forms of analgesia or anaesthesia than is vacuum extraction.

With adequate experience and proper placement of the vacuum cup, most deliveries that require instrumental rotation of the head can be accomplished by vacuum extraction, thus obviating the need for painful and potentially traumatic forceps rotations. This experience should not be difficult to obtain, and should form part of all residency training programmes in obstetrics.

The widely held belief that vacuum extraction is too slow to be useful when rapid delivery is required for fetal distress can now firmly be laid to rest. With proper technique, the interval between deciding on the need for instrumental delivery and delivery itself is no longer with vacuum extraction than with forceps.

Although there is no adequate evidence on which to judge the difference between these instruments on long-term outcomes of neonatal morbidity, there is a distinct difference in short-term outcomes. Although cephalhaematoma occurs more frequently with vacuum extraction, all other types of injuries of the head and face are more frequently observed after forceps delivery.

On balance, it would appear that for most instrumental rotational deliveries vacuum extraction is to be preferred over forceps. The same may hold, albeit to a lesser extent, for most other operative vaginal deliveries as well. Reserving one instrument for routine applications and the other for especially difficult situations would be ill-advised. Difficult extractions, whether by forceps or by vacuum extraction, should not be undertaken unless the operator has considerable expertise with the instrument chosen. Delivery by caesarean section should then be considered as an alternative.

39

Labour and delivery after previous caesarean section

This chapter is derived from the chapter by Murray Enkin (70) in EFFEC-TIVE CARE IN PREGNANCY AND CHILDBIRTH.

1 Introduction

Although in recent years the dogma of 'once a caesarean always a caesarean' has come under both professional and public scrutiny, in many countries the practice is still carried out, and remains a stated policy in many institutions.

Two general propositions underlie the widespread practice of repeat caesarean section: that trial of labour, with its inherent risk of uterine rupture, represents a significant hazard to the wellbeing of mother and baby; and that planned repeat caesarean operations are virtually free of risk. It is important to examine the validity of these propositions.

2 Results of a trial of labour

No controlled trials have compared the results of elective caesarean section versus trial of labour for women who have had a previous caesarean section. In the absence of such trials, the best available data on the relative safety of trial of labour comes from the prospective comparative studies that have been reported. In these studies, including a total of almost 9000 pregnant women with a history of one caesarean section, over two-thirds were allowed a trial of labour. Of these women almost 80 per cent gave birth vaginally. Thus, for the series for which total data are available, well over half of all women with a previous caesarean section gave birth vaginally.

A large number of retrospective studies have also compared the effects of elective caesarean section versus trial of labour in women who have had one previous caesarean section. There is far greater potential for bias in these retrospective studies than in the prospective studies, and one should be cautious in drawing conclusions from them; nevertheless, it is interesting to note that their results are similar to, and support the conclusions from the prospective studies.

Uterine dehiscence (wound breakdown) or rupture (the data available do not allow these two conditions to be quantified separately) occurred in 0.5 to 2.0 per cent of the women who had elective caesarean sections, and in 0.5 to 3.3 per cent of the women in the trial of labour groups in the prospective cohort studies. Most of these dehiscences were minor in nature, and had no sequelae.

Data from the prospective studies show that febrile morbidity rates were consistently and substantially higher in the groups of women who underwent elective caesarean section (range 11 to 38 per cent) than in the groups of women who had a trial of labour, including both those who had an emergency caesarean section and those who had a vaginal delivery (range 2 to 23 per cent). Although the febrile morbidity rates were highest among women who underwent caesarean section after a trial of labour, these were more than counterbalanced by the lower rate in the two-thirds of women who give birth vaginally after a trial of labour.

Blood transfusions, endometritis, abdominal wound infections, thrombo-embolic phenomena, anaesthetic complications, pyelonephritis, pneumonia, and septicemia were also less common in women who had a vaginal delivery following low transverse caesarean section than in women who underwent a repeat caesarean section.

Perinatal mortality and morbidity rates were similar with trial of labour and elective caesarean section in the studies that report these data. Such comparisons, however, are of little value, because the groups compared are not equivalent. The decision to perform a repeat caesarean section or to permit a trial of labour may be made on the basis of whether or not the fetus is living or dead, anomalous, or immature.

3 Risks of caesarean section

3.1 *Risks to the mother*

Large series of caesarean sections have been reported with no associated maternal mortality. One should not be lulled into a false sense of security by this. The risk of a mother dying with caesarean section is small, but is still considerably higher than with vaginal delivery.

The rate of maternal death associated with caesarean section (approximately 40 per 100 000 births) is four times that associated with vaginal delivery (10 per 100 000 births). The maternal death rate associated with elective repeat caesarean section (18 per 100 000 births), although lower than that associated with caesarean sections overall, is still almost twice the rate associated with all vaginal deliveries, and nearly four times the mortality rate associated with normal vaginal delivery (5 per 100 000 births).

The rate of maternal mortality attributable to caesarean section *per se* is difficult to estimate, as some of the deaths observed are caused by the condition which necessitated the caesarean section in the first place. While it is not possible to quantitate exactly the extent of increased risk of death to the mother from elective caesarean section, the data available suggest that it is between two and four times that associated with vaginal delivery.

Most forms of maternal morbidity are higher with caesarean section than with vaginal delivery. In addition to the risks of anaesthesia attendant on all surgery, there are risks of operative injury, febrile morbidity, and effects on subsequent fertility, and of psychological morbidity as well.

3.2 *Risks to the baby*

The major hazards of caesarean section for the baby relate to the risks of respiratory distress contingent on either the caesarean delivery itself, or on preterm birth as a result of miscalculation of dates. Babies born by caesarean section have a higher risk of respiratory distress syndrome than babies born vaginally at the same gestational age.

The availability of more accurate and readily available dating with ultrasound may decrease the risk of unexpected preterm delivery. Nevertheless, it is unlikely that this risk can ever be completely eliminated.

4 Factors to consider in the decision about a trial of labour

A mathematical, utilitarian approach comparing the balance of risks and benefits of trial of labour with those of planned caesarean section will not always be the best way to choose a course of action. Such an approach can, however, provide important data that may be helpful in arriving at the best decision.

The technique of decision analysis has been used to determine the optimal delivery policy after previous caesarean section. The probabilities and utilities of a number of possible outcomes, including the need for hysterectomy, uterine rupture, iatrogenic 'prematurity', need for future repeat caesarean sections, prolonged hospitalization and recovery, additional cost, failed trial of labour, discomfort of labour, and inconvenience of awaiting labour can be put into a mathematical model comparing different policies. Over a wide range of probabilities and utilities, which included all reasonable values, trial of labour proved to be the logical choice.

4.1 *More than one previous caesarean section*

Data on the results of trials of labour in women who have had more than one previous caesarean section tend to be buried in studies of trial of labour after previous caesarean section as a whole. The available data on delivery outcome for trial of labour in women who have had more than one previous caesarean section show that the overall vaginal delivery rate is little different from that seen in women who have had only one previous caesarean section. Successful trials of labour have been carried out on women who have had three or more previous caesarean sections.

The rate of uterine dehiscence (wound breakdown) in women who have had more than one previous caesarean section is slightly higher than the dehiscence rate for women with only one previous caesarean, but all dehiscences in the reported series were without symptoms and without serious sequelae. There was no maternal or perinatal mortality associated with any of the trials of labour after more than one previous caesarean section reported in these series. No data have been reported on other maternal or infant morbidity specifically associated with multiple previous caesarean sections.

While the number of cases reported is still small, the available evidence does not suggest that a woman who has had more than one previous caesarean section should be treated any differently from the woman who has had only one caesarean section.

4.2 *Reason for the primary caesarean section*

The greatest likelihood of vaginal delivery is seen when the first caesarean section was done because of breech presentation; vaginal delivery rates are lowest when the initial indication was failure to progress in labour, dystocia, or cephalopelvic disproportion. Even when the indication for the first caesarean section was disproportion, dystocia, or failure to progress, successful vaginal delivery occurred over 50 per cent of the time in most published series, and the rate was over 75 per cent in the largest series reported. It is clear that a history of caesarean section for dystocia is not a contraindication to a trial of labour, and has only a small effect on the likelihood of vaginal birth when a trial of labour is permitted.

4.3 Previous vaginal delivery

Mothers who have had a previous vaginal delivery in addition to their previous caesarean sections are more likely to deliver vaginally after trial of labour than mothers with no previous vaginal deliveries. This advantage is increased even further in those mothers whose previous vaginal delivery occurred after rather than before the primary caesarean section.

4.4 Type of previous incision in the uterus

Modern experience with operative approaches other than the lower segment operation for caesarean section is limited. There is, however, a growing trend towards the use of vertical incisions in preterm caesarean sections. This, and the inverted T incision sometimes necessary to allow delivery, show that consideration of the type of uterine scar is still relevant.

The potential dangers of uterine rupture are related to the rapid 'explosive' rupture which is most likely to be seen in women who have a classical midline scar. The majority of dehiscences found following lower segment transverse incisions are 'silent', 'incomplete', or incidentally discovered at the time of repeat caesarean section. While scars found at repeat caesarean section can be described as 'dangerous' (meaning thin or 'windowed'), only a small proportion of them actually demonstrated a rupture. What the fate of these 'dangerous' scars would actually have been, had labour been permitted, can only be surmised.

Following a classical caesarean section, rupture of the scar is not only more serious than rupture of a lower segment scar, it is also more likely to occur. Rupture may occur suddenly during the course of pregnancy, prior to labour, and before a repeat caesarean section can be scheduled. A review of the literature at a time when classical caesarean section was still common showed a 2.2 per cent rate of uterine rupture with previous classical caesarean, and a rate of 0.5 per cent with previous lower segment caesarean sections. That is, the scar of the classical operation was more than four times more likely to rupture in a subsequent pregnancy than that of the lower segment incision.

Unfortunately, even in the older literature, there are very few data on the risk of uterine rupture of a vertical scar in the lower segment.

One 1966 study reported an incidence of rupture of 2.2 per cent in classical incision scars, 1.3 per cent in vertical incision lower segment scars and 0.7 per cent in transverse incision lower segment scars. The distinction between the risk of rupture of vertical and transverse lower segment scars may be related to extension of the vertical incision from the lower segment into the upper segment of the uterus.

The uncertain denominators in the reported series make it difficult to quantify the risk of rupture with a previous classical or vertical incision lower segment scar. It is clear, however, that the risk that such a rupture may occur, that it may occur prior to the onset of labour, and that it may have serious sequelae, are considerably greater with such scars than with transverse incision lower segment scars. It would seem reasonable that women who have had a hysterotomy, a vertical uterine incision, or an 'inverted T' incision should be treated in subsequent pregnancies in the same manner as women who have had a classical caesarean section, and that trial of labour, if permitted at all, should be carried out with great caution, and with acute awareness of the increased risks likely to exist.

4.5 *Gestational age at previous caesarean section*

During the past decade improved neonatal care has increased the survival rate of preterm babies, and this in turn has led to a reduction in the stage of gestation at which obstetricians are prepared to perform caesarean sections for fetal indications. This has resulted in caesarean sections being used to deliver babies at or even before 26 weeks. At these early gestations the lower segment is poorly formed, and so-called 'lower segment' operations at this period of gestation are, in reality, transverse incisions in the body of the uterus. Whether or not such an incision confers any advantage over a classical incision remains in doubt. Indeed, some obstetricians now recommend performing a classical incision under these circumstances.

Whichever of these incisions is used at these early gestational ages, their consequences for subsequent pregnancies are currently unknown. It is quite possible, in theory at least, that they may result in a greater morbidity in future pregnancies than that associated with the lower segment operation at term.

4.6 *Integrity of the scar*

The decision to advise for or against a trial of labour may be influenced by an assessment of the integrity of the scar. This assessment may be helped by knowledge of the operative technique used at the previous caesarean section, the operative findings at the time of surgery, whether an extension of the operative incision had occurred, and the nature of the postoperative course.

5 Care during a trial of labour

5.1 *Use of oxytocics*

The use of oxytocin or prostaglandins for induction or augmentation of labour in women who have had a previous caesarean section has remained controversial, because of speculation that there might be an increased risk of uterine rupture or dehiscence. This view is not universally held, nor is it strongly supported by the available data. A number of series have been reported in which oxytocin or prostaglandins were used for the usual indications with no suggestion of increased hazard. Review of the reported case series shows that any increased risk of uterine rupture with the use of oxytocin is likely to be extremely small.

Such comparisons, of course, are rendered invalid by the fact that the cohorts of women who received, or did not receive, oxytocin may have differed in many other respects in addition to the use of oxytocin. Nevertheless, the high vaginal delivery rates and low dehiscence rates noted in these women suggest that oxytocin can be used for induction or augmentation of labour in women who have had a previous caesarean section, with the same precautions that should always attend its use.

5.2 *Regional analgesia and anaesthesia*

The use of regional (caudal or epidural) analgesia in labour for the woman with a previous caesarean section has been questioned because of fears that it might mask pain or tenderness, which are considered to be early signs of rupture of the scar. The extent of the risk of masking a catastrophic uterine rupture is difficult to quantify. It must be minuscule; only one case report of this having occurred was located. In a number of reported series regional block is used whenever requested by the woman for pain relief, and no difficulties were encountered with this policy.

There does not appear to be any increased hazard from uterine rupture associated with the use of regional anaesthesia for women who have had a previous caesarean section. It is sensible, safe, and justified to use analgesia for the woman with a lower segment scar in the same manner as for the woman whose uterus is intact.

5.3 *Manual exploration of the uterus*

In many reports of series of vaginal births after previous caesarean section, mention is made of the fact that the uterus was explored postpartum in all cases, in a search for uterine rupture or dehiscence without symptoms. The wisdom of this approach should be seriously challenged.

Manual exploration of a scarred uterus immediately following a vaginal delivery is often inconclusive. It is difficult to be sure whether or not the thin, soft lower segment is intact. In any case, in the absence of bleeding or systemic signs, a rupture without symptoms discovered postpartum does not require any treatment, so the question of diagnosis would be academic.

No studies have shown any benefit from routine manual exploration of the uterus in women who have had a previous caesarean section. There is always a risk of introducing infection by the manual exploration, or of converting a dehiscence into a larger rupture. A reasonable compromise consists of increased vigilance in the hour after delivery of the placenta, reserving internal palpation of the lower segment for women with signs of abnormal bleeding.

6 Rupture of the scarred uterus in pregnancy and labour

Complete rupture of the uterus can be a life-threatening emergency. Fortunately the condition is rare in modern obstetrics despite the increase in caesarean section rates, and serious sequelae are even more rare. Although often considered to be the most common cause of uterine rupture, previous caesarean section is involved in less than half the cases.

Excluding symptomless wound breakdown, the rate of reported uterine rupture has ranged from 0.09 per cent to 0.22 per cent for women with a singleton vertex presentation who underwent a trial of labour after a previous transverse lower segment caesarean section. To put these rates into perspective, the probability of requiring an emergency caesarean section for other acute other conditions (fetal distress, cord prolapse, or antepartum haemorrhage) in any woman giving birth, is approximately 2.7 per cent, or 30 times as high as the risk of uterine rupture with a trial of labour.

Treatment of rupture of a lower segment scar does not require extraordinary facilities. Hospitals whose capabilities are so limited that they cannot deal promptly with problems associated with a trial of labour are also incapable of dealing appropriately with other obstetrical emergencies. Any obstetrical department that is prepared to look after women with much more frequently encountered conditions such as placenta praevia, abruptio placentae, prolapsed cord, and acute fetal distress should be able to manage a trial of labour safely after a previous lower segment caesarean section.

7 Gap between evidence and practice

Obstetric practice has been slow to reflect the scientific evidence confirming the safety of trial of labour after previous caesarean section. The degree of opposition to vaginal birth after caesarean section, in North America in particular, is difficult to explain, considering the strength of the available evidence that trials of labour are, under proper circumstances, both safe and effective. Two national consensus statements and two national professional bodies, in Canada and the United States, have recommended policies of trial of labour after previous caesarean section.

Increasing numbers of pregnant women, as well as professionals, are vehemently protesting the status quo. For a variety of reasons many women prefer to attempt a vaginal birth after a caesarean section. Their earlier caesarean experience may have been emotionally or physically difficult. They may be unhappy because they were separated from their partners or from their babies. They may wonder if it was all necessary in the first place. They may be aware of the accumulated evidence on the relative safety and advantages of trial of labour, and simply be looking for a better experience this time.

In recent years a number of consumer 'shared predicament ' groups have appeared, with the expressed purposes of demythologizing caesarean section, of combatting misinformation, and of disseminating both accurate information and their own point of view. Special prenatal classes are available for many parents who elect to attempt a vaginal birth after a caesarean section.

8 Conclusions

A trial of labour after a previous caesarean section should be recommended for women who have had a previous lower segment transverse incision caesarean section, and have no other indication for caesarean section in the present pregnancy. The likelihood of vaginal birth is not significantly altered by the indication for the first caesarean section (including 'cephalopelvic disproportion' and 'failure to progress'), nor by a history of more than one previous caesarean section.

A history of classical, low vertical, or unknown uterine incision or hysterotomy carries with it an increased risk of uterine rupture, and in most cases is a contraindication to trial of labour.

The care of a woman in labour after a previous lower segment caesarean section should be little different from that for any woman in labour. Oxytocin induction or stimulation, and epidural analgesia, may be used for the usual indications. Careful monitoring of the condition of the mother and fetus is required, as for all pregnancies. The hospital facilities required do not differ from those that should be available for all women giving birth, irrespective of their previous history.

40

Caesarean section

This chapter was derived from the chapters by Jonathan Lomas and Murray Enkin (69) and Jim Pearson and Gareth Rees (72) in EFFECTIVE CARE IN PREGNANCY AND CHILDBIRTH.

1 Introduction

The term caesarean section refers to the operation of delivering the baby through incisions made in the abdominal wall and uterus. It has an enormous potential for the preservation of life and health, probably greater than that for any other major surgical operation.

The caesarean section rate varies considerably among countries, from about 5 per cent to over 20 per cent of all deliveries. The optimal rate is not known, but from national data available, little improvement in outcome appears to occur when rates rise above about 7 per cent. Despite this, rates of caesarean section well above this level exist in many parts of the world.

Many caesarean sections are carried out for unequivocal indications, such as placenta praevia or transverse lie. The majority of these operations, however, are carried out for rather ambiguous indications. Criteria for the diagnoses of dystocia (prolonged labour) and fetal distress, two of the most commonly given reasons for performing a caesarean section, are by no means clear. No data are available to suggest what proportion of babies presenting as a breech would benefit from delivery by caesarean section. Previous caesarean section, the most rapidly increasing reason given for the operation, is rarely an adequate indication by itself.

The extent to which obstetricians differ in the use of this major operation to deliver babies suggests that the obstetrical community is uncertain as to when caesarean section is indicated. It also suggests that other factors, such as the socio-economic status of the woman, the influence of malpractice litigation, women's expectations, financial considerations, and convenience may sometimes be more important than obstetrical factors in determining the decision to operate.

2 Anaesthesia for caesarean section

When caesarean section is required, its safety depends on the care with which the anaesthetic is administered and the operation performed.

Caesarean section can be carried out under either regional (epidural or spinal block) or general anaesthesia. Regional anaesthesia has many advantages. It largely avoids the risk of regurgitation and aspiration of stomach contents associated with general anaesthesia. It allows the mother to remain awake, and permits early contact between mother and baby at birth.

The main disadvantages of using regional anaesthesia for caesarean section relate to the extensive block required for the operation. This may result in a drop in blood-pressure which may be dangerous unless promptly recognized and treated.

Despite the increasing popularity of regional anaesthesia, general anaesthesia is sometimes required. Regional anaesthesia is contraindicated if the mother has any coagulation disorder. If the reason for the caesarean section relates to a bleeding complication in the mother, the drop in blood-pressure with regional anaesthesia can be particularly dangerous. General anaesthesia can be more rapidly administered, and therefore is of value when speed is important, such as when the fetus is severely distressed. Some women prefer to be asleep for the operation.

The disadvantages of general anaesthesia relate to the serious problems that are sometimes associated with it, such as pulmonary aspiration, inadequate airway control, and neonatal depression. If improperly managed, these can lead to significant maternal and fetal morbidity, and sometimes mortality. Aspiration of gastric contents is an important cause of maternal death associated with general anaesthesia. Aspiration of acidic gastric contents can cause acid pneumonitis (Mendelson's syndrome), the severity of which depends on the acidity of the aspirate.

The most important measure in preventing pulmonary aspiration is occlusion of the oesophagus by cricoid pressure. The manoeuvre requires an assistant who is knowledgeable and capable, and it loses its effectiveness unless skilled help is available. Deaths from Mendelson's syndrome usually result from not applying cricoid pressure, relaxing the pressure before intubation, or applying pressure inefficiently.

An equally important problem with general anaesthesia arises when the anaesthetist is unable to intubate the trachea. Deaths due to Mendelson's syndrome or failed intubation are largely preventable, and can be almost eradicated by improvements in clinical care.

Whatever form of anaesthesia is chosen, it is important for the woman to be in a 15–20 degree lateral tilt position, rather than lying flat on her back. This relieves the pressure of the pregnant uterus on the vena cava. It has been shown in controlled trials to reduce the fall in blood-pressure that may occur with anaesthesia or surgery, and to improve the oxygenation of the baby.

3. Surgical technique

Details of operative technique vary from surgeon to surgeon, and few of these have been evaluated in controlled trials. This is sometimes of little consequence, as little difference in results can be expected; but some controlled comparisons have provided important information.

When a transverse rather than a vertical skin incision is used, average operating time is longer, and more women require blood transfusions. On the other hand, febrile morbidity occurs somewhat less frequently with the transverse skin incision, and many women find the transverse scar more acceptable cosmetically. The uterine incision should always be made transversely in the lower uterine segment, except in extremely rare circumstances. The initial incision is made with a scalpel. Whether scissors or fingers should be used to extend the incision, and whether the suture material or technique used for closure influences the post-operative result, has not been evaluated.

A controlled trial has shown that repairing the uterine incision after bringing the uterus out through the abdominal wound results in somewhat lower blood loss than repairing it within the pelvis. No adverse effects of this technique were detected, so it would seem sensible to use it, if difficulty in exposure is likely to interfere with the repair.

4 Conclusions

Caesarean section is a major operation, with great potential benefit, but also with substantial risks for both mother and baby. The hazards can be kept to a minimum, first, by avoiding unnecessary use of the operation, and, second, by meticulous attention to proper anaesthetic and surgical techniques.

41

Prophylactic antibiotics with caesarean section

This chapter is derived from the chapter by Murray Enkin, Eleanor Enkin, Iain Chalmers, and Elina Hemminki (73) in EFFECTIVE CARE IN PREGNANCY AND CHILDBIRTH.

1 Introduction
2 Effects of infection and febrile morbidity
3 Choice of antibiotic preparation
4 Timing, dose, and frequency of administration
5 Route of administration
6 Potential adverse consequences of antibiotic prophylaxis
7 Conclusions

1. Introduction

Maternal morbidity after caesarean section has not been studied as systematically as has the maternal mortality associated with the operation, but the problem of post-operative infection is undoubtedly substantial. Febrile morbidity, a proportion of which is likely to be caused by factors other than infection, appears to be an inevitable sequel to caesarean section for at least one in five women. More importantly, serious infections such as pelvic abscess, septic shock, and septic pelvic vein thrombophlebitis are not rare.

Labour and ruptured membranes are the most important factors associated with an increased risk of infection, the risk rising with increased duration of each. Obesity appears to be a risk factor of particular importance for wound infection.

The potential for reducing maternal morbidity following caesarean section by administering antibiotics prophylactically has been investigated systematically in the past two decades, and over 90 reports of randomized controlled trials have now been published. There is very little usable information on the extent to which toxic or allergic effects of antibiotics cause maternal morbidity, or information on the effects of antibiotic prophylaxis at caesarean section on infants. In the more recent trials, this may be because prophylaxis has been started after the umbilical cord has been clamped. In spite of these limitations, the information that is available provides useful guidelines for practice.

2 Effects on infection and febrile morbidity

There is now overwhelming evidence that antibiotic prophylaxis markedly reduces the risk of serious post-operative infection, such as pelvic abscess, septic shock, and septic pelvic vein thrombophlebitis. A protective effect of the same order of magnitude is seen for endometritis. The degree of reduction in the risk of wound infection is somewhat less, but it is still substantial.

Because the rates of infection associated with caesarean section performed after the onset of labour or after ruptured membranes are higher than those following elective operations, the absolute numbers of serious infections avoided by prophylactic administration of antibiotics in association with emergency caesarean sections will be greater than those avoided by a similar policy for elective sections. Enough evidence has now accumulated to show that prophylactic antibiotics may achieve as great reductions in the relative risk of both endometritis and wound infection among women having planned operations as among those having emergency procedures.

Although there may be more dispute about the clinical importance of post-operative febrile morbidity than about the importance of the more serious infections discussed above, its higher incidence as an outcome means that it is possible to distinguish effects of antibiotic prophylaxis in smaller, more homogeneous groups of trials.

3 Choice of antibiotic preparation

The risk of post-operative febrile morbidity is reduced by a comparable amount by both broad-spectrum penicillins and cephalosporins. The only trial to have assessed the prophylactic effect of trimethoprim and sulphamethoxazole in these circumstances also found a statistically significantly reduced risk of post-operative febrile morbidity. The most striking risk reduction in post-operative febrile morbidity was achieved when a combination of broad-spectrum penicillins and aminoglycosides were used for prophylaxis.

There is currently no good evidence that the antiprotozoal drug metronidazole reduces the risk of post-operative febrile morbidity following caesarean section.

Studies directly comparing different antibiotic preparations can be divided into two groups: those comparing broad spectrum penicillins with cephalosporins, and those comparing a combination of broad-spectrum penicillins plus aminoglycosides with broad-spectrum penicillins alone.

The evidence from trials in which broad-spectrum penicillins and cephalosporins have been compared directly suggest that they have similar effects on the risk of post-operative febrile morbidity.

Trials comparing a combination of broad-spectrum antibiotics and aminoglycosides with placebo show a greater effect than trials comparing broad-spectrum antibiotics used alone with placebo. This suggests that the combination might be a more effective prophylactic. The results of trials in which direct comparisons between the two regimens were made point in the same direction, but the evidence is not sufficiently strong to warrant adoption of a regimen that is more complicated (and costly) and associated with some increased risk of ototoxicity and nephrotoxicity from the aminoglycosides.

4 Timing, dose, and frequency of administration

Relatively short courses of antibiotics are less effective than longer courses, and single-dose regimens are less effective than multiple-dose regimens. There is also a trend, not statistically significant, suggesting that larger doses of antibiotics achieve prophylaxis more successfully than smaller doses.

5 Route of administration

Intra-operative irrigation with antibiotics has been shown to be more effective than irrigation with placebo in reducing the risk of post-operative febrile morbidity, and indirect comparisons suggest that this route of administration may be as effective (and possibly more effective) than systemic administration. Evidence from direct comparisons of the two routes of administration provides no strong evidence that one route of administration is superior to the other.

6 Potential adverse consequences of antibiotic prophylaxis

Only a minority of the reports of controlled trials included information about adverse effects of the prophylactic agents used, and even in these reports the reference was usually rather casual. It is thus not surprising that the reported incidence of adverse reactions was very low—1 per cent or less. This is well below the rate of adverse reactions that one would expect of antibiotics, especially broad-spectrum antibiotics given intravenously.

Drug effects on the infant (which might include protective as well as unwanted effects) have not been studied systematically by the majority of investigators. Preventing exposure of the baby to antibiotics by starting them after the umbilical cord has been clamped would seem to be a sensible precaution, even if there is some slight, as yet undetected, loss of prophylactic efficacy. Not only will babies be spared any unwanted effects of drugs that have crossed the placenta; they will also be spared the intensive investigations and neonatal administration of antibiotics which many paediatricians feel are mandatory, because they are concerned that intrapartum fetal exposure to antibiotics may suppress microbial growth and thus mask neonatal sepsis.

Antibiotics received by the mother can also reach the baby through breast milk. The drug levels involved seem likely to be very low, particularly if the course of prophylactic antibiotics has been relatively short.

An important argument of those who have objected to routine antibiotic prophylaxis has been their concern about the effects of this practice on the bacterial flora, namely replacement of non-pathogenic bacteria with pathogenic ones, and a rise in resistance of bacteria in treated patients and in the hospital environment generally. At least some antibiotics appear to cause these changes with relatively few doses. There is some suggestion that certain prophylactic regimens, for example, trimethoprim and sulfamethoxazole, may be less disruptive of flora, yet remain effective.

7 Conclusions

The first step that should be taken to reduce the infectious morbidity that is so common following caesarean section is to minimize the numbers of unnecessary operations. The second step requires attention to the variety of factors that reduces the risk of infection following justified use of the operation. These include minimizing the length of hospital admission prior to surgery; delaying shaving of the operation site until immediately before the operation; sterilizing swabs and instruments, the hands of the operating team, the skin of the woman, and the air of the operating theatre; and paying attention to good surgical technique.

Decisions about whether or not to institute a policy of antibiotic prophylaxis should no longer depend on uncertainties about whether reductions in the risks of serious infections can be achieved in this way; they can. If the level of post-caesarean infectious morbidity is very low without a policy of antibiotic prophylaxis, the ratio of benefits to costs, in absolute terms, might argue against instituting such a policy. Such circumstances are rare, and the evidence justifies far wider adoption of antibiotic prophylaxis than currently exists. Although the incidence of adverse drug effects among women receiving prophylactic antibiotics has probably been underestimated, it is inconceivable that it could outweigh the reduction in serious maternal morbidity which can be achieved by a policy of antibiotic prophylaxis. Adverse drug effects in the baby can be lessened by beginning prophylaxis after the umbilical cord has been divided.

Adverse ecological effects on bacterial flora are more difficult to quantify and predict, but are potentially of greater concern than adverse drug reactions in individual mothers and babies. If prophylactic antibiotics are used routinely, genital tract cultures and drug-sensitivity studies should be performed in all women who become infected despite receiving prophylaxis, and the hospital bacteriology laboratory should conduct a periodic review of the susceptibility patterns of commonly isolated organisms to detect gradual changes in antibiotic resistance.

The risk of these adverse ecological effects is likely to be reduced if the total load of antibiotics is reduced. The evidence suggests that single-dose or short regimens are not as effective as multiple-dose or longer regimens. Even so, the disadvantages of longer courses of antibiotics in terms of the resulting increase in the total antibiotic load, the numbers of women experiencing side-effects, and the additional cost in financial terms may actually outweigh the advantages of their greater prophylactic efficacy relative to shorter or single-dose regimens.

As far as choice of antibiotic is concerned, the broad-spectrum penicillins are as effective as the cephalosporins. No strong case for adding aminoglycosides to broad-spectrum penicillins can be made; on the basis of current evidence any increase in effectiveness that may result is likely to be marginal and would add the risk of ototoxicity and nephrotoxicity associated with these drugs. Metronidazole currently has no place in antibiotic prophylaxis for caesarean section because there is no convincing evidence that it is effective.

It is now clear that withholding prophylactic antibiotics from women having caesarean section will increase the chances that they will experience serious morbidity, and further trials including no-treatment controls would not be justified.

Preparing for induction of labour

This chapter is derived from the chapters by Iain Chalmers and Marc J. N. C. Keirse (60) and Marc J. N. C. Keirse and A. Carla C. Van Oppen (61) in EFFECTIVE CARE IN PREGNANCY AND CHILDBIRTH.

1 Introduction

The decision to bring pregnancy to an end before the spontaneous onset of labour is one of the most fundamental ways of intervening in the 'natural history' of pregnancy and childbirth. The indications for such 'elective deliveries' (which may be achieved either by inducing labour or by elective caesarean section) range from those that are life-saving, to those that are trivial. Research has concentrated almost exclusively on evaluating methods of induction, rather than on the more important question of when induction or elective caesarean is preferable to waiting for the spontaneous onset of labour.

There is little purpose in assessing the relative merits of different ways of achieving elective delivery if there is no need for elective delivery in the first place. Although the effects of elective delivery are closely bound up with the effects of the methods used to achieve it, comparisons of these methods should be seen as a secondary goal to the more fundamental question of when elective delivery is indicated.

2 Preparing the cervix

The state of the cervix at the time that induction of labour is attempted is the most important determinant of the subsequent duration of labour. An 'unripe' cervix fails to dilate adequately in response to uterine contractions. Attempted induction when the cervix is not ripe may result in high rates of induction failure, protracted and exhausting labours, a high caesarean section rate, and a variety of other complications. These include intrauterine infection and pyrexia when amniotomy is employed, and uterine hypertonus and drug-induced side-effects (due to the high doses needed) with the use of oxytocics.

Realization of the importance of the state of the cervix for induction has led both to the development of various methods to assess cervical 'ripeness' and to the search for methods that decrease cervical resistance prior to induction. A variety of methods have been used in attempts to influence the success of induction by modifying ('ripening') the state of the cervix. Assessment of the state of the cervix is highly subjective, and even experienced examiners may differ in their appraisal of cervical features. Several cervical scoring systems have been developed in an attempt to establish more comparable guidelines for cervical assessment. The best known of these is the score proposed by Bishop, which rates five different qualities (cervical effacement, dilatation, and consistency, position of the cervix relative to the axis of the pelvis, and descent of the fetal presenting part) on a total score from 0 to 13. Most other scoring systems use the same components, although with different weighting.

3 Prostaglandins for cervical ripening

A few years after the introduction of prostaglandins for inducing labour in the late 1960s, doses which by themselves were insufficient to induce labour successfully were found to produce a marked softening of the uterine cervix. There is evidence that this softening results from a direct effect of prostaglandins on the cervix, rather than being a result of uterine contractions.

The effects of prostaglandins in ripening the cervix prior to induction of labour have been assessed in a large number of controlled trials. These studies show that prostaglandin treatment, by any route, is more likely than placebo or no treatment to achieve an increase in the cervical score, and to facilitate induction of labour. In all trials, labour commenced before the start of induction (during the period

allocated for cervical ripening) more often in women receiving prostaglandins for cervical ripening than in women who received placebo
or no medication.

'Induction failure' tended to occur less frequently in the prostaglandin-treated than in the control groups. The likelihood of not
being delivered within 12 or 24 hours after the start of induction, and
of not having a vaginal delivery within 12 or 24 hours after the start
of induction, was considerably reduced in prostaglandin-treated
women.

Very few reports provide data on the frequency with which pharmacological or epidural analgesia was used in the active treatment
and control groups. In those reports that do provide data, the use of
epidural analgesia is statistically significantly lower among prostaglandin-treated women than among women in the control group.

'Uterine hypertonus' or 'uterine hyperstimulation', either during
the period of cervical ripening or during the subsequent induction of
labour, occurred statistically significantly more often in prostaglandin-treated women than among women who received placebo or no
treatment prior to induction. Whether for this or for other reasons,
fetal heart rate abnormalities also tended to occur more frequently
with prostaglandin treatment, although the difference compared to
placebo or no treatment was not statistically significant. Neither of
these trends led to an increase in the rate of operative delivery.

On the contrary, the trials show a modest, but statistically significant decrease in the caesarean section rate with prostaglandin
treatment as compared with placebo or no treatment. A more marked
effect was seen on the incidence of instrumental vaginal delivery.
Overall, prostaglandin treatment results in a major reduction in the
incidence of operative delivery.

Only 7 trial reports provided data on the incidence of postpartum
haemorrhage and/or the use of blood transfusion. The data do not
suggest that these outcomes are influenced by the use of prostaglandins for cervical ripening, but the estimate is not precise.

There is a trend towards fewer low Apgar scores in babies born to
mothers who received prostaglandins, although this effect is compatible with chance. Few trial reports provide data on the more
substantive infant outcome measures, such as resuscitation of the
newborn, admission to a special-care nursery, and perinatal death.
None of these outcome measures suggested any influence, good or
bad, of cervical ripening.

There is no convincing evidence that prostaglandins PGE_2 and
$PGF_{2\alpha}$ have clinically important differential effects on cervical ripening when used in equipotent doses. However, the much lower drug
dose needed for PGE_2 would suggest this compound may be superior
to $PGF_{2\alpha}$.

3.1 *Oral prostaglandins*

Oral prostaglandins have shown little or no beneficial effect when compared with either placebo or no treatment for cervical ripening. The drug must be administered repeatedly over a period of several hours in order to have effects that, on the whole, are not very impressive. Overall, the data suggest that oral prostaglandins are not a suitable approach to ripening of the cervix.

3.2 *Vaginal prostaglandins*

Prostaglandins administered by the vaginal route for cervical ripening have been studied more extensively. The results are similar to those of prostaglandins by any route: an increase in the frequency of labour onset during the ripening period, a decrease in the incidence of failed induction, and an increase in the likelihood of 'hypertonus' or 'hyperstimulation' (excessive uterine contractility). The rate of instrumental vaginal delivery was slightly decreased with the use of vaginal prostaglandins, but no effect was demonstrated on the overall use of caesarean section. As expected, there was no effect on infant outcomes such as Apgar scores, or need for resuscitation.

Women receiving vaginal prostaglandins for cervical ripening were more likely to undergo caesarean section during the time interval allowed for cervical ripening than women receiving the control treatment. This higher incidence of caesarean section during cervical ripening was apparently compensated for by a lower caesarean section rate during induced labour, since the overall caesarean section rate tended to be lower rather than higher with the prostaglandin treatment.

3.3 *Endocervical prostaglandins*

Endocervical administration of prostaglandin in a viscous gel (injected in the cervical canal) has been explored most thoroughly in controlled comparisons. Both the number of controlled trials reported and the number of women included is larger than for any other method of cervical ripening. Most of the investigations have been conducted with 0.5 mg PGE_2, a dose that is much smaller than those used with either the oral or vaginal routes of administration.

As for prostaglandins by any route, endocervical administration is more likely than either placebo or no treatment to result in uterine activity, in the onset of labour, in a reduction of the need for formal induction of labour at the end of the ripening period, and in delivery during the ripening period. More women undergo caesarean section during the ripening period with prostaglandin treatment, but this is compensated for by a reduction in the rate of caesarean during labour, and thus does not lead to a higher caesarean section rate overall. The number of women who were not delivered within 12 hours and within 24 hours after the beginning of induction was reduced in the trials that provided data on this outcome. The trends toward a lower incidence of caesarean section, instrumental vaginal delivery, and the overall rate of operative delivery are similar to those observed with prostaglandins administered by any route.

3.4 *Extra-amniotic prostaglandins*

Only three placebo-controlled trials have been reported on extra-amniotic administration of a prostaglandin for cervical ripening. Overall, there are too few data to permit adequate judgement of either the merits or the hazards of extra-amniotic prostaglandin administration for ripening the unfavourable cervix.

3.5 *Direct comparisons between different routes*

The results of the two reasonably well-conducted comparisons of endocervical with vaginal PGE_2 for cervical ripening suggest that the endocervical approach is somewhat more effective in terms of the number of women going into labour or delivered during ripening (if this is considered to be a desirable outcome). No statistically significant effects were found on other outcomes.

The three trials which compared extra-amniotic with vaginal administration show that labour is more likely to occur during ripening when the extra-amniotic rather than the vaginal route of administration is selected. None of the other outcome measures on which data were available indicate any differential effect between these two routes of administration, but the precision of these estimates is low.

The results of the single trial which has reported on a comparison between extra-amniotic and endocervical administration show that 75 per cent of women receiving the PGE_2 extra-amniotically went into labour, compared to 32 per cent of those who received the drug endocervically. This would suggest that the extra-amniotic route, if used at all, should be reserved for women in whom immediate induction of labour is warranted.

4 Other methods for cervical ripening

4.1 Oestrogens

Much of the interest in oestrogens for cervical ripening has come from the idea that these agents might ripen the cervix without concomitant effects on uterine contractility. Pooled overviews of the available data offer no suggestion that labour is more likely to occur during oestrogen treatment than it is with placebo treatment. No case of 'uterine hypertonus' or 'hyperstimulation' was reported (among 110 oestrogen-treated women) in the three trials that referred to this complication. Notwithstanding the apparent lack of contraction-enhancing activity of the oestrogen treatment, it was associated with a statistically significant reduction in the incidence of caesarean section. Data on infant outcomes are lacking in most of the reports. The two trials that provided categorical data on low 1-minute Apgar scores suggest a decrease with oestrogen treatment, but this reduction is compatible with chance.

4.1 Oxytocin

An overview of the trials comparing the effects of oxytocin with no treatment for an unripe cervix shows no significant effect on labour onset during ripening or on the incidence of any form of operative delivery.

All the information currently available indicates that oxytocin administration to ripen the cervix (rather than to induce labour) serves no useful purpose. Oxytocin infusions for prolonged periods of time (as is usually the case when the aim is to ripen the cervix) are unpleasant, limit the woman's mobility, and may lead to water-intoxication when administered in large doses. This practice should be abandoned.

4.3 Mechanical methods

In recent years mechanical devices which were formerly used for induction of labour have also been applied in attempts to achieve cervical ripening. In addition to laminaria tents, new synthetic hydrophilic materials were developed with the same aims in mind. Only one of these, polyvinyl alcohol polymer sponge that behaves like a synthetic laminaria tent (Lamicel®), has so far been tested in controlled comparisons for ripening the cervix prior to induction. The comparison has been with other ripening agents, however, rather than with no treatment.

The use of these mechanical methods of ripening the cervix has been shown to increase cervical ripeness scores, to increase the proportion of women going into labour or delivering during ripening, and to decrease the proportion of women who did not have a vaginal delivery within 12 hours. No effect has been shown on the incidence of caesarean section, puerperal pyrexia, or low Apgar scores.

Overall the data do not suggest that the insertion of various mechanical devices into the cervix, or the extra-amniotic space, is a useful approach to ripening the cervix prior to induction of labour.

4.4 Relaxin

Porcine relaxin, a polypeptide hormone extracted from corpora lutea of sows and capable of relaxing the pelvic ligaments of the guinea pig, was first thought to be involved in remodelling the collagenous structure of the cervix in the 1950s. Placebo-controlled trials failed to reveal a shortening of labour following the administration of relaxin, and the use of relaxin disappeared from obstetric practice.

With the development of better techniques to purify the compound, relaxin has made a comeback for cervical ripening. Three controlled trials have compared relaxin with placebo for cervical ripening. The only differences that reached statistical significance were a greater increase in Bishop score and a higher incidence of labour starting during relaxin treatment than that observed in the control groups. All three trials appear to indicate a lower incidence of caesarean section with than without relaxin treatment, but these observations are compatible with the play of chance. The few categorical data on infant outcome measures that are available from these three trials offer no evidence for any effect, good or bad.

Although, theoretically, the merits of the treatment might be to enhance cervical softening without a concomitant effect on uterine contractility, the sparse data that are available do not suggest that this actually occurs in practice. About 25 per cent of women will go into labour during ripening with relaxin treatment.

The available evidence does not suggest that relaxin is a worthwhile treatment for ripening the cervix prior to induction of labour. It should not be adopted into clinical practice unless larger, properly controlled trials show that it does more good than harm.

4.5 Breast stimulation

In an attempt to explore 'natural' methods for ripening the cervix, two groups of investigators have evaluated the effects of breast stimulation. In each of these trials, the intervention consisted of self-applied gentle massage of the breasts for 3 hours a day (spread over 2 to 3 sessions) on 3 consecutive days. Women in the control group were instructed to avoid breast stimulation. Both trials report that women allocated to breast stimulation were more likely to go into labour during the intervention period than those allocated to the control group. Both studies reported statistically significant increases in the mean Bishop score in the 3 days of breast stimulation, but neither of the two reports mentions whether this resulted in easier labour or delivery.

5 Prostaglandins versus other methods

A number of controlled comparisons have been conducted in which prostaglandins have been compared with alternative methods, such as oxytocin or oestrogen administration, or the insertion of mechanical devices. Most of these comparisons have involved small numbers of women.

5.1 *Prostaglandins versus oestrogens*

The four controlled trials that compared prostaglandins with oestrogens for cervical ripening indicate that women are more likely to experience labour during cervical ripening with a prostaglandin than with oestradiol. Otherwise no differences were found between the treatment groups; but data on the different outcomes were only available for some of the trials, and all estimates lack precision.

5.2 *Prostaglandins versus oxytocin*

As might be expected from the indirect comparisons, when the effects of prostaglandins are compared with those of oxytocin for ripening the cervix, there is a statistically significantly greater likelihood of labour starting, and of women delivering, during cervical ripening with the prostaglandin preparation than with oxytocin. Thus the number of women who were not delivered within 24 hours and within 48 hours after induction of labour was smaller in prostaglandin-treated than in oxytocin-treated women. The number of caesarean sections, although tending to be smaller with prostaglandin than with oxytocin treatment, was not statistically significantly different.

The data lend further support to the conclusion that oxytocin is not effective for ripening the cervix prior to induction of labour.

5.3 *Prostaglandins versus mechanical methods*

Randomized comparisons between vaginally administered prostaglandins and mechanical devices such as laminaria, Foley catheters, and Lamicel have shown prostaglandins to be more effective in increasing the cervical score. Prostaglandin administration is more likely to result in the onset of labour by the end of the ripening period than is the insertion of mechanical devices. Of the three trials that provided information on the incidence of 'fetal distress', two detected no difference in incidence and one found the incidence to be statistically significantly higher in prostaglandin-treated women than in women receiving Lamicel®. It is difficult to judge whether this represents a real difference between the two types of methods, as the dose of PGE_2 (4 mg in cellulose gel) used in that study may be considered high for the objective of cervical ripening.

There is no evidence for any differential effects in other maternal outcomes on which data were reported (such as the incidences of caesarean section, instrumental vaginal delivery, and pyrexia during labour and the puerperium), but all of these estimates are rather imprecise. The same applies to infant outcomes, for which very few data were available.

6 Hazards of cervical ripening

From the evidence reviewed for this chapter it is clear that ripening of the cervix, with any of the methods that have been used for this purpose, is not a trivial intervention. The risks of the ripening itself include a (small) danger of intrauterine infection with mechanical procedures and extra-amniotic drug administration; an increased likelihood of uterine hypertonus and of fetal heart rate abnormalities; and a non-negligible degree of discomfort and inconvenience for the mother. Some of these hazards, uterine 'hypertonus' and fetal heart rate 'abnormalities' in particular, are ill-defined and of unclear significance for the baby. Yet they are known to have prompted caesarean sections during cervical ripening, and are therefore important to the mother.

The risks of cervical ripening are not limited to those of the intervention itself, but include those associated with other aspects of induction of labour. The greatest hazard is that awareness among clinicians that it is possible to ripen the cervix will result in unnecessary induction of labour in women for whom an artificial ending of pregnancy would not otherwise have been contemplated. This can only increase the numbers of women exposed to any serious hazards of these procedures without a concomitant expectation of benefit.

7 Conclusions

None of the methods that are successful in ripening the unripe cervix are trivial interventions. None of them act exclusively on the cervix, and all of them tend to increase myometrial contractility. Cervical ripening should not be viewed as anything other than the first step in induction of labour, and it should not be used unless there are valid grounds for ending pregnancy artificially.

The occasional need to induce labour in the presence of an unripe cervix requires methods that have not only been shown to increase cervical compliance, but which increase the likelihood of spontaneous vaginal delivery of a healthy baby within a reasonable period of time. Of the various interventions used only the prostaglandins, which have also been the most extensively studied, have so far approached this goal. Use of prostaglandins in these circumstances decreases the likelihood of 'failed induction', decreases the incidence of prolonged labour, and increases the chances of a spontaneous vaginal delivery. Despite the many studies on the use of prostaglandins for preinduction cervical ripening, there are still insufficient data to allow any confident statements about the effects on the baby.

The use of prostaglandins for ripening the cervix is not a harmless procedure, and it is certainly inappropriate to administer prostaglandins for cervical ripening for trivial reasons, and without careful monitoring of maternal and fetal wellbeing.

Currently available data do not permit firm conclusions about the relative merits of E and F prostaglandins for this indication, although PGE2 is likely to be superior to PGF2α. Oral administration of prostaglandins, in order to have any effect, requires repeated administration over a long period of time, and may be associated with unpleasant maternal side-effects; it has no place in cervical ripening. Apart from this, there is at present no basis for believing that any one of the other routes of administration (vaginal, extra-amniotic, or endocervical) that have been used is superior to any other route. It is, of course, essential that doses should be adapted to take into account the particular route of administration.

On balance, and in the light of current evidence, the most appropriate route would be the one that entails least discomfort for the mother. When choice of the extra-amniotic route involves the use of an indwelling Foley catheter, for example, the discomfort and inconvenience experienced by the mother might be sufficient reason to choose either endocervical or vaginal administration.

Of the other approaches to cervical ripening, only oestrogens have been studied with any consistency. Although they are known to affect cervical compliance, the available evidence does not allow confident conclusions about their effects on substantive outcomes. In particular, it is unclear whether oestrogen pretreatment actually increases the likelihood that women will be delivered within a reasonable time interval after induction of labour.

There is even less information to allow an assessment of the possible place of relaxin, the mechanical methods, and breast stimulation. None of these can currently be recommended for the care of women with an unripe cervix for whom there is a need to bring pregnancy to an end. The same applies to the use of oxytocin for ripening the cervix before a formal induction attempt is undertaken; this use is troublesome and unpleasant for the mother, and confers no benefits. The direct randomized comparisons between prostaglandins and these other methods are consistent with these observations and suggest that prostaglandins currently represent the approach of choice for ripening the unfavourable cervix.

Methods of inducing labour

This chapter is derived from the chapters by Michel Thiery, Cornelia J. Baines, and Marc J. N. C. Keirse (59); Marc J. N. C. Keirse and Iain Chalmers (62); and Marc J. N. C. Keirse and A. Carla C. van Oppen (63) in EFFECTIVE CARE IN PREGNANCY AND CHILDBIRTH.

1 Introduction

For practical purposes, modern obstetric practice uses only three broad approaches to the induction of labour: stripping (sweeping) of the membranes; amniotomy; and oxytocic drugs (oxytocin or a prostaglandin). Other methods, although still occasionally reported, have generally been abandoned.

2 Sweeping (stripping) the membranes

Sweeping (stripping) the membranes from the lower uterine segment has been widely used to induce labour. There are good theoretical reasons to suggest that it may be effective. Although it is now rarely considered as a formal method of induction, the procedure is still frequently used at term in the hope that it will circumvent the need to induce labour formally with amniotomy or oxytocic drugs.

Despite its long history and its wide use, we are aware of only one formal attempt to assess the effects of digital stripping of the membranes at term. Women who had the membranes stripped daily for three days were more likely to go into labour within 24 hours following the third stripping than were the women who served as controls. The author felt that the apparent success of the method in inducing labour was counterbalanced by the unpredictable interval between stripping and the onset of labour, and by 'a definite increase in maternal morbidity', details of which were not provided.

It is remarkable that stripping the membranes has been the subject of so little controlled research. Randomized trials could easily be mounted to assess the effects of this commonly performed procedure.

3 Amniotomy

The membranes may be artificially ruptured in two ways: low amniotomy (forewater rupture), and high amniotomy ('hindwater' rupture). A number of advantages have been claimed for high amniotomy, including reduced risks of infection and cord prolapse, controlled release of amniotic fluid, and the possibility of rupturing the membranes when the cervix is too firmly closed to allow forewater rupture; but none of these claims have been assessed in controlled comparisons. The procedure can undoubtedly cause damage to the fetus, the placenta, and the genital tract of the mother. High amniotomy, if it is to be used at all, should be reserved for those situations in which there is polyhydramnios in addition to a strong indication for induction of labour.

3.1 Amniotomy used alone

Although debate continues as to whether amniotomy performed *during* labour increases or decreases uterine contractility, there is no doubt that this procedure, when performed *before* the onset of labour, can induce labour. It embodies a firm commitment to delivery; once the membranes have been ruptured, there is no turning back.

The main disadvantage of amniotomy when used alone for the induction of labour is the unpredictable, and occasionally long, interval to the onset of labour-like uterine activity, and thus to delivery.

3.2 Amniotomy with oxytocic drugs versus amniotomy alone

In order to shorten the interval between amniotomy and delivery, oxytocic drugs are usually used either at the time that the membranes are ruptured or after an interval of a few hours, if labour has not started. Evidence from controlled trials shows that women who receive oxytocics from the time of amniotomy are more likely to be delivered within 12 hours and within 24 hours, and less likely to be delivered by caesarean section or forceps, than those who have had amniotomy alone.

Women with the early oxytocin administration require less analgesia than those having late oxytocin administration. This does not necessarily mean that induction of labour is less painful for these women; it may simply reflect the shorter interval between amniotomy and delivery. In both of the trials for which data are available, the incidence of postpartum haemorrhage was lower when amniotomy was followed by early oxytocin administration.

Depressed Apgar scores are seen less frequently with a policy of using oxytocin from the time of amniotomy. No other differential effects on the baby have been noted in controlled trials.

3.3 *Amniotomy with oxytocic drugs versus oxytocic drugs alone*

In the only controlled trial in which a policy of routine amniotomy at the time of starting oxytocic drugs to induce labour was compared with a policy in which the membranes were left intact, a higher proportion of women in the amniotomy group were in established labour within six hours of starting the induction. No significant differences were detected in the proportions of women delivered within 24 and 48 hours, nor in the caesarean section rate.

This trial, despite involving just over 200 women, may have been too small to detect clinically important differences between the two policies compared. Observational data derived from studies conducted in the 1960s suggest that about a third of women in whom induction of labour is attempted with oxytocin administration but without concurrent amniotomy will remain undelivered 2 to 3 days after the beginning of the induction attempt. Not surprisingly, in the light of these observations, amniotomy has come to be used routinely at the time that oxytocic drugs to induce labour are started.

3.4 *Hazards of amniotomy*

A number of undesirable consequences have been attributed to artificial rupture of the membranes. These include intrauterine infection (occasionally leading to septicaemia); early decelerations in the fetal heart rate; umbilical cord prolapse; and bleeding, either from fetal vessels in the membranes, from the cervix, or from the placental site.

Any instrument (or a finger) passing up the vagina in order to rupture the amniotic sac will carry some of the vaginal bacterial flora with it. The risk of clinically significant intrauterine infection ensuing from these procedures is largely dependent on the interval between amniotomy and delivery.

The view that amniotomy predisposes to fetal heart rate deceiera-tions is largely based on the results of a study of its use in labour of spontaneous onset. There was considerable potential for bias in this study, and the results are impossible to interpret with any confidence.

4 Oxytocin

4.1 Routes and methods of administration

Intravenous infusion of oxytocin is currently the most widely used method for inducing labour. No formal comparisons between the intravenous route and other routes of administration have been reported.

Intravenous oxytocin has been administered in a variety of dif-ferent ways, ranging from simple, manually adjusted, gravity-fed systems, through mechanically or electronically controlled infusion pumps, to fully automated closed-loop feedback systems, in which the dose of oxytocin is regulated by the intensity of uterine contrac-tions. Gravity-fed systems have the disadvantage that the amount of oxytocin infused may be difficult to regulate accurately, and may vary with the position of the woman. A further disadvantage is that the amount of fluid administered intravenously may be large, and may thus increase the risk of water-intoxication. Automatic oxytocin in-fusion equipment, by contrast, delivers oxytocin at a well-regulated rate, in a small volume of fluid. In theory it should optimize efficacy and safety during oxytocin administration, but there is no evidence that these theoretical advantages confer any benefit in practice.

The only formal comparisons of different methods for administer-ing oxytocin to induce labour are two small trials comparing automat-ic oxytocin infusion systems with 'standard' infusions. A total of only 131 women were studied in these two trials, an insufficient number to detect differences in any substantive outcomes. Experience with early versions of automated infusion systems indicated enough problems to make it clear that their merits and risks must be more thoroughly evaluated before their place, if any, in clinical practice can be determined.

4.2 Hazards of oxytocin administration

The possible hazards of oxytocin *per se* must be distinguished from the hazards associated with any attempt to induce labour, and those associated with any artificial stimulation of uterine contractions.

The antidiuretic effect of oxytocin can result in water retention and hyponatraemia, and may lead to coma, convulsions, and even mater-nal death. These risks are mainly associated with oxytocin infusions at early stages of pregnancy, when uterine sensitivity to oxytocin is far less than it is at term, and when large doses are thus required to stimulate uterine contractions. In women with an already reduced urinary output the danger of water-intoxication is an important consideration at any stage of gestation.

Any agent that causes uterine contractions, whether it be a drug such as oxytocin or a prostaglandin, or a practice such as nipple stimulation, may also cause excessive uterine contractility. If the myometrial contraction force exceeds the levels of venous pressure, the venous circulation through the myometrium will become compromised. Blood flow from and to the placenta will be affected, which will in turn result in inadequate fetal oxygenation. Uterine rupture is a further, though much rarer consequence of excessive stimulation of uterine activity. The balance of evidence suggests that induction of labour with oxytocin increases the incidence of neonatal hyperbilirubinaemia.

These hazards will be minimized firstly, by restricting the use of elective delivery to circumstances in which it can be justified, and secondly, by appropriate regulation of uterine contractility, regardless of the method through which it is stimulated artificially.

5 Prostaglandins

5.1 Comparisons with placebo

Not surprisingly, the 'failure' rate of induction and the proportion of women needing a second induction attempt is lower following prostaglandin administration (in various doses, formulations, and routes) than with placebo treatments. There were fewer caesarean sections in the prostaglandin than in the placebo groups in the reported trials, but the rates of instrumental vaginal delivery were similar. Most of the trials mentioned specifically that 'uterine hypertonus' and/or 'uterine hyperstimulation' were not observed, and several commented on the low incidence of gastro-intestinal side-effects encountered.

Very few infant outcomes were reported in any of these trials. Among those in which they were reported, none showed any differences between the prostaglandin and placebo groups.

5.2 Prostaglandin E versus prostaglandin F

Both E and F prostaglandins stimulate uterine contractility. Among these two series of prostaglandins, only PGE_2 and $PGF_{2\alpha}$ (which are also naturally formed during spontaneous labour) have been used to any extent for the induction of labour.

In order to achieve a similar effect on uterine contractility, $PGF_{2\alpha}$ must be administered in a dose eight to ten times as large as that needed when PGE_2 is used. This difference in potency applies to the stimulating properties of these compounds on the myometrium. It does not apply to the same extent to their effects on other organ systems, such as the gastro-intestinal tract. Consequently, for a comparable uterotonic effect the incidence of other, undesired effects tends to be larger with $PGF_{2\alpha}$ than with PGE_2.

There are two exceptions to the general rule that PGE_2 is preferable to $PGF_{2\alpha}$ as far as side-effects are concerned: hyperthermia and venous erythema are more often observed with PGE_2 than with $PGF_{2\alpha}$ administration. Venous erythema which relates to dilatation of the vasa vasorum of the venous system, is seen virtually only with intravenous PGE_2 infusions. Although on occasions alarming from a visual point of view, venous erythema is painless, and disappears after the end of the infusion period.

5.3 *Routes and methods of administration*

Early studies of prostaglandins for the induction of labour used the intravenous route of administration. From these studies, few, if any, advantages of using prostaglandins for induction of labour emerged. Compared with oxytocin they appeared to offer no advantage and were considerably more expensive.

Oral administration of PGE_2 (in repeat doses increasing from 0.5 to 2 mg) became widely used as an alternative to intravenous infusions of prostaglandins for inducing labour, particularly when combined with amniotomy and in women with a favourable cervix. Because of its gastro-intestinal side-effects, $PGF_{2\alpha}$ is not suitable for oral administration. Even with oral PGE_2, gastro-intestinal side-effects occur, although they are usually confined to one or two episodes of vomiting.

Probably the most widely adopted mode of administration of PGE_2 (and of $PGF_{2\alpha}$ in countries where PGE_2 is not available) has become the vaginal route.

Because intravenous, oral, and vaginal administration of prostaglandins all lead to high levels of these drugs in the blood, the gastrointestinal tract, or both, intrauterine (extra-amniotic) routes of administration have been used in attempts to reduce the side-effects associated with the other routes. Continuous or intermittent extra-amniotic infusion of a solution of PGE_2 is effective for inducing labour, but as the procedure is cumbersome and inconvenient for the mother, it was later replaced by extra-amniotic injection of PGE_2 suspended in a viscous gel.

There have been only two controlled comparisons of the extra-amniotic route with other routes of prostaglandin administration. Neither of the two trials showed that the more invasive extra-amniotic route offered any advantage; but the precision of that estimate is low.

Another route of local administration, endocervical injection of PGE_2 in a viscous gel, has been used mainly for ripening the cervix rather than for induction. The relative merits and hazards of endocervical administration compared to other routes of administration for the induction of labour have not yet been adequately assessed.

5.4 Hazards of prostaglandin administration

The specific hazards attributable to prostaglandins *per se* relate mainly to their effects on the gastro-intestinal tract. These effects are minimal when the drugs are administered endocervically or extra-amniotically, and maximal when routes of administration (intravenous, oral, and vaginal) are used that lead to high levels of the drugs in either the blood or the gastro-intestinal tract. These problems may affect up to about 10 per cent of women.

Pyrexia may result from a direct effect of prostaglandins on thermoregulating centres in the brain. This is particularly a problem with systemic prostaglandin E_2 administration, and may give rise to concern that intra-uterine infection has supervened. This concern may be further fuelled by a rise in the leucocyte count, which can also be stimulated by prostaglandin administration.

More worrying than the specific hazards associated with prostaglandins are concerns that the simplicity of their administration may encourage their use for trivial indications, or that inadequate attention may be paid to careful monitoring of uterine contractility.

6 Prostaglandins versus oxytocin for inducing labour

Oxytocin administration, combined with amniotomy, remains the most widely used approach to the induction of labour. During recent years prostaglandins have become more widely used for induction, particularly when the cervix is 'unripe'. The important question is whether prostaglandins are, on balance, superior to oxytocin for the induction of labour.

6.1 Effects on time and mode of delivery

The proportions of women who remained undelivered 12 hours after the start of induction are similar for women induced with prostaglandins and for those induced with oxytocin. By 24 hours, however, fewer women remain undelivered when they had been induced with prostaglandins. The proportion of women who remain undelivered after 48 hours shows an even larger difference in favour of prostaglandins. When only women who deliver vaginally are considered, the superiority of prostaglandins is even more striking.

There is no clear evidence of a differential effect of prostaglandins and oxytocin on the caesarean section rate. The rate of instrumental vaginal delivery is lower in the women induced with prostaglandins, as is the incidence of operative delivery overall.

6.2 *Effects on the mother*

There are some major differences between the effects of these two classes of drugs on organ systems other than the uterus. A larger proportion of women experience gastro-intestinal side-effects, such as nausea, vomiting, and diarrhoea, when prostaglandins rather than oxytocin are used for the induction of labour. Pyrexia during labour is also more likely to occur with prostaglandins than with oxytocin, although the differential effect appears to be attributable to intravenous PGE_2.

Uterine hyperstimulation occurs more frequently with prostaglandin than with oxytocin administration, although in many trials this complication was not observed. A diagnosis of hyperstimulation may lead to a variety of interventions, ranging from changes in position, through fetal scalp blood sampling, to administration of betamimetic agents and caesarean section. Thus the condition is important to the mother, irrespective of whether or not it directly jeopardizes the mother or the fetus.

Data on the incidence of retained placenta, of postpartum haemorrhage, and of pyrexia during the puerperium show no difference in the effects of prostaglandins and oxytocin.

6.3 *Effects on the infant*

In view of the increased incidence of uterine hyperstimulation associated with induction using prostaglandins, it is reassuring to note that the incidence of fetal heart rate abnormalities is similar among the fetuses of women receiving prostaglandins and among fetuses of women receiving oxytocin.

Unfortunately, few trials provide data on substantive infant outcomes, such as resuscitation of the newborn, admission to a special-care nursery, or early neonatal convulsions. Even data on perinatal death are only available from half the trials. From those trials that provide data, no differential effects of prostaglandins and oxytocin emerge. The precision of these estimates, however, is extremely low.

Somewhat more data are available on the incidence of low 1-minute and 5-minute Apgar scores. There may be a trend towards slightly more low 1-minute Apgar scores in the prostaglandin-induced babies, but thus is not statistically significant, and no difference is noted in 5-minute Apgar scores.

The incidence of neonatal hyperbilirubinaemia is lower among infants born after induction of labour with prostaglandins than among those born after induction with oxytocin, but the difference is compatible with chance.

7 Conclusions

The most important decision to be made when considering the induction of labour is whether or not the induction is justified, rather than how it is to be achieved. Whatever method is chosen to implement a justified decision to induce labour, uterine contractility and maternal and fetal wellbeing must be monitored carefully.

Amniotomy alone is often inadequate to induce labour. When amniotomy is used to induce labour and fails to result promptly in adequate uterine contractility, oxytocic drugs should be administered. The administration of oxytocin without amniotomy is also associated with an unacceptable failure rate.

If prostaglandins are used to induce labour, prostaglandin E_2 is likely to lead to fewer gastro-intestinal side-effects than is prostaglandin $F_{2\alpha}$. The use of oral prostaglandin $F_{2\alpha}$ should be abandoned. If the cervix is 'ripe' and a decision has been made to use prostaglandins to induce labour, the two main alternatives are oral or vaginal administration of prostaglandin E_2. There is currently no satisfactory evidence on which to base a rational choice between these two routes.

Prostaglandins are more likely than oxytocin to result in vaginal delivery within a reasonable length of time after the start of the induction, and to reduce the incidence of operative delivery associated with induction of labour. The extent to which this may reflect the greater mobility possible with some forms of prostaglandin administration than with intravenously administered oxytocin is unknown.

These positive effects of prostaglandins must be balanced against their negative effects. Depending on the route, type, and dose of prostaglandin used, between 5 and 20 per cent of women will experience troublesome gastro-intestinal side-effects, or pyrexia. With the types and formulations of the drugs that are currently available, there is also an important difference in the cost of prostaglandin and oxytocin inductions.

There is too little evidence to allow any judgement about whether prostaglandins are more or less safe for the baby than oxytocin.

Preterm delivery

This chapter is derived from the chapter by Marc J. N. C. Keirse (74) in
EFFECTIVE CARE IN PREGNANCY AND CHILDBIRTH.

1 Introduction

There is no greater risk for a normally formed infant than to be born too early. Preterm birth is the most important single determinant of adverse outcome of pregnancy, in terms of both the likelihood of survival and the quality of life.

Preterm delivery, defined as the birth of an infant with a gestational age of less than 37 completed weeks, is not a single homogeneous entity. In comparison to birth at term, it is more frequently associated with other conditions, such as inadequate fetal growth, prelabour rupture of the membranes, multiple pregnancy, placenta praevia, placental abruption, fetal congenital malformations, abnormal fetal lie, and severe disease of the mother, all of which add their own hazards to the baby.

Only a few decades ago the prognosis for the survival of very preterm infants was so poor that obstetricians were not inclined to consider special care for their delivery. The prevailing belief was that any measures taken to increase the survival rate would result only in increasing numbers of handicapped children who would be a burden to their families and society. In the last two decades the pendulum has swung from therapeutic nihilism to over-zealous intervention. Current recommendations such as 'caesarean section may be preferable to vaginal delivery for all singleton infants of very low birthweight', now suggest that it is mothers, not infants whose interests should be ignored, an equally untenable thesis.

2 Nature and range of preterm delivery

2.1 Types of preterm delivery.

There are substantial differences in the apparent outcome of preterm delivery, depending on the vantage point of those who accumulate the data. Many reported data from the neonatal perspective do not include stillbirths or grossly malformed infants, and they rarely contain reference to the significant pathology that may be present in mother or fetus before delivery. This is particularly relevant to the provision of care for preterm delivery. Many aspects of that care are determined by data on the outcomes of liveborn infants who have received modern intensive neonatal care, rather than on the outcome of fetuses for whom the obstetrician must make a decision.

2.1.1 *Antepartum death and lethal malformations* There have been surprisingly few attempts to distinguish what can and what cannot be achieved by care for preterm delivery. Studies, conducted in widely different settings, have shown that, for between 10 and 15 per cent of all preterm deliveries, none of the different forms of care available have any influence on the outcome for the baby, since all of these infants had either died before the onset of labour or before admission, or had malformations that were incompatible with life. These 10 to 15 per cent of preterm births accounted for well over 50 per cent of the total perinatal mortality associated with preterm delivery.

For these preterm deliveries, at the very least, the objectives of care should be directed at maternal rather than at fetal or neonatal interests. The prognosis for the baby is already determined, but the form of care chosen can have a profound effect on the mother's wellbeing.

The frequency with which preterm delivery occurs in the presence of a dead or malformed fetus is ample justification for a careful ultrasound examination before undertaking any form of care that carries a substantial risk of maternal morbidity.

2.1.2 *Multiple pregnancy* Multiple births are 15 times more frequent among preterm births than among births at term, and preterm multiple births constitute nearly half of all multiple births. These infants, 20 per cent of all liveborn preterm infants, have a higher incidence of respiratory distress syndrome and a higher mortality rate than singleton infants, even after correcting for differences in gestational age. Infants from multiple pregnancies, when born alive, have gestational age-specific mortality rates which are comparable to singleton infants who are at least one to two weeks less mature.

2.1.3 *Elective delivery* Infants with antepartum fetal death, lethal malformations or multiple pregnancy make up about 25 per cent of preterm births. About a third of the remainder result from a deliberate obstetric decision to end pregnancy, either by induction of labour or by elective caesarean section. This category of preterm birth is becoming increasingly important. It constitutes an entirely different obstetric problem from that of delivery following the spontaneous onset of labour. The issue of how best to achieve delivery is secondary to that of whether or not one should attempt to achieve delivery at that time.

One cannot assume that the prognosis for the baby, if elective delivery is undertaken, will be similar to that after preterm delivery following the spontaneous onset of labour. While there is a great deal of data on survival, morbidity, and follow-up of low birthweight, very low birthweight (<1500 gram), and less than 1,000 gram infants, there is a dearth of information on how relevant these data are to the outcome of electively delivered infants, compared to infants born after the spontaneous onset of labour.

2.1.4 *Maternal and fetal pathology* Thus, for more than half the infants delivered preterm, care decisions for delivery are dominated by considerations such as the absence of any chance of infant survival, the complexities of multiple pregnancy, and the question of whether and how to put an end to a pregnancy that is at no inherent risk of spontaneous preterm labour and delivery.

For about half the remaining preterm infants, preterm delivery ensues, causally or incidentally, from pathological processes in the mother, such as hypertension or antepartum haemorrhage, or in the baby, such as retarded fetal growth. Not surprisingly, the occurrence of preterm labour in these circumstances is often interpreted as demonstrating that nature is trying to remove the fetus from a hostile intrauterine environment. Whether that interpretation is or is not correct may be difficult to ascertain, but it can influence profoundly the type of care provided.

2.2 Gestational age

2.2.1 *Range of gestation.* The likelihood of preterm delivery increases with increasing gestational age up to the internationally defined cut-off point of 37 weeks, and less than a quarter of preterm births occur before 32 weeks. The delivery of the very preterm infant (gestational age of less than 32 completed weeks) presents the greatest challenge; but this arbitrary cut-off point has little relevance to clinical care. There is no specific gestational age or estimated fetal weight at which a 'hands-off approach' suddenly changes from being negligent to being appropriate. Nor is there a specified gestational age or estimated fetal weight above or below which a 'hands-on approach' should automatically result in the use of surgical procedures to effect delivery.

Measures that have been clearly demonstrated to be beneficial for the infant and safe for the mother, such as corticosteroid administration, can be applied with far greater confidence at very low gestational ages than other measures, such as non-selective caesarean section, which confer far more dubious, if any, benefits to the infant, and substantial hazards to the mother.

2.2.2 *Estimated weight or gestational age as basis for care options* Most of the available data on outcomes of preterm delivery, which are based on weight rather than gestational age categories, are of limited clinical utility. Although a wealth of information is available on short- and long-term outcomes of infants weighing less than 1000 grams, less than 1500 grams, less than 2000 grams or less than 2500 grams, experienced clinicians are aware of the pitfalls inherent in the birthweight-specific data on which they sometimes are expected to base their care options. These data include infants whose intrauterine growth was restrained, and who were therefore born at a more mature gestational age than would be expected from birthweight alone. They refer to infants delivered to neonatal units after all the selection processes that occur between the decision for delivery and arrival in a neonatal unit.

Moreover, estimates of what the actual weight of the baby will be at delivery are notoriously inaccurate. Clinical estimates are often far off the mark. While great advances have been made in the accuracy of fetal weight estimation by ultrasound, in most hands its accuracy is still far from satisfactory. This applies in particular to the low weight ranges, and, as is often the case for preterm delivery, when the measurements must be made with some urgency and by whoever happens to be available.

Even if birthweight could be estimated with 100 per cent accuracy before birth, the available evidence still suggests that this information would be inferior to gestational age as a determinant of infant outcome and care options. Although birthweight is a better predictor of mortality than gestational age when the whole range of gestation from 20 to over 40 weeks is considered, this does not apply in the very preterm infant, where maturity is more important than organ weight. For these infants, estimated gestational age is a better predictor of both neonatal mortality and risk of intraventricular haemorrhage than birthweight.

A carefully taken menstrual history and ascertainment of any prior assessment of gestational age during pregnancy will be more useful for the woman in preterm labour than attempts to determine fetal weight. In the absence of any evidence that estimation of fetal weight improves outcome, it is not justified to substitute weight estimation for a careful assessment of the menstrual history and gestational age as *the* basis for care decisions.

3 Place of and preparations for delivery

3.1 *Place of delivery*

The most dangerous place for a preterm baby to be delivered is in a hospital with caregivers who believe that they have, but do not in reality have, the equipment and skills necessary to care effectively for these tiny babies before and after birth. Misplaced self-confidence can result in failure of timely referral to institutions where such facilities are available.

Whenever possible, delivery of the very young and very small fetus should be in a centre with adequate facilities and equipment, persons capable of managing and handling the equipment, manpower to ensure around the clock utilization of its resources, and professionals in various disciplines ready and willing to collaborate in care of the mother and baby.

3.2 *Preparations for delivery*

The woman at imminent risk of preterm delivery requires an immediate assessment concerning the appropriateness of transfer to a perinatal centre. This will depend on gestational age, on the facilities that are available (which may, for example, be sufficient for delivery at 36 but not at 31 weeks), and on the imminence of the expected delivery.

If the woman is in labour, it is wise to inhibit labour with betamimetic drugs in order to postpone delivery at least until after she arrives at the perinatal centre. Administration of corticosteroids should be commenced before transfer, unless delivery is likely to be delayed for more than 48 hours, or gestational age has advanced beyond the stage at which respiratory distress syndrome is likely to be a problem.

Given the frequency with which preterm delivery is associated with maternal disease, the institutions where preterm delivery is undertaken should be able to draw on the expertise not only of neonatologists or perinatologists, but on that of other professionals who may be needed to provide counselling or advice. Ultrasound equipment should be available for every preterm labour or delivery, along with persons who can handle the equipment and interpret its findings correctly. Full laboratory facilities should be available at all times. Resuscitation equipment should be available on the spot, and the presence and proper working order of this equipment should be verified before each delivery.

Fetal assessment prior to delivery should identify multiple pregnancy; assess whether or not the fetus is alive and well; differentiate the normally formed from the congenitally malformed fetus; and assess fetal presentation. As mentioned earlier, careful review of the gestational data is mandatory. All of these are prerequisites for proper care for preterm delivery. A policy of caesarean section for all is not an adequate substitute.

A professional who is skilled in resuscitation and who can devote all his or her attention to the infant should be in attendance at all preterm deliveries. This is readily achieved where labour and neonatal wards are adjacent (as they should be). Where distances present a problem, every effort should be made, first, to ensure that these distances are phased out in the foreseeable future, and, second, to increase staffing levels so that no preterm baby in the mean time will be delivered without appropriate neonatal attention.

3.3 *Prevention of intraventricular haemorrhage*

Intraventricular haemorrhage is an important cause of mortality and morbidity in the very preterm infant. The risk of haemorrhage is inversely related to gestational age, ranging from more than 70 per cent under 26 weeks to less than 10 per cent after 33 weeks. More than 90 per cent of these haemorrhages occur in infants below 35 weeks of gestation. Two trials have addressed the possibility of reducing the incidence of intraventricular haemorrhage in preterm infants by administration of phenobarbitone to the mother before delivery. Both trials indicate that this treatment has potential for reducing the incidence of intraventricular haemorrhage and neonatal mortality in preterm infants. Unfortunately, neither of the two trials used methodology of sufficient rigour to exclude the possibility of selection bias, but in both trials the diagnosis of intraventricular haemorrhage was made without knowledge of the type of treatment received. The reduction in the incidence of both intraventricular haemorrhage and neonatal death in these two trials is such that confirmation or denial of the benefits of this treatment is required urgently.

4 Route of delivery

One of the main decisions about care for preterm delivery, and certainly the most controversial one, is the choice between vaginal delivery and caesarean section. From the volume of literature that has been published on this issue one would expect a wealth of evidence to be available for selecting the best of these approaches. This is not the case. Calls for clinical trials to provide unbiased comparisons between vaginal and abdominal routes of delivery have been published for more than a decade. Yet there have been very few attempts to put these recommendations into practice, and those that have been attempted were abandoned before, or soon after, they started.

To date, no unbiased information is available to shed light on the question of when a caesarean section might add sufficient benefits to the infant to warrant the operation.

Much of the discussion regarding route of delivery has centred on the preterm breech. Breech presentation is far more common in preterm infants than it is in term infants, and for a variety of reasons breech presentation at delivery carries a higher risk for the infant than does cephalic presentation. This increased risk has paved the way for instituting 'prophylactic caesarean section' for the preterm baby presenting as a breech, as a presumably safer method of delivery. In some centres the supposed benefits of this approach have been extended to all preterm babies, without adequate evidence that the assumed gain in safety is indeed a gain and not a loss.

The many, mostly retrospective, observational studies that have compared the outcome of vaginal breech delivery with that following caesarean section have usually found higher survival rates after caesarean section than after vaginal delivery. Unfortunately, even when they made genuine attempts to control as much as possible for confounding factors, none of these studies have compared like with like.

Infants delivered vaginally are more likely to be those who are considered to be too small, of too low gestational age, or too sick to receive sufficient benefit from caesarean section. They may be those whose mothers arrived too late in second stage labour to have a caesarean section. They are also more likely to be those who have forgone the benefits of antenatal corticosteroid treatment, because delivery occurred too quickly for these drugs to be administered or to have their full effect.

Infants delivered vaginally are also more likely to have been born in the absence of a senior obstetrician and neonatologist, and to have received less dedicated care at vaginal delivery. If the general policy favours caesarean section, vaginal delivery is likely to be assisted by a person without the necessary technical skills and experience of breech delivery of tiny infants.

In contrast, infants delivered by caesarean section are more likely to be those for whom delivery could be planned in advance. They are more likely to be born as the result of elective obstetric intervention to end pregnancy. Delivery is more likely to have been preceded by thorough assessment of the fetal condition, possibly including ascertainment of lung maturation, and after full preparations were made for whatever special neonatal care is required. These infants are more likely to be born later in gestation and to have birthweights that are higher than those of infants born vaginally.

This lack of comparability between the infants born vaginally and by caesarean section makes plain the futility of observational studies in this field, and emphasizes the need for properly controlled studies to answer this important question.

5 Abdominal delivery

Although caesarean section is considered to be one of the safest of the major surgical procedures, it still carries an important risk of mortality and morbidity. Some special considerations apply to a preterm caesarean section.

A careful ultrasound examination is essential before caesarean delivery of a preterm infant. First, it is important to determine whether or not the fetus is normally formed; a caesarean to deliver a fetus with a lethal abnormality would be a double tragedy. Second, an exact diagnosis of the fetal presentation may allow correction of malpresentation before the uterus is incised, and this may make all the difference between an easy caesarean delivery and a traumatic extraction of a malpositioned infant through a poorly formed and thick lower uterine segment. Third, it is useful to know whether or not the placenta will be in the way. Little gain can be made in avoiding trauma to the aftercoming head, for example, when this relatively large head needs to be delivered through a small incision in a thick uterine segment, which has the placenta as well as the body of the baby bulging through it.

At caesarean section, particularly when it is performed for breech presentation, it is important to assess whether the lower uterine segment is sufficiently wide to permit easy delivery of the head. Often, and particularly in elective preterm delivery, there will be little lower uterine segment, and whatever incision is made will be made through the body of the uterus. Some authors therefore recommend a vertical rather than a transverse incision; but no controlled experiments have been conducted to evaluate the relative merits of the alternative policies.

If the presentation is not longitudinal it is advisable to correct it before the uterine incision is made, preferably to a vertex presentation. This is usually not too difficult, especially when there is a normal volume of amniotic fluid, and the uterine relaxant effect of betamimetic treatment can be maintained up to the moment of delivery with this aim in mind. It is just as important to strive for easy and gentle delivery of the fetal head at caesarean delivery as it is at vaginal delivery.

6 Vaginal delivery

The head of the preterm baby, with its soft bones and wide skull sutures, is more vulnerable than that of the term baby to compression by the maternal pelvic tissues, and to sudden decompression when the baby emerges from the birth canal. Several measures have been proposed to minimize the occurrence of these changes in intracranial pressure. These include liberal use of epidural analgesia to lower resistance in the birth canal; routine use of 'prophylactic forceps' delivery to counteract both compression before and decompression after birth; and routine use of early episiotomy to remove the resistance of rigid perineal tissues.

6.1 Epidural and other analgesia

Adequate analgesia is just as important for the mother giving birth preterm as for the mother delivering at term. The main difference may be that the woman in preterm labour may be less well prepared for birth, and may be overcome by the suddenness of it all and the increased risk of delivering preterm. It is important to respond to her anxiety and discomfort in ways that do not depress the baby. When, as is often the case, pharmacological analgesia is required, an epidural block is probably safer than narcotics, although there have been no controlled studies to substantiate this recommendation.

The routine use of epidural, particularly for the preterm breech, has also been suggested as a means of abolishing the urge to push before the cervix is fully dilated, and to reduce the resistance of the pelvic musculature. This is a reasonable hypothesis, but as yet there is no evidence to support it. Similar or greater protection might be gained by close communication with, and careful instructions to, the women.

6.2 Elective forceps delivery

Prophylactic forceps have become accepted practice for preterm vaginal delivery in many places, but there have been few attempts to assess the value, if any, of this practice. The postulated protection of the baby's head can be questioned on theoretical grounds. Forceps are effective levers, and any compression applied at the handles is transmitted directly to the blades and hence to the fetal head. In addition, a substantial part of the traction force during delivery is transmitted as compression force to the fetal head. This may be particularly damaging to a preterm baby with soft skull bones and wide skull sutures.

Only one trial has compared elective forceps with spontaneous delivery for the preterm infant. The outcomes addressed were limited to retinal haemorrhages, which may or may not be indicators of (traumatic) intracranial haemorrhages in the preterm neonate. Retinal haemorrhages were observed in 2 of 23 infants in the forceps group and in 1 of 23 infants in the spontaneous group. There is at present no valid evidence to suggest that routine use of forceps to deliver the preterm baby confers more benefit than harm.

6.3 Routine use of early episiotomy

Only one small, and inadequately controlled, trial has attempted to address the question of whether or not routine use of episiotomy for delivery of the preterm baby improves neonatal outcome. Whether a policy of routine episiotomy confers any benefit cannot be deduced with any confidence from this trial, although the authors stated that their results 'do not support the use of episiotomy in preterm delivery'.

7 Immediate care at birth

The physiological consequences of early versus late cord clamping have not been studied as well in the preterm infant as they have been at term. In the preterm infant, delayed cord clamping is associated with a 50 per cent increase in red cell volume and 56 per cent of this placental transfusion occurs within the first minute after birth. Proponents of early clamping suggest that the large transfusion may encourage pulmonary oedema and increase the risk of intracranial haemorrhage and hyperbilirubinaemia. Those who advocate delayed clamping point out that the placental transfusion may expand the pulmonary bed and prevent respiratory distress, prevent hypovolaemia and hypotension, and increase haemoglobin concentrations and total body iron stores.

It remains unknown whether alternative policies of cord clamping with preterm birth will have a significant impact on neonatal outcome. Only one small trial has been reported, and it had inconclusive results. From the available evidence (admittedly gathered predominantly in infants who were not born preterm) there does not seem to be any justification for rushing to clamp the cord.

A paediatrician should be present at all preterm deliveries. For the very preterm and very small infant, the paediatrician should be an experienced neonatologist, and decisions with regard to resuscitation and suctioning should be his or her prerogative, taken in harmony with the parents and the obstetrician.

The simple measure of providing adequate heat in the delivery room can contribute more to subsequent neonatal wellbeing than any of the other measures that, in many places, are routinely applied to effect delivery of the preterm infant.

8 Conclusions

The expression 'preterm delivery' encompasses a variety of different clinical presentations. In some the risk is little different from that of delivery at term; in others the utmost sophistication of facilities and skills is necessary if the infant is to have even a remote hope of intact survival. Many of these small babies are already compromised by other factors, such as congenital malformations, multiple pregnancy, or complicating maternal illness. Care for preterm delivery must, therefore be carefully individualized, taking all these factors into consideration.

The plan of care for the preterm baby should be governed by consideration of gestational age rather than of estimated weight, because gestational age is a better indicator of prognosis.

The baby should be delivered in an institution that has all the necessary facilities and skilled personnel readily available. Transfer of the baby after birth is not as likely to be effective as birth in a centre that is adequately equipped and staffed to ensure that the fetus is alive and well, rule out congenital malformation, establish fetal presentation before delivery, and perform the skilled resuscitation that is necessary at the moment of birth. Even for the woman in active labour, inhibition of labour with betamimetics may be successfully used to delay delivery long enough to permit transfer of the mother to such a centre.

The choice of the best route of delivery, vaginal or caesarean section, is by no means easy. The observational data on the differential effects of abdominal and vaginal delivery are all subject to such major biases, that their results should be totally ignored. In the absence of guidance from controlled trials, caesarean section, with its known risks to the mother, should be the exception rather than the rule. This applies to the fetus presenting as a breech as well as to that presenting as a vertex.

A careful ultrasound examination is essential before caesarean delivery of a preterm infant, to ensure that the baby is free of lethal congenital malformations, to determine fetal presentation and allow correction if necessary before the uterus is incised, and to determine the position of the placenta, which may interfere with the extraction of the baby. It is important that the uterine incision is adequate in size, in spite of the fact that this is sometimes difficult with the poorly developed lower segment characteristic of the preterm uterus. Extraction of the baby through an inadequate incision may be far more traumatic than vaginal delivery.

The head of the preterm baby is more vulnerable to injury, either from compression or sudden expansion, than that of the baby at term. There is no evidence to suggest that either elective forceps delivery or performing an episiotomy reduces this risk. The routine use of both of these procedures should be abandoned, except in the context of controlled trials.

As the evidence in favour of early or late clamping of the umbilical cord is conflicting, decisions about when to perform this should be based on the urgency of the need for resuscitation.

A paediatrician should be in attendance at all preterm deliveries, and for the very preterm or very small infant, he or she should be an experienced neonatologist capable of making the decisions and performing the skilled resuscitation that may be necessary.

Meticulous attention to all the features that should be present for all births, such as a warm environment and careful consideration, is even more important for the preterm birth than for the birth at term without complications.

45

Immediate care of the newborn infant

This chapter is derived from the chapters by Jon Tyson, William Silverman, and Joan Reisch (75) and Howard Berger (83) in EFFECTIVE CARE IN PREGNANCY AND CHILDBIRTH.

1 Introduction

Given the success of human evolution and the exceptionally high survival rate of human newborn infants, it is apparent that, for the vast majority of newborn babies, little more than a clear airway and adequate warmth are required to support the first few minutes of adaptation to extra-uterine life. Despite this, there are striking variations in the patterns of care of newborn babies in the immediate post-delivery period. These variations reflect both the inherent resilience and adaptability of the newborn infant and the lack of consensus among caregivers as to what constitutes appropriate care.

2 Immediate care of the normal newborn infant

2.1 Welcoming the newborn infant

In his book *Birth without violence*, Frederick Leboyer described a number of measures designed to minimize 'the shock of the newborn's first separation experiences': the use of a dark delivery room, delayed clamping of the umbilical cord, gentle massage, and a warm bath for the infant. Leboyer claimed that infants so treated would grow up to be healthier and 'free of conflict'. Superior development was reported in an uncontrolled case series of children who had been delivered in this way.

These claims have been tested in three randomized controlled trials assessing the effect of 'Leboyer deliveries' on infant neurobehavioural status in the first hour of life, at 24 and 72 hours after birth, and at eight months of age. In two of three studies, no statistically significant effects, either beneficial or harmful, were found. In a third and as yet unpublished study, 'Leboyer deliveries' were associated with increased infant alertness in the delivery room and changes in maternal–infant interaction (increased maternal smiling and talking to the infant) on the second postpartum day. No effect on subsequent infant development was identified.

The fact that no long-term advantages of the specific measures advocated by Leboyer have been demonstrated does not mean that the newborn should not be treated with the regard and respect due to any human being.

2.2 Ensuring a clear airway

The common practice of routine suctioning to remove secretions from the newborn infant's oral and nasal passages is not without potential hazards. These include cardiac arrhythmias, laryngospasm, and pulmonary artery vasospasm. Possible benefits include improved air exchange, reduced likelihood of aspiration of secretions, and, perhaps, reduced acquisition of any pathogens present in the amniotic fluid or birth canal.

If nasal and pharyngeal suctioning is used, care should be taken to minimize pharyngeal stimulation. Suction bulbs rather than catheters should be used, because suction bulbs are less likely to induce cardiac arrhythmias.

The practice of routine gastric suctioning was introduced into practice following the poorly tested suggestion that the respiratory distress of infants of diabetic women often resulted from regurgitation and aspiration that might have been prevented by gastric suctioning. As the passage of the tube during the immediate neonatal period may produce bradycardia or laryngospasm and disruption of prefeeding behaviour, there is no justification for routine gastric suctioning in the delivery room.

2.3 Maintaining body temperature

The recommendation that all babies be kept warm immediately after birth is based on extrapolation from an extensive body of evidence about thermal physiology of newborn animals and human neonates. With the possible exception of extremely small infants, there is solid observational evidence that neonates maintain their body temperature in a cool environment at the metabolic cost of increased energy expenditure.

A variety of studies have demonstrated that the postnatal fall in infant temperature can be reduced by skin-to-skin contact between the infant and mother, as it can also be reduced by the use of an incubator or a radiant warmer, by drying the infant, or by covering the infant's body or head with insulated material.

2.4 Prophylactic administration of vitamin K to prevent haemorrhagic disease

Most textbooks recommend routine parenteral administration of vitamin K to all newborn infants, yet there is a continuing debate about whether or not it is necessary to administer vitamin K to healthy, formula-fed infants. The concentration of vitamin K in cow's milk or infant formula appears to be considerably greater than in human milk, and prothrombin levels in infants given parenteral vitamin K at birth are similar to those in comparable infants fed on cow's milk for only 24 hours.

The usually quoted incidence rates of haemorrhagic disease of the newborn in the absence of vitamin K administration range from 0.25 per cent to 0.50 per cent. These rates are derived from studies done many years ago, at a time when traumatic deliveries were more common, and when first feeds were often delayed. The risk of healthy formula-fed infants developing haemorrhagic disease today seems likely to be considerably smaller. These considerations have led some paediatricians to abandon routine prophylaxis in normal formula-fed infants. Breastfed infants are at greater than average risk of developing haemorrhagic disease of the newborn, and failure to administer vitamin K to these infants may predispose them to serious bleeding, for example, intracranial haemorrhage.

2.5 Prophylactic measures to prevent eye infections

The Credé procedure of silver nitrate conjunctival prophylaxis, introduced in 1881, was credited with the control of gonococcal ophthalmia of the newborn in the last century. Many countries have a legal requirement that one of a list of approved chemical agents should routinely be instilled into the eyes of all newborn infants, with the aim of preventing infectious conjunctivitis. No controlled trials have been carried out to ascertain whether or not this is a more effective means of preventing blindness than careful observation of the newborn, followed by adequate treatment of any conjunctivitis that should appear.

When routine chemical prophylaxis is advised or required, the next question concerns the choice of the most effective and least harmful agent. The routine use of silver nitrate has been questioned recently because it results in a higher frequency of conjunctivitis than other agents; because of its uncertain efficacy against the gonococcus; and because of its ineffectiveness against *Chlamydia* (which in many areas is the most common cause of neonatal ophthalmia). In addition to 1 per cent silver nitrate, erythromycin (0.5 per cent ophthalmic ointment or drops in single-use tubes or ampoules) and tetracycline (1 per cent ophthalmic ointment or drops in single-use tubes or ampoules) are considered to be 'acceptable' agents. A rational choice of agent is difficult. There have been no trials involving adequate numbers of infants with bacterial or chlamydial eye infections to permit evaluation of their relative merits.

Concern has been voiced that immediate application of topical agents to the eyes of newborn infants would disrupt the visual inter-action between mother and baby during the first hour of life, during much of which time the baby is in the 'quiet alert' state. While there is no evidence that this would have any long-term detrimental effects on maternal–infant relationships, there is equally no evidence to suggest that topical agents must be given within the first minutes after birth.

3 Prophylactic measures in newborns considered to be at above average risk

3.1 *Suctioning of infants who have passed meconium in utero*

It may be possible to reduce the likelihood of postnatal aspiration of meconium by suctioning applied to nostrils, mouth, and pharynx of infants before the chest has been delivered and the umbilical circulation has been interrupted. Whether this strategy has any important effect on the incidence of severe meconium aspiration syndrome is unknown, but it would seem to have somewhat less potential for doing harm than an alternative policy, tracheal intubation of all infants born after meconium passage. The low rate of morbidity following intubation reported by experienced resuscitators cannot be reproduced by others with a lesser level of skill.

Meconium passage *in utero* occurs in a substantial proportion of infants born with pulmonary artery hypertension, and even relatively mild stimuli may produce intense pulmonary vasospasm in these infants. Infection may also be a risk. Hypoxia, bradycardia, and increased intracranial pressure are not unusual during intubation.

Because of these risks, and because there have been no demonstrated benefits, it would seem unwise to perform tracheal intubation for infants who are not depressed simply because they have been born following meconium passage *in utero*. Careful tracheal suction should be carried out only for infants who are depressed at birth (heart rate less than 80–100 beats per minute at birth) and have meconium in the pharynx.

3.2 *Elective tracheal intubation for very-low-birthweight infants*

A policy of elective tracheal intubation at birth has been compared with selective intubation in only one clinical trial, and this involved infants weighing 1500 grams or less at birth, regardless of whether they showed signs of asphyxia or respiratory disease. The better outcome of the electively intubated group may have resulted either from a 'skilled intubator' effect, or from selection bias resulting from exclusion of infants who delivered precipitously or during times of the day or night when the resuscitation team was less likely to be available.

Because of the potential hazards of intubation, routine delivery-room intubation of all infants below 1500 grams is unjustified on the basis of current evidence.

3.3 *Prophylactic administration of surfactant to immature infants*

A number of controlled trials of bovine, human, or artificial surfactant provide encouraging evidence that immediate post-natal administration of surfactant can reduce the morbidity and mortality of infants born before pulmonary maturation has occurred. Babies who receive surfactant are less likely to develop moderate or severe respiratory distress and pneumothorax. They are also less likely to develop periventricular haemorrhage. Most importantly, the evidence currently available suggests that administration of calf-lung surfactant may increase the chances of survival without bronchopulmonary dysplasia.

The quality of the evidence which supports the administration of surfactant to high-risk newborns is higher than for any other immediate prophylactic treatment method for newborn infants, or indeed for any other method of delivery-room care.

4 Immediate resuscitation of ill newborn infants

The availability of professionals skilled in neonatal resuscitation has increased with the growth of neonatology as a specialty. This change has meant that the birth of an immature, asphyxiated, or otherwise high-risk neonate is more likely to be attended by someone who is experienced in giving care to such infants. A proportion of ill and high-risk infants will continue to present as unpredicted emergencies, however, and it will often fall to a midwife, nurse, general practitioner, or trainee obstetric specialist to initiate and continue neonatal resuscitation.

Whenever possible, a person skilled in resuscitation, who can devote all of his or her attention to the infant, should be in attendance at high-risk deliveries. Basic resuscitation equipment (a radiant warmer, resuscitation bags and masks, endotracheal tubes, laryngoscope, stethoscope, oxygen source, and tubing) should be readily available in every delivery room. Because the need for resuscitation is not recognized prior to the delivery of approximately half of all infants requiring resuscitation, the presence and proper working order of this equipment should be verified before each delivery.

While anaesthesia bags are likely to be required for the optimal resuscitation of severely asphyxiated infants, their hazards if used improperly (for example, the application of dangerously high airway pressures) make them unsuitable for routine use by inexperienced personnel. Likewise, the hazards of umbilical artery catheters and trochars for endotracheal tubes should preclude their use in delivery rooms, except by highly experienced resuscitators.

4.1 *Resuscitation*

Artificial ventilation should be initiated promptly for infants with a heart rate less than 100 beats per minute following birth, and oxygen should be administered to any infant with generalized cyanosis. Regardless of heart rate or colour, artificial ventilation should also be begun for infants with inadequate chest excursion and poor breath sounds, especially small preterm infants likely to have surfactant deficiency.

Proper ventilation of the infant is the single most important aspect of neonatal resuscitation, and the heart rate is the most useful and easily measured criterion for its success. A poor response to bag-and-mask ventilation is the most common indication for endotracheal intubation.

Before intubation is performed in an infant whose heart rate does not rise promptly with bag-and-mask ventilation, attention should be given to the following points: proper positioning of the head ('sniffing position'); ensuring that the upper airway is clear; using sufficient pressure to produce adequate chest excursions; and administering an adequate inspired oxygen concentration. Observing distention of the neck as the resuscitation bag is squeezed indicates that a proper head position and clear airway (allowing delivery of gas to the level of the glottis) has been established. The careful use of an anaesthesia bag may be required to deliver more pressure, or a greater oxygen concentration, than can be delivered by self-inflating bags. Persistent bradycardia may be caused by applying excessive pressure to the infant's head through the face mask.

Although there is evidence that ventilation by endotracheal tube is more efficient than ventilation by face mask, in view of the known hazards of intubation, resuscitation should be initiated using a face mask rather than an endotracheal tube, except when skilled personnel are in attendance.

4.2 *Oxygen*

Supplemental oxygen (100 per cent concentration of the warm and humidified gas) is recommended for artificial ventilation of neonates who have not established effective spontaneous respiration by one minute of age. No comparative studies of the benefits and risks of various oxygen concentrations for the management of such infants have been reported.

Some concern has been expressed that blowing oxygen across the face of a newborn infant might result in bradycardia, but most concern has been focused on whether the risk of severe retinopathy would be appreciably increased in immature infants who experience short periods of exposure to high blood-oxygen levels. There is no satisfactory evidence, however, to suggest that the risk is any greater than that associated with the relatively high blood-oxygen levels that occur at birth in all babies with the onset of air breathing.

4.3 *Cardiac massage*

Cardiac massage, used for infants born with an absent heart beat, can at times be life-saving. The use of cardiac massage through the intact chest wall of the newborn baby was originally recommended by investigators who studied a small number of term infants, and who noted that the procedure increased blood-pressure without any evidence of trauma to the skeleton or organs. With more widespread use it became clear that the method occasionally causes rib fractures and trauma to the liver or lung. Since the original recommendation, cardiac massage of the newborn baby has received little systematic study, and there is little information of the kind needed to recommend precise indications and methods.

4.4 *Naloxone*

Naloxone hydrochloride is a narcotic antagonist, believed to be virtually free of side-effects. It may be administered as an adjunctive measure *after* assisted ventilation has been established, if depression is thought to be the result of a narcotic drug given to the mother before delivery. It is probably wise not to give naloxone to infants of narcotic-dependent mothers for fear of precipitating withdrawal illness in the baby.

Because of concern about the potential importance of endogenous opioid substances in newborn infants, and the observations in one study of less optimal maternal ratings of infant behaviour among naloxone-treated infants than among controls, administration of naloxone should be restricted to infants who have not only been exposed to narcotics *in utero*, but who also require active resuscitation in the immediate neonatal period.

4.5 Sodium bicarbonate

Randomized trials have failed to detect any benefit from either rapid or slow administration of sodium bicarbonate to neonates. In the absence of any demonstrated benefits of giving this drug in the immediate postnatal period, its use cannot be recommended.

4.6 Blood-volume expanders

The only clear-cut indication for the use of blood-volume expanders in the early neonatal period is the combination of unmistakable signs of shock with evidence of acute blood loss, including feto–maternal haemorrhage. In this circumstance, shock may be treated with repeated infusions of blood-volume expanders (usually 5–10 ml) and the infant's response assessed after each infusion. The volume expander may be 5 per cent albumin, Ringer's lactate, saline, or heparinized placental blood.

Volume-expanders have also been used in the presence of hypotension unaccompanied by other signs of shock or blood loss. This practice is of far more dubious validity.

5 Indications for withholding or discontinuing resuscitation

The issue of when to withhold or discontinue resuscitation concerns the most difficult treatment decision to be made in the delivery room. Much of the information needed to define appropriate indications for using intensive care is lacking: the effect of intensive care on mortality and the quality of life of survivors, and the cost of care for severely impaired or malformed infants.

Ultimately, decisions to withhold or withdraw aggressive care involve value judgements about what is considered an acceptable outcome and an acceptable cost. Although much has been written to express the views of health care professionals, lawyers, and ethicists concerning aggressive care of extremely high-risk infants, little has been done to explore the views of the parents, who, apart from the child, have most at stake in such decisions.

Given the limited amount of useful information which is available for reaching decisions about instituting or withholding aggressive neonatal care, a liberal policy of resuscitation must be recommended whenever doubt exists. This allows the physician time to gather important information about the infant, and the distressed parents time and opportunity to participate more effectively in joint decisions about subsequent therapy.

6 Conclusions

For the vast majority of infants, the only needs immediately after delivery are vigilance, a clear airway, and a warm welcome.   No benefits have been demonstrated for routine suctioning of the newborn's oral and nasal passages, and the practice has potential hazards. If suctioning is carried out, a bulb is preferable to a catheter. There is no justification for routine gastric suctioning in the delivery room.

Breastfed babies should receive supplemental vitamin K routinely to prevent haemorrhagic disease of the newborn. Although the evidence is not conclusive, it is probably best to administer vitamin K to formula-fed infants as well.

Topical ophthalmic preparations to prevent infective ophthalmia are required by law in many countries. Erythromycin causes less chemical conjunctivitis than silver nitrate, and is more effective against *chlamydia* infection. There is no evidence to suggest that these medications must be given immediately after birth. Where not required by law, observation for and prompt treatment of ophthalmia may be as effective as routine prophylaxis, and may save many babies from unnecessary medication.

Endotracheal suction should be carried out on all depressed babies who are born with meconium in the pharynx. For non-depressed babies born after the passage of meconium, the hazards of intubation seem likely to outweigh any potential benefits. Routine delivery-room intubation of all infants below 1500 grams is unjustified on the basis of current evidence.

Despite the very limited information from clinical trials of resuscitation, the great majority of ill or depressed infants can be successfully managed simply by appropriate ventilation, without the need to consider the use of drugs, volume-expanders, or other adjuncts. The most common serious error in neonatal resuscitation is the failure to recognize and correct hypoventilation, a problem which is preventable with sufficient staff training and experience. Each hospital must establish appropriate methods to facilitate the most effective care for asphyxiated or depressed neonates.

46

Care of the new mother and baby

This chapter is derived from the chapters by Molly Thomson and Ruta Westreich (77) and Janet Rush, Iain Chalmers, and Murray Enkin (78) in EFFECTIVE CARE IN PREGNANCY AND CHILDBIRTH.

1 Introduction

Most societies recognize that a new mother needs both emotional support and practical help in the days following childbirth. The form that this help takes, and the way that it is given, varies from culture to culture, and changes with the passage of time. The major change in most industrialized societies has resulted from the shift of the place of birth from home to hospital. This has influenced the pattern of mother–baby interaction in at least two ways. First, women giving birth in unfamiliar surroundings and attended by caregivers with whom they are not familiar may feel inhibited, and may thus not behave towards their newborn child as they would have done had they been at home among familiar faces. Second, institutional rules and policies may obstruct immediate postnatal social interaction between newly delivered mothers and their babies.

The only justification for retaining practices that restrict a woman's autonomy, her freedom of choice, and her access to her baby, would be clear evidence that these restrictive practices are likely to do more good than harm.

2 Restriction of early mother–infant contact

Evidence concerning the possible adverse consequences of routine separation of mothers and their newborn infants in the early postnatal period has been accumulating throughout the period of thirty years or more during which this practice has become widespread. Relevant data is available from controlled trials published as long ago as 1952.

In general, the pertinent controlled trials have compared the effects of the restricted early contact that was standard in most forms of institutional care, with those of more liberal early contact between mothers and their newborn infants. The effects on maternal affectionate behaviour have been the focus of much of this research.

Several controlled trials have compared the effects of institutional policies that result in restricted interaction between mothers and their newborn babies within two hours of delivery, with policies that encourage interaction at that time. A majority of the methodologically sound trials showed that maternal affectionate behaviour was significantly less common among mothers whose contact with their babies had been restricted than among mothers cared for more liberally.

Other trials have compared standard hospital practices with attempts to encourage mother-infant interaction after the immediate postnatal period. The additional interaction in these trials ranged from a small amount of care-taking in the intensive-care nursery by mothers of premature infants, to full rooming-in for mothers of normal infants. The few statistically significant differences that were observed suggested that restrictive policies were associated with less affectionate maternal behaviour and more frequent maternal feelings of incompetence and lack of confidence. Perhaps most important of all, the results of one well-conducted study suggested that, compared with a policy of rooming-in, the routine hospital policy of separating mothers from their babies led to an increase in the subsequent risk of child abuse and neglect among socially deprived, first-time mothers.

The effect of policies tending to restrict early or frequent mother–infant interaction on subsequent breastfeeding patterns has been examined in ten trials. The women participating in these trials all wished to breastfeed their babies, and, in all but one of the trials, they were having their first child. The restrictive policies were characterized by delays in permitting mother–infant interaction for anything between 4 and 48 hours after delivery. These delays were then followed (in most studies) by scheduled breastfeeding.

Although these trials involved women from a range of socioeconomic backgrounds and a variety of countries, the results were remarkably consistent: the proportion of women who had discontinued breastfeeding one to three months after delivery was substantially higher in the women who had been subjected to the more restrictive policies.

3 Control of infection

Many of the regulations and routines in postpartum care in hospital have been instituted in attempts to prevent or contain cross-infection. Until the decline in virulence of the streptococcus, and the arrival of effective antimicrobial therapy in the late 1940s, the major risk associated with hospital delivery was puerperal sepsis in the mother. As hospital nurseries began to fill up with members of the baby boom that followed the Second World War, staphylococcal skin disease among neonates became the major infectious problem. A variety of measures were taken in attempts to deal with this problem. These included isolation, segregation, rules of dress and entry to the nursery, medicated bathing, special treatment of the umbilical cord, and routine vaccination against staphylococcal disease,

The inflexible use of central nurseries in which a number of babies were kept in close proximity to each other, but apart from their mothers, may actually have increased the very risk which its adoption as a policy was intended to decrease. A 1959 study showed lower rates of colonization and infection in babies who spent between eight and twelve hours a day with their mothers than in babies who were kept in a nursery, and were rarely in contact with their mothers.

It is sad that the results of this controlled study appeared to have had so little impact on the almost universal policy of routinely separating mothers and babies in this way. Instead, the problem of cross-infection and nursery epidemics of staphylococcal infection was addressed using a variety of more technological approaches.

The use of gowns, hats, and masks in normal newborn and intensive-care nurseries became routine in spite of the lack of any evidence from several controlled trials that these practices had a beneficial effect on infant colonization and infection rates. With the obvious failure to control neonatal infection by segregation and isolation, the mainstay of infection prophylaxis came to involve regimens of treatment of the umbilical cord and medicated bathing.

The first controlled trial mounted to assess any of these new regimens showed that staphylococcal colonization of the skin could be reduced by daily applications of triple dye to the umbilical cord stump. This effect was confirmed in a number of studies conducted over the subsequent two decades.

A rather more complex approach to the problem involved the use of 3 per cent hexachlorophene in detergent to wash babies immediately after birth, and then daily until discharge from hospital. Compared with dry care or care with medicated soap, 3 per cent hexachlorophene bathing was shown to reduce staphylococcal skin colonization and, more importantly, pyoderma.

Unfortunately no direct comparisons were made initially between the simpler regimen of painting the umbilical cord with triple dye, and the more elaborate policy of daily bathing with hexachlorophene (with its known attendant risk of hypothermia). Evidence derived more than a decade later suggests that the two regimens have similar effects on staphylococcal skin-colonization rates, but this did not become available until after 1971, when it was realized that hexachlorophene could be neurotoxic in the newborn.

Hexachlorophene remains in use in some neonatal nurseries, because of a view that, in the concentrations at which it is currently in contact with neonatal skin, its advantages in controlling staphylococcal colonization outweigh its likely disadvantages. The fundamental question is not 'what medication should be put in the baby's bath water?', but 'is routine medicated bathing of neonates justified at all in the light of the available evidence?'. The available evidence suggests that it is not justified. A controlled trial showed that infants bathed routinely in a bath with 'Savlon' were statistically significantly more likely than controls to develop an infection.

Of the variety of methods used to treat the umbilical cord, only neomycin has been shown to reduced colonization rates more effectively than triple dye. Convincing evidence exists that silver sulphadiazine offers no advantage over triple dye with respect to colonization rates, and there appears to be little if any difference between them in infection rates. Other preparations currently in use for treating the umbilical cord have simply not been adequately compared with the triple dye 'standard', and their introduction into clinical practice probably reflects commercial interests rather than scientific evidence.

Many restrictive and costly practices remain in force in hospital nurseries today. Gowning rules persist in almost three-quarters of newborn nurseries, despite the lack of evidence that this ritual has any beneficial effect. Many hospitals invoke concern about infection as a reason for restricting or forbidding siblings to visit, although studies using concurrent and historical control groups have been unable to detect any adverse effect of this on infant colonization rates.

It would be extremely dangerous to take a cavalier attitude to the undoubted reality of hospital-spread infection among new mothers and babies. Means for preventing or containing such infections must be kept under constant review. But maintaining or instituting restrictive measures without assessing whether or not they accomplish these ends should no longer be tolerated.

4 Routine observations

Making and recording regular measurements of temperature, pulse, blood-pressure, fundal height, and observations of lochia and the various wounds that a woman may sustain during delivery is still common practice in the days following childbirth. The intensity of this screening activity varies arbitrarily, and depends more on the hospital in which a mother happens to give birth, and on the length of time she happens to spend in it, than on her individual needs. It would certainly seem prudent to screen women in this way when they are known to be at increased risk of either infection or haemorrhage. It is more difficult to see how this deployment of resources could be justified as a routine for all women.

5 Drugs for relief of symptoms

The postpartum period is often accompanied by a number of discomforts. Pain in the perineum and breasts is common, and women not infrequently count these symptoms among the most unpleasant memories they have of childbirth.

In most hospitals medication for such discomforts tends to be under the direct control and supervision of hospital personnel. This policy is valid in the case of dangerous drugs, drugs that might interact with other medications, or those that would normally be available only on a doctor's prescription. It is hardly rational in the case of drugs which, outside hospital, are readily available to the woman without a prescription. Because these medications are usually for the relief of symptoms, it would be more sensible for women to use them when they feel the need.

In many hospitals non-prescription drugs intended for the relief of symptoms are still administered routinely and at set times. Professional belief in the value of early and regular bowel evacuation, for example, has led to some rather obsessional concerns on this matter. Laxatives, stool-softeners, enemas, and anal ointments remain routine components of postpartum care in some hospitals. Controlled trials have confirmed that, in the puerperium, as at other times, routinely prescribed laxatives and medicated enemas do result in earlier bowel movements, and that bulk-forming laxatives are less likely to cause unpleasant cramps and diarrhoea than are irritant laxatives. None of the reported results in this small body of research, however, could be regarded as justification for administering any of these preparations routinely.

In an attempt to provide a more rational basis for care (including self-care), a number of hospitals have developed programmes to provide mothers with information about the drugs they may use, and have given them access to their own supply of medications. These descriptive studies all suggest that women are usually pleased with these arrangements, and that staff time was used more efficiently after their introduction.

6 General support and education

Fragmentation of care is almost inevitable when the care of mothers is the responsibility of midwives or postpartum nurses and obstetricians, while that of the babies is the responsibility of nursery nurses and paediatricians. Consistent advice and continuity of care are prerequisites for giving effective support to mothers and their newborn babies. Although not demonstrated by controlled evaluation, it would seem likely that the desired consistency of care would be easier to achieve if mother and baby were accommodated together, or at the very least, if the same people were looking after mother and baby.

The implementation of such programmes at the present time, however, is far from easy. A number of observational studies have described attempts to implement changes in the direction of greater coherence and continuity of care, as well as pointing out some of the difficulties and pitfalls encountered. The only controlled study that has been reported described the difficulties involved in instituting a major change in nursing assignment. Nursing staff had concerns about their workload, their knowledge, and their competence to carry out the procedures that would be necessary to provide more comprehensive care to both mothers and babies postpartum. The enthusiasm for change in this direction among the head nurses and nursing consultant was not shared by the core nursing staff. After implementation of the programme, women in the experimental ward required less formal instruction in feeding and changing the nappies of their babies than women in a control ward, but no differences were detected between the two groups of women in terms of enjoying their time with their babies, obtaining rest, or their feelings of readiness for discharge home.

The postpartum stay in hospital presents obvious opportunities for imparting information that may be of help to new mothers. Although there is little agreement on what should be the content of formal postpartum educational programmes, a number of studies, several of them controlled trials, have addressed the methods of postpartum education. These studies have concerned educational programmes relating to subjects ranging from contraception, through feeding and immunization advice, to information about child safety. Although the demonstrable effects of teaching were rarely as dramatic as the investigators had hoped, this body of research shows that postpartum educational programmes can and do affect parental behaviour and health outcomes.

7 Length of hospital stay

How long should a healthy woman and baby remain in hospital after childbirth? The generally accepted 'correct' length of postnatal stay has varied greatly from time to time, and at present it varies equally widely among institutions. It appears to be determined more by fashion and the availability of beds than by any systematic assessment of the needs of recently delivered women and their new babies.

The period of 'lying in' in industrialized societies had its institutional foundations with the establishment of charitable lying-in hospitals in the mid-eighteenth century. In these first maternity hospitals, women were, quite literally, confined to bed for a period of 28 days following delivery. By the 1950s the usual hospital lying-in period was 12–14 days, but since then it has fallen in most countries.

Several formal early-discharge programmes (even within 24 hours), often with strict inclusion criteria, have been instituted as a deliberate change from standard hospital policies. The most common impetus for initiating such programmes seems to have been the needs of the institution (because of a shortage of beds or personnel), although some programmes appear to have been inspired by the preferences of childbearing women.

Two randomized trials, and a number of observational studies, have shown that few women or babies are readmitted to hospital after early discharge. These low readmission rates demonstrate that early discharge from hospital is feasible, and that healthy mothers and babies who have help at home and follow-up care and guidance available, may safely go home within 6–48 hours of birth.

Although there have been no demonstrable adverse consequences of early postnatal discharge from hospital in terms of maternal and child health, it is important to note that there is also no evidence that such programmes, on balance, save money or scarce resources if care continues in a domiciliary setting. The costs of the home support given to women discharged early have been estimated to be about the same as the savings in hospital costs that result from earlier discharge. Also, when healthy women go home earlier, those remaining in hospital are, on average, more sick, require more intensive care, and involve additional work and strain for the staff. Early hospital-discharge programmes inevitably put an additional load on the primary care sector and on the family or friends of the woman. The additional resources required to cope with this load must obviously be assessed in any credible attempt to assess the costs of early discharge from hospital.

Demands for increased early-discharge programmes have been made by a variety of commentators who believe themselves to be speaking on behalf of childbearing women, but when such programmes have been instituted they have not always been popular. The extent to which women who have recently given birth in hospital want early discharge may have been overestimated.

Women's physical, social, and psychological circumstances after delivery vary greatly. It would seem sensible for professionals to be as flexible as possible in trying to respond to this variation. The exercise of choice may well be the crucial issue. A substantial proportion of women surveyed feel that the length of their hospital stay was 'wrong', usually because it had been too long, but, for some women because it had been too short. Some of the latter felt that a more extended escape from duties at home would have helped them to recover from childbirth more effectively.

The available evidence suggests that although early discharge from hospital is feasible and safe, it is neither clearly beneficial (in health or economic terms), nor wanted by the majority of women. Firm decisions about when a woman should go home after childbirth should be delayed until after she has delivered, and, as far as possible, should be based on her individual needs and preferences rather than on any predetermined formula.

8 Conclusions

Because the available evidence suggests that most of the restrictive practices still perpetuated in some hospitals are ineffective if not harmful, the ball is in their court to provide good evidence to justify their continuation. Unless or until they do so, mothers should have unrestricted access to their babies; caps and masks should be abolished, and aprons and gowns used only by those who wish to protect their own clothing from the various kinds of messes that babies make. Bathing the baby should be seen, not as a measure for preventing infection, but as an opportunity for a mother to interact with and gain confidence in handling her child.

There is no evidence to suggest that the restriction of early postnatal mother–infant interaction, which has been such a common feature of the care of women giving birth in hospitals, has any beneficial effects. On the contrary, the available evidence suggests that any effects that these restrictive policies have are undesirable. Disruption of maternal–infant interaction in the immediate postnatal period may set some women on the road to breastfeeding failure, and, possibly, altered subsequent behaviour towards their children. The data suggest the plausible hypothesis that women of low socioeconomic status may be particularly vulnerable to the adverse effects of restricting contact.

The importance of maternal care-taking behaviour is so essential to the newborn baby that a variety of biological and social mechanisms must have evolved to promote it. The mutually reinforcing affectionate behaviour that appears to occur during early postnatal mother–infant contact is only one such mechanism. Because it is not the only mechanism, it is important to recognize that many mothers who are constrained from early contact with their babies, whether through illness, misguided hospital policies, or personal preference are likely to overcome any effects of this separation.

There is no solid scientific basis upon which to select from the variety of measures used to treat the umbilical cord, because the available trials have not been large enough to distinguish differences in infection rates (as opposed to colonization rates). Based on the available evidence concerning colonization rates, triple dye is an inexpensive and effective prophylactic for routine use. Neomycin powder is a somewhat more expensive and effective alternative. There is currently no evidence to justify the use of alcohol or powders containing hexachlorophene or other medications, outside the context of randomized controlled trials to assess whether they offer any advantages over triple dye or neomycin powder.

For some women, the postpartum period in hospital can serve a valuable function. The physical, emotional and educational needs of the new mother can be met. Incipient problems, whether physical, psychological, or social, can be recognized, identified, resolved, or referred appropriately. The role of the caregiver can change from that of performer of tasks to that of teacher and counsellor. This can only be accomplished, however, by a flexible approach to care, recognizing the special needs of each individual woman. To accomplish this, many long-standing routines and attitudes must be challenged.

The standard hospital setting, with its orientation towards sickbed protocols and procedures, and its division of care along the lines of the separate medical disciplines of obstetrics and paediatrics, is not conducive either to helping the new mother develop the skills and self confidence she needs to care for herself and her new baby, or to enhancing her sense of personal worth and self-esteem. It is unlikely that any single scheme of care will prove to be right for all women. Treating the new mother as a responsible adult, giving her accurate and consistent information, letting her make her own decisions and supporting her in those decisions is the essence of effective postpartum care.

47

Breastfeeding

This chapter is derived from the chapters by Sally Inch (21); Sally Inch and Sally Garforth (80); and Sally Inch and Mary Renfrew (81) in EFFECTIVE CARE IN PREGNANCY AND CHILDBIRTH.

1 Introduction

Many elements of care during pregnancy and childbirth can foster or jeopardize the successful establishment and maintenance of breastfeeding. Efforts made to provide social and psychological support to mothers during pregnancy, for example, may increase the likelihood that mothers will breastfeed their babies successfully. In contrast, sedative and analgesic drugs given during labour, by altering the behaviour of the newborn infant, can compromise the crucial role of the baby in the initiation of lactation.

The establishment of lactation may be jeopardized at the time of delivery in other ways as well. Routine gastric suctioning and administration of silver nitrate eye drops in the immediate postnatal period have both been shown by controlled trials to alter infant behaviour in a way that prejudices the infant's role in establishing lactation. Separating babies from their mothers, either because of entrenched hospital routines or for necessary treatment of the baby, reduces the likelihood that breastfeeding will be established successfully.

Important factors in establishing and maintaining breastfeeding after birth include antenatal care, the time of the first feed, positioning, feeding frequency and duration, supplements for babies and mothers, and support for breastfeeding mothers.

2 Antenatal preparation

The majority of women who decide to breastfeed seem to make this decision prior to, or early in pregnancy. Those who choose to bottle-feed tend to make up their minds later in pregnancy. That this effect is not mediated by knowledge alone was demonstrated by two randomized controlled trials. Giving women well-designed, written, and illustrated information about breastfeeding, was found to increase their knowledge of the subject, but had little effect on their choice of feeding method, or on the duration of breastfeeding. The data suggest that once a woman has decided how she will feed her baby, she is unlikely to change her mind subsequently.

While information alone, at least in a written form, may not affect the *decision* to breastfeed, antenatal information given to women who have already decided to breastfeed may be beneficial in some circumstances. The available data suggest that antenatal classes may be effective in promoting breastfeeding, but more evidence is undoubtedly needed to assess which elements of the information and what kind of classes women find helpful.

Several research studies have attempted to assess the efficacy of antenatal nipple 'conditioning'. No statistically significant differences were found, either objectively or subjectively, between the different methods of conditioning or between the use of Massé cream, expression of colostrum, or the unprepared nipple. A number of less adequately controlled studies have also failed to showed any effects of antenatal nipple conditioning.

3 Early versus later suckling

Early contact between mother and baby has, in addition to other important benefits, beneficial effects on breastfeeding. It is difficult to separate the effects of early suckling *per se* from the effects of other early mother–baby behaviours, such as touching and gazing. No research has demonstrated a 'critical period' for the first feed in terms of breastfeeding success; that is, there is no evidence to suggest that if a mother does not feed her baby immediately after birth, then her subsequent breastfeeding will suffer. There are therefore no research-based grounds for replacing traditional dogma ('no baby should breastfeed until four hours after delivery') with new dogma ('all babies should feed immediately after delivery'). Babies have a wide range of behaviour following spontaneous delivery, and are not all ready to feed at the same time. Until more evidence is available, interventions aimed either at delaying or speeding up the time of the first feed should be avoided.

These findings suggest that skilled professional help at the first *feed* after delivery (as opposed to the immediate post-delivery nuzzle at the breast) would be useful. This should be done at a time when the baby is receptive, in privacy, and after the newly delivered mother and baby have been made comfortable. If possible, it should be done while the father or someone else whom the mother has found supportive, is still present. The baby's behaviour and needs can be explained to the new parents, who will usually be receptive at this time. A brief explanation of the importance of correct positioning and the concept of supply and demand can be given before the mother positions the baby accurately at the breast. This can be followed by a little more information, including the importance of unrestricted feeding, potential problems, and how (and why) to summon help.

4 The importance of correct positioning

Correct positioning of the baby on the breast plays a crucial role both in the prevention of sore nipples and in the successful establishment of breastfeeding. The ability of a woman to position her baby correctly on her breast is a learned and predominantly manual skill, which the mother must acquire from observation and practice. Industrialized societies, on the whole, do not provide women with the opportunity to observe other breastfeeding women before they attempt breastfeeding themselves. This deficiency is compounded by the frequent lack of experienced breastfeeding mothers in the woman's immediate social sphere.

Professionals must understand the underlying mechanisms of suckling, and acquire the skill and experience to help a mother to position her baby correctly, before they can be of real value to the mother. The fragmentation of postnatal care that is so common today prevents many professionals from acquiring these skills.

When the baby is properly attached to the breast (see Fig. 1) the nipple, together with some of the surrounding breast tissue, is drawn out into a teat by the suction created within the baby's mouth. Breaking this suction causes the nipple to recoil abruptly. The teat thus created extends as far back as the junction of the baby's hard and soft palate, with the nipple itself forming only about one third of the teat. At its base, the teat is held between the upper gum and the tongue, which covers the lower gum. It lies in a central trough formed by the raised edges of the tongue, which directs the expressed milk backwards into the pharynx, using a roller-like, peristaltic movement of the tongue. The peristaltic action begins as the front edge of the tongue curves upwards, closely followed by the raising of the lower jaw,

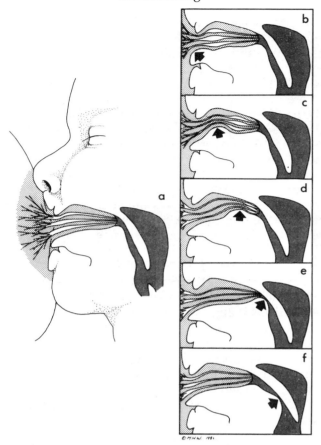

Fig. 1 (a–f): Diagrams of accurate positioning of the baby on the breast (from Woolridge 1986a).

which follows the tongue's movement with pressure from the lower gum. This wave of compression moves progressively backwards beyond the tip of the nipple, thus directing the milk into the pharynx and on into the oesophagus. Meanwhile, a fresh cycle of compression by the tongue has been initiated from its tip.

It is thus the breast tissue opposed to the baby's lower jaw and tongue which is the critical region in the transfer of milk: the tongue applies peristaltic force to the underside of the teat. The hard palate simply provides the necessary resistance to the tongue's action. Once sufficient breast tissue has been formed into the 'teat', there should be virtually no movement of this teat in and out of the baby's mouth. Similarly, friction from the tongue and gums against the skin of the breast and nipple should be minimal; only the milk within the sinuses of the breast should move across the border of the baby's mouth, not the breast tissue itself. If, on the other hand, the baby is incorrectly positioned at the breast and is unable to form a teat out of the breast tissues as well as the nipple, then the nipple is likely to incur frictional damage as the teat is repeatedly drawn in and out of the mouth between the tongue and gums by the cyclical application of suction.

The mother needs to be taught how to elicit and use the two components of the baby's rooting reflex, the moving of the head towards the source of stimulation when the skin around the mouth is touched, and the accompanying gaping of the mouth preparatory to receiving the breast. She should be shown how to move the baby towards the breast and 'plant' the lower rim of the baby's mouth well below the nipple at the moment that the baby's mouth gapes widely. This should be followed by moving the baby close to the breast as it takes a good mouthful of breast tissue. The mother cannot rely, as her helper does, on seeing where the baby's lower lip and jaw are in relation to her nipple, for she has a poor view of the underside of the breast, the critical area of attachment. Observation of the baby's sucking pattern, as well as the sensations that the mother herself experiences (she should feel no pain), will serve to confirm that the baby is correctly positioned (see Fig. 2).

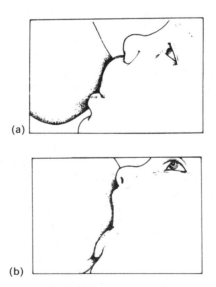

Fig. 2 (from Fisher 1981):
(a) Baby incorrectly positioned at breast.
(b) Baby correctly positioned at breast.

More widespread acquisition and use of the skills needed to achieve correct positioning of the baby on the breast would probably do more than anything else to reduce the frequency of the problems currently experienced by so many breastfeeding mothers.

5 The importance of flexibility in breastfeeding practices

A baby needs to eat and sleep according to his or her own individual rhythms, rather than by those imposed by arbitrary regimens. Feeds are usually infrequent in the first day or so, but the frequency rapidly increases between the third and seventh day, and then decreases more slowly. Although some babies are content to feed as infrequently as every four hours, most babies want to be fed more frequently than this. The interval between feeds, for the first few weeks of life at least, is variable, ranging from one to eight hours. Babies who are permitted to regulate the frequency of their feeds themselves gain weight more quickly, and remain breastfed for longer than those who have external limitations imposed on them. There are no data providing any justification for the imposition of breastfeeding schedules.

Similar comments apply in respect of the duration of feeds. The fact that limitation of suckling time is still being advocated in books addressed both to mothers and to professionals reflects the deeply ingrained belief that the nipples need to be 'toughened' to permit pain-free feeding. Mothers and professionals are often instructed that the baby should be permitted to feed for only 2 minutes at each breast for the first day, increasing the time by 2–3 minutes daily, so that at the end of the first week the baby has reached a maximum of 10 minutes on each side. These admonitions are based on the belief that this practice will 'break the nipples in gradually', prevent their exposure to prolonged sucking, and thus prevent nipple soreness and cracks.

Controlled studies show that this is not the case. Comparison of restricted and unrestricted duration of·feeds shows no significant differences between the two groups in the proportion of women who develop sore or cracked nipples; but significantly more mothers in the regulated groups give up breastfeeding altogether by six weeks.

The still commonly given advice to limit sucking time to 10 minutes on each breast has repercussions beyond its failure to prevent nipple damage. The composition and the rate of flow of milk changes over time. The fat content increases and the flow rate decreases as the feed progresses. Thus, at the start of a feed the baby takes a large volume of low-calorie foremilk; this changes to a smaller volume of high-calorie hindmilk at the end of the feed. Babies feed for differing lengths of time at the breast if left undisturbed. The length of the feed is probably determined by the effectiveness and rate of milk transfer between mother and baby. While many babies will terminate a feed spontaneously in under 10 minutes, those who have a slow rate of intake may well take longer than this. Even though the volume of milk that they consume after 10 minutes have elapsed may not be very great, it may be sufficiently high in calories to make a significant contribution in energy value. The external imposition of a time limit for feeding will thus result in some babies having their calorie intake significantly curtailed.

Babies are driven to feed by the need to obtain calories, and thus take much larger volumes of low-calorie milk than they would of high-calorie milk, in an attempt to gain the required number of calories. Babies who are taken from the first breast before they spontaneously terminate the feed may take a much larger volume of milk from the second breast than they might otherwise have done, in order to try to 'make up' their calories. For the same reason these babies may also require feeding much more frequently than they would have required if they were allowed to finish feeding spontaneously.

In addition, interference with spontaneous feeding patterns may result in the baby being deprived of essential vitamins. Vitamin K, for example, is especially concentrated in colostrum and hindmilk, and this may explain the increased incidence of haemorrhagic disease of the newborn in breastfed babies.

There is still a need, in some institutions, for more intensive policy discussions and in-service training to ensure that a policy that supports and encourages flexible breastfeeding is translated effectively into practice.

6 'Supplementing' the baby

There is no evidence to support the widespread practice of giving breastfed babies supplementary feeds of water, glucose, or formula. A healthy baby has no need for large volumes of fluid any earlier than these become available physiologically from the breast. There is no evidence to support the widespread belief that giving additional fluids to breastfed babies prevents or helps to resolve physiological jaundice. In the only randomized controlled trial to have examined the question, there was no statistically significant reduction in mean plasma bilirubin levels associated with giving water supplements, nor any evidence that babies receiving extra fluids were any less likely to develop 'breast milk jaundice' or require phototherapy.

The practice of giving breastfed babies formula while lactation is becoming established is also misconceived and unsupported by evidence. Women whose babies receive supplements are up to five times more likely to give up breastfeeding in the first week, and twice as likely to abandon it during the second week as women who are not supplemented, but encouraged to feel that their own colostrum and milk are adequate.

Those hospitals that allow breastfeeding mothers to be given free samples of formula also prejudice the chances of successful establishment and maintenance of breastfeeding. The four randomized evaluations of this policy show that it increases the chances that breastfeeding will have been abandoned within a few weeks of delivery.

7 'Supplementing' the mother

Advice given to breastfeeding women concerning their own fluid intake has been inconsistent and has led to confusion and misinformation. The results of controlled studies provide no evidence that increased fluid intake by breastfeeding mothers will result in improved lactation. Some women find it unpleasant to drink when they are not thirsty because it makes them feel 'turgid' and 'unwell'. Women with perineal and labial trauma may have their discomfort increased by the diuresis associated with greater fluid intake.

8 Combined oestrogen-progestogen contraceptives

Combined oestrogen-progestogen contraceptives may affect the composition of breast milk. Their effect on milk volume is not clear, probably because of limitations in the methods used to estimate milk volume. What is clear is that their use increases the incidence both of breastfeeding failure and of supplementation with breast milk substitutes.

All the evidence from the controlled trials suggests that combined oestrogen-progestogen contraceptives are unsuitable for women who wish to breastfeed their babies. This finding is of particular importance in parts of the world in which use of breast-milk substitutes poses a threat to infant life and health. Lactation itself, particularly if breastfeeding is unrestricted, has a contraceptive effect. In developing countries, breastfeeding prevents more pregnancies than all other methods of contraception combined. If breastfeeding women wish to enhance the contraceptive effect of lactation itself, they should use non-hormonal methods.

9 Supporting breastfeeding mothers and babies

A large proportion of women who wish to breastfeed begin to do so, but discontinue long before their babies are four months old. Perhaps the most important factor in the efforts to achieve successful breastfeeding is that those who attempt it should succeed. Many of the problems that confront women who are trying to breastfeed are avoidable. Fewer women would experience these problems if all breastfeeding women had access to accurate information, and appropriate and practical help and support when they needed it. More pregnant women would then know of others who had breastfed successfully, and be more confident that they themselves would succeed.

A number of controlled trials have assessed the effects of various forms of support for breastfeeding mothers. Although the results were not totally consistent, most show that the duration of breastfeeding can be increased by regular and frequent contact with the mother by the same caregiver, either in person or by visits followed by telephoning. Advice and support for mothers who wish to breastfeed can be important in helping them to achieve their objectives. If the advice given is flawed it is unlikely to be helpful.

10 Nipple trauma

The most widely held explanation for the prevalence of nipple pain in industrialized cultures is the supposed thinness or sensitivity of the nipple epithelium. This probably explains the widespread belief, unsupported by the studies that have examined the question, that women with fair skin or red hair are more likely to experience problems. Most nipple damage could be prevented by skilled care from the very first feed.

A number of treatments, including ointments, tinctures, and sprays have been used for the treatment or prevention of nipple damage. None that have been evaluated have been shown to be of benefit. The use of a nipple shield for any length of time, even by those who find its use acceptable, may add to a mother's problems by suppressing her milk production.

The only factor that has been shown to both prevent and treat nipple trauma is good positioning of the baby at the breast.

11 Problems with milk flow

If the milk is not removed as it is formed (as regulated by the baby's need to go to the breast) the volume of milk in the breast will exceed the capacity of the alveoli to store it comfortably. Over-distension of the alveoli with milk causes the milk-secreting cells to become flattened and drawn out, and even to rupture. If severe, this will cause secondary vascular engorgement. Once the alveoli become distended, further milk production begins to be suppressed.

Engorgement results from limitations on feeding frequency and duration, and from problems with positioning the baby at the breast. A number of different treatments have been advocated. Some, such as the use of moist heat or ice packs, have not been evaluated.

The controlled evaluations of the effects of oxytocin on engorgement failed to find any beneficial effect of oxytocin in relieving engorgement. Two early studies seem to indicate that manual expression, started antenatally and continued postnatally, will help to relieve engorgement and increase the duration of breastfeeding; both of these studies, however, were carried out under conditions where feeding was restricted and engorgement was, as a result, very common.

Oral proteolytic enzymes have been tested in placebo-controlled studies, which suggest that they may provide effective relief for women with breast pain, swelling, and tenderness. Both trials found statistically significant improvements in the groups of women receiving the proteolytic enzymes.

Treatment of severe engorgement has included both administration of stilboestrol and binding of the breasts, two measures also advocated for suppression of lactation in women who do not wish to breastfeed. No controlled trials have evaluated their effectiveness in the treatment of breast engorgement in breastfeeding women.

Allowing the baby unrestricted access to the breast still appears to be the most effective method of treating, as well as of preventing, breast engorgement.

The other common difficulty caused by milk-flow problems is mastitis. Milk flow can be limited by restriction of feeding, by a badly positioned baby, or when some obstacle is placed in the way of milk draining from one section of the breast. This obstacle can result from such factors as blocked ducts, compression from fingers holding the breast, bruising from trauma or rough handling, or because a brassiere is too small or too tight. In consequence, the milk collects in the alveoli and the pressure in the alveoli rises. The distension of the alveoli can often be felt as a tender lump in the breast tissue. If this distension is not relieved the pressure may force substances from the milk through the cell walls into the surrounding connective tissue, setting up an inflammatory reaction. The mother develops a swollen, red, and painful area on her breast, a rise in her pulse and temperature, and an aching, flu-like feeling, often accompanied by shivering attacks and rigors. At this stage the process is not infective, and the problem can be resolved by relieving the obstruction. If this is not speedily accomplished bacterial infection may supervene, and may ultimately give rise to a breast abscess.

Perhaps understandably, the immediate response of the professional confronted with the symptoms of localized breast tenderness, redness, and fever in breastfeeding women is often the prescription of antibiotics. What begins as a non-infective, inflammatory process may, if not treated appropriately, rapidly progress to an infective process and delay in treating an infective process: will adversely affect the outcome. Nevertheless, a substantial proportion of women with mastitis do not have an infection.

For women with milk stasis, simple continuation of breastfeeding gives the best results; expression of breast milk has not been shown to confer any advantage. The outcome for women with non-infective mastitis is best with continuation of breastfeeding supplemented by breast milk expression. For women with infective mastitis, antibiotics are necessary, and for them expression of breast milk improves the outcome.

12 Problems with milk supply

The most common reason given for discontinuing breastfeeding is insufficient milk. There is no information, however, about the extent to which this insufficiency is inevitable, as opposed to iatrogenic and thus preventable. Objective evidence of insufficient milk is hard to obtain, but it is likely that the high reported incidence reflects over-diagnosis of the problem. Observations in traditional societies suggest that less than 1 to 5 per cent of women would be physiologically incapable of producing an adequate milk supply.

It is important to be able to diagnose the occurrence and aetiology of insufficient milk accurately. Accurate measurement of milk production is possible with expensive and sophisticated research techniques, but the only clinically available method for this measurement is test weighing of the baby before and after feeds, then calculating the breast milk intake by the difference in weights. Such test weighing, which is grossly inaccurate, has been used to estimate the baby's intake in case of anxiety about milk supply, and as a routine practice in some hospitals.

The rationale for test weighing is to determine whether babies are taking 'too much' or 'too little' milk. If too little they can receive supplements, if too much the duration of breastfeeding can be curtailed. The hazards of these inappropriate responses to an inherently inaccurate test have already been discussed. In the one study mounted to examine this question directly, the effect of routine test weighing and supplementary feeding was compared with infants who were neither weighed or supplemented. The total duration of breastfeeding was almost the same in both groups, but the mothers in the test-weigh group were five times more likely to stop breastfeeding in the first week, and twice as likely to stop in the second week as those in the group whose babies were not test weighed.

The decision to give a healthy term breastfed baby supplementary feeds as a result of information gained by assessing milk intake is based on the unwarranted assumption that it is possible to know how much breastmilk an individual baby needs. It would be more relevant to monitor the general condition of a baby (health, contentment/behaviour, colour and consistency of stools, colour of urine, etc.) and note his or her progress (change in body weight).

The best means of preventing the occurrence of insufficient milk is unrestricted feeding by a well-positioned infant while giving good practical and emotional support to the breastfeeding mother. This is also the basis for the treatment of insufficient milk, and is likely to solve the problem in a high proportion of, but not all, mothers.

Professionals should be alive to the possibility that milk insufficiency may persist. Babies may become seriously undernourished because of a dogged, but mistaken, belief that the problem will always be resolved by physiological means. When mothers and babies do not respond to the fundamental elements of good breastfeeding practice, other treatments should be considered.

In the past, when a baby's life depended on breastmilk, many remedies were sought for those who seemed unable to produce enough milk. In addition to some rather bizarre prescriptions a variety of herbal infusions, such as the seeds of fennel *(Foeniculum vulgare)* and the flowers of goat's rue *(Galega officinalis)* were, and still are, recommended to increase milk production. We have been unable to identify any controlled evaluation of the effects of these preparations. Four main types of drugs have, however, been evaluated in attempted treatment of insufficient milk: dopamine antagonists, iodine, thyrotropin-releasing hormone, and oxytocin.

Since dopamine has been shown to have a critical role in the mechanisms which control prolactin production, several researchers have experimented with drugs that block dopamine receptors, including metoclopramide (Maxalon), sulpiride (Dolmatil), and domperidone (Motilium).

There is some evidence that these drugs may be of use for women who are temporarily unable to feed their sick or premature babies. Further research is required to clarify this.

As the let-down reflex, which is primed by oxytocin release from the posterior pituitary, is essential for successful breastfeeding, some investigators have reasoned that to give oxytocin may improve problems with milk supply. A variety of outcomes have been studied, but the most crucial information concerns weight changes in the baby. The trials conducted have produced conflicting results, and to date there is no strong evidence that oxytocin administration has a beneficial effect on milk supply.

13 Conclusions

Those who care for women during pregnancy and childbirth have a crucial role to play in enabling a woman to breastfeed successfully. Now that sound, research-based information is readily available to them, the professional ignorance which may have been acceptable in the past is no longer tolerable. If the potential for helping women to breastfeed their babies is to be realized, professionals must reject much of the received wisdom in this field and pass on to women only those practices which have been demonstrated to be effective.

Those who are most likely to be closely involved with mothers at the time that breastfeeding is becoming established should have a clear understanding of how a baby breastfeeds. They should recognize that although separation of babies from their mothers after delivery jeopardizes the successful establishment of lactation, there is no evidence to suggest that the timing of the first feed, in itself, is crucial to success.

Professionals should know how a mother can be helped to position her baby correctly on the breast. They should impose no restrictions on the duration or the frequency of feeds, and neither offer nor recommend additional fluids or formula for healthy breastfed babies, particularly by giving free samples of formula to women in hospital.

Normal lactating women with access to adequate fluid can depend on their thirst to regulate fluid intake effectively. Urging women to drink more than their thirst dictates has no justification.

Use of combined oestrogen-progestogen contraceptives compromises lactation. If women wishing to breastfeed also wish to enhance the contraceptive effect of lactation, they should use either non-hormonal methods, or preparations containing only progestogens.

Women can be helped to establish and maintain breastfeeding in a number of ways, but the experimentally-derived evidence suggests that continuity of personal support from an individual who is knowledgeable about breastfeeding is most effective.

The main reasons women give for discontinuing breastfeeding are nipple trauma, breast engorgement, mastitis, and insufficient milk. The majority of these problems can be prevented by unrestricted breastfeeding by a baby who has been well-positioned from the first feed on, and by giving mothers excellent practical and emotional support.

If a woman does sustain nipple trauma, she should continue to breastfeed, express milk if necessary, and receive help with positioning. Discontinuing breastfeeding, and the application of any of a variety of preparations to the nipple, does not help. Indeed, some of these interventions have been shown to prejudice the success of breastfeeding.

Problems with milk flow can result in engorgement and possibly in mastitis. Oral proteolytic enzymes may help in the treatment of engorgement. If mastitis does not resolve rapidly with good feeding and expression, then antibiotic treatment should be instituted. In all cases of engorgement and mastitis, however, the key to successful treatment is good drainage of the breast. This is best achieved by unlimited feeds by a well-positioned baby.

Mothers and health professionals who suspect insufficient milk as a result of signs and symptoms in the baby or the mother face a challenging problem. Identifying the problem and its cause is always difficult and often impossible. Until diagnostic precision improves, the basis of the treatment offered when insufficient milk is suspected remains unrestricted breastfeeding by a well-positioned baby, together with practical and emotional support for the mother.

48

Perineal pain and discomfort

This chapter is derived from the chapter by Adrian Grant and Jennifer Sleep (79) in EFFECTIVE CARE IN PREGNANCY AND CHILDBIRTH.

1 Introduction

Perineal pain constitutes a major problem for mothers in the early days following vaginal delivery, especially if they have sustained perineal trauma. Sometimes this pain persists for a long time; pain during intercourse as long as three years after delivery may have its origin in suboptimal postpartum care.

Avoidance of trauma when possible, and proper repair when trauma occurs, are the primary approaches to avoiding or reducing these problems. In addition, a wide range of measures and active treatments are advocated for secondary prevention, or relief.

2 Local applications

2.1 *Non-pharmacological applications*

Sprays, gels, creams, solutions, ice packs, baths, and douches are all commonly recommended for the relief of perineal discomfort after vaginal delivery, but they have had little, if any, formal evaluation.

Cooling with ice or sprays is often used in postnatal care in the belief that pain and oedema are reduced. Ice packs in the puerperium do give immediate symptomatic relief by numbing the perineum, but this is usually short-lived, and there is no evidence of any longer-term benefit. Sprays have been reported also to relieve perineal discomfort, probably by a cooling effect, although they occasionally cause a stinging discomfort.

There is evidence from a randomized trial that cold sitz baths are more effective than warm sitz baths in relieving perineal discomfort; but the differential effect is limited to the first half-hour after bathing, and the cold baths are not popular with women.

The warmth of a hot bath may give some comfort in the immediate puerperium. In a recent survey, over 90 per cent of women reported that bathing had relieved perineal discomfort. This observation was uncontrolled, however, and there is no knowing whether a similar proportion of women would have gained relief if they had not bathed at all, or had used showers rather than baths. With the current trend towards showers and bidets rather than baths in modern maternity hospitals the question of the difference in comfort resulting from these different approaches is important.

The growing popularity of locally applied herbal substances for relief of perineal pain probably reflects both a belief that 'time-honoured natural medicines must be safe', and their increased availability from many retail outlets. No controlled studies of their use have been reported. Witchhazel soaked into gauze swabs or other pads and applied directly to the perineal tissues is commonly recommended for the relief of pain, but a randomized trial showed no evidence that it was any more effective than tap water.

Salt added to bathwater is one of the oldest claimed 'remedies' for perineal and other trauma, and is still very popular. The salt is believed to soothe discomfort and to promote healing, although a precise mode of action is unclear. Claims that it has antiseptic or antibacterial properties have not been confirmed. There is no consensus as to the type of salt preparation or quantity which should be used. Recommendations about the quantity range from a heaped tablespoon in a small bath to 3 lbs in 30 gallons of water (about 10 grams per litre). In a large controlled trial, the addition of salt to the bath water had no detectable effect either on perineal pain or on the patterns of perineal wound healing.

2.2 Local antiseptics

The addition of antiseptic solution, particularly 'Savlon' concentrate, to the bath water is also a common practice during the postnatal period. This too was studied in the large trial mentioned above, women having been asked to add Savlon to a daily bath for the first ten days after delivery. There was no evidence that this addition improved symptomatic relief from bathing, or that it reduced perineal discomfort. Similarly, a study comparing antiseptic solution with unmedicated tap water for 'jug douching' showed also no differential effect on symptoms, healing, or infection rates.

The use of vaginal creams containing sulphonamides, once recommended for routine use in the postpartum period, has been evaluated in two controlled studies. The results suggested that minor benign cervical abnormalities, such as erosion or ectropion, were less common in the women who had used the sulphonamide creams, and that these women reported less use of vaginal douches. Equal proportions of women in each group had resumed sexual intercourse by six weeks after delivery.

2.3 Local anaesthetics

Local anaesthetics are commonly applied as sprays, gels, creams, or foams. Double blind comparisons of local anaesthetics show them to be clearly more effective for relief of perineal pain than placebo. On the evidence of several well-controlled studies it is safe to conclude that local anaesthetics are useful for relief of perineal pain in the immediate postpartum period. Aqueous 5 per cent lignocaine spray or lignocaine gel appears to be the most rational first choice of agent and formulation.

2.4 Combinations of local anaesthetics and topical steroids

Based on the assumption that much of the pain from perineal trauma arises from local oedema and inflammation, a local anaesthetic (pramoxine) has recently been combined with a steroid (hydrocortisone) as a single topical agent. Early uncontrolled studies gave very encouraging results, but two well-controlled studies produced conflicting findings. Whereas the first study reported less pain, better pain relief, and less use of oral analgesia in the pramoxine/hydrocortisone group, the other reported more oedema and a greater use of oral analgesia, particularly after the third day. Wound breakdown was also more common in the actively treated group in this study. As steroids are known to impair wound healing, the latter finding is biologically plausible. It would not seem sensible to use this combination except in the context of further properly controlled trials.

3 Local physiotherapies

3.1 Relief of pressure on the perineum

A variety of simple aids may be used during sitting or lying as a means of relieving pressure on the sore perineum. When a mother is resting in bed, a wedge or pillow may be used to support her on her side.

These should be covered in a waterproof fabric so that they can be easily cleaned. Rubber or foam-rubber rings have been widely advocated in the past, especially for mothers needing to sit comfortably to feed their babies. Rubber rings have largely been withdrawn from use, as they are believed to compress venous return, thereby increasing the risk of thrombosis in women already at higher risk postpartum. The fact that they are no longer supplied in hospital does not prevent many women from buying their own or substituting children's swimming rings. The popularity of this simple measure suggests that it gives relief to many women.

3.2 *Ultrasound and pulsed electromagnetic energy*

Recent developments in the physical treatments of soft-tissue injuries have lead to the increased use of electrical therapies for the traumatized perineum. Two such treatments are currently in common use—ultrasound, and pulsed electromagnetic energy.

Evidence about the effectiveness of therapeutic ultrasound for other soft-tissue injuries is not wholly consistent, and the precise mode of action is not properly understood. Ultrasound therapy requires constant operator attendance during treatment, and hence is costly in physiotherapist's time. The transducer is applied directly to the skin, and must be moved during transmission as a safeguard against tissue damage; conduction is aided by a jelly or cream. This gentle movement of the transducer head over the injured tissues may alone provide some therapeutic or psychological benefit.

Similar benefits to those seen following ultrasound therapy have been claimed, on the basis of observational studies, for pulsed electromagnetic energy. The interrupted transmission of the energy allows high-intensity waves to be used while minimizing local heat. The main advantage of pulsed electromagnetic energy is its ease of application. It may be transmitted through a sanitary towel, thus avoiding the need for constant operator attendance.

The effects of this therapy on perineal healing have been assessed in two published trials. Maternal reporting of perineal pain before and after treatment revealed no benefit from the active therapy. The physiotherapists who operated the machines, however, observed a reduction in the extent of perineal bruising which they ascribed to pulsed electromagnetic energy.

A randomized controlled trial has compared ultrasound, pulsed electromagnetic energy, and placebo therapy given in the immediate postpartum period for the treatment of the 'severely traumatized' perineum. Preliminary analyses have not shown any clear differences in the major measures of outcome among the groups. About 90 per cent of women in each group, including the placebo group, felt that the treatment had made the pain better, underlining both the necessity for well-designed comparative studies, and the power of the placebo effect on the condition.

These preliminary analyses provide no basis for the widespread use of these two expensive modalities in the treatment of perineal problems. Further randomized trials would be needed to justify any continued use of these technologies in the postnatal ward, and would provide an opportunity to assess the size of the placebo effect.

3.3 Pelvic floor exercises

The usual rationale for advising post-natal exercises of the pelvic floor muscles is the belief that the exercises will reduce the risk of urinary stress incontinence and genital prolapse. In the only large controlled trial in which the effects of post-natal exercises on incontinence rates has been assessed, the rate of incontinence (three months after delivery) among women who had received intensive instruction and reinforcement for pelvic floor exercises was similar to that among other women who had received the usual level of information and no special reinforcement. Although no beneficial effects of post-natal exercises on subsequent incontinence rates were detected, some other outcomes did appear to be affected. Women who received the intensive post-natal exercise programme and reinforcement were significantly less likely to have perineal pain. They were also less likely to be depressed. This latter difference may have been mediated either by the greater attention paid to their progress postpartum, or simply because they were in less pain.

4 Treatments taken by mouth

4.1 Herbal preparations

A range of herbal preparations for oral use, aimed at relieving perineal symptoms, is available. For example, arnica (leopard's bane) supplied as tablets, and comfrey as a tablet or a tea are claimed to reduce bruising. As far as we know, they have never been formally evaluated.

4.2 Proteolytic enzymes

Some of the pharmacologically active proteolytic enzymes occur naturally; ananase, for example is an extract of Hawaiian pineapple plants. Three such enzyme preparations (bromolain, chymotrypsin alone, and chymotrypsin plus trypsin) have been evaluated in controlled trials. Although the trials individually gave somewhat conflicting results, an overview of the results shows significant decreases in oedema, in pain on sitting, and in pain on walking by the third day. These results suggest that oral proteolytic agents may have an important effect on perineal discomfort. Nevertheless, the trials are different in terms of quality, prevalence of outcomes, and estimates of treatment effect, so this conclusion can be only tentative. Firm conclusions must await the results of better controlled studies.

4.3 Oral analgesics

A bewildering choice of pharmacologically active preparations can be taken by mouth to relieve perineal pain. Despite the large number of randomized trials in which these agents have been evaluated, the experimental evidence is relatively unhelpful. There are two main reasons for this. First, most trials show that the active preparations are superior to placebo, but fail to distinguish clinically important differences between alternative analgesics. Second, many of the drugs included in the trials are no longer commercially available.

A number of factors must be considered when making a choice of oral analgesic preparations. One is the severity of the pain being treated. Another is whether the formulation is likely to cause constipation, which is particularly important to avoid when treating perineal pain. Some oral preparations can cause gastric upset, and this should be avoided if possible. Whether the drug or drugs are carried in breast milk, and, if so, whether this has any potential danger for the baby, is a further important consideration. In addition, some drugs have more serious, albeit rare, adverse effects. Finally, the relative costs of the alternative preparations should be taken into account.

On the basis of these criteria, paracetamol (acetaminophen) is probably the drug of choice for mild perineal pain. It has a useful analgesic effect and is largely free of unwanted side-effects. Aspirin is less satisfactory because it can cause gastric irritation, prolongs bleeding time, and poses a potential risk to the baby because of its carriage in breast milk.

Of the other non-steroidal anti-inflammatory drugs, ibuprofen would seem to be the most appropriate, if an alternative to paracetamol is required for treating perineal pain. Unlike some of the other non-steroidal anti-inflammatory drugs it appears to be largely free of unwanted side-effects, and very little is excreted in breast milk.

The choice of analgesics is less satisfactory when perineal pain is insufficiently relieved by paracetamol or ibuprofen. The opioid dextropropoxyphene may cause dependence and cannot be recommended. One option is to give paracetamol in combination with lower doses of codeine or dihydrocodeine than would be the case if the latter were being used on their own. Although it seems reasonable to combine the two types of analgesia, it is uncertain whether the analgesic effect is greater than with paracetamol on its own.

If perineal pain does not respond adequately to paracetamol, it seems sensible to consider the additional use of local therapies such as heat and local anaesthetics. If the pain is likely to be associated with local inflammation, a non-steroidal anti-inflammatory agent, such as ibuprofen or aspirin, may be helpful. If stronger analgesia is still required there is no obvious first choice. There are differences in individual susceptibility to different analgesic formulations. Codeine derivatives are less suitable for perineal pain than for other types of pain because they predispose to constipation. For this reason the combinations of paracetamol (acetaminophen) with a stronger opioid analgesic may have a special place for the relief of perineal pain.

5 Conclusions

Cooling with crushed ice, witchhazel, or tap water gives short-term symptomatic relief from perineal pain and discomfort. Locally applied anaesthetics such as aqueous 5 per cent lignocaine spray or lignocaine gel are also effective, and may last longer. Adding a steroid to such local anaesthetics may do more harm than good. The addition of salt or antiseptic solution to bathwater has no further effect on perineal pain or healing.

The quality of personal care during the puerperium is likely to be a major determinant of postpartum perineal discomfort. On the basis of currently available evidence the therapeutic effects noted from physiotherapies, such as therapeutic ultrasound, pulsed electromagnetic energy, and the teaching of postnatal exercises, may derive from the personal attention involved, rather than from the treatment modalities themselves.

Paracetamol (acetaminophen) is the oral analgesic of choice for mild perineal pain. If paracetamol in conjunction with the local therapies mentioned fails to control the pain, a non-steroidal anti-inflammatory agent such as ibuprofen or aspirin is a useful alternative. The oral proteolytic enzymes may also be considered for relatively intractable perineal pain, although their effectiveness has still not been clearly established. There is no obvious oral analgesic for more severe pain which is inadequately controlled by paracetamol. The tendency for codeine derivatives to cause constipation makes these drugs less suitable for perineal pain than for pain in other sites.

Until recently, the prevention and treatment of perineal pain following childbirth using approaches other than systemic analgesia have been the subject of little formal evaluative research. Yet postpartum perineal pain is so common that alternative strategies can be compared in statistically powerful, single-centre, randomized controlled trials. Such trials are needed if more effective treatments for this common problem are to be developed.

49

Breast symptoms in women who are not breastfeeding

This chapter is derived from the chapter by Fabio Parazzini, Flavia Zanaboni, Alessandro Liberati, and Gianni Tognoni (82) in EFFECTIVE CARE IN PREGNANCY AND CHILDBIRTH.

1 Introduction

Women may not breastfeed their babies after childbirth for a variety of reasons, ranging from stillbirth to personal choice. The decision not to breastfeed may lead to considerable breast pain and engorgement during the days after childbirth, until lactation becomes spontaneously suppressed. A number of approaches have been adopted in attempts to hasten the suppression of lactation and reduce the symptoms that accompany it.

2 Non-pharmacological approaches

Until forty years ago tight binding of the breasts and fluid restriction were the most common approaches to the suppression of lactation. They remain among the most frequently adopted of the non-pharmacological methods. Almost no formal investigation of these methods has been undertaken, although the results of one small randomized trial showed that breast pain was less frequent in women who restricted their fluid intake than in those just wearing brassieres.

Non-pharmacological methods of inhibiting lactation have been implicitly compared with pharmacological methods in trials of different drug agents. In one study, in which breast binders were compared with bromoergocriptine, the drug was shown to be more effective in controlling symptoms during the first week postpartum;

by the second week the two groups were equally likely to experience symptoms; three weeks postpartum problems were more frequent in the group that had received bromoergocriptine. It is probable, therefore, that there may be short-term disadvantages, but longer-term benefits of non-pharmacological approaches to suppress lactation.

3 Pharmacological approaches

3.1 Sex hormones

The use of stilboestrol reduces the incidence of continuing lactation, breast pain, and engorgement during the first week postpartum. However, there appear to be long-term costs of this short-term efficacy. More women given stilboestrol than women given placebo required additional treatment after discharge from hospital, and four times as many in the stilboestrol-treated group reported abnormal bleeding after the end of treatment. These unwanted effects of the drug outweighed its short-term benefits.

Trials comparing the effects of different oestrogens show that stilboestrol suppresses lactation and pain more effectively than quinoestrol. Chlorotrianisene, another stilboestrol analogue, has also been shown to reduce lactation, breast pain, and engorgement in placebo-controlled trials.

Various combinations of an oestrogen and testosterone have been shown to have dramatic short-term effects on lactation, breast pain, and breast engorgement. The only trial in which long-term effects have been reported shows a reversal of the short-term effects by the end of the second week.

The risk of thromboembolic complications is increased with oestrogen use, but the absolute level of risk is quite low. Withdrawal bleeding after hormonal treatment is reported by about 15 per cent of women, irrespective of the type of drug used.

3.2 Bromoergocriptine

The short-term effects of bromoergocriptine, compared with placebo, have been well established. The results of well-controlled trials show that it greatly decreases lactation, breast pain, and engorgement in the first postpartum week. Only limited data are available on effects during the second week, but the effects by this time are much less dramatic. Comparisons show that bromoergocriptine suppresses lactation and breast engorgement in the first postpartum week more effectively than stilboestrol.

No major adverse effect has been reported in women treated with bromoergocriptine for suppression of lactation. The reported frequency of nausea is less than 5 per cent.

3.3. *Other drugs*

Pyridoxine has been compared with placebo in three studies; the few data available show a limited effect on continued lactation.

In the early 1960s the effects on lactation and breast symptoms of spraying synthetic oxytocin intranasally were studied in at least three trials, one of them unpublished. None of these studies provided any evidence that the treatment was effective.

4 Conclusions

The available evidence suggests that fluid restriction may reduce symptoms among women who do not wish to breastfeed. Physical methods of lactation suppression, like breast binding, are associated with more pain in the first week after delivery than pharmacological methods, but they appear to be more effective in the longer term. Women should be made aware of these relative advantages and disadvantages when a method to suppress lactation is chosen.

If it is decided to use one of the pharmacological approaches, the available evidence suggests that, in the short term, stilboestrol may be superior to quinoestrol, and bromoergocriptine superior to stilboestrol. The thrombogenic potential of oestrogens, although small, is another reason for selecting bromoergocriptine from among the various pharmacological options available.

Bromoergocriptine, and newer drugs like dihydroergocriptine, should be compared formally with physical methods of suppressing lactation in well-designed controlled trials that have adequate sample sizes and duration of follow-up. Women's views of the relative merits and disadvantages of the alternative methods should constitute an essential element in the evaluation, and more serious attention should be given to documenting the frequency of short- and long-term adverse reactions.

50

Effective care in pregnancy and childbirth: a synopsis

*This chapter is derived from the final chapter in EFFECTIVE CARE IN
PREGNANCY AND CHILDBIRTH.*

The underlying thesis of this book is that evidence from well--
controlled comparisons provides the best basis for choosing among
alternative forms of care for pregnancy and childbirth. This evidence
should encourage the adoption of useful measures and the abandon-
ment of those that are useless or harmful. It is probably worth noting
that the systematic review of evidence on which the book has been
based has, at times, shattered our own preconceptions about the
effects of care.

In this final chapter we have tried to summarize the main conclusions reached in earlier chapters. This summary takes the form of
four Appendices which list, respectively, forms of care that have been
shown to reduce negative outcomes of pregnancy and childbirth;
forms of care that appear promising, but require further evaluation;
forms of care that have unknown effects; and finally, forms of care
that we think should be abandoned in the light of the available
evidence.

We hope that the explicit form in which these conclusions have
been stated will be useful, and that the advantages of the Appendices
will outweigh their drawbacks. A tabulated summary such as this is
necessarily selective, and, to some extent, subjective. Nuances discussed in earlier chapters cannot find expression in tables. A few of
the apparently causal associations listed may have arisen by chance;
others may appear to be implausible. Many of the conclusions will be
controversial. Our conclusions must obviously be judged in the light
of the methods used by our collaborators and ourselves to assemble
and review the evidence on which they are based.

Before discussing the Appendices in more detail, we would like to
discuss some of the ways in which the results of research may, and
may not, be applicable in practice. First, because research based on
the study of groups generates evidence about how people respond to
particular forms of care on average, they may be relevant in guiding
the development of broad policies for care during pregnancy and
childbirth. For example, there is strong evidence that continuity of

personal care, combined with efforts to provide social and psychological support during pregnancy and childbirth, is preferred by women, and that it has a number of other beneficial effects; furthermore, there is no evidence that it has any adverse effects. This evidence should be used to support efforts to ensure that continuity of care and the provision of social and psychological support is pursued as a matter of policy. Similarly, there is strong evidence that, compared with other suture materials, catgut used to repair perineal trauma leads to more short-term perineal discomfort, and that it has no compensating advantages. As a matter of policy, therefore, catgut should be abandoned for suturing perineal trauma.

Second, the results of research must be considered in relation to decisions about the care of individuals. Once again, evidence from controlled comparisons will usually identify the form of care that is best for most women and babies. Nevertheless, forms of care that appear to be desirable for the majority of women and babies may be wrong for some of them; conversely, forms of care that do not appear to be effective overall may be effective for some women or babies. Improvements in diagnostic accuracy should help caregivers to identify individual women and babies who are likely to respond in an atypical way to particular forms of care. Although advances in diagnostic accuracy will undoubtedly occur, tailoring care to meet the specific needs of individuals will continue to be more of an art than a science. This art can be improved by listening more carefully to what women have to say, and by involving them to a greater extent in decisions about their care.

Lastly, there is an important additional dimension to be considered in assessing the implications for care of the results of the reviews presented earlier. This is that different people will use the evidence presented in this book in different ways because of the different values they assign to particular forms of care and their effects. Their judgements will differ when it comes to assessing whether the benefits of a particular form of care are sufficient to outweigh its costs, whether the latter are assessed in terms of unwanted physical or psychological effects, inconvenience, or resource consequences. In other words, the differing circumstances and values of different individuals may provoke different reactions to the same quality of evidence—as common sense would suggest they should. Knowledge of the effects of care, however, is a necessary prerequisite if the choices made by individuals about care are to be properly informed. We hope that the four Appendices that follow, used in conjunction with the chapters on which they have been based, will assist this process of informed choice.

Appendix 1 lists forms of care that, in our opinion, have been shown to reduce negative outcomes of pregnancy and childbirth. We do not pretend that it is comprehensive, because there are many aspects of care (transfusions for haemorrhagic shock, for example) that are so obviously worthwhile that their inclusion would have appeared trite. Our decision to include forms of care in Appendix 1 was usually made because the estimates of their beneficial effects derived from controlled trials were statistically significant. Other evidence was used when we considered it to be sufficiently strong.

The inclusion of a particular form of care in Appendix 1 does not necessarily imply that it should be adopted in practice. Whether the forms of care included in this Appendix are adopted will depend on assessments of the importance of the likely benefits weighed against the importance of the likely costs. For a variety of reasons, as noted above, perceptions of this relationship between benefits and costs will vary from individual to individual, and from situation to situation. Although the available evidence suggests that the forms of care included in Appendix 1 do indeed reduce the negative outcomes listed, these welcome effects are sometimes achieved at the cost of increasing unwanted effects. Thus, genetic amniocentesis, although it leads to improved detection of fetal chromosomal abnormalities, increases the risk of miscarriage and neonatal respiratory morbidity; epidural anaesthesia, while providing very effective relief of pain during labour, increases the chances that instrumental assistance will be used for delivery; and pharmacological suppression of lactation, although reducing unpleasant symptoms in the short term, may result in 'rebound' lactation and breast symptoms two or three weeks after delivery.

In addition, although a certain form of care may well be able to reduce the frequency of a particular negative outcome, the outcome may already be so rare (or be considered so trivial) that adoption of this form of care would seem unwarranted. These considerations might apply to screening for gonorrhoea during pregnancy to reduce the incidence of gonococcal ophthalmia; or to the routine use of continuous electronic fetal heart rate monitoring with fetal scalp blood sampling during labour to reduce the incidence of early neonatal seizures; or to routine ultrasonography in early pregnancy to reduce the incidence of induction of labour for 'post-term' pregnancy.

Appendix 2 lists those forms of care that appear to be promising in the light of the available evidence, but which, in our opinion, require further evaluation before informed decisions can be made about whether or not they should be adopted in practice. Some of the forms of care in Appendix 2 were included because the estimates of their effects did not quite reach conventional levels of statistical significance; others were included because we felt that a statistically significant reduction in negative effects may have reflected bias because of the quality of the available evidence. Some of the possible effects of forms of care included in Appendix 2 could be of great relevance for improving the effectiveness of care, and it is important that they should receive some priority in future research.

Appendix 3 lists forms of care for which we feel there is simply too little good evidence to permit an informed judgement about their effects one way or the other. Some of the forms of care listed may reduce the likelihood of substantive negative outcomes of pregnancy and childbirth; others may have valuable placebo effects. Other forms of care included in Appendix 3 may have no important beneficial effects, or may, on balance, actually do more harm than good. Because of these uncertainties, those who use or advocate the forms of care listed in Appendix 3 should be aware of their inadequately evaluated status, and should collaborate in well-designed studies to assess their effects. This should apply especially to those forms of care that are costly in terms of resources. Those who do not use these forms of care should not introduce them, unless this is done within the context of properly controlled trials to assess whether they do more good than harm. Such assessment should be made in terms of substantive, not intermediate outcomes. A reasonable 'rule of thumb' for deciding whether a particular outcome should be regarded as substantive is to ask whether parents regard it as important.

Finally, Appendix 4 lists those forms of care which, in our view, should be abandoned. Inclusion of a form of care in this Appendix does not imply that no woman or baby could ever derive benefit from it. Forms of care have been included in Appendix 4 either because we feel that the evidence suggests that their adverse effects are likely to outweigh any conceivable beneficial effects that they may have; or because alternative forms of care, which we judge to be preferable, are available. Many of the forms of care included in Appendix 4 are unjustified routines and policies, which, applied inflexibly, result in the differing needs of individual women being ignored.

As stated in our Preface, there is still scope for considerable disagreement about many of the conclusions that we and our collaborators have reached. While we have made great efforts to ensure that the data presented are comprehensive and accurate, it is likely that some important studies have been overlooked, and that errors and misinterpretations have crept in. We conclude by reiterating our invitation to readers to bring omissions and mistakes to our attention for inclusion and correction in later editions of this book. We shall ensure that those who help us in this way are appropriately acknowledged.

Appendix 1.

Forms of care that reduce negative outcomes of pregnancy and childbirth.

Intervention	Effects	Chapters
Enhanced social and psychological support from caregivers	Reduced: —poor communication with staff —dissatisfaction with care —not feeling 'in control' —worries and unhappiness —feeding problems with baby —feeling physically unwell 6 weeks postpartum	3
Various anti-smoking interventions, particularly behaviour modification techniques and psychological support	Reduced: —smoking during pregnancy —low average birthweight	4
Carbohydrate supplements for malnourished women	Reduced: —low average birthweight	5
Antenatal classes	Reduced: —use of pharmacological analgesia in labour	6
Serum alpha-feto-protein estimation	Improved: —detection of neural tube malformations —detection of Down's syndrome	8
Genetic amniocentesis	Diagnosis of: —chromosomal disorders —neural tube malformations	8
Measurement of blood pressure during pregnancy	Improved: —detection of pre-eclampsia	9

Appendix 1   Forms of care that reduce negative outcomes of pregnancy and childbirth.

Selective use of ultrasonography	Improved: —confirmation of fetal life —estimation of gestational duration —estimation of fetal size —estimation of amniotic fluid volume —detection of fetal malformation —location of placenta —investigation of pelvic masses —establishment of fetal presentation	12
High *vs.* low feedback to mother during ultrasonography	Reduced: —negative feelings about examination	12
Routine ultrasonography in early pregnancy	Reduced: —induction of labour for 'post-term' pregnancy	12
Antiemetics (antihistamines, Debendox/Bendectin) for nausea/vomiting	Reduced: —nausea and vomiting	15
Antacids for heartburn	Reduced: —heartburn	15
Increased dietary fibre intake	Reduced: —constipation	15
Bulking agents and stool-softeners	Reduced: —constipation	15
Prophylactic diuretics for woman at increased risk of pre-eclampsia	Reduced: —hypertension	16
Methyldopa for hypertension	Reduced: —severe hypertension	16
Beta-blockers for hypertension	Reduced: —severe hypertension	16
Antihypertensive therapy for severe hypertension	Reduced: —hypertensive encephalopathy —cerebral haemorrhage	16

Appendix 1 Forms of care that reduce negative outcomes of pregnancy and childbirth.

Screening and treatment for asymptomatic bacteriuria	Reduced: —persistent/recurrent bacteriuria —pyelonephritis	17
Screening and treatment for syphilis	Reduced: —congenital syphilis	17
Screening and treatment for gonorrhoea	Reduced: —gonococcal disease in mother and baby	17
Clotrimazole for candidiasis	Reduced: —persistent candidiasis —infant colonization	15
Imidazoles *vs.* nystatin for candidiasis	Reduced: —persistent candidiasis	15
Metronidazole (after organogenesis complete) for symptomatic trichomonal vaginitis	Reduced: —symptomatic vaginitis	15
Intrapartum antibiotics for group B strep. colonization	Reduced: —infant colonization —infant sepsis with group B strep	17
Rubella vaccination postpartum	Reduced: —rubella embryopathy in subsequent pregnancy	17
Anti-D postpartum for Rh-negative women with Rh-positive babies	Reduced: —isoimmunization after 6 months —isoimmunization in subsequent pregnancy	18
Screening for Rh status and anti-D Rh globulin for Rh-negative women during pregnancy	Reduced: —positive Kleihauer test at 32–35 weeks —positive Kleihauer test at delivery —isoimmunization 6 months postpartum	18

Appendix 1   Forms of care that reduce negative outcomes of pregnancy and childbirth.

Tight *vs.* moderate control of diabetes	Reduced: —urinary tract infection —caesarean section —preterm birth —macrosomia —respiratory distress syndrome —perinatal mortality	19
Cervical cerclage for history of previous second trimester miscarriage	Reduced: —delivery before 33 weeks —miscarriage or perinatal death	21
External cephalic version at term for breech presentation	Reduced: —non-cephalic births —caesarean section	14
Antibiotics after prelabour rupture of membranes	Reduced: —puerperal infectious morbidity	24
Effecting delivery when signs of infection after prelabour rupture of membranes	Reduced: —infectious morbidity	24
Betamimetic tocolytics in preterm labour	Reduced: —delivery within 24 hours —delivery within 48 hours —delivery before 37 weeks	23
Indomethacin in preterm labour	Reduced: —delivery within 48 hours —delivery within 7–10 day —delivery before 37 weeks —birthweight below 2500 grams	23
Oral betamimetics for maintenance after inhibition of preterm labour	Reduced: —recurrent preterm labour	23
Corticosteroids prior to preterm delivery	Reduced: —respiratory distress syndrome —periventricular haemorrhage —necrotizing enterocolitis —early neonatal death	22, 44

Appendix 1 Forms of care that reduce negative outcomes of pregnancy and childbirth.

Social and psychological support during labour	Reduced: —augmentation of labour —caesarean section	28
Antacids before general anaesthesia	Reduced: —gastric acidity	30
Vaginal *vs.* rectal examinations to assess progress in labour	Reduced: —maternal discomfort from examination	32
Electronic fetal heart monitoring + scalp sampling *vs.* intermittent auscultation	Reduced: —early neonatal seizures	31
Intravenous preloading before epidural anaesthesia	Reduced: —maternal hypotension —fetal heart rate abnormalities	31
Upright *vs.* recumbent position during first stage of labour	Reduced: —use of narcotics/epidural	30
Systemic narcotics during labour	Reduced: —pain	34
Epidural *vs.* systemic narcotics during labour	Reduced: —pain	34
Scheduled top-ups of epidural *vs.* top-ups at maternal request	Reduced: —episodes of severe pain	34
Epidural *vs.* placebo after 8 cm.	Reduced: —pain in second stage	34
Methoxyflurane *vs.* nitrous oxide	Reduced: —nausea and vomiting	34
PGE2 for cervical ripening	Reduced: —induction-delivery interval 24 hours —operative delivery	42
PGF2α for cervical ripening	Reduced: —induction-delivery interval 24 hours —operative delivery	42

Appendix 1 Forms of care that reduce negative outcomes of pregnancy and childbirth.

Oestrogens for cervical ripening	Reduced: —caesarean section	42
Amniotomy + early *vs.*+ late oxytocin for induction	Reduced: —induction-delivery interval 24 hours —operative delivery —postpartum haemorrhage	43
Oxytocin + amniotomy *vs.* oxytocin alone for induction	Reduced: —induction-delivery interval >24 hours	43
Prostaglandins *vs.* placebo for induction	Reduced: —induction-delivery interval >24 hours —caesarean section	43
Prostaglandins *vs.* oxytocin for induction	Reduced: —induction-delivery interval >24 hours —operative delivery	43
Prostaglandins/ analogues for induction after fetal death	Reduced: —failure to deliver vaginally	26
Low dose *vs.* high dose prostaglandin analogues for induction after fetal death	Reduced: —maternal morbidity	26
Upright *vs.* recumbent position during second stage of labour	Reduced: —abnormal fetal heart rate patterns —severe pain —low umbilical artery pH (<7.25)	35
Lateral tilt *vs.* dorsal position during second stage of labour	Reduced: —mean umbilical arterial pH	35
Exhalatory *vs.* sustained bearing down during second stage labour	Reduced: —abnormal fetal heart rate patterns —low Apgar scores	35
Late *vs.* early pushing with epidural during second stage of labour	Reduced: —use of rotational forceps	35

Appendix 1 Forms of care that reduce negative outcomes of pregnancy and childbirth.

Restricted *vs.* liberal use of episiotomy at delivery	Reduced: —overall trauma —perineal trauma	35
Active management of third stage of labour	Reduced: —postpartum haemorrhage	36
Free bleeding from placental end of cord	Reduced: —feto-maternal transfusion	36
Early cord clamping	Reduced: —length of third stage	36
Prophylactic oxytocics in third stage	Reduced: —postpartum haemorrhage	36
Prostaglandins for otherwise uncontrollable postpartum haemorrhage due to uterine atony	Reduced: —emergency hysterectomy —internal iliac artery ligation	36
Continuous *vs.* interrupted sutures for perineal trauma	Reduced: —short term perineal pain	37
Polyglycolic acid *vs.* catgut sutures	Reduced: —short term perineal pain	37
Polyglycolic acid *vs.* silk or nylon sutures	Reduced: —short term perineal pain	37
Policy of trial of labour after previous caesarean section	Reduced: —caesarean section —maternal morbidity	39
Vacuum extraction *vs.* forceps delivery (all indications)	Reduced: —maternal injury —use of major anaesthesia	38
Vacuum extraction *vs.* forceps for rotational deliveries	Reduced: —maternal injury —use of major anaesthesia	38
Cricoid pressure during induction of general anaesthesia	Reduced: —aspiration of gastric contents	40

Appendix 1 Forms of care that reduce negative outcomes of pregnancy and childbirth.

Uterine exteriorization *vs.* intraperitoneal repair at caesarean, when exposure is difficult	Reduced: —serious infection	40
Prophylactic atibiotics with emergency caesarean section	Reduced: —endometritis —serious infection —wound infection —febrile morbidity	41
Prophylactic antibiotics with elective caesarean section	Reduced: —endometritis —serious infection —wound infection —febrile morbidity	41
Antibiotic *vs.* placebo irrigation with caesarean section	Reduced: —febrile morbidity	41
Ultrasound examination prior to preterm delivery	Reduced: —unnecessary caesarean sections for babies with lethal malformations	44
Referral to institution with intensive care facilities for very preterm birth	Reduced: —neonatal mortality —neonatal morbidity	44
Neonatologist for immediate care of very preterm infant	Reduced: —neonatal morbidity	44, 45
Prevention of neonatal hypothermia in delivery room	Reduced: —acidosis	45
Prophylactic calf or human surfactant for preterm infants	Reduced: —moderate/severe respiratory distress syndrome —pneumothorax —periventricular haemorrhage —neonatal death	45

Appendix 1 Forms of care that reduce negative outcomes of pregnancy and childbirth.

Prophylactic 'artificial lung-expanding compound' for preterm infants	Reduced: —moderate/severe respiratory distress syndrome —neonatal death	45
Silver nitrate for prophylaxis against gonococcal conjunctivitis	Reduced: —gonococcal conjunctivitis	45, 17
Antibiotic prophylaxis against neonatal gonococcal conjunctivitis	Reduced: —gonococcal conjunctivitis	45, 17
Erythromycin ointment *vs.* silver nitrate for prophylaxis against bacterial conjunctivitis	Reduced: —chemical conjunctivitis	45, 17
Unrestricted mother— infant contact following delivery	Reduced: —breastfeeding failure	46
Prophylactic triple dye on umbilical cord	Reduced: —staphylococcal skin colonization	46
Prophylactic neomycin on umbilical cord	Reduced: —staphylococcal skin colonization	46
Local anaesthetic in aqueous form for perineal pain	Reduced: —perineal pain	48
Unrestricted breastfeeding	Reduced: —breastfeeding failure	47
Social support and information for breast-feeding mothers	Reduced: —breastfeeding failure	47
Bromocriptine for non-breastfeeding mothers	Reduced: —breast pain during first week —continued lactation during first and second weeks —engorgement during first and second weeks	49

Appendix 1 Forms of care that reduce negative outcomes of pregnancy and childbirth.

Synthetic oestrogens for non-breastfeeding mothers	Reduced: —breast pain during first week —continued lactation during first week —engorgement during first week	49
Oestrogen/testosterone combination for non-breastfeeding mothers	Reduced: —breast pain during first week —continued lactation during first week —engorgement during first week	49
Bromocriptine *vs.* breast binders for non-breastfeeding mothers	Reduced: —breast pain during first week —continued lactation during first week —engorgement during first week	49
Enhanced care for bereaved parents	Reduced: —depression at 6 months postpartum —anxiety at 6 months postpartum	27

Appendix 2.

Forms of care that appear promising, but require further evaluation.

Intervention	Possible beneficial effects	Chapters
Folate supplements for malnourished/ still growing pregnant women/girls	Possibly reduced: —low birthweight —stunted maternal growth	5
Antenatal classes	Possibly reduced: —low self esteem —dissatisfaction in pregnancy and childbirth	6
Antenatal expression of colostrum	Possibly reduced: —breast engorgement —damaged nipples —breastfeeding failure	47
Anticipatory guidance for women wishing to breastfeed	Possibly reduced: —breastfeeding failure	47
Home monitoring of uterine contractions in women at increased risk of preterm labour	Possibly reduced: —preterm labour	23
Routine ultrasound placentography in third trimester	Possibly reduced: —low Apgar score —perinatal death	12
Routine fetal movement counting	Possibly reduced: —stillbirth	13
Dilute hydrochloric acid for heartburn	Possibly reduced: —heartburn	15

Appendix 2   Forms of care that appear promising, but require further evaluation.

Prostigmine for heartburn	Possibly reduced: —heartburn	15
Sodium chloride for leg cramps	Possibly reduced: —leg cramps	15
Anti-platelet agents for increased risk of pre-eclampsia and fetal growth retardation	Possibly reduced: —proteinuria —severe pre-eclampsia —recurrent fetal growth retardation —perinatal death	16
Plasma volume expansion for severe pre-eclampsia	Possibly reduced: —oliguria —severe hypertension	16
Plasmapheresis in severe Rhesus disease	Possibly reduced: —perinatal morbidity and mortality	18
Hospitalization and bed rest for multiple pregnancy	Possibly reduced: —diastolic BP >109 mm. Hg.	21
Abdominal decompression for compromised fetus	Possibly reduced: —proteinuria/pre-eclampsia —fetal distress in labour —birthweight less than 2500 grams —low Apgar score at 1 minute —perinatal death	21
Ultrasonography for surveillance after prelabour rupture of membranes preterm	Possibly reduced: —perinatal morbidity	24
Using prophylactic antibiotics with corticosteroids after prelabour rupture of membranes preterm	Possibly reduced: —maternal infectious morbidity —neonatal infectious morbidity	24
17-alpha hydroxy-progesterone caproate i.m. in women at increased risk of preterm delivery	Possibly reduced: —preterm delivery —low birthweight	23

Appendix 2   Forms of care that appear promising, but require further evaluation.

Prophylactic progestogens for women at increased risk of preterm labour	Possibly reduced: —perinatal morbidity	23
Thyroid releasing hormone in addition to corticosteroids prior to preterm delivery	Possibly reduced: —days on artificial ventilation —days in supplementary oxygen	23
Amnioinfusion for intrapartum 'fetal distress'	Possibly reduced: —persistent fetal heart rate abnormality	31
Intravenous betamimetics for intrapartum 'fetal distress'	Possibly reduced: —persistent fetal heart rate abnormality	31
Piracetam for intrapartum 'fetal distress'	Possibly reduced: —caesarean section —neonatal morbidity	31
Self administered *vs.* scheduled narcotics	Possibly reduced: —total dose of pethidine —pain	34
Amniotomy to augment spontaneous labour	Possibly reduced: —use of oxytocin —instrumental vaginal delivery	33
Prostaglandins when induction required after prelabour rupture of membranes	Possibly reduced: —operative delivery	24
Syntometrine *vs.* oxytocin for third stage of labour	Possibly reduced: —postpartum haemorrhage	36
Multiple *vs.* single doses of antibiotics with caesarean section	Possibly reduced: —febrile morbidity	41
Maternal phenobarbitone prior to preterm delivery	Possibly reduced: —intraventricular haemorrhage —perinatal death	44

Appendix 2   Forms of care that appear promising, but require further evaluation.

Tracheal suction for depressed meconium-stained neonates	Possibly reduced: —severe meconium aspiration syndrome	45
Elective intubation for neonatal resuscitation	Possibly reduced: —asphyxial damage	45
Routine administration of vitamin K to neonates	Possibly reduced: —haemorrhagic disease —intracranial haemorrhage	45
Antiobiotic prophylaxis against neonatal chlamydial conjunctivitis	Possibly reduced: —chlamydial conjunctivitis	45
Oral proteolytic enzymes for perineal trauma	Possibly reduced: —short term perineal pain —perineal oedema	48
Correct positioning of baby at breast	Possibly reduced: —breast engorgement —sore nipples —breastfeeding failure	47
Oral proteolytic enzymes for breast engorgement	Possibly reduced: —breast engorgement	47
Bromocriptine *vs.* stilboestrol for lactation suppression	Possibly reduced: —continued lactation during first week —breast pain during first week —engorgement during first week	47

Appendix 3

Forms of care with unknown effects, which require further evaluation.

Intervention	Assessment of effects required in terms of:	Chapters
Modification of working patterns during pregnancy	—material and perinatal morbidity	3, 4
Periconceptional pre/proscriptions for women without overt problems	—maternal and perinatal morbidity	4
Periconceptional multivitamins and folate	—neural tube defects	4
Advice to abstain from coitus and alcohol during pregnancy	—perinatal morbidity	4
Nutritional advice and/or supplements	—pre-eclampsia —maternal and perinatal morbidity —childhood morbidity	5
Routine iron and/or folate supplements	—maternal and perinatal morbidity	5
Different types of antenatal classes	—maternal and perinatal morbidity —paternal lack of involvement with child	6
Woolwich shells for inverted nipples	—breastfeeding failure	47
Hoffman's exercises for inverted nipples	—breastfeeding failure	47
Frequency and timing of antenatal visits	—diagnosis of pre-eclampsia —antenatal hospital admission —maternal and perinatal morbidity	9

Appendix 3 Forms of care with unknown effects, which require further evaluation.

Formal risk scoring	—maternal anxiety —maternal and perinatal morbidity	7
Routine pelvic examination with antenatal visits	—preterm labour —perinatal morbidity	7
Chorion villus sampling *vs.* amniocentesis	—miscarriage —maternal and perinatal morbidity —childhood morbidity	8
Glucose tolerance testing	—maternal and perinatal morbidity —perinatal mortality	10
Serial fundal height/ girth measurements	—perinatal morbidity	11
Routine ultrasound for fetal anthropometry and congenital malformations	—maternal and perinatal morbidity	12
Doppler ultrasound for fetal and uteroplacental blood flow	—maternal and perinatal morbidity	12
All biochemical tests of fetal wellbeing	—perinatal morbidity	13
All biophysical tests of fetal wellbeing	—perinatal morbidity	13
X-ray pelvimetry with breech presentation	—caesarean section —maternal and perinatal morbidity	14
Calcium for leg cramps	—leg cramps	15
Vitamin D for leg cramps	—leg cramps	15
Quinine for leg cramps	—leg cramps	15
Routine screening for chlamydia	—neonatal infection	17
Routine screening for toxoplasmosis	—neonatal infection	17

Appendix 3   Forms of care with unknown effects, which require further evaluation.

Routine screening for HIV infection	—neonatal infection	17
Alternative treatment regimens for vaginitis	—symptomatic vaginitis	15
Treatment of mycoplasma colonization	—maternal and perinatal morbidity	17
Screening for and treatment of chlamydia	—chlamydial infection of newborn	17
Alternative treatments for chlamydial infection	—chlamydial infection of newborn	17
Antiviral agents for active genital herpes	—persistent infection —herpes infection of newborn	17
Caesarean section for herpes with no clinical evidence of active disease	—herpes infection of newborn —maternal and perinatal morbidity	17
Repeated viral cultures for history of herpes	—herpes infection of newborn	17
Hospitalization for uncomplicated multiple pregnancy	—perinatal morbidity	21
Hospitalization for non-proteinuric hypertension	—development of proteinuria —severe hypertension —maternal and perinatal morbidity	21
Strict bed rest for proteinuric hypertension	—fulminating pre-eclampsia —maternal morbidity —perinatal morbidity and mortality	21
Cervical cerclage, other than for history of second trimester miscarriage	—preterm delivery —admission to hospital —maternal and perinatal morbidity	21
Postural management for breech presentation	—non-cephalic birth —caesarean section —maternal and perinatal morbidity	14

Appendix 3 Forms of care with unknown effects, which require further evaluation.

Amniocentesis after prelabour rupture of membranes preterm	—maternal and perinatal morbidity	24
Routine digital or speculum examination after prelabour rupture of membranes	—maternal and perinatal morbidity	24
Amnioinfusion during preterm labour after prelabour rupture of membranes	—caesarean section —perinatal morbidity	24
Betamimetics after prelabour rupture of membranes preterm	—maternal and perinatal morbidity	24
Prophylactic oral betamimetics for twin pregnancy	—perinatal morbidity	23
Prophylactic oral betamimetics for women at increased risk of preterm labour	—perinatal morbidity	23
Routine magnesium supplementation to prevent preterm delivery	—perinatal morbidity	23
Magnesium sulphate for inhibition of preterm labour	—maternal and perinatal morbidity	23
Diazoxide for inhibition of preterm labour	—maternal and perinatal morbidity	23
Oxytocin analogues for inhibition of preterm labour	—maternal and perinatal morbidity	23
Calcium antagonists to counteract side-effects of betamimetics	—maternal and perinatal morbidity	23
Beta-blockers to counteract side-effects of betamimetics	—maternal and perinatal morbidity	23

Appendix 3   Forms of care with unknown effects, which require further evaluation.

Fetal weight estimations as a guide to care for preterm delivery	—caesarean section —perinatal morbidity	44
Elective induction of labour at 42+ weeks	—caesarean section —maternal and perinatal morbidity	25
Routine withholding of food and oral fluids during labour	—aspiration of gastric contents —maternal morbidity —operative delivery	30
Non-pharmacological methods of pain relief	—labour pain —use of pharmacological analgesia —maternal and perinatal morbidity	34
Epidural narcotics with or without local anaesthetic agents	—pain relief —maternal and perinatal morbidity	34
Early oxytocin to augment spontaneous labour	—use of analgesia —hyperstimulation —operative delivery —perinatal morbidity	33
Alternative oxytocic regimens for augmenting spontaneous labour	—use of analgesia —hyperstimulation —operative delivery —perinatal morbidity	33
Relaxin for cervical ripening	—caesarean section —perinatal morbidity	42
Sweeping (stripping) of membranes at term	—need for formal induction of labour —maternal morbidity —perinatal morbidity	43
Automatic oxytocin infusion apparatus for induction	—maternal discomfort and morbidity —perinatal morbidity	43
Prostaglandins *vs.* oxytocin for induction	—maternal discomfort and morbidity —perinatal morbidity	43
Induction of labour for prelabour rupture of membranes at term	—caesarean section —maternal and perinatal morbidity	24

360

Appendix 3 Forms of care with unknown effects, which require further evaluation.

Alternative regimens for prostaglandin analogues for induction after fetal death	—maternal morbidity	26
Perineal massage in labour	—perineal trauma —maternal discomfort	35
Midline *vs.* mediolateral episiotomy	—perineal pain —dyspareunia —longer-term maternal morbidity	35
Intraumbilical vein oxytocin for retained placenta	—manual removal of placenta —maternal morbidity	36
Non-absorbable synthetic suture *vs.* polyglycolic acid suture for subcuticular skin closure	—perineal pain —perineal irritation	37
Apposition vs. suturing of perineal skin for perineal trauma	—perineal pain —delayed wound healing	37
Vacuum extraction *vs.* forceps delivery	—short and long term effects on baby	38
Alternative designs of vacuum extractor	—instrument failure —maternal and fetal injury	38
Different antibiotic regimens for prophylaxis with caesarean section	—maternal morbidity —prevalence of commensal flora	41
Shorter *vs.* longer courses of antibiotics with caesarean section	—maternal morbidity	41
Routine *vs.* selective caesarean section for very preterm delivery	—maternal and perinatal morbidity	44
Routine *vs.* selective forceps for vaginal delivery preterm	—maternal and perinatal morbidity	44

Appendix 3   Forms of care with unknown effects, which require further evaluation.

Routine *vs.* selective episiotomy for vaginal delivery preterm	—maternal and perinatal morbidity	44
Routine pharyngeal suctioning of neonates at birth	—gas exchange —aspiration —colonization	45
Tracheal suction for non-depressed, meconium-stained neonates at birth	—meconium aspiration syndrome —pulmonary artery hypertension —infectious morbidity	45
Sodium bicarbonate administration to asphyxiated neonates	—intracranial haemorrhage —sequelae of asphyxia	45
Alcohol-based dressings for umbilical cord	—neonatal infection	46
Routine observations of maternal temperature, pulse, blood-pressure, fundal height, lochia	—maternal morbidity	46
Ultrasound therapy for perineal pain	—perineal pain	48
Pulsed electromagnetic energy therapy for perineal pain	—perineal pain	48
Postnatal pelvic floor exercises	—perineal pain —urinary incontinence	48
Steroids added to local anaesthetics for perineal pain	—perineal pain —perineal wound infection	48
Dopamine antagonists for inadequate milk supply	—breastfeeding failure	47
Nipple shields for nipple trauma	—nipple pain —nipple healing —breastfeeding failure	47

362

Appendix 3 Forms of care with unknown effects, which require
further evaluation.

Appendix 4

Forms of care that should be abandoned in the light of the available evidence.

Forms of care	Chapters
Failing to involve women in decisions about their care	3
Failing to provide continuity of care during pregnancy and childbirth	3
Leaving women unattended during labour	3, 28
Involving doctors in the care of all women during pregnancy	3
Involving obstetricians in the care of all women during pregnancy	3
Insisting on universal institutional confinement	3
Prescribing high-density protein supplements during pregnancy	5
Advising restriction of weight gain during pregnancy	5
Measuring maternal weight routinely throughout pregnancy	5
Advising restriction of salt intake during pregnancy	5
Measuring haemoglobin at every antenatal visit	5
'Conditioning' nipples during pregnancy	47
Performing X-ray pelvimetry in cephalic presentations	14
Prescribing saline cathartics or lubricant oils for constipation	15
Prescribing stilboestrol during pregnancy	21
Using external cephalic version electively before term	14
Inducing labour for uncomplicated prelabour rupture of membranes preterm	24
Expanding plasma volume before using betamimetics in preterm labour	23
Prescribing ethanol for inhibition of preterm labour	23
Prescribing progesterone for inhibition of preterm labour	23
Prescribing aspirin for inhibition of preterm labour	23
Inducing labour routinely at less than 42 weeks gestation	25
Shaving the perineum routinely prior to delivery	29
Administering enemas or suppositories routinely during labour	29
Limiting duration of second stage of labour arbitrarily	35

Appendix 4   Forms of care that should be abandoned in the light of the available evidence.

Appendix 4   Forms of care that should be abandoned in the light of the available evidence.

Index